ISLAMIST MOVEMENTS DURING THE TUNISIAN TRANSITION AND SYRIAN CRISIS

Edinburgh Studies of the Globalised Muslim World

Series Editor: **Frédéric Volpi**, Director, Prince Alwaleed Bin Talal Centre for the Study of Contemporary Islam, University of Edinburgh

This innovative series investigates the dynamics of Muslim societies in a globalised world. It considers the boundaries of the contemporary Muslim world, their construction, their artificiality or durability. It sheds new light on what it means to be part of the Muslim world today, for both those individuals and communities who live in Muslim-majority countries and those who reside outside and are part of a globalised ummah. Its analysis encompasses the micro and the macro level, exploring the discourses and practices of individuals, communities, states and transnational actors who create these dynamics. It offers a multidisciplinary perspective on the salient contemporary issues and interactions that shape the internal and external relations of the Muslim world.

Published and forthcoming titles

Salafi Social and Political Movements: National and Transnational Contexts
Masooda Bano

A Political Theory of Muslim Democracy
Ravza Altuntaş-Çakır

Literary Neo-Orientalism and the Arab Uprisings: Tensions in English, French and German Language Fiction
Julia Wurr

Why Islamists Go Green
Emmanuel Karagiannis

Islamic Modernities in World Society: The Rise, Spread and Fragmentation of a Hegemonic Idea
Dietrich Jung

Islamist Movements during the Tunisian Transition and Syrian Crisis: The Power of Practices
Teije H. Donker

edinburghuniversitypress.com/series/esgmw

ISLAMIST MOVEMENTS DURING THE TUNISIAN TRANSITION AND SYRIAN CRISIS

The Power of Practices

Teije H. Donker

EDINBURGH
University Press

Edinburgh University Press is one of the leading university presses in the UK. We publish academic books and journals in our selected subject areas across the humanities and social sciences, combining cutting-edge scholarship with high editorial and production values to produce academic works of lasting importance. For more information visit our website: edinburghuniversitypress.com

Edinburgh University Press Ltd
13 Infirmary Street
Edinburgh EH1 1LT

Typeset in 11/15pt EB Garamond by
Cheshire Typesetting Ltd, Cuddington, Cheshire, and
printed and bound in Great Britain

A CIP record for this book is available from the British Library

ISBN 978 1 3995 0618 2 (hardback)
ISBN 978 1 3995 0620 5 (webready PDF)
ISBN 978 1 3995 0621 2 (epub)

CONTENTS

FIGURES

ABBREVIATIONS

ANC	Assemblée Nationale Constituante, National Constituent Assembly
AQIM	Al-Qaeda in the Islamic Maghreb
Colibe	Commission des Libertés Individuelles et de l'Egalité; Individual Freedoms and Equality Committee
CPA	contentious practices approach
CPR	Congrès pour la République, Congress for the Republic
Ettakatol	Forum Démocratique pour le Travail et les Libertés; Democratic Forum for Labour and Liberties, also abbreviated as FTDL
FSA	Free Syrian Army
HTS	Hayat Tahrir al-Sham; The Committee for the Liberation of the Levant
IFEDA	Le Centre d'Information, de Formation, d'Études et de Documentation sur les Associations; The Centre for Information, Formation, Study and Documentation of Associations
IJCA	Integrated Judicial Council of Aleppo
ISI	Islamic State in/of Iraq
ISIS	Islamic State (in Iraq and Sham); Daesh
MTI	Mouvement de la Tendance Islamique; the Movement of Islamic Tendency

OTT	Organisation Tunisienne du Travail; the Tunisian Labour Organisation
SAF	strategic action field
SIC	Syrian Islamic Council
SIG	Syrian Interim Government
SMB	Syrian Muslim Brotherhood
SOC	Syrian Opposition Coalition
Türkiye	Republic of Türkiye, Turkey
UGTT	Union Générale Tunisienne du Travail; the Tunisian General Labour Union

ROMANISATION OF ARABIC

The romanisation of Arabic, often referred to as its transliteration, is a balancing act between consistency and custom. To what extent does one apply the same set of romanisation rules to all Arabic sentences, concepts, individuals and geographic names? Or does one also account for local and individual conventions? I opted for the following. When romanising normal sentences, I followed the American Library Association and Library of Congress approach to romanisation of Arabic script. The romanisation table can be found on the website of the Library of Congress.[1] To save time and ensure consistency, I used a python tool, developed by Fadhl Eryani and Nizar Habash.[2] Following this approach, I romanised the sentence الشعب يريد إسقاط النظام as *al-sha'b yurīd isqāṭ al-niẓām*: the people want the fall of the regime.

For names of individuals, towns and organisations, I opted to romanise according to local and individual conventions. This meant I often romanised individual names following a French approach and sometimes excluded articles. The name of [الخطيب الإدريسي] appears as Khatib Idrissi not al-Khaṭīb al-Idrīsī and [نور الدين الخادمي] as Noureddine Khadmi not Nūr al-Dīn al-Khādimī. But the name of [أبو محمد الجولاني] appears as Abu Muhammad al-Julani. It is Aleppo, not Ḥalab, and it is Sfax, not Ṣafāqis. In cases where multiple options exist – [محمد العفاس], for example, is romanised as Mohamed Afess, Affess, Afes and Affes, with the latter two options used by Mohamed

Afes himself – I opted for the most common approach. References apply the Library of Congress approach to romanisation consistently.

Notes

1. See https://www.loc.gov/catdir/cpso/romanization/arabic.pdf.
2. Eryani and Habash, 'Automatic Romanization of Arabic Bibliographic Records'. See the website at romanize-arabic.camel-lab.com.

ACKNOWLEDGEMENTS

While I am writing these acknowledgements, during the summer of 2023, most of the dreams that drove Tunisians and Syrians to the streets in 2011 have been dashed. One by one, Arab countries normalised relations with the Syrian regime of Bashar al-Assad and ended up readmitting it to the Arab League. In Tunisia, during a recent visit, the Dutch and Italian Prime Ministers, together with the European Union's President Ursula von der Leyen, signed a deal with Tunisia's new autocrat, Kais Saied, promising hundreds of millions of euros in investments in return for controlling migration to Europe. Kais Saied's ever widening crackdown on opposition parties and activists remained unmentioned in press statements. Almost cynically so, a movement for change in the Arab world finds itself sidelined domestically and internationally.

The debts I accrued during my research reflect the highs and lows of the Syrian crisis and Tunisian transition. In the weeks and months after the January 2011 revolution, Tunisians throughout the country – journalists, activists, politicians, students, imams and random strangers – shared their memories, hopes and dreams for a future Tunisia. People from all social groups, political leanings and religious convictions were open to talking to me. This remained true in the years after, even as their expectations turned more pessimistic. Most of the Syrians I interviewed after March 2011 were, initially, travelling back and forth between Syria and Turkey or Jordan. As time passed, and border policies became more stringent, many of the Syrians

I met were forced to live in exile. I am grateful to all that met and talked to me in these trying circumstances. Several people met me multiple times, several others became friends. Because of the ever deteriorating social and political situation, I will name no one here, but in every case: thank you.

Turning to academia, I am grateful to my two PhD supervisors at the European University Institute, Donatella della Porta and Olivier Roy, for all their guidance during and after my PhD project. I also have to thank them for allowing me to change my research focus, at the last minute, from Algeria to Tunisia following the revolution. Without it, this book would never have happened. For making my time at the European University Institute, the EUI, an unforgettable and stimulating one, I have to thank Oriana, Jess, Tiago, Georges, Leila, Olli, Kevin, Emre, Kıvanç, Virginie, Tim, Emin, Emre, Nadia, Magnus and Karolina. A special thanks to Kasper Netterstrøm for the (sometimes heated but always rewarding!) research collaboration. At Princeton University, my gratitude goes to Bernard Haykel, Mirjam Künkler and all the students at the Near East Studies Department who made my stay both enlightening and fun. A special thanks to Cole Bunzel for providing me with several crucial primary documents.

While residing in Syria, the (former) Dutch Academic Institute in Damascus (NIASD) gave me an academic home: thank you to Kim Duistermaat, Astrid Rijbroek and Taco van der Zwaag for their support. At the Center for Maghrib Studies in Tunis, I would like to thank Laryssa Chomiak, Tom deGeorges and Riadh Saadaoui for their invaluable help and kindness during my Tunisian fieldwork periods. I also thank Bob Parks for providing the initial welcome at the US research institutes in the Maghreb region.

A postdoc at the department of Comparative Politics at the University of Bergen, Norway, provided time for additional fieldwork and to develop my knowledge of the work of Pierre Bourdieu. Thank you to Gunnar Grendstad and Jan Oskar Engene for giving me the freedom to pursue my research interests and to Johs Hjellbrekke for introducing me to multiple correspondence analysis. It was in Bergen that I transformed my PhD into what became this book. For their friendship (and kind advice about how to keep sane in a city as dark and rainy as Bergen!), thank you Georg, Yvette, Michael, Vegard, Gyda, Ingvild, Olav, Magnus and Maja.

A three-year lectureship at the Department of Sociology at the University of Cambridge gave me an introduction to UK academia and access to an amazing community of scholars. A thank you to Patrick Baert and Hazim Kandil for the opportunity and advice along the way. For providing me with an academic home at Cambridge, thank you Murray Edwards College and its President Dame Barbara Stocking. For their feedback on drafts and friendships, thank you Rin, Jeff, Helena, Matthew and Harald. Finally, a thank you to my amazing students on my Soc8 'Religion and Contentious Mobilisation' course and my Hughes Hall supervisees for the wonderful and insightful debates.

During the drafting stages, I held an Associate Fellowship at the Alwaleed Centre for the Study of Islam in the Contemporary World at the University of Edinburgh. A big thank you goes to the participants in the workshops where I presented my work, and to Frederic Volpi for the opportunity to write and publish this book at Edinburgh University Press. I could not have asked for a better editorial team: Louise Hutton and Isobel Birks. The same goes for Eddie Clark, who worked in-house on production, and freelance editor Olivia Ralphs for the final copy-editing. They never pressured me when I needed more time to write, while speeding along the editing process. Thank you! I am also very grateful to the reviewer for their critical and extensive comments. The book was revised substantially as a result and, I hope, is all the better for it. Also, a thank you to Christiaan Triebert for allowing me to use one of his pictures as a front cover for the book.

Last, but definitely not least, I would like to thank my parents for supporting me to go out, explore and experiment, while tagging along with my older sister and brother: Afke and Tjibbe. Thank you to my Dutch friends, Marcel, Thomas, Jeroen, Sjors (and all the others!) for reminding me of my Dutch roots. And I saved the best for last: thank you, Neci, for allowing me all the time in the world to write this monograph and patiently listening and commenting on the draft chapters. I started drafting when our first daughter was just born. I finished when the second approached her first birthday. My heartfelt thanks to both, for bringing joy to my life and (thanks to morning daycare and very long afternoon naps!) still allowing me to write this book. Ada & Lara: een kus van mij.

With all this said and done: all remaining mistakes are mine and mine alone.

CAST OF CHARACTERS

Names are in alphabetical order by first name. If only a first name is listed, it means a pseudonym is used to ensure anonymity and biographical information is intentionally generic. This also applies to names used elsewhere in the book.

Adnan al-Aroor. Born in 1948 in Hama, Syria. He fled his hometown in 1982 and settled in Saudi Arabia. Not widely known before the uprising, he became famous after 2011 for his outspoken support for the uprising. In 2012, he returned to the region and since then visited Syria occasionally.

Ahmed Hussein al-Shar'a, a.k.a. *Abu Muhammad al-Julani*. Born in Saudi Arabia, in 1982, to Syrian parents. His father worked as an oil engineer in Riadh. The family returned to Damascus in 1989 and settled in the middle-class Mezzeh neighbourhood. He travelled to Iraq in 2003 to fight the US occupation and gradually rose among the ranks of al-Qaeda in the country. His ascent came to a halt between 2005 and 2008, while incarcerated by the Americans in Camp Bucca, but continued afterwards in the Islamic State in Iraq organisation, or ISI. Following a high-level decision by ISI to establish a representation of the global jihad in Syria, he returned and, in January 2012, established the Nusra Front. He is currently the leader of Hayat Tahrir al-Sham, a successor to the Nusra Front, that controls Idlib and much of its province.

Hamza. An activist from Sfax, born in the 1980s. He became active in religious groups during his youth. After the revolution, he became an imam until being barred in 2015 during the Unity Government of Habib Essid. He remained a well-known local activist throughout the period covered in this book.

Hassan Aboud a.k.a *Abu Abdullah al-Hamawi*. Born 1979 in Hama, Syria. He studied English and pedagogy and took part in the jihadist uprising against the occupation of Iraq. On his return, the Syrian regime incarcerated him at the Sednaya prison close to Damascus where he lived through its 2008 uprising. The Syrian regime released him in the spring of 2011. At the end of that year, he established the Ahrar al-Sham Brigades that transformed into the Ahrar al-Sham Movement and became one of the most powerful jihadist organisations during the Syrian crisis. He died on 9 September 2014 following an explosion that decimated Ahrar al-Sham's leadership.

Hussein Obeidi. Born in Tunis, Tunisia, in 1942 or 1943. He became Grand Imam of the Zaytuna Mosque after the 2011 revolution.

Khatib Idrissi. Born in August 1954 in Sidi Ali Ben Aoun, a town 10 km south-west of Sidi Bouzid. He studied nursing in Gafsa. Between 1985 and 1994, he worked in Saudi Arabia, concurrently studying sharia sciences. On his return to Sidi Aoun, he became a leading voice in Tunisian Islamism. Following the 2011 revolution, he was often described as the main ideologue of Ansar Sharia, a Tunisian jihadist group. He always maintained he was not affiliated with the group.

Marouan. Born in the early 1980s in Deir ez-Zor, Syria. He was studying at the University of Aleppo when the uprising started. He worked as a media activist with the Army of Mujahideen and the Fastaqim Union.

Omar. Born in early 1980 and studied engineering. During the 1990s, his family faced problems with the security services because of Islamist activities, although they were never formally members of an Islamist party. Following the revolution, he started a popular Islamic school with branches across Tunisia. The school was forced to cease its activities in the summer of 2014.

Rached Ghannouchi. Born in 1941 in El Hamma (Gabès Governorate in South Tunisia). He received a degree from Zaytuna University in 1962 and a philosophy degree from the university of Damascus, Syria, in 1968. He established the Movement of Islamic Tendency together with Abdelfattah Mourou and Hmida Ennaifer in 1981 and the Ennahda party in 1989. During the rule of Habib Bourguiba, the regime incarcerated him for several years. During a brief period of political liberalisation after Ben Ali's ascent to power in 1987, he was released, but went into exile in 1989 as repression returned. He spent 22 years in exile in the United Kingdom until his return to Tunisia following the revolution of January 2011.

Ratib. A popular sheikh and imam from Daraa. He and his extended family had experienced problems with the Assad regime for years. From the start of the uprising, he called for freedom during his Friday sermons. Within weeks, a regime sniper shot him. He went into exile, became a member of the Syrian National Council for several years and, subsequently, a senior representative of the Syrian Islamic Council.

Ridha Jaouadi. A secondary teacher and imam from Sfax. He received his baccalaureate in Literature in 1983 and an MA in the Foundations of Religion (*Uṣūl al-Dīn*) from Zaytuna University in 2011. He was barred from preaching under the Ben Ali regime in 1991. After the January 2011 revolution, representatives of the Lakhme Mosque, the largest mosque in Sfax, appointed him as their Friday imam. He quickly made a name for himself as an outspoken and activist imam. In September 2015, the regime barred him – again – from preaching. He became a Member of Parliament in 2019.

Seifallah Ben Hassine, a.k.a *Abu Iyadh al-Tunisi.* Born in November 1965 in Tunisia. He was active in the Afghan jihadist uprising in the 1980s and set up the al-Qaeda-linked Tunisian Combat Group in the early 2000s. Multiple sources place him close to al-Qaeda's leadership throughout these years. In 2003, he was arrested in Türkiye, extradited to Tunisia and sentenced to 43 years in prison. Finding himself freed after the 2011 revolution, he established Ansar Charia and began public activities in May 2011. Ansar Charia and Abu Iyadh became ubiquitous names in public debates in between 2011 and 2013. Following repression of his organisation, he fled to Libya where he was killed in 2015.

Taha Subhi Falaha, a.k.a *Abu Muhammad al-Adnani.* Born in 1977 in the Idlib province, Syria. During the early 2000s, the Syrian regime arrested him multiple times for proselytisation and jihadist activities. In 2003, he moved to Iraq to fight against the US occupation and became active in al-Qaeda. American forces incarcerated him between May 2005 and 2010, reportedly at

Camp Bucca. In 2012, together with Abu Muhammad Julani and others, he travelled to Syria and set up the Nusra Front, of which he became its spokesperson. In 2013, he publicly chose the side of Baghdadi and became one of ISIS's top leaders. It was Adnani who declared the establishment of the caliphate in 2014 with Baghdadi as its caliph. He was killed in August 2016.

Tarif al-Sayed Issa. Born May 1959 and grew up in the Idlib countryside. From an early age, he became active in the Syrian Muslim Brotherhood and took part in protests against Hafez al-Assad in Idlib in March 1980. After the regime abducted his younger brother to pressure him to turn himself over, he fled to Jordan. He lived in Jordan, Iraq and Yemen in the following years – always remaining engaged as an activist in the Syrian Muslim Brotherhood. Eventually, he claimed asylum in Sweden. Following the 2011 uprising, he returned to Syria and became active in charity work, the Syrian National Council, local councils and – at fifty-five years old – as a fighter in the liberation of his home town. He died in March 2018, after driving his car over a landmine in Idlib two months earlier.

Osama al-Rifai. Born in Damascus, Syria, in 1944. He is the eldest son of a famous Damascene religious scholar: Karim al-Rifai. He studied English at the University of Damascus and after his graduation preached at the mosque of his father. In 1981, regime repression forced him into exile. He was allowed to return in the late 1990s and built up a powerful charitable movement in the capital. Following the start of protests in 2011, he became a vocal supporter of the uprising. Regime repression forced him, again, into exile. From Türkiye, he was involved in the establishment of the Syrian Islamic Council in 2014. In 2021, the Syrian Interim Government appointed him as the Mufti of the Republic. His younger brother, Saraya, is also a well-known sheikh and supporter of the uprising.

TIMELINE OF EVENTS

Year	*Month*	*Tunisian Transition*	*Syrian Crisis*
2011	Jan	14: President Zine El Abidine Ben Ali leaves for Saudi Arabia. 30: Rached Ghannouchi returns from exile.	
	Feb	19: General amnesty for political prisoners. 27: Mohammad Ghannouchi government dissolved; Beji Caid Essebsi appointed as interim Prime Minister.	
	Mar	1: Formal recognition of Ennahda as political party. 15: Ridha Jaouadi takes over as Friday imam at the Lakhme Mosque.	15: Youth arrested in Daraa, start of uprising. 26: 260 inmates released from the Sednaya prison, among them many Islamists.
	Apr	2: Hizb al-Tahrir public prayer and protest in Tunis.	26–27: Opposition meeting in Istanbul, Turkey.
	May	21: First public statement from Ansar Charia.	9: EU imposes sanctions against Syrian regime. 31–3 June: Antalya opposition meeting.
	June		6: Collective violence aimed at police and army in Jisr al-Shughur.

Year	*Month*	*Tunisian Transition*	*Syrian Crisis*
	July	1: Protest in Sfax in defence of Islam.	16: National Salvation Congress held in Istanbul, Turkey. 29: Free Syrian Army (FSA) established.
	Sep		15: Syrian National Council established.
	Oct	Nessma TV airs Persepolis, protests follow. Protests at Sousse University against barring of niqab turn violent. 23: National Constituent Assembly (ANC) elections.	2: Burhan Ghalioun elected President of the Syrian National Council.
	Nov	Protests start at Manouba University, Tunis. 21: Agreement on formation of Troika government. 22: First plenary session of the ANC.	Sectarian violence in Homs. 11: Ahrar al-Sham Brigade established. 16: Syria suspended from Arab League.
	Dec	12: Moncef Marzouki appointed as President of the ANC. 24: Troika government inaugurated, with Hamadi Jebali as Prime Minister.	
2012	Jan		24: First statement from the Nusra Front.
	Feb	3: ANC starts deliberations.	
	Mar	16 & 23: Protests demanding inclusion of sharia in constitution.	24: FSA signs agreement with Syrian National Council.
	May	12: Agreement on Zaytuna Mosque's autonomy between Hussein Obeidi (Grand Imam of the Zaytuna Mosque), Ministries of Education, Higher Education and Religious Affairs.	25: Houla massacre.
	June	12: Attack on art exhibition in La Marsa. 16: Nidaa Tounes established. 16: Ninth General Conference of the Ennahda party.	

Year	*Month*	*Tunisian Transition*	*Syrian Crisis*
	July	6 July: Nidaa Tounes receives formal recognition as political party.	12: Tremseh massacre. 18: Bomb attack on National Security Headquarters in Damascus. 18: Rebel attack on Damascus starts. 19: Rebel attack on Aleppo starts.
	Aug	13: Draft constitution leaked. 13: Protest for gender equality in the constitution.	
	Sep	14: Attack on US embassy, and involvement of Ansar Charia reported.	Syrian Islamic Liberation Front established. 1: Transitional Council of Aleppo established.
	Oct	18: Lotfi Naguedh assassinated.	Integrated Judicial Council of Aleppo starts work.
	Nov		11: Founding of National Coalition for Syrian Revolutionary and Opposition Forces.
	Dec	14: First draft constitution published.	Sharia Committee in Aleppo established. 7: Supreme Military Council founded. 11: US designates the Nusra Front as terrorist organisation. 12: Founding of Syrian Islamic Front, incorporates Ahrar al-Sham Brigades among other Islamist rebel factions.
2013	Jan		31: The Islamic Ahrar al-Sham Movement established as part of the Syrian Islamic Front.
	Feb	6: Chokri Belaid murdered. 19: Hamadi Jebali resigns as Prime Minister.	
	Mar	14: Ali Laarayedh appointed as Prime Minister.	5: Opposition forces capture Raqqa. Attack led by Nusra Front and Ahrar al-Sham. 6: Aleppo Transitional Council dissolves itself into the Local Council of Aleppo. 19: Syrian Interim Government established, Ghassan Hitto elected as Prime Minister. 21: Ramadan al-Bouti assassinated.

Year	*Month*	*Tunisian Transition*	*Syrian Crisis*
	Apr	22: Second draft constitution published.	8: Islamic State in Iraq and Sham (ISIS) established; Nusra Front declares allegiance to al-Qaeda.
	May	20: Supporters of Ansar Charia clash after being barred from holding a national congress.	
	June	1: Third draft constitution published. 18: UGTT proposes national reconciliation process.	
	July	25: Mohamed Brahmi assassinated.	
	Aug	Tunisian National Dialogue Quartet formed. Tunisian government designates Ansar Charia as a terrorist organisation. 1–7: Ramadan protests. 8: Organisation Tunisienne du Travail (the Tunisian Labour Organisation, OTT) established.	21: Ghouta chemical attack by the Syrian regime kills hundreds.
	Sep	Commission of Consensus established within the ANC. 23: Destourian Movement established.	24: Shared statement by the Nusra Front, Ahrar al-Sham and other Islamist groups: we only support armed violence in the name of Islam.
	Oct	25: National dialogue convention: consensus on technocratic government to replace Troika government in ANC.	
	Nov		14: Abdel Qader Saleh killed. 22: Islamic Front established.
	Dec		1: Anti-ISIS Army of Mujahideen established.
2014	Jan	26–27: New constitution ratified by the ANC. 29: Mehdi Jomaa government inaugurated.	13: ISIS takes control of Raqqa. 22: Geneva II Conference starts.
	Mar	State of emergency (which started in January 2011) ends. 29: Mounir Tlili becomes Minister of Religious Affairs.	2: ISIS retreats from Aleppo city. 16: ISIS retreats from Idlib region.

Year	*Month*	*Tunisian Transition*	*Syrian Crisis*
	Apr	3: United States and Tunisia launch strategic dialogue on economy, security, governance. 30: Transitional Justice law passed.	13: Founding of Syrian Islamic Council (SIC).
	June		26: Supreme Military Council formally disbanded. 29: ISIS's Caliphate established.
	July	22: Twenty mosques closed by Ministry of Religious Affairs.	11: Nusra's declaration of establishing emirate.
	Aug	6: 157 associations closed by Ministry of Interior.	
	Sep		9: Explosion kills leadership of Ahrar al-Sham. 15: Nusra Front creates Dar al-Qadaa. 22: Start of US-led intervention against ISIS.
	Oct	26: First post-revolutionary democratic parliamentary elections.	
	Nov	23: First round of presidential elections.	29: Sharia Committee in Aleppo is reformed into a Sharia Court, services are placed in the hands of the Local Council. The Nusra Front establishes General Management of Services in Aleppo.
	Dec	21: Second round of presidential elections. Beji Caid Essebsi wins against Moncef Marzouki.	25: Levant Front established.
2015	Jan	22: Hussein Obeidi deposed as Grand Imam of the Zaytuna Mosque.	
	Feb	4: Formation of Government of National Unity: coalition of Nidaa Tounes, Ennahda, Free Patriotic Union and Afek Tounes. Othman Battikh becomes Minister of Religious Affairs.	
	Mar	18: Bardo National Museum attack by ISIS. 20: Essebsi proposes Economic Reconciliation Act.	24: Jaish al-Fatehm, or Army of Conquest, established with the aim to attack Idlib.
	June	26: Sousse terrorist attack.	Army of Conquest captures Idlib.

Year	*Month*	*Tunisian Transition*	*Syrian Crisis*
	July	1: Abu Iyadh al-Tunisi killed in Libya. 14: Introduction of Reconciliation Act to parliament. 25: Counter-Terrorism Act passes in parliament.	Supreme Judicial Council established in Aleppo.
	Sep	First Manich Msamah protests organised: the protest campaign continues for two years. 15: Ridha Jaouadi barred from preaching.	18: The five principles of the Syrian Revolution published. 30: Russian intervention starts.
	Oct	25: State of emergency reimposed.	30: Vienna peace talks.
	Dec		8: Riyadh conference held as an attempt to unify opposition.
2016	Jan	6: Othman Battikh replaced as Minister of Religious Affairs.	
	Feb		2: Aleppo surrounded, soon after a ceasefire is agreed that holds until July.
	Mar	7–9 ISIS commandos storm the military barracks and national guard post in Ben Guardene. 22: National Counter-Terrorism Commission set up.	17: Democratic Federation of Rojava established in Northern Syria.
	Apr		Regime bombing of Aleppo increases in severity.
	May	25: Tenth general conference of Ennahda.	
	July		26: Jabhat Fatah al-Sham established, succeeds the Nusra Front and severs relationship with al-Qaeda.
	Aug	13: Abir Moussi appointed President of the Free Destourian Party. 26: New Unity Government inaugurated. Prime Minister is Youssef Chahed.	Abu Muhammad al-Adnani killed in Syria. 24: Turkish intervention in Syria starts: the Euphrates Shield operation.
	Nov	7: National Security Council adopts anti-terrorism and anti-extremism strategy.	
	Dec		14: Syrian regime recaptures Aleppo.

Year	*Month*	*Tunisian Transition*	*Syrian Crisis*
2017	Jan		Clashes between Ahrar al-Sham and Jabhat Fatah al-Sham. 28: Hayat Tahrir al-Sham (HTS) established, successor to Nusra Front and Jabhat Fatah al-Sham.
	May		4: Astana de-escalation zones established through agreement between Türkiye and Russia.
	July	19: Parliament approves seven articles of the Reconciliation Act.	22: HTS gains full control over Idlib city.
	Aug		24: The Civil Administration Initiative held in Idlib, a prelude to establishment of the Syrian Salvation Government.
	Sep	13: Reconciliation Act passed in parliament.	
	Nov		2: Syrian Salvation Government established, which challenges the Syrian Interim Government.
2018	Feb		18: Founding of National Front for Liberation: merger of Nour al-Din al-Zenki and Ahrar al-Sham. 27: Hurras ad-Din established: representation of al-Qaeda in Syrian crisis.
	Apr		14: Regime forces recapture Eastern Ghouta.
	June	1: Publication of Colibe report, results in populist backlash.	
	Sep		17: Türkiye and Russia sign demilitarisation agreement for Idlib.
	Dec		12: Attack by Türkiye on Rojave; US President Trump pulls out US troops from Syria.
2019	Jan	27: Dignity Coalition established.	1–9: Attack by HTS on National Front for Liberation (and Ahrar al-Sham) in the Idlib region. HTS takes over all their positions. Soon after, Local Councils forced to formally recognise Syrian Salvation Government.

Year	*Month*	*Tunisian Transition*	*Syrian Crisis*
	Mar		High Fatwa Council established in Syrian Salvation Government.
	June	20: Qalb Tounes established, President is Nabil Karoui. 27: Bombings in Tunis aimed at police.	
	July	25: Beji Caid Essebsi dies.	
	Sep	15: Kais Saied wins presidential elections. 19: Ben Ali dies in exile in Saudi Arabia.	
	Oct	6: Parliamentary elections.	27: US forces assassinate Abu Bakr al-Baghdadi.
2020	Jan	26: Ridha Jaouadi resigns from the Dignity Coalition.	
	Feb	27: New government formed. Elyes Fakhfakh is Prime Minister, and Rached Ghannouchi is Speaker of Parliament.	
	Mar		Russian–Turkish ceasefire takes hold in north-west Syria and stabilises front lines.
	July	15: Elyes Fakhfakh resigns as Prime Minister. 30: Vote of no confidence against Ghannouchi fails.	
	Sep	2: Hichem Mechichi becomes Prime Minister. 16: Letter with 100 signatories sent to Ghannouchi opposing his upcoming third term as party leader.	
2021	Feb		
	May	12: Dignity Coalition recognised as party.	
	July	21: Kais Saied suspends parliament.	

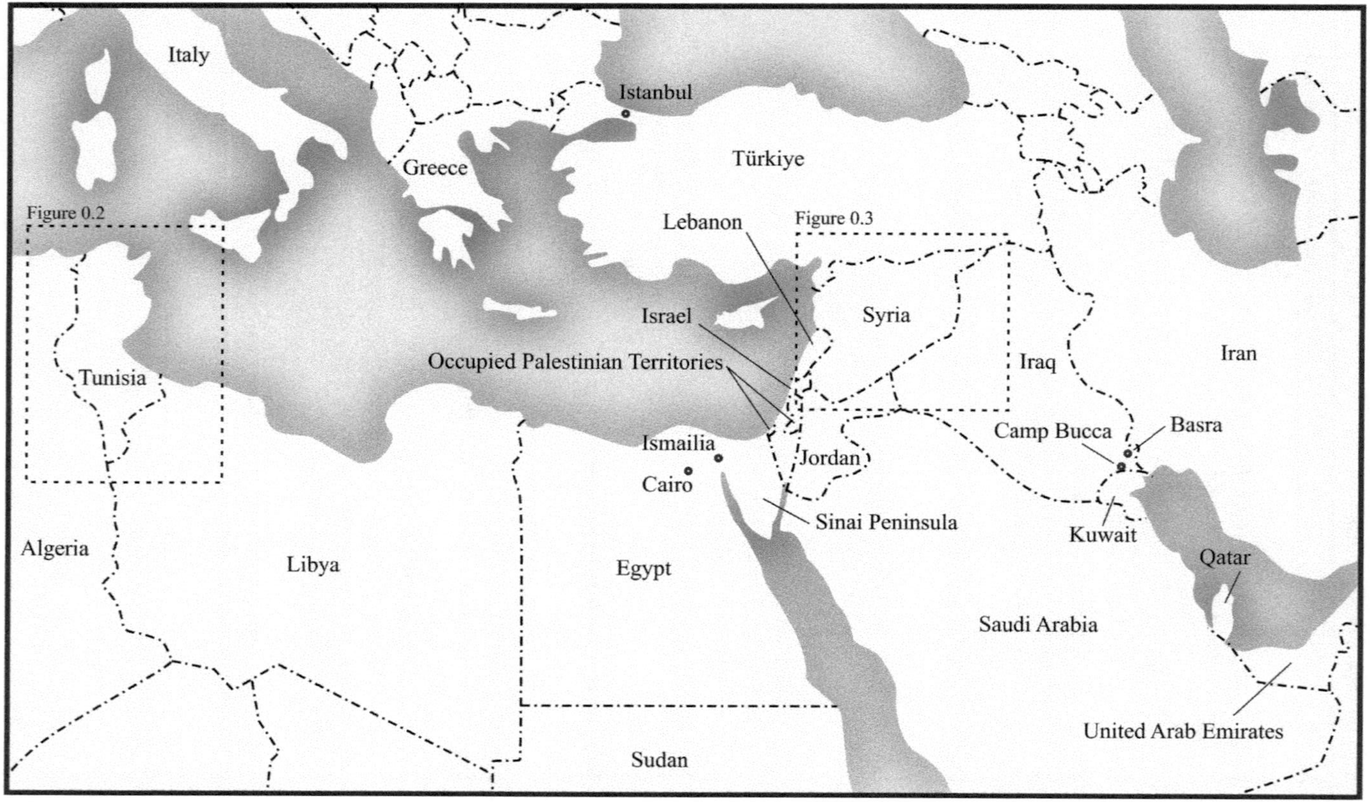

Map 1 Southern Europe, Middle East and North Africa.

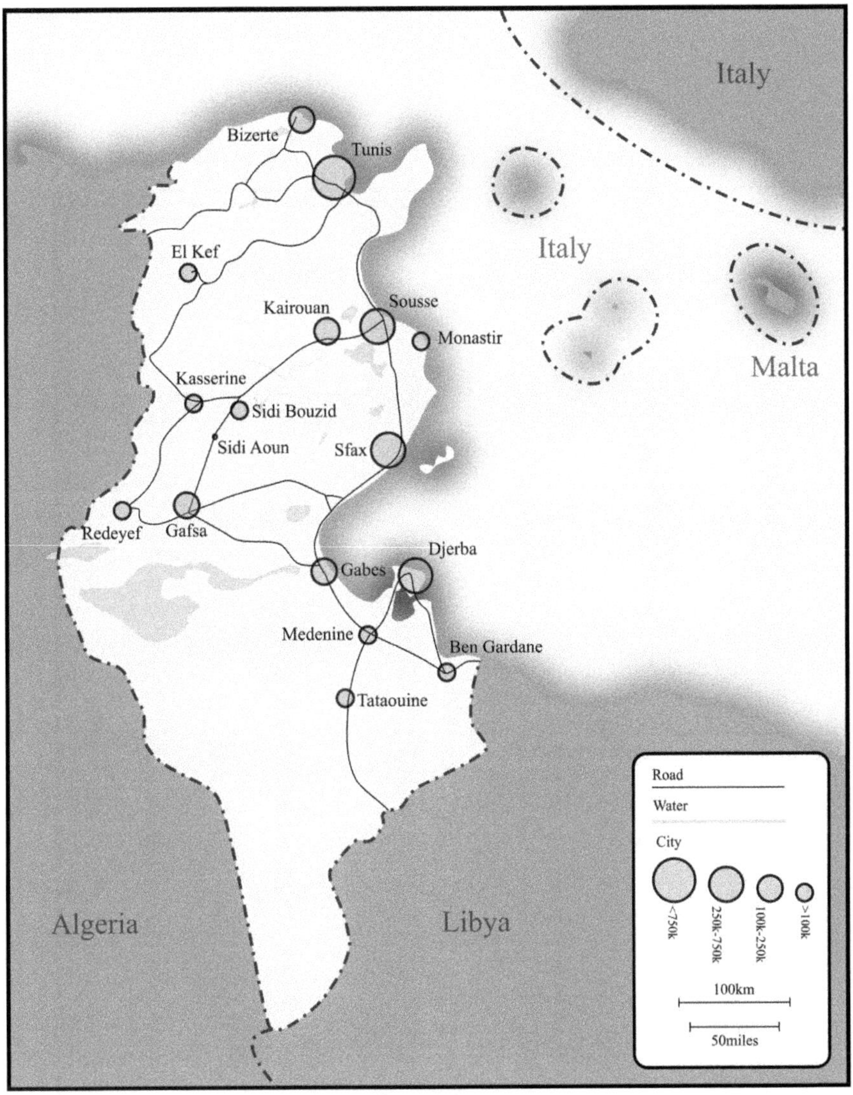

Map 2 Tunisia.

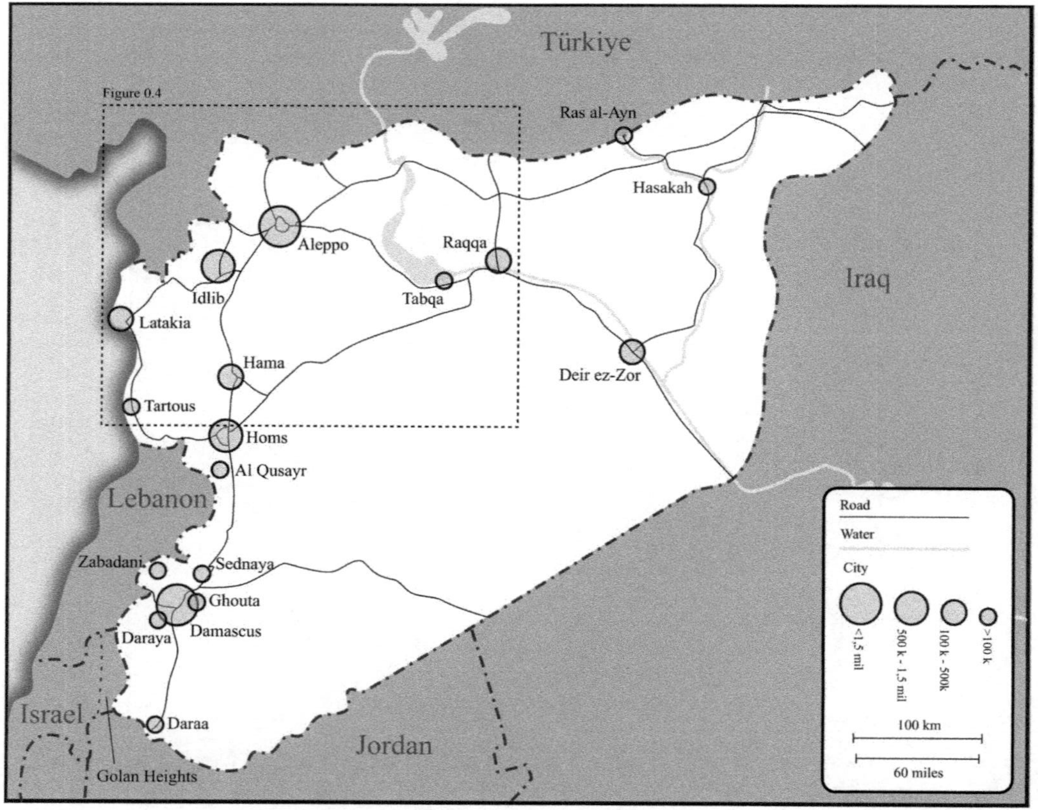
Türkiye
Figure 0.4
Ras al-Ayn
Hasakah
Aleppo
Raqqa
Idlib
Tabqa
Latakia
Iraq
Hama
Deir ez-Zor
Tartous
Homs
Al Qusayr
Lebanon
Zabadani
Sednaya
Ghouta
Damascus
Daraya
Israel
Daraa
Jordan
Golan Heights
Road
Water
City
<1,5 mil
500 k - 1,5 mil
100 k - 500k
>100 k
100 km
60 miles

Map 3 Syria.

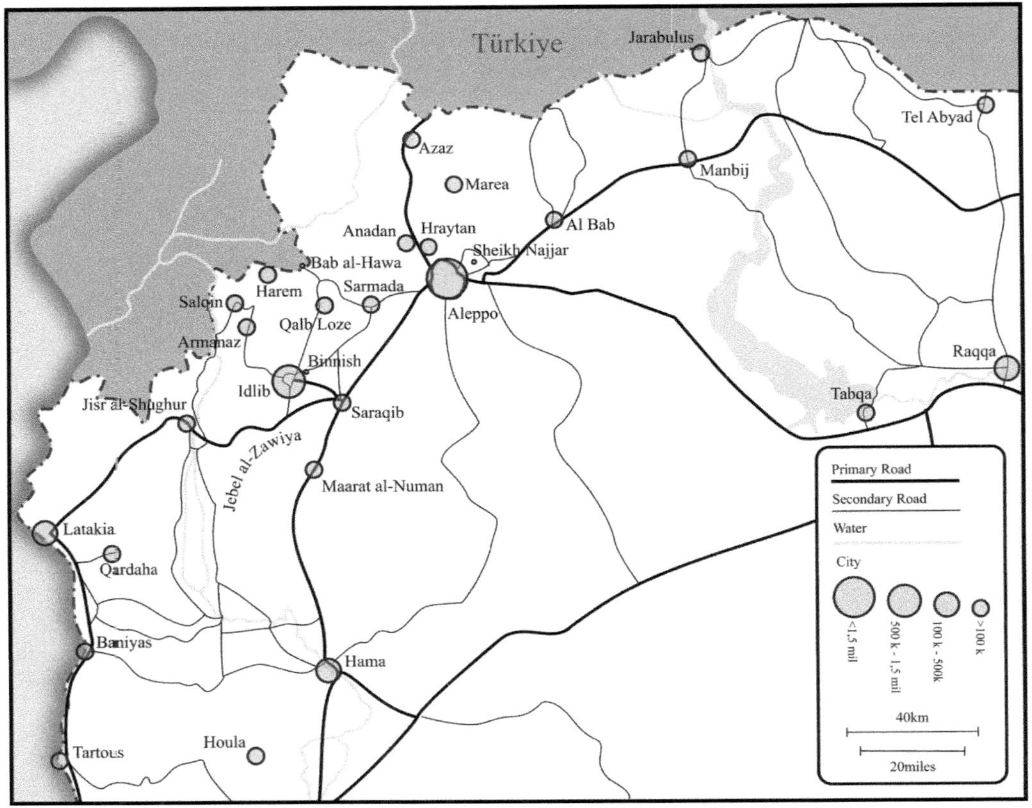

Map 4 North-West Syria.

1

INTRODUCTION

The summer seems to have arrived. It is the beginning of April 2011, and the temperature outside is thirty degrees Celsius. I am sitting in the back of a Tunisian *louage* (a minivan taxi) as we are travelling from Sidi Bouzid to Sidi Ali Ben Aoun in the inland of Tunisia. The landscape is dry and dusty, with endless olive groves lining the roads. Packed in the *louage* as canned sardines, we are leaving the town where the revolution began. It has been less than three months since the former autocrat Zine El Abidine Ben Ali fled to Saudi Arabia into exile. In those twelve weeks, Tunisians lived through momentous political changes: there was a successful second uprising against the Interim Government, continued violence in Tunisia's interior regions and a general amnesty for political prisoners. Revolutionary graffiti covered the walls everywhere, and the hope for a better future was palpable.

I am hoping to meet Khatib Idrissi. Multiple activists mentioned him as a leader of the Salafist movement in the country. I heard that he lives in Ben Aoun. After the *louage* arrives at the bus station, I walk to the closest shop and ask for Khatib Idrissi. A customer replies with a friendly 'just come along, I'll show you where he lives'. The town is like any other in Tunisia's inland, with one main street that has a gas station and some coffee shops serving cafe direct (the Tunisian version of a latte). Sideroads are lined with plastered houses and walled inner gardens. In less than ten minutes, we arrive at his house. Next door, a few youngsters are busy building, all distinct from others in the town by their clothing and long beards. We ring the doorbell, and a man in his thirties opens the door. He walks me around the house and, while I wait, calls the sheikh. Khatib Idrissi is waiting for me when he lets me in. He hears me enter the house – he is blind – and says: 'It's almost noon. You must be hungry. Want to have lunch?'

Khatib Idrissi had already made a name for himself before the revolution. He was born in Sidi Aoun in 1954 and studied nursing in Gafsa. In 1985, he left for Saudi Arabia to work in a hospital and ended up studying sharia sciences while living there. When he returned in 1994, he began teaching sharia sciences in and around Sidi Aoun. At the time, the Tunisian regime repressed political, and especially Islamist, activism. Soon after he started teaching, the political police intervened: they barred him from teaching in any formal (mosque) setting. He continued informally at his house, but oversight from the political police increased and pervaded every aspect of his life. It eventually led him into early retirement. It was around this time that he lost his sight.[1] In 2006, the regime incarcerated him because of his home-based religious education. They released him in 2009.

After the revolution, Khatib Idrissi immediately resumed teaching classes in *taḥfīẓ* (memorisation), *tafsīr* (exegesis), *ʿaqīdah* (creed), *fiqh* (jurisprudence) and *al-sīrah* (prophetic biography) at the local mosque. The Ben Ali regime did not allow these topics to be taught except for *taḥfīẓ*. When I visited him, he had not yet been reinstated as a Friday imam but was busy building a mosque next to his house, where he hoped to become its imam and use it for religious classes. Every weekend, he travelled with a small group of students to give sermons and lessons at local mosques. They visited Sidi Bouzid, Bizerte, Hay Tadamun in the capital and other places around the country.[2]

I begin this book with the example of Khatib Idrissi for three reasons. First, he is an example of the subject of this book. It centres on a deceptively simple question: What is the impact of Islamist movements on post-2011 Arab activism? To answer this question, I compare an Islamist movement during two episodes of social and political conflict, the Tunisian transition and the Syrian crisis, between 2011 and 2021. Many perceived Khatib Idrissi as an outspoken activist in a Tunisian Islamist, and specifically Salafist, movement. His activities seem to warrant such an assessment. He empowered Islam through *daʿwah* (proselytisation) activities, reinstating an autonomous religious sphere after the revolution, building his own mosque and teaching on issues with political relevance. He explicitly opposed labelling himself as a Salafist or Islamist and considered himself an expression of true Islam as it existed among Tunisian people. He explicitly critiqued Sufism – which he did not accept as being part of Islam – and the political Islam of Ennahda.[3] Khatib Idrissi turned into a polarising public figure soon after that fateful January of 2011.

The second reason is that Khatib Idrissi illustrates the importance of a focus on concrete practices when investigating the impact of an Islamist movement. Journalists and scholars alike have described Khatib Idrissi as an ideologue – as someone providing the ideological foundations for a Tunisian jihadi Salafist movement – but the examples show the importance of what he practically did.[4] Khatib Idrissi studied sharia sciences in Saudi Arabia, taught in mosques and at home, and after the revolution restarted classes, built his own mosque and went across the country to teach and proselytise. These concrete activities produced economic and symbolic resources, enacted a way of life as an example to others and fostered social networks between like-minded people. Ideas only have meaning when enacted as concrete practices. To investigate the impact of Islamist movements, I study their distinct practices, such as establishing Islamic schools and charity organisations, articulating Islamic collective identities, enforcing public norms, producing knowledge, creating Islamic political parties, service organisations and courts and engaging in an Islamic jihad.

Third, Khatib Idrissi's life exemplifies the importance of taking the intersection between individual biography and contextual history seriously when investigating Islamist movements. Popular and academic debates are replete with culturalist explanations that explain the popularity and character of such movements based on some particular element of Sunni Islam.[5] However, this makes it impossible to trace how history and biography explain the impact of these movements today. Some scholars analyse Islamist movements as if they exist in a temporal vacuum. In contrast, I show the concrete, practical ways in which biographies of activists, and histories of the contexts in which they are active, shaped the impact of Islamist movements on Arab activism after the 2011 uprisings.

Keeping the above in mind, in this book I describe an Islamist movement during the Tunisian transition and Syrian crisis, follow the life stories of those involved and trace the histories of the context in which they are active. One example is Taha Subhi Falaha. He was a jihadist fighter born in Idlib in 1977 who left for Iraq in order to fight the US occupation and was incarcerated for years by American forces. He returned to Syria in 2012 and made a name for himself as the spokesperson for the Nusra Front and later ISIS. Some readers will know him by his *nom de guerre* of Abu Muhammad al-Adnani. The US killed him in 2016. Another example is Ratib, a local sheikh and imam from Daraa. At the start of the Syrian uprising – undeterred by repeated threats from the Syrian regime – he called for freedom for his people during his Friday sermon. A regime sniper shot him, but he survived. There are many others. They range from jihadist leaders to foot soldiers, from charity workers to politicians, from media activists to Sunni Islamic *'ulamā'* (Islamic scholars). The front matter provides brief descriptions of sixteen individuals who return repeatedly throughout the pages of this book. It is undeniable that Islamist activists, their biographies and the contexts in which they are active are immensely diverse.

A Contentious Practices Approach

However, my goal with this book is to propose an analytical approach that investigates the process through which these diverse examples are drawn together into something we can call an Islamist movement, rather than providing isolated descriptions of individuals and groups that are active 'to support Muslim causes'.[6] When we enquire about the impact of an Islamist movement on Arab activism, we are essentially asking how Islamism gains a unique relevance in episodes of social and political conflict despite its internal diversity.

To investigate this process, I propose the concept of distinct practices. With this concept, I denote the practices (such as establishing associations, producing knowledge, organising protests, coordinating collective violence) that constitute a sociopolitical conflict but are related to a specific stake (something that matters in this conflict, such as liberal values, LGBTQ+ rights or religion) that renders these practices distinct. For example, we can observe the establishment of liberal associations or Christian knowledge production and organisation of Islamic, jihadist, collective violence.

The distinctiveness of practices is not fixed; there are constant struggles to define the legitimate ways in which practices can be set apart and made relevant in episodes of conflict. I analyse the struggles around constructing distinctly Islamic education, associations, judiciary, collective violence, politics, protests, service provision and more. I argue that political Islam is not defined by the characteristics of an Islamist ideology but by the particular, historical and biographical, trajectories along which Islamism is constructed as a distinct type of practice in social conflict. In summary, I place the investigation of contemporary Islamist movements firmly in the concrete practices of contentious collective action.

In doing so, I propose, what I call, a contentious practices approach (CPA) to Islamist movements. Chapter two provides a detailed discussion, but suffice it to say that it draws on the relational sociology of Pierre Bourdieu. The book provides a study of how a distinct set of relational interactions – a social field in Bourdieu's language – emerges around Sunni Islam during episodes of social and political conflict.[7] To do so, I investigate concrete struggles between individuals and organisations about the position of Sunni Islam in relation to the practices that constitute such conflict episodes. These struggles emerge as social movements. They are social processes through which agents share a distinct collective identity, engage in collective action and construct enduring conflictual relations with clearly identified opponents.[8]

Using the contentious practices approach and drawing on a comparison between the Tunisian transition and Syrian crisis, this book proposes that:

1. The impact of Islamist movements is relationally practised. The empirical chapters demonstrate how activists establish Islamic associations, schools, charities and governance institutions; articulate Islamic collective identities; organise Sunni Islamic, jihadist forms of collective violence, produce distinct Islamic knowledge and enforce Islamic public norms. Or, more precisely, they render practices distinct by situating Sunni Islam in relation to education, service delivery, charity, national identities and armed insurrections – to name but a few examples. As a result, alternative educational spheres are created, the authority of established executive authority is challenged, local identities are bridged to transnational ones and a global, jihadist framework is provided for funding and organising collective violence. Contentious interactions become patterned along an Islamic

distinction. By rendering practices distinct, Sunni Islam gains political relevance in relation to local, national and regional conflicts – it turns Islamist.

2. Islamist movements consist of a two-fold struggle to define their impact. When Islamists engage in Islamic educational, political or charitable practices, they inadvertently clash with non-Islamist counterparts in related fields. However, by doing so, they also become embroiled in internal struggles about legitimate ways to render practices distinct. This two-fold struggle, counterintuitively, acts as the binding force that holds an Islamist movement together in relation to a contentious episode. Only those who have a stake in defining the social and political impact of Sunni Islam engage in these struggles, situating them as a distinct collective during conflict episodes.
3. The impact of an Islamist movement is historically and biographically situated. The use of distinctly Islamic practices in prior conflicts shapes how Islam is used to make educational, political or charitable practices distinct in contemporary ones. They inform individual views of the possible and desirable ways to render practices distinct, concurrently shaping the institutional, cognitive and social contexts in which activists operate. In short, when activists use Islam to distinguish their practices, they draw on preexisting resources and perceptions – situating their practices in relation to, first, a history of an Islamist movement and, second, their own past experiences with distinctly Islamic forms of collective action.

Rather than approaching Islamist movements as a substantive phenomenon emerging around a particular ideology, the notion of distinct practices urges more research into the relational mechanisms that make up the process through which an Islamist movement evolves. It tilts research toward genealogies of conflicts around Sunni Islam as a stake, the mechanisms of their evolution across time and space and scenarios of future change. The concluding chapter provides a more detailed discussion of these propositions.

Why Sunni Islam in the Tunisian Transition and Syrian Crisis?

Religious movements are actively involved in conflicts worldwide. The Indian Hindutva movement, a religious-nationalist movement, and the conservative right-wing movement in the US are two examples. In both cases, activists link religion to social and political conflicts. For instance, in India, activists challenge the multi-ethnic character of Indian national identity while emphasising an idealised vision of a harmonious Hindu family – middle class, upper caste and well-educated.[9] They have used violence against Muslim minorities to defend this image of the Indian nation.[10] In the US, activists challenge primary school teaching related to Darwinism, critical race theory and LGBTQ+ rights.[11]

We cannot understand this activism, and the motives of activists involved, without being sensitive to their historical particularities. For example, in India, the partition from Pakistan in 1947, the initial political hegemony of the Congress Party and their economic liberalisation policies during the 1990s are crucial to understanding contemporary Hindu nationalism.[12] In the US, a history of depression-era migration from Texas to California – placing a pious community in a mostly liberal context – gave birth to the politicisation of an evangelical movement that enabled the rise of Richard Nixon and subsequently Ronald Reagan. It produced the polarised liberal–conservative dichotomy that characterises US activism today.[13] The same applies to the emergence of religion as a stake in conflicts between Uygurs and the Chinese government, the civil war in Northern Ireland, Jewish settlers in Palestine or Catholic nationalism in Eastern Europe. All these conflicts have their own historical particularities. The Arab world is no different: religion also emerged in the Arab world as something that matters, as a stake, in social and political conflict.

However, two elements are particular to Sunni Islam as a stake in the Arab world compared with the other examples. First is the breadth and extent of conflict in the region. Historically, the region has been far from stable: the Arab–Israeli conflict has festered since the establishment of Israel in 1948, and the Iran–Iraq war (1980–8), Lebanese civil war (1975–90), Algerian civil war (1991–2002) and US occupation of Iraq (2003–11) are all examples of wars in the Arab region. But, between 2011 and 2021, the number of conflicts in the region has been immense: the revolutions (and counter coups) in Tunisia, Egypt and Sudan; a wave of popular protest in Algeria; the civil war in Libya, Iraq and Yemen; the war in Syria and the political and economic implosion of Lebanon. The region is going through a series of crises the like of which it has not seen since the creation of contemporary Arab nation-states around the First World War.

Second is the historical salience of religion as a stake in the region. Contemporary Arab nation-states emerged when Western ideas of modernity, nationalism and state bureaucracy became more dominant and the power of the Ottoman empire declined while European colonial dominance increased. In this context, religion emerged as a form of authentic resistance to these social and political changes: anti-colonial uprisings invoked Islam (and the notion of jihad), for example, and conservative groups used religious language to oppose social changes that were informed by European ideas.[14] Contemporary Arab states cannot be understood without taking the historical development of, and conflicts about, religious identities and authorities into account. Vice versa, Islamist movements are deeply embedded within Arab nations and states as they exist today. It makes the Arab world and Sunni Islam a perfect case study to investigate how history and biography intersect in shaping the impact of social movements.

Two Case Studies

This book is a comparative study of the Tunisian transition and the Syrian crisis. These two cases were selected because they share a phenomenon of continuous contentious interactions between 2011 and 2021, during which Islamist movements emerged. At the same time, the two cases have different characteristics as they are from different geographical contexts, North Africa versus the Middle East, and have different preceding histories in relation to modern state formation and social transformation. Additionally, while the Tunisian transition is a conflict over defining the character of a future Tunisian nation-state, the Syrian crisis turned into an armed insurgency aimed at overthrowing the regime of Bashar al-Assad. Although both episodes involved deaths, injuries, social fragmentation, foreign interventions and migration, their extent was much greater in the Syrian crisis than in the Tunisian transition. According to the Syrian Network for Human Rights, the conflict resulted in almost 230,000 civilian deaths as of March 2022. The uprising and revolution in Tunisia resulted in fewer than 400 casualties.[15] Because of these differences, when we find similar causal mechanisms explaining the process of Islamist movements, it can suggest that these mechanisms travel beyond these two cases to other conflict episodes.

Having said this, there are multiple historical and biographical connections between these two cases. For instance, Islamists in both episodes often refer to the same historical figures – either as positive or negative inspirations. Individual activists have been involved in both cases due to their travels, resulting in them becoming part of multiple conflicts throughout their lives. Many Syrian youngsters travelled to Iraq in 2003 to fight in a jihad against the US occupation of the country. After the 2011 uprisings, Tunisians travelled to Libya to take part in the civil war there, and many Libyans fled to Tunisia in return. Additionally, between 2012 and 2015, thousands of Tunisians travelled to Syria to fight a jihad. Therefore, we cannot approach these cases as entirely independent from each other. To assess the generalisability of the causal mechanism observed in both cases, we need to build a historically informed and empirically rich understanding of each case study.

Data and Methods

The research for this book began in 2011 and continued until 2021, involving thirteen fieldwork trips to Tunisia, Jordan, and Türkiye between February 2011 and October 2016. During these trips, I conducted interviews with 170 people, some of whom I interviewed multiple times. I selected interviewees based on their activism, participation in protests, affiliation to opposition or rebel groups or involvement in service provision and governance organisations. Many were participants in an Islamist movement, but not all of them were. Besides targeted sampling, I selected interviewees through a process of snowball sampling. The combination of these two methods resulted in a sample that included individuals who were relevant to the study but were still diverse. Interviewees ranged in age from their early twenties to early sixties, and their highest educational attainment ranged from elementary education to PhD level. There was an imbalance for gender, with the large majority of interviewees being men. In addition to these interviews, I also observed protests, public discussions and educational and charitable activism, which were recorded as videos and images. Some of these appear in the empirical chapters.

The biographies of individual activists are a crucial part of my argument in this book. Interviewees consented to be used in an academic study – anonymously. I ensured their anonymity by describing their individual characteristics and biographies in generic terms, which does mean that sometimes a point cannot be made as precisely as would otherwise have been possible. A partial solution is that the study also draws on biographies of public figures, who are discussed with full names and detailed biographies, from publicly available data. Whenever I interviewed a public figure, I asked for consent to disclose the interviewees name, only doing so after receiving consent.

The analysis also relies on hundreds of primary documents, such as videos, speeches, declarations and statements from individuals and organisations, collected through justepaste.it, YouTube.com, Telegram, Facebook pages and websites from relevant organisations. I also created a corpus of self-descriptions and founding statements of around 100 Syrian opposition groups for a related side-project, some of which are also included in this project. I supplemented these sources with a wide range of secondary documents: mainly Syrian and Tunisian newspaper articles, as well as policy papers and analysis articles in Arabic, French and English. Newspaper repositories, such as the Tunisian Turess and the Syrian prints archive were particularly useful in this regard.[16]

Finally, I use descriptive statistics to highlight contextual developments in the Arab world, the Tunisian transition and Syrian crisis. These descriptions draw on multiple sources: the World Bank, the Syrian Observatory for Human Rights and Syrian and Tunisian statistical yearbooks. However, as quantitative data related to the Arab world is notoriously unreliable, I only use this data for descriptive purposes.

The Book

In this book, I describe the Syrian crisis and Tunisian transition through the lens of Islamist movements. As a result, I do not provide a comprehensive description of collective action during these two episodes. I do not discuss the role of unions in the Tunisian transition, nor do I cover the Kurdish politics in Syria and the foreign policies of Türkiye, Iran, Russia and the US in the region. Kenneth Perkins, Nadia Marzouki and Larissa Chomiak already covered the former,[17] and Charles Lister, Gilles Dorronsoro et al., Yassin-Kassab and al-Shami have covered the latter.[18] Moreover, I do not focus on a particular Islamist individual, movement or organisation as there are already numerous publications that do so.[19] While writing this book, I ensured that each chapter can be read independently, but together they provide a comprehensive argument that is more significant than the sum of its parts.

Chapter two introduces the book's topic and specifies its central question. It emphasises its relevance for studies on the politicisation of Islam and relational approaches in studies on social movements. It then details a conceptual and analytical approach based on the notion of distinct practices and explains its indebtedness to Bourdieusian relational sociology. The chapter ends with an outline of what I call a contentious practices approach (CPA) to Islamist movements.

Chapter three provides an introduction to the genesis and evolution of Islamist movements, tracing their development from the fall of the Ottoman Empire, at the beginning of the nineteenth century, to the rise of transnational Islamist movements at the beginning of the twenty-first. The chapter argues that we cannot understand the character of contemporary Islamist movements without considering the historical contexts in which they developed.

Chapter four provides a detailed empirical description of the Tunisian political transition, offering a relational analysis of an Islamist movement and tracing its rise, transformation and decline during this conflict episode. In the first part, it observes how situating Islam as distinct practice in relation to an associational, educational and political field reshaped access to symbolic, institutional and material resources, imbuing it with political relevance. In the second part, it traces several conflicts about how Islam could and should render practices distinct. These conflicts brought together activists who had a stake in defining Islam as a distinct practice, inadvertently setting them apart as a distinct Islamist movement. In the last section, we trace how distinctly Islamic practices became increasingly rare towards 2021, reflecting the decline of the movement.

Chapter five does the same for the Syrian crisis, observing how activists used Islam to render public services, collective violence, justice and governance distinct. In the second part, it traces conflicts that pitted organisations such as the Syrian Islamic Council, the Syrian Muslim Brotherhood, Ahrar al-Sham, the Nusra Front, the Islamic State in Iraq and Syria – and their representatives – against each other. Islam as a stake drew them together into an Islamist movement. The last section narrates how, towards 2020, foreign powers increasingly defined the dynamics of the Syrian crisis, leaving less space for local agents to enact distinct practices, resulting in the movement's decline.

Chapter six compares the life cycle of an Islamist movement during the Tunisian transition and Syrian crisis. In the first section, it offers a taxonomy of positions that activists took in struggles about how to use Islam to render practices distinct. This taxonomy demonstrates that these positions reflect the diverse expression, and enduring traits, of an Islamist movement that transcends the temporal and geographic boundaries of a single conflict episode. Second, an Islamist movement during the Tunisian transition and Syrian crisis is compared, using the taxonomy of relational positions. The chapter concludes with a preliminary outline of the causal mechanisms that can elucidate the life cycle of an Islamist movement in one contentious episode and its evolution across multiple ones.

Chapter seven revisits the book's central questions and its propositions. It discusses each in light of the data presented in the preceding chapters. It concludes with an outline of the broader relevance of these propositions for studies on social movements and political Islam.

Notes

1. It was due to a hereditary illness that affects the pigment of the eyes.
2. Interview with Khatib Idriss, 4 April 2011, Sidi Ali Ben Aoun, Tunisia.
3. Ibid.
4. See for instance Babnet, 'al-Khaṭīb al-Idrīsī yanfī I'tiqālhu'; Qilālah, 'Tamma A'tiqālhu Wa-Al-Īfrāj 'anhu Fī Ẓurūf Ghāmiḍah: Min Huwa Al-Khaṭīb Al-Idrīsī Shaykh Al-Salafiyīn Fī Tūnis Wa-Ū'stādh Abū 'Iyāḍ'; Allani, 'The Islamists in Tunisia between Confrontation and Participation: 1980–2008'; A., 'Tunisie: Le Prédicateur Salafiste Jihadiste Al-Khatib Al-Idrissi Arrêté et Relâché'; Merone, Blanc and Sigillò, 'The Evolution of Tunisian Salafism after the Revolution: From La Maddhabiyya to Salafi-Malikism', 463.
5. To give just one infamous example: Lewis, *The Crisis of Islam: Holy War and Unholy Terror*.
6. Wiktorowicz, *Islamic Activism: A Social Movement Theory Approach*, 2.
7. Bourdieu, *Practical Reason: On the Theory of Action*.
8. For this definition of a social movement, see Della Porta and Diani, *Social Movements: An Introduction*, 20.
9. Banerjee, 'Armed Masculinity, Hindu Nationalism and Female Political Participation in India: Heroic Mothers, Chaste Wives and Celibate Warriors'.
10. BBC News, 'Uttar Pradesh: India's Muslim Victims of Hate Crimes Live in Fear'.
11. Casas, 'One Mother's Mission to Ban "Vulgar" Books"'.
12. Chacko, 'The Right Turn in India: Authoritarianism, Populism and Neoliberalisation'; Jaffrelot, *Hindu Nationalism: A Reader*.

13. Dochuk, *From Bible Belt to Sunbelt: Plain-Folk Religion, Grassroots Politics, and the Rise of Evangelical Conservatism*.
14. See for example Heyd, *Foundations of Turkish Nationalism: The Life and Teachings of Ziya Gökalp*; Gökalp, *Turkish Nationalism and Western Civilization: Selected Essays*; Hourani, *Arabic Thought in the Liberal Age 1798–1939*; Tripp, 'Islam and The Moral Economy: The Challenge of Capitalism'.
15. AFP, 'Tunisia Revolution: 129 Died, 634 Injured, Official Count Shows'; SNHR, 'On the 11th Anniversary of the Popular Uprising'.
16. See turess.com and en.syrianprints.org, respectively.
17. Chomiak and Entelis, 'The Making of North Africa's Intifadas'; Marzouki, 'Tunisia's Wall Has Fallen'; Perkins, *A History of Modern Tunisia*.
18. Lister, *The Syrian Jihad: Al-Qaeda, the Islamic State and the Evolution of an Insurgency*; Baczko, Dorronsoro, and Quesnay, *Civil War in Syria: Mobilization and Competing Social Orders*; Yassin-Kassab and Al-Shami, *Burning Country: Syrians in Revolution and War*.
19. See for instance Meddeb, *Ennahda's Uneasy Exit From Political Islam*; Merone and Cavatorta, 'Salafist Mouvance and Sheikh-Ism in the Tunisian Democratic Transition'; Lefèvre, *Ashes of Hama: The Muslim Brotherhood in Syria*; Bunzel, 'From Paper State to Caliphate: The Ideology of the Islamic State'; Gerges, 'ISIS and the Third Wave of Jihadism'; Wolf, *Political Islam in Tunisia: The History of Ennahda*; Tamimi, *Rachid Ghannouchi: A Democrat within Islamism*; Hamdi, *The Politicisation Of Islam: A Case Study Of Tunisia*.

2

THE DISTINCT PRACTICES OF ISLAMIST MOVEMENTS

> We had to threaten with a protest asking for the resignation of the Minister to get an appointment with him. When we met the Minister we asked: are you an Ennahda Ministry or a Ministry for all Tunisians? The answer was, of course, all Tunisians. We then asked: then why are there no Salafists working here? They should also be represented in government agencies![1]

What Are We Talking About?

To investigate its impact on Arab activism, it is necessary to define what Islamist movements are. Many scholars, implicitly or explicitly, define Islamist movements as a network of agents (either individuals or organisations) who share an ideology and collective identity derived from Sunni Islam, which forms the basis for sustained conflicts with secular states and the global political order.[2] There are several problems with this understanding of Islamist movements that have a direct impact on how we define them and investigate their impact on Arab activism.

The first issue relates to the emphasis on their opposition to secular states. Multiple studies have shown that Islamist movements do not have to be antagonistic to them. One example is the Justice and Development Party in Türkiye, which embedded itself in Turkish bureaucracy and used the power of the state to implement a programme of societal transformation.[3] Another example is the quote above, in which a young activist, Omar (a pseudonym), argues for the representation of Salafists within Tunisian bureaucracies because they are part of Tunisian society. Instead of disengaging and challenging the Tunisian nation-state, he engages and attempts to cooperate with secular ministries in order to empower the movement. Most political scientists today agree that politics is not only about shaping government policies but includes struggles to construct social categories and individual identities and attempts to transform economic, cultural and social structures. Islamist movements reflect this diversity: activities range from charity activism, education to lobbying, party politics and armed insurrection. It follows that the political impact of Islamist movements might not be enacted in direct reference, and opposition, to state but through projects aimed at social change.

A second issue relates to Islamism as an ideology. A popular definition defines Islamism as an ideology that claims to recreate a true Islamic society by establishing an Islamic State through political action. It implies that there is a particular influence of Sunni Islam on the social and political ideas of Islamists. It proposes a distinct type of state formation, based on Sunni Islamic politics, economy, social justice and so on.[4] In reality, this translation of Sunni Islam to social and political ideas is far from straightforward. There is an immense amount of literature on individuals, parties and movements that attempt to transform society and politics based on Sunni Islam, with much of this literature revolving around ideologies of Islamism,[5] Salafism[6] and Salafi–jihadism.[7] Despite the amount of studies, a causal relationship between the content of these ideologies and types of social, economic and political has not been established. The relationship between notions such as caliphate, sharia, jihad, *tawheed* (unity of faith) and *manhaj an-nabawi* (method, of the prophet and his companions) on the one hand, and Islamist, Salafist or jihadist education, charity, justice, governance and collective violence on the other hand remains unclear.[8]

Consider the notion of Salafism as mentioned in the quote above. It is said to be an ideology build on the idea of return to the authentic version of Islam of *al-salaf al-ṣāliḥ* (or the pious ancestors, often understood as the first three generations of Muslims). It argues for a direct interpretation of the Quran and hadith (implying a unity of faith) and urges individuals to imitate social and political practices, or the methods, of the prophet Muhammad and his companions.[9] Despite a clear ideological core, scholars make subdivisions within the Salafist movement: for example into a purist, politico and jihadi current.[10] The reason is simple: the diversity of Salafist religious interpretations and concrete practices makes it impossible to subsume them within one single movement. In practice, the interpretation of religious texts is flexible, the implementation of ideas around the unity of faith diverse and the translation of the Prophet's actions to concrete practices dynamic. It makes it challenging to relate Sunni Islamic terms such as jihad, *tawheed* and *manhaj an-nabawi* to a distinct type of political ideology.[11] Salafism – as well as Islamism – is not a distinct type of ideology but a label applied to diverse forms of activism.

This observation highlights an issue in the study of Islamist movements: how can we speak of Islamist movements being distinct from other types of social movements when it is impossible to link Sunni Islam to particular types of social and political activism? Does this diversity of activism not render the notion of a distinctly Islamist social movement irrelevant?

In this book, I turn this issue around. I argue that Islamist movements exist because they render their own practices distinct. When a movement draws together a range of social and political practices and comprises a distinct set of participants with their own authority structures and worldviews around Sunni Islam, it is an Islamist movement and has impact. If not, Islamism remains an ideology with individual adherents but without real-life impact or cohesion. Omar, quoted above, through his demand for social representation in a Tunisian bureaucracy, places his activism in a broader Islamist movement that he argues is a distinct but integral part of Tunisian society. Such distinctness can be empirically observed – not in the least because it is highly contentious. Attempts to enact distinctly Islamic practices, as we will see, are subject to constant challenge and struggles. Activists constantly fight among each other to define how Sunni Islam shapes their practices. Ironically, it is these fights that provide the glue that holds an Islamist movement together: only agents who have a stake in defining the social and political impact of Sunni Islam engage in these struggles – situating them as a distinct collective in episodes of social and political conflict.

Islamist movements, as a result, are best approached as a social process through which distinct types of collective action emerge, transform and decline. Such an approach follows much of the recent scholarship that defines social movements as 'a distinct social process' through which agents engage in collective action that comprises 'conflictual relations with clearly identified opponents', 'dense informal networks' and that shares 'a distinct collective identity'.[12] By focusing on their distinct practices, I identify and investigate the life cycle, so to speak, of Islamist movements.

Questions

My aim is to investigate the impact of Islamist movements on post-2011 Arab activism, taking the Tunisian transition and Syrian crisis as case studies. I ask the following questions:

1. In the Tunisian transition and Syrian crisis, what were conflicts around constructing distinctly Sunni Islamic practices?
2. How did these conflicts reflect the emergence, transformation and decline of an Islamist movement?
3. What does the comparison between an Islamist movement in the Syrian crisis and Tunisian transition teach us about the impact of social movements on episodes of social and political conflict?

The rest of this chapter lays out a conceptual and theoretical framework to investigate Islamist movements through the lens of distinct practices. The framework is called the contentious practices approach (CPA). I will first describe the aims of this approach and discuss its relevance for recent studies on political Islam and social movements. This is followed by an introduction of the concepts that make up this approach and a discussion on how the relational sociology of French social scientist Pierre Bourdieu informs the CPA. Finally, I outline the analytical implementation of the CPA and the theoretical questions it enables.

So What?

In writing this book, I have three aims. The first is to add to critical conceptual approaches of Islamism. I investigate Islamist movements as a dynamic process through which distinctly Islamic practices emerge: distinct ways to articulate national identity, for instance, provide public services, administer justice, engage in party politics, create associations, organise collective violence or march in protests. The construction of such distinctness is inherently contentious and defined in relation to other issues at stake in episodes of collective contentious action. It implies that the character of political Islam is not fixed, but morphs with the dynamics of the conflict episode in which it is constructed. By tracing such conflicts, I provide an empirically grounded and historically sensitive account of the social construction of political Islam during the Syrian crisis and Tunisian transition.

My second aim is to bring studies on Islamist movements in direct conversation with relational approaches in social movement studies (SMS). In the last two decades, an increasing number of scholars have applied insights from SMS to Islamist groups and parties. These scholars have drawn mostly on classic approaches revolving around the concepts of political processes and opportunity structures,[13] collective action frames and framing tasks,[14] resource mobilisation theory[15] and social network analysis.[16] Far fewer scholars have drawn on the more recent relational turn in SMS, such as the mechanistic approach from Tarrow, Tilly and McAdam,[17] the strategic approach from James Jasper[18] or strategic action fields from McAdam and Fligstein.[19] In this book, I add to these relational approaches an awareness of situational distinctness. Islamist movements revolve around the construction of Sunni Islam as a distinct stake in, in this case, the Tunisian transition and Syrian crisis. In other words, by rendering it the basis of a distinct type of practice, activists situate Sunni Islam in relation to the broader dynamics of these two episodes of contentious collective action.

My third aim is to argue for the concept of distinct practices to analyse the life cycle of Islamist movements in conflict episodes. The construction of distinct practices results in the creation of alternative educational spheres, challenges to established executive authority, situating local identities among transnational ones and providing a global, jihadist framework for funding and organising collective violence. As a result, Sunni Islam emerges as something that matters – as a stake – in struggles around reforming education, providing public services, drafting a constitution or creating courts. It challenges existing institutional and material structures while reshaping worldviews of individual activists. With the notion of distinct practices, we can trace the trajectory along which Sunni Islam gains political relevance, how this political relevance transforms and, possibly, how it eventually declines.

The Concepts of Political Islam and Islamism

During the last two decades, scholars studying the relationship between politics and religion have increasingly focused on the historical development of, and struggles around, the idea that religion is, and should be, an apolitical and private affair. Talal Asad, through a hermeneutical lens, highlighted the western European genealogy of the idea of religion as apolitical and distinct from public affairs.[20] Jose Casanova, taking a more institutional lens, argued for the struggles that ensue when religion goes through a process of deprivatisation.[21] Saba Mahmood demonstrated how Egyptian women acquired agency by internalising a conservative normative framework through their participation in an Egyptian mosque movement. It stands in contrast to Western feminist ideas of the relation between individual liberation and sociopolitical empowerment.[22] These scholars persuasively show how ideas about what is political and religious are situationally contingent and vary across time and space.

These insights also apply to political Islam. Muhammad Qasim Zaman has written extensively on the notion of *al-amr bi-al-maʿrūf wa-al-nahy ʿan al-munkar* (to enjoin what is right and forbid what is wrong) to show how this notion for a moral-religious imperative transforms with social and political changes brought on by modernisation.[23] Charles Tripp traced the changing discursive responses from activist Muslims to the impact of capitalism in the Arab world. He shows how Muslim intellectuals were, and still are, constantly re-articulating the position of Islamic concepts (for example that of *al-maṣlaḥah al-ʿāmmah*, or public interest) in relation to the development of capitalism.[24] Sarah Tobin investigates how conservative Muslims in Amman attempt to ease tensions between piety and globalised capitalism while trying to be good Muslims. She observes how economic practices, such as banking and finance, are cast as distinctly Islamic and how piety is increasingly subjected to economic calculations through 'evaluations of value, profit, and risk; rationalisation of processes and outcomes [and] audits of "performance indicators"' applied to assess who and what is a good Muslim.[25] The notion of piety is recast, so to speak, through a global capitalist cognitive frame. These practical examples of flexible interpretations of key Sunni Islamic terms put into doubt any clear and fixed distinctions between religion, society, state and politics.

Rather, the boundaries between these concepts, and their interrelations, are constantly being renegotiated and fought over. As Fredric Volpi notes:

> Religion and politics remain two open-ended and interlocked interpretive fields that are consistently redefined in order to meet the explicit or implicit needs of their users. [. . .] Political Islam is thus a contextual construct that refers to what individuals in a particular sociohistorical context think about the political and the religious.[26]

The above insights render the concept of political Islam problematic. The concept assumes a default separation between public politics and private religion: a default that is transgressed through the Islamisation of politics – the process that forms the basis of political Islam as ideology. If the separation between politics and religion varies across time and space, political Islam cannot be anything but one of many variable relational connections between what is seen to be politics and what is seen to be religion. In short, the reason for a generic concept of political Islam is lost.

This study turns this issue around. Instead of assuming the Islamisation of politics and society matters because it transgresses a norm of separation between religion and public life, it investigates how this connection emerges as something that matters. My contribution to the above studies is to propose an empirical study of how relational connections between politics, society and religion emerge as being distinct: as particular and important for social and political affairs. To do so, I investigate the practical ways through which people enact such relational mappings, analysing the concrete struggles of constructing, and positioning, Sunni Islam in relation to politics, social activism, governance, education and justice. Empirically, these struggles emerge as social movements: social processes through which agents share a distinct collective identity, engage in collective action and construct enduring conflictual relations with clearly identified opponents.[27]

Studies on Islamist Movements

During the last two decades, there has been an increased focus on Islamist movements in SMS.[28] The edited volume by Quintan Wiktorowicz, *Islamic Activism,* published in 2004, proved a step change for this increased focus.[29] In the volume, Diane Singerman engages with debates on collective identity and social networks in studies on social movements when she analyses Islamist movements in Egypt. She shows that under the authoritarian rule of Mubarak in Egypt, it is the networked character of associational life that explains the emergence and organisational power of Islamist movements.[30] Mohammed Hafez investigates the relation between changing political opportunity structures and radicalisation of the Groupe Islamique Armé in Algeria – drawing on the social movement work of Charles Tilly, Sidney Tarrow and Doug McAdam.[31] He argues that it is the sequence of initial political liberalisation followed by a sudden closure that set the stage for the radicalisation of Islamism in the country. Hakan Yavuz draws on similar works to argue that the impact of changing political opportunities differs between Islamist movements. He emphasises the importance of disaggregating Islamist movements into their constituent elements to enable an assessment of these diverse consequences of opening opportunity spaces.[32] There have been many related studies since.[33]

These scholars provide a critical reply to studies that imply an Islamic exceptionalism on the behaviour and identity of Islamist movements. Instead, they show that Islamist movements are very much subject to the same political constraints, social dynamics and pragmatic considerations as other social movements. They show that many existing approaches in SMS can be applied to Islamist movements, for example those revolving around collective identity formation, social networks and political processes.[34]

Having said this, because these scholars apply existing approaches to Islamist movements, they tend not to challenge the conceptual frameworks on which they build. The added value to SMS remains somewhat underdeveloped.[35] In the following years, some notable exceptions emerged. Cihan Tuğal, for instance, builds on the case of Islamist movements in Istanbul, Türkiye, to observe how an integration with state power is crucial to their contentious project of societal transformation.[36] It is an observation that is at odds with mainstream political process approaches in SMS that revolve around analysing social movements as challengers to, and distinct from, state institutions.[37] It opens up a new field of social movement theorisation on the causes and consequences of social movements embedding themselves in state power, for instance, around the notion of hegemony.[38] Asef Bayat approaches Islamism not as a well-defined movement but as a type of discursive practice to highlight the varied individual, institutional, social, economic and political interactions that shape relations between state and societal power.[39] It highlights that the collective activism of social movements does not have to be embodied by explicitly political claims but can be embodied by everyday practices: a politics of presence in which the social logic of movements is weaved into society at large, undercutting the power of (authoritarian) states without directly challenging them.[40]

These contributions show that concrete practices of Islamist movements challenge taken-for-granted conceptual boundaries in SMS: boundaries between state and social movements, between social and political activism, and between individual conviction and collective action. They provide empirically rich accounts of the dynamic ways in which the emergence of Islamist movements transforms concrete practices of politics, social activism and state governance. Both Cihan Tuğal and, more explicitly, Asef Bayat, are testament to the fact that scholars can use concrete practices to investigate the relational, interactive construction of Islamist movements.

Even though the relational perspective was conceptually and theoretically novel to SMS, the extent that Bayat and Tuğal engaged with contemporaneous debates remained limited. This was probably because relational approaches in SMS were still relatively new and underdeveloped. Tilly, Tarrow and McAdam published the *Dynamics of Contention*, proposing a relational approach around mechanisms and processes, only a few years before. The same goes for Jasper's strategies approach. McAdam and Fligstein's *Theory of Fields* was still a few years away. The current study can draw on these seminal relational contributions and, crucially, the range of debates, empirical studies and analyses that they started: studies from Nick Crossley,[41] Donatella della Porta,[42] Suzanne Staggenborg,[43] Eitan Alimi et al.,[44] Marcos Ancelovic[45] and Florence Passy[46] are just a few of many examples. It is safe to state that I am writing this chapter at a time when relational approaches are close to becoming dominant in SMS.

Relational Approaches in Social Movement Studies

In the past two decades, SMS have made a so-called relational turn. Three popular relational approaches in these studies revolve around the mechanisms and processes that make up so-called contentious episodes,[47] the formations and transformations of social fields[48] and the strategic interactions between agents and organisations.[49] Together, these approaches analyse social movements as a dynamic process, observe the formations and transformations of social fields and place interactions between agents front and centre in their analyses. They also highlight that relational approaches in studies on social movement have a tendency to focus on dynamic interactions: explaining processes through causal mechanisms, observing change and transformation of fields and theorising strategic interactions. Situating these interactions among broader relational patterns of contentious episodes – for example among broader social processes, other strategic action fields or the historical development of contextual structures – has received less attention. It makes comparative analyses based on these relational approaches challenging.

In the *Dynamics of Contention*, Tilly, Tarrow and McAdam propose a relational approach based on the notion of causal mechanisms, or types of 'events that alter relations among specified sets of elements in identical or closely similar ways over a variety of situations'.[50] Mechanisms are concrete causal explanations for changing relations between agents (or organisations) that travel beyond a particular empirical case: for example, the constitution of agents, scale-shift and polarisation. Regular sequences of these mechanisms combine into social processes. The varied ways in which mechanisms combine into social processes explains the different outcomes of similar processes across cases.[51] These mechanisms proved to be very useful in theorising the processes through which relational interactions change.

Having said this, causal mechanisms and processes often lack a situational embeddedness in an empirical reality: they provide descriptions of empirical events but lack the conceptual depth to set them apart from broader social dynamics.[52] It limits the explanatory power of mechanisms: they end up retelling a historical narrative, without showing the analytical particularity – and importance – of the events that are narrated. Take the paired comparison between the 1950s Mau Mau revolt in Kenya with the 1980s Philippines Yellow Revolution as analysed in the *Dynamics of Contention*. In both these cases, the authors observe mechanisms of 'collective attribution of threat or opportunity', 'social appropriation' and 'brokerage'.[53] But without conceptual specification of what social change each mechanism constitutes, it is difficult to assess the extent that brokerage in the Mau Mau revolt is distinct from, say, mechanisms of coalition building or institutionalisation or to what extent attribution of threat reflects a similar empirical change in social relations in the 1950s Mau Mau revolt in Kenya with the 1980s Philippines Yellow

Revolution. Because of the lack of conceptual depth, it is difficult for scholars to make mechanisms empirically distinct and compare them between episodes.

Doug McAdam and Neil Fligstein build on the concept of strategic action fields (SAFs) to create their relational approach. They define an SAF as a 'meso-level social order where actors interact' around a commonly recognised 'stake', with 'knowledge of one another under a set of common understandings about the purposes of the field, the relationships in the field and the field's rules'.[54] They argue that the formation and transformations of SAFs can be easily empirically observed: when two or more organisations 'attempt to attain ends that are sufficiently similar' and if that compels them to 'take one another's actions into account' then, McAdam and Fligstein argue, you are observing an attempt at field formation.[55]

What remains unclear is how to assess if ends are sufficiently similar to approach interactions between organisations as a distinct SAF. Or, to turn the phrasing around, it is unclear how to assess if a stake is sufficiently distinct to warrant giving analytical importance to related social interactions and the SAF they make up. If we observe interactions between, for instance, the universities of Oxford, Cambridge, Durham and St Andrews around a campaign of state funding of colleges, how can we assess if these interactions are separate from, say, funding campaigns by other (noncollegiate) UK universities? This issue is further complicated because the stake of a field is often subject to challenge, and with it, who and what does and does not belong to mutually shared interactions. It makes it challenging to define boundaries of SAFs and to compare them across cases.[56]

A final, third, approach is the strategic interaction approach by James Jasper.[57] The approach revolves around an analysis of how micro-level social interactions shape strategies for contentious action.[58] It builds on the notion of players[59] on the one hand and arenas[60] on the other. Players can be individuals or organisations: examples of arenas are courts, the street, organisations or any other social setting. The range of strategies available to agents is constrained by the rules and resources of an arena. These arenas are the outgrowth of preceding strategic interactions. As Jasper notes: the 'strategic approach highlights the trade-offs, choice points and dilemmas that players face as they negotiate arenas'[61] and that, in turn, arenas 'embody past decisions, invested resources and cultural meanings' of players.[62]

The strategic interaction approach pivots questions regarding the causes and consequences of collective action to who did what, when and where – and how previous actions shape strategies available to players today.[63] It means that it becomes difficult to situate the development of resources – and related structural differentiations and inequalities – in local, regional or global histories. The value of local political resources in Idlib, for instance, declined with the increased military cooperation between Russia and Türkiye in Northern Syria in 2017. Having access to foreign alliances became more important to the detriment of controlling local governance institutions – a change that was not the result of strategic interactions in Idlib. In other words, the value of political resources was shaped indirectly by regional dynamics. Because Jasper's approach emphasises individual interactions, it is challenging to analyse how local arenas of strategic interactions are situated in, and shaped by, such local, regional or global structural developments.

In short, these scholars approach social movements as a dynamic process: observing the formations and transformations of social fields and placing interactions between agents front and centre in their analyses. Having said this, situating these interactions among general relational patterns – situating a distinct set of social mechanisms among a broader set of social processes or a particular strategic action field among others – received less attention. It makes it challenging to compare mechanisms, fields or patterns of strategic interactions across cases and articulate theoretical arguments that travel beyond the case studies at hand.

The Contentious Practices Approach

I use the concept of distinct practices – defined below – to analyse the relational trajectories along which Islamist movements emerge, transform and decline. The concept enables an analysis of the concrete struggles around constructing Sunni Islam as something that matters in social and political conflict and how these struggles are situated among broader dynamics of contentious episodes. In doing so, it adds to critical conceptual approaches in studies on political Islam and relational approaches in studies on social movements.

The CPA draws on the work of French philosopher and social scientist Pierre Bourdieu.[64] First, it builds on his relational philosophy of science: social entities and their properties exist only through their position in relation to the other entities that make up an interactive context, or a social field. Individuals, organisations and their characteristics do not exist on their own but exist in relation to other individuals and organisations that make up a social space. Second, it builds on his dispositional philosophy of action. The range of potential actions of a social agent is embodied: they are the outcome of lived experiences of interactions in social fields that inscribe field structures onto social agents.[65] It implies that the actions of agents are not the result of a rational assessment of interests but, rather, of individual biographies, made up from internalised, lived structural positionalities, or dispositions, that reflect in the horizon of perceived possible actions.

Bourdieu uses the notions of capitals, habitus and fields as a conceptual toolkit to investigate the 'two-way relationship between objective structures (those of social fields) and incorporated structures (those of habitus)' and look at how it shapes the reproduction and transformation of social life.[66] Anglophone scholars have used the approach extensively: from studies on social inequality[67] and organisational sectors[68] to the embodied experience of boxing[69] and many other topics.[70]

The combination of a relational view of social reality and a dispositional approach to social action enables an analysis of the struggles to construct Islamist movements and their impact on collective contentious action. In doing so, this book is heavily indebted to Bourdieu but does not faithfully apply a Bourdieusian relational sociology to Islamist movements. Instead, I draw on his philosophy of science and action and translate the concepts of capitals, habitus and fields to fit more closely with traditional approaches in SMSs. As a result, although the relational and dispositional elements remain mostly intact, the concepts I use in the CPA are more selective and movement-centric than capitals, habitus and social fields as used by Pierre Bourdieu. I also forego the use of his rather state-centric notion of field of power to allow for more flexibility regarding the temporal and geographical context in which movements are active. The concepts I use are distinct practices, contextual resources, individual dispositions and social stakes. I will discuss each in turn, before specifying the type of relational theories that we can construct using these concepts.

Concepts

I use the term distinct practices to highlight practices that revolve around a particular stake – something that matters – in social and political conflict. A stake can be education, political liberalisation, workers' rights or any other sociopolitical issue. To revolve around a particular stake, practices need to be set apart from, while being positioned and prioritised in relation to, dynamics of a broader conflict. In short, practices need to be rendered distinct. Examples of distinct practices are LGBTQ+, liberal, labour, Islamic or Christian (or other) ways of making claims, establishing organisations, raising money, dressing, talking, articulating collective identities, organising collective violence and producing knowledge. The construction of distinct practices implies the construction of distinct sets of structured resources and individual dispositions and struggles to define the legitimate principles that govern interactions between participants involved in this stake.[71]

With contextual resources, I mean the symbolic, material and institutional assets that are produced through, used in and provide the structure to a social context. Examples are financial capital – money – in an economic field, authority in a political field and institutional access in an organisational field. Resources are the staple of traditional analysis of social movements around the concepts of political opportunity structures,[72] the rational actor models of the resource mobilisation theory[73] and its cultural translation as cognitive frames.[74] In these approaches, scholars tend to approach social, political or economic resources as substantive entities that have characteristics of their own: a political opportunity structure is open or closed, resources are present or they are not. Instead, the CPA builds on the view that resources, and the social structures they reflect, exist because of being enacted relationally. A religious field, for example, exists as a distinct pattern of social interactions around the production of the authority to consecrate. This authority is structured by – and structures in return – religious elitism and marginalisation. Practical examples of such structuration are notions of orthodoxy and heterodoxy, church hierarchy and different levels of authority among Muslim scholars, the *'ulamā'* (religious scholars) and sheikhs.[75]

When I mention individual dispositions, I am referring to individuals' internalised categorisations of social life and expectations of the principles that govern social interactions.[76] I use dispositions to highlight the internalised boundaries and frames that help make sense of social space and the expectations of behaviour that go along with it: who you belong to, who the other is and what action is seen as possible, legitimate and necessary. Dispositions become explicit when enacted: they make up the horizon of possible actions in relation to other agents in a situation.[77] An individual that lives according to a schedule set by five prayers a day, for example, is not just setting a daily schedule according to religion, but is allowing religion to shape how this person socialises, learns, works and interacts with their community. Since the cultural turn in studies on social movements, scholars have taken cognition more seriously in their analyses. The notion of cognitive frames,[78] cognitive liberation,[79] discursive opportunities[80] and narratives[81] have all been used to assess cognition-related issues in the emergence and development of social movements.[82] Individual dispositions, as used here, emphasises the cognitive elements of relational positionality and their enactment through concrete individual actions.

With social and political stakes, I refer to the contentious interactions that emerge around the reconstruction of a particular resource and related dispositions. For a stake to emerge, these contentious interactions need to be set apart, and positioned in relation to, other stakes in a social setting. They need to define their own autonomous dynamics while having a broader social and political importance. The notion of social stake echoes the Bourdieusian notion of social field: a set of historical relations between social positions anchored in a certain form of power that prescribes its own particular values and possesses its own regulative principles.[83] A religious field exists, for instance, in the extent that it has its own distinct structured hierarchy around access to religious authority and inculcates its own distinct ways of viewing social life. Both of which are enacted through concrete practices of their participants. Social fields emerge when they ascribe, and are structured by, their own dispositional logics. Bourdieu approached art, journalism, religion and the family all at some point in his career as a social field.[84] A social stake emerges when structural hierarchies become unstable and dispositional logics are questioned. Such struggles and challenges are always situated within a broader setting that comprise other stakes and fields. Well-known examples of changing structural hierarchies and dispositional logics in religious fields are the European reformation and the emergence of contemporary Salafism. Both these stakes – the social and political nature of Christianity and Islam – cannot be seen in independence from broader social, political and economic changes that are taking place around them.

Relational Theories

The questions that these concepts enable us to ask revolve around the relationships between contextual resources and individual dispositions and how they shape the emergence, transformation and decline of distinctly Sunni Islamic practices in contentious episodes. A first set of questions relates to correspondences between individuals' structural positionality and their cognitive dispositions. How are people's practices shaped by the structural context in which they live? This type of question relates closely to classic Bourdieusian studies on the relationship between taste and social class or the role of Catholic religion as a type of symbolic resource used to legitimate and reinforce social inequalities.[85] There are an impressive number of academics who have investigated the relation between social behaviour and class position using this approach.[86]

The second approach revolves around questions about how divergences, conflicts and change emerge between structural positionality and individual dispositions, tracing the trajectories of challenges to and conflicts around dispositional logics of social fields. There are two reasons why contextual resources and individual dispositions can be considered dissimilar while also being mutually constituted. The first relates to time. In the words of Bourdieu:

> To understand the practices of [field participants], and not least their products, entails understanding that they are the result of a meeting of two histories: a history of the position they occupy and the history of their dispositions. Although position helps to shape dispositions, the latter, in so far as they are the product of independent conditions, have an existence and efficacy of their own and can help to shape positions. In no field is the confrontation between positions and dispositions more continuous or uncertain than in the literary and artistic field.[87]

The historical development of resources across time is individual agnostic but field specific; while biographical dispositional change is field agnostic but individual specific. Individuals are shaped by all the social fields in which they have taken part throughout their lifetimes, while resources are shaped by all the individuals that produce them. Practically, this means there is no mechanical relation between structural positionality of an individual and their dispositions in that field. When two individuals share a structural position in the same field, they will not exhibit the same behaviour because their reactions to the situation they find themselves in is shaped by their own life histories. Let us say that two jihadists are released from prison around March 2011 and find themselves in the middle of the Syrian crisis. Despite having a similar age, class and regional background, when faced with a particular situation – say the choice to establish a rebel group – their individual life histories (their experiences with adversity and success in prior jihadist struggles, family dynamics and discussion with fellow imprisoned jihadists) will shape their dispositions to quietism or whether they embed their organisation in the national uprising or international networks of a global jihadist movement. Because of differences in individual dispositions, individuals react differently to similar structural positions they hold. Instead of assuming that field position defines individual dispositions, it is better to approach structural positionality as a prism that refracts individual dispositions into a unique horizon of possible actions.[88]

A second reason relates to space. As noted above, groups, institutions and other organisations are agents. At the same time, they can be approached as fields. It means that fields are like matryoshka dolls that fit within each other.[89] This vertical integration can turn a social field into a stake in and of itself. Take, for instance, al-Qaeda as a representative of a global jihadist field that included, at one point in time, organisations such as al-Qaeda in the Islamic Maghreb (AQIM) in North Africa and the Nusra Front in Syria. These groups can all be considered social fields in and of themselves. It raises a tension of vertical integration: how are similarities constructed between these subfields when they are active in such very different contexts? AQIM is active in North Africa, the Nusra Front in Syria. AQIM is a transnational regional movement. The Nusra Front is local and engaged in governance initiatives. These organisations are subject to different pressures and incentives because of the different situations in which they exist – while constantly interacting based on a shared understanding of what it means to be part of a global jihadist movement. It raises tensions around the construction of a collective jihadist identity, the aims of a jihadist movement and who can speak in name of global jihadism. Jihadism itself becomes a stake. Sometimes conflicts around jihadism become so intense to breakdown any shared understanding of what a global jihadist movement is and who belongs to it: the fall out between al-Qaeda and the Islamic State in Iraq and Syria is an example.

In its analysis of social movements, the CPA focuses on how a stake endures despite – and partially because of – being subjected to these temporal and spatial forces. It does not theorise the mechanisms that constitute a process of contentious episodes, as was the case with the *Dynamics of Contention*. It also does not place the emergence and internal governance of a field at the centre of studies on social movements, as was the case with the *Theory of Fields*, or individual interactions, as with the *Strategic Action Approach*. Instead, the CPA takes distinct practices as a central concept to investigate the life cycle of a stake in episodes of social and political conflict, and theorises its evolution across time and space. In doing so, it draws on these previous approaches, in addition to the work of Pierre Bourdieu: it investigates the mechanisms through which a social stake is situated as a distinct field of social, strategic interactions in relation to broader episodes of conflict. On the one hand, it implies we need to analyse how individual biographies and contextual histories shape these interactions. On the other, it implies we need to analyse how these interactions are situated in local, regional and global settings. It tilts research toward an analysis of genealogies of conflicts, the mechanisms of their evolution and the scenarios of future change.[90] Scholarship on this line of relational research is not as large as those focusing on issues of reproduction and socialisation, but it does exist. Philip Gorski and Bradford Verter have explored similar questions.[91] It is this latter set of questions that is central to the CPA.

The Praxis of CPA Analyses

What are the conflicts around constructing Sunni Islam as a distinct stake in these conflicts? How is Sunni Islam situated in relation to other stakes? How do such struggles relate to local, national or global conflicts? How do individual biographies situate participants in relation to these conflicts? These are just some questions that scholars can ask using a CPA in studies on social movements. To answer these questions, we have to trace relational trajectories that explain the emergence of a distinct practice that makes up a social movement. If we can identify and compare such relational trajectories, we will gain an understanding of the how and why of the impact of movements on contentious episodes.

A CPA analysis unfolds in three steps:

1. Describe conflicts around the construction of distinct practices. What are the distinct dispositions, resources and contentious interactions that make up these conflicts?
2. Trace the trajectories of these conflicts across time and space. Drawing on individual biographies and contextual histories, identify the varied ways that a particular distinct practice – and related stake – emerged, transformed and declined in local, regional and global settings.
3. Theorise the relational mechanisms that make up the process through which distinct practices emerge, transform and decline across time and space.

What is the impact of Islamist movements on post-2011 Arab activism? I started this chapter with a quote from Omar that problematised popular perceptions of Islamist movements. As a solution, the CPA provides an approach that places concrete practices front and centre in its analysis and adds a focus on distinction as the central contentious issue of analytical concern. The outcome is a relational analysis of social movements that emphasises situational positionality, in contrast to existing relational approaches in social movement studies, without neglecting the interactive dynamics as the basis of the emergence and transformation of collective contentious action. Meanwhile, it enables a detailed empirical study of the construction of Sunni Islam as a social and political stake, adding to critical studies of political Islam. Together, as an answer to the question guiding this book, it results in a paired comparison of the trajectories along which Islamist movements emerged, transformed and declined during the Tunisian transition and Syrian crisis between 2011 and 2021.

Notes

1. Interview with Omar, 2 October 2012, Tunis, Tunisia.
2. See for the application of such an approach Brachman, *Global Jihadism: Theory and Practice*.

3. Tuğal, 'Transforming Everyday Life: Islamism and Social Movement Theory'; White, *Islamist Mobilization in Turkey: A Study in Vernacular Politics*.
4. Roy, *Globalized Islam: The Search for a New Ummah*, 58.
5. Tibi, 'The Islamist Venture of the Politicization of Islam to an Ideology of Islamism: A Critique of the Dominating Narrative in Western Islamic Studies'; Eligür, *The Mobilization of Political Islam in Turkey*; Kepel, *Jihad: The Trail of Political Islam*.
6. Wiktorowicz, 'Anatomy of the Salafi Movement'; Meijer, *Global Salafism: Islam's New Religious Movement*; Lacroix, 'Between Revolutionaries and Apoliticism: Nasir Al-Din Al-Albani and His Impact on the Shaping of Contemporary Salafism'; Pierret, 'Salafis at War in Syria: Logics of Fragmentation and Realignment'.
7. Tibi, 'The Totalitarianism of Jihadist Islamism and Its Challenge to Europe and to Islam'; Drevon, 'Embracing Salafi Jihadism in Egypt and Mobilizing in the Syrian Jihad'; Wagemakers, *A Quietist Jihadi: The Ideology and Influence of Abu Muhammad Al-Maqdisi*; Hegghammer, *Jihad in Saudi Arabia: Violence and Pan-Islamism since 1979*; Brachman, *Global Jihadism: Theory and Practice*; Gerges, 'ISIS and the Third Wave of Jihadism'; Khosrokhavar, *Inside Jihadism: Understanding Jihadi Movements Worldwide*.
8. Rupesinghe, Naghizadeh, and Cohen, 'Reviewing Jihadist Governance in the Sahel'; Hegghammer, 'Jihadi-Salafis or Revolutionaries? On Religion and Politics in the Study of Militant Islamism'; Li, 'A Jihadism Anti-Primer'.
9. Haykel, 'On the Nature of Salafi Thought and Action'.
10. Wiktorowicz, 'Anatomy of the Salafi Movement'; see also Haykel, 'On the Nature of Salafi Thought and Action'; Pierret, 'Salafis at War in Syria: Logics of Fragmentation and Realignment'; for an alternative preference-based typology, see Hegghammer, 'Jihadi-Salafis or Revolutionaries? On Religion and Politics in the Study of Militant Islamism'.
11. For a similar observation see Volpi, *Political Islam Observed*, 208.
12. Della Porta and Diani, *Social Movements: An Introduction*, 20.
13. Kitschelt, 'Political Opportunity Structures and Political Protests: Anti-Nuclear Movements in Four Democracies'; Tarrow, *Power in Movement: Social Movements and Contentious Politics*; Goldstone, 'More Social Movements or Fewer? Beyond Political Opportunity Structures to Relational Fields'; McAdam, *Political Process and the Development of Black Insurgency, 1930–1970*.
14. Benford and Snow, 'Framing Processes and Social Movements: An Overview and Assessment'; Snow et al., 'Frame Alignment Processes, Micromobilization,

and Movement Participation'; Snow and Benford, 'Ideology, Frame Resonance and Participant Mobilization'.

15. McCarthy and Zald, 'Resource Mobilization and Social Movements: A Partial Theory'; Jenkins, 'Resource Mobilization Theory and the Study of Social Movements'.
16. Diani, 'Networks and Social Movements: A Research Programme'; Castells, *Networks of Outrage and Hope: Social Movements in the Internet Age*; Passy, 'Social Networks Matter. But How?'; Mische, 'Cross-Talk in Movements: Reconceiving the Culture-Network Link'; Snow, Zurcher and Ekland-Olson, 'Social Networks and Social Movements: A Microstructural Approach to Differential Recruitment'.
17. McAdam, Tilly and Tarrow, *Dynamics of Contention*.
18. Jasper, 'A Strategic Approach to Collective Action: Looking for Agency in Social-Movement Choices'; Jasper and Duyvendak, *Players and Arenas*.
19. Fligstein and McAdam, 'Toward a General Theory of Strategic Action Fields'; Fligstein and McAdam, *A Theory of Fields*.
20. Asad, *Formations of the Secular: Christianity, Islam, Modernity*; see also Soares and Osella, 'Islam, Politics, Anthropology'.
21. Casanova, *Public Religions in the Modern World*.
22. Mahmood, *Politics of Piety: The Islamic Revival and the Feminist Subject*; see also Abu-Lughod, 'Do Muslim Women Really Need Saving? Anthropological Reflections on Cultural Relativism and Its Others'.
23. Qasim Zaman, *The Ulama in Contemporary Islam: Custodians of Change*; Mahmood, *Politics of Piety: The Islamic Revival and the Feminist Subject*, 60; Cook, *Commanding Right and Forbidding Wrong in Islamic Thought*.
24. Tripp, 'Islam and The Moral Economy: The Challenge of Capitalism'.
25. Tobin, *Everyday Piety: Islam and Economy in Jordan*, 5.
26. Volpi, *Political Islam Observed*, 18.
27. Paraphrased from Della Porta and Diani, *Social Movements: An Introduction*, 20.
28. One earlier example is Lapidus and Burke, *Islam, Politics, Social Movements*.
29. Wiktorowicz, *Islamic Activism: A Social Movement Theory Approach*.
30. Singerman, 'The Networked World of Islamist Social Movements', 143–44.
31. Hafez, 'A Political Process Explanation of GIA Violence in Algeria'.
32. Yavuz, 'Opportunity Spaces, Identity, and Islamic Meaning in Turkey'.
33. Sutton and Vertigans, 'Islamic "New Social Movements"? Radical Islam, Al-Qa'ida and Social Movement Theory'; Gunning, *Hamas in Politics: Democracy, Religion, Violence*; Gunning and Baron, *Why Occupy a Square?:*

People, Protests and Movements in the Egyptian Revolution; Karagiannis, 'Political Islam and Social Movement Theory: The Case of Hizb ut-Tahrir in Kyrgyzstan'; Meijer, 'Taking the Islamist Movement Seriously: Social Movement Theory and the Islamist Movement'; Lacroix, *Awakening Islam: Religious Dissent in Contemporary Saudi Arabia*; Eligür, *The Mobilization of Political Islam in Turkey*.

34. Several of these studies were a direct reply to calls for broadening empirical material in studies on social movements. See McAdam and Tarrow, 'Dynamics of Contention Ten Years On', 18.
35. See for example Lacroix, *Awakening Islam: Religious Dissent in Contemporary Saudi Arabia*; Gunning and Baron, *Why Occupy a Square?: People, Protests and Movements in the Egyptian Revolution*; Karagiannis, 'Hizballah as a Social Movement Organization: A Framing Approach'.
36. Tuğal, 'Transforming Everyday Life: Islamism and Social Movement Theory'.
37. Tarrow, *Power in Movement: Social Movements and Contentious Politics*; Fligstein and McAdam, 'Toward a General Theory of Strategic Action Fields', 5.
38. Tuğal, 'Transforming Everyday Life: Islamism and Social Movement Theory', 430.
39. Bayat, *Making Islam Democratic: Social Movements and the Post-Islamist Turn*, 4–5.
40. Ibid., 203.
41. Crossley, *Making Sense of Social Movements*.
42. Della Porta and Diani, *Social Movements: An Introduction*; della Porta, 'Radicalization: A Relational Perspective'.
43. Meyer and Staggenborg, 'Thinking about Strategy'.
44. Alimi, Bosi and Demetriou, *The Dynamics of Radicalization: A Relational And Comparative Perspective*.
45. Ancelovici, 'Bourdieu in Movement: Toward a Field Theory of Contentious Politics'.
46. Passy and Monsch, *Contentious Minds: How Talks and Ties Sustain Activism*.
47. McAdam, Tilly and Tarrow, *Dynamics of Contention*.
48. Fligstein and McAdam, 'Toward a General Theory of Strategic Action Fields'; Fligstein and McAdam, *A Theory of Fields*.
49. Jasper, 'A Strategic Approach to Collective Action: Looking for Agency in Social-Movement Choices'; Jasper, *Getting Your Way: Strategic Dilemmas in the Real World*; Jasper and Duyvendak, *Players and Arenas*.
50. McAdam, Tilly and Tarrow, *Dynamics of Contention*, 24.

51. Ibid., 24, 305–47.
52. For a similar criticism Koopmans see, 'A Failed Revolution-But a Worthy Cause'.
53. McAdam, Tilly and Tarrow, *Dynamics of Contention*, 95, 102.
54. Fligstein and McAdam, 'Toward a General Theory of Strategic Action Fields', 3.
55. Fligstein and McAdam, *A Theory of Fields*, 167–68.
56. Ibid., 215–22.
57. Jasper, 'A Strategic Approach to Collective Action: Looking for Agency in Social-Movement Choices'.
58. Jasper and Duyvendak, *Players and Arenas*, 9–10.
59. '[T]hose who engage in strategic action with some goal in mind', see Ibid., 10.
60. A 'bundle of rules and resources that allow or encourage certain kinds of interactions to proceed, with something at stake', see Ibid., 14.
61. Ibid., 20.
62. Ibid., 17.
63. See Ibid.
64. Bourdieu, *Distinction: A Social Critique of the Judgement of Taste*; Bourdieu and Wacquant, *An Invitation to Reflexive Sociology*; see also Gorski, 'Bourdieusian Theory and Historical Analysis: Maps, Mechanisms, and Methods'; Emirbayer, 'Manifesto for a Relational Sociology'; Bottero and Crossley, 'Worlds, Fields and Networks: Becker, Bourdieu and the Structures of Social Relations'. I am not the first, nor will I be the last, to draw on Bourdieu in studies on social movements. See for instance Ancelovici, 'Bourdieu in Movement: Toward a Field Theory of Contentious Politics'; Crossley, *Making Sense of Social Movements*; Krinsky, 'Fields and Dialectics in Social Movement Studies'; Mathieu, 'L'espace des mouvements sociaux'; Mathieu, 'The Space of Social Movements'.
65. Bourdieu, *Practical Reason: On the Theory of Action*.
66. Ibid., vii.
67. Savage, *Social Class in the 21st Century*; Hjellbrekke et al., 'The Norwegian Field of Power Anno 2000'; Ljunggren, 'Elitist Egalitarianism: Negotiating Identity in the Norwegian Cultural Elite'.
68. Fligstein, *The Architecture of Markets: An Economic Sociology Of Twenty-First-Century Capitalist Societies*.
69. Wacquant, *Body & Soul: Notebooks Of an Apprentice Boxer*.
70. For an overview, see Sallaz and Zavisca, 'Bourdieu in American Sociology, 1980–2004'.
71. The notion of distinct practices is somewhat related to the debate on the construction of collective identity and its relation to postmodernist structural

transformation: see Melucci, *Challenging Codes: Collective Action in the Information Age*; Melucci, *The Playing Self: Person and Meaning in the Planetary Society*; Touraine, *The Voice and the Eye: An Analysis of Social Movements*; Touraine and Mercy, *Critique of Modernity*.

72. Tarrow, *Strangers at the Gates: Movements and States in Contentious Politics*; Tarrow, *Power in Movement: Social Movements and Contentious Politics*.
73. Jenkins, 'Resource Mobilization Theory and the Study of Social Movements'; McCarthy and Zald, 'Resource Mobilization and Social Movements: A Partial Theory'.
74. Benford, 'An Insider's Critique of the Social Movement Framing Perspective'; Snow and Benford, 'Ideology, Frame Resonance and Participant Mobilization'.
75. Iannaccone, 'Religious Practice: A Human Capital Approach'; Verter, 'Spiritual Capital: Theorizing Religion With Bourdieu Against Bourdieu'; Rey, *Bourdieu on Religion: Imposing Faith and Legitimacy*; Furseth, 'Religion In the Works of Habermas, Bourdieu, and Foucault'; Dianteill, 'Pierre Bourdieu and the Sociology of Religion: A Central and Peripheral Concern'.
76. Bourdieu, *Practical Reason: On the Theory of Action*, 8.
77. Maton, 'Habitus'.
78. Snow and Benford, 'Ideology, Frame Resonance and Participant Mobilization'.
79. McAdam, *Political Process and the Development of Black Insurgency, 1930–1970*.
80. Giugni et al., 'Institutional and Discursive Opportunities for Extreme-Right Mobilization in Five Countries'; Koopmans and Statham, 'Ethnic and Civic Conceptions of Nationhood and the Differential Success of the Extreme Right in Germany and Italy'.
81. Polletta, 'It Was like a Fever . . .' Narrative and Identity in Social Protest'; Polletta, *It Was like a Fever: Storytelling in Protest and Politics*.
82. The notion of agents' dispositions relates to causal mechanisms, such as the 'attribution of threat' in the *Dynamics of Contention*, the importance of emotion in Jasper's arenas of interactions and the notion of individual skills in Fligstein and McAdams SAFs. See McAdam, Tilly and Tarrow, *Dynamics of Contention*, 46–47; Jasper, 'A Strategic Approach to Collective Action: Looking for Agency in Social-Movement Choices', 6; Fligstein and McAdam, *A Theory of Fields*, ch. 1 and 2.
83. Bourdieu and Wacquant, *An Invitation to Reflexive Sociology*, 16–17.
84. Bourdieu, *The Rules of Art: Genesis and Structure of the Literary Field*; Bourdieu, 'The Field of Cultural Production, or: The Economic World Reversed'; Bourdieu, 'Genèse et Structure Du Champ Religieux'; Bourdieu, *Practical Reason: On the Theory of Action*, ch. 3.

85. Bourdieu, 'Symbolic Power'; Bourdieu, *Distinction: A Social Critique of the Judgement of Taste*. See also Bourdieu, 'Genesis and Structure of the Religious Field'.
86. Friedland, 'The Endless Fields of Pierre Bourdieu'; Savage et al., 'A New Model of Social Class? Findings from the BBC's Great British Class Survey Experiment'; Savage, *Social Class in the 21st Century*; Skeggs, 'Context and Background: Pierre Bourdieu's Analysis of Class, Gender and Sexuality'; regarding the use of Bourdieu in US sociology, see Sallaz and Zavisca, 'Bourdieu in American Sociology, 1980–2004'.
87. Bourdieu, *The Field of Cultural Production: Essays on Art and Literature*, 61.
88. Bourdieu and Wacquant, *An Invitation to Reflexive Sociology*, 17; Bourdieu, 'The Field of Cultural Production, or: The Economic World Reversed'; see also Gorski, 'Bourdieusian Theory and Historical Analysis: Maps, Mechanisms, and Methods'. For a study that emphasises the importance of biography in Islamist mobilisation, see Arat, *Rethinking Islam and Liberal Democracy: Islamist Women in Turkish Politics*.
89. Fligstein and McAdam, 'Toward a General Theory of Strategic Action Fields', 3.
90. Note that in a formula, the analytical framework then reads as follows: [(History) (Biography)] + Events = Social Movement.
91. Gorski et al., *The Post-Secular in Question: Religion In Contemporary Society*; Gorski and Altınordu, 'After Secularization?'; Verter, 'Spiritual Capital: Theorizing Religion With Bourdieu Against Bourdieu'.

3

THE EVOLUTION OF ISLAMISMS

> What humanity strives for is the obliteration of humiliation and deprivation in society, and that every human being can achieve a living standard that is worthy of human dignity. It is this that the various schools [*madhāhib*] of socialism strive for; and that Islam's programme [*al-Islām barnāmijuhu*] offers to achieve.[1]

How can we narrate the history of an Islamist movement when the relationship between politics and religion is situational and contingent? The concept of Islamism assumes a default separation between public politics and private religion, which is transgressed through the politicisation of religion. This allows for a history of transgressive ideas, ideologues or organisations. However, several scholars have convincingly shown that ideas about what is political and religious vary across time and space, meaning that any default separation is but one of many variable relational connections between the two.[2] As a result, a *raison d'être* for the concept of political Islam disappears – as there is no default separation to transgress – and with it the focus for a historical narrative. At its most extreme, the relevance of narrating a history of Islamism, Salafism or jihadism disappears completely as they disappear as empirical objects of study altogether. In Frederic Volpi's *Political Islam Observed*, for example, the only history left to narrate is that of the study of political Islam – not political Islam itself.[3]

However, it is undeniable that a group of individuals and organisations share a background of collective activism around Islam. We see this in the shared institutional history around organisations such as the Muslim Brotherhood, Palestinian Hamas and Tunisian Ennahda as well as the Groupe Islamique Armé (Armed Islamic Group) in North Africa, al-Qaeda and ISIS. Or we see this in historical figures who serve as ideational reference points, such as Ibn Taymiyya, Hassan al-Banna, Sayyid Qutb, Yusuf al-Qaradawi, Bin Baz and al-Albani, and references to historical events, ranging from decolonial struggles, the Afghan war, Iranian revolution and the Algerian and Bosnian civil wars to the Egyptian repression of Islamist activism. Regardless of whether they refer to these events positively or negatively, activists share a repertoire of references to organisations, individuals and struggles. Despite their diversity, it seems there is something that brings them together around a shared history of collective activism.

How to square the circle? Following the contentious practices approach (CPA), I do not approach Islamism as a transgression of a division between private religion and public politics. Instead, I approach it as the attempt to make connections between politics, society and religion particular and important in relation to social and political issues. It means a history of Islamism traces how Islam has been situated as something that matters, as a stake, in relation to social and political issues. The result is an eventful history of situations in which Islam became a contentious issue with real world – social, political and economic – consequences. An example is Mustapha al-Siba'i's (1915–64) quote above, in which he intentionally mixes the notion of Islamic schools of jurisprudence (the *madhāhib*) with the civil notion of political programme (*barnāmij*) to argue that it is both the *madhāhib* of socialism and the *barnāmij* of Islam that strive for the obliteration of social deprivation. The quote comes from his book *The Socialism of Islam*, which was first published in 1959. It is impossible to see his argument, that Islam strengthens socialism, in isolation from the popularity of socialist movements in the Arab world in the 1950s. He rendered Islam relevant to the social and political conflicts of the day.

This chapter provides a narrative of events around which Islam became a contentious issue. It comprises several brief descriptions of historical situations in which individuals situated Islam as relevant in relation to state power, national identities, social activism and collective violence. We will observe how activists, during the 1950s, used Islam to create a distinct type of social activism while they turned to postcolonial Arab states for their empowerment. After this, during the 1960s and 1970s, several activists used Islam to create a distinct type of revolutionary challenge to (Arab) states, while during the 1980s and 1990s they related individual morality to political legitimacy through situating Islam in relation to citizenship, democracy and resistance. Finally, we will see how, in the 1990s and 2000s, Islamists created a global, performative resistance movement based on Islam. The chapter highlights how we can only understand these innovative ways to position Islam in the context in which they were first enacted. Meanwhile, these positions persist as individual dispositions and contextual resources of a contemporary Islamist movement. In brief, the chapter provides an introduction to the evolution, and internal diversity, of an Islamist movement.

The chapter focuses on issues that are relevant in this book. It does not aim to be comprehensive. The chapter provides a general introduction and is wide in scope but shallow in depth. Starting out with the decline of the Ottoman empire and ending at the eve of the 2010 Arab uprisings, it covers about 150 years in fewer than 6,000 words. It caters to readers with little prior knowledge of Arab history. For those who desire more information, there are references in the endnotes to further readings.

Discovering Society

What is today Tunisia and Syria, historically fell within the Ottoman Empire. Ruled from Constantinople (renamed Istanbul in 1930), it covered a territory from Algiers in the west to Basra in the east, and from the border of today's Ukraine in the north to Yemen in the south. People living in the Ottoman empire were subjects to a ruler, not citizens of a nation-state, and their relation to the ruler varied between regions and social groups. It meant that religion legitimated the rule of the Ottoman caliph over his subjects but did not inform any specific (social, educational, etc.) policies. The caliph claimed to represent God's will on earth; he did not represent or act in the name of a Sunni Muslim nation. There was a social class of Sunni Islamic scholars, the *'ulamā'*, from which were drawn the *qāḍīs* (Islamic judges) and *muftīs* (someone who issues fatwas, or religious rulings). They did not, apart from exceptional cases, question the public authority of the caliph. Whenever they did, for example with Ibn Taymiyya and Ibn Qayyim, they challenged the authority of Sunni Islamic scholars and that of the caliph – invariably landing them in prison. There was no uniform framework to manage relations with non-Muslim subjects, or *dhimmī's*, a term that covered a wide range of bespoke financial and legal relationships of non-Sunni groups to the ruler.[4] To further emphasise this, the Ottoman caliph did not directly rule several regions. Today's Tunisia, for example, was ruled by a bey who recognised the authority of the Ottoman caliph but was to a large degree independent. The same went for what is Egypt today. Syria was an Ottoman province that did not have its own independent ruling class. In short, people living in the Ottoman empire were subjects not citizens, and the relation to political rule varied across regions and social groups.

When Ottoman rulers began to centralise their bureaucracy, modernise the economy, standardise education and reform taxation in order to strengthen the empire and hold off foreign incursions, they unintentionally transformed this relationship between political authority and society: a previously distant relationship between caliph and his subjects transformed into a much closer relationship between a population and its state. In this context, scholars such as Khair ad-Din al-Tunsi, Jamal Ad-Din al-Afghani and Muhammad Abduh explored the connections between Islam and emerging nation-states. It transformed Sunni Islam from a religious legitimation of the authority of a ruler to a malleable, symbolic, discursive and institutional resource in social and political conflict.

These reforms had already started in the sixteenth century but accelerated during the eighteenth and nineteenth centuries as foreign powers increasingly challenged the Ottoman empire. Through what later came to be known as the *tanẓīmāt* policies, Ottoman rulers created centralised taxation systems, conscripted armies, created local councils and set up commercial and criminal law courts and nonreligious educational systems.[5] Implementing these *tanẓīmāt* policies varied across the empire: in Syria, tax was increasingly paid directly to the Ottoman state instead of through local intermediaries, and taxation differed between religious groups.[6] Ottoman authorities created a *millet* system for non-Muslim groups – initially Greek Orthodox, Armenian and Jewish but over time more were added – who were given distinct legal positions and ethnic-religious courts and were subject to different tax regimes. In Tunisia, England and France forced the adoption of a security covenant on the bey in 1857 that codified all Tunisian citizens as being equal in the state – with all citizens, irrespective of faith, being subject to one tax law – while creating separate courts for religious minorities and Europeans.[7] The *tanẓīmāt* reforms transformed the previously distant interactions between the caliph and his subjects into a far closer relationship between a population and its state but did so along different paths.

These transformations had immense social impact. In Tunisia, for example, Khair ad-Din al-Tunsi, a famous Muslim reformer, created a Habus council in 1874 that centralised the management of land controlled by religious authorities (almost 25 per cent of Tunisian territory). He also reformed education at the Zaytuna mosque-university and established a Western-inspired Sadiqi college in 1875.[8] In Syria, the *tanẓīmāt* period saw the power of local lords and local Muslim notables in rural areas and mount Lebanon decline in favour of a centralised government in Damascus and Istanbul. In Egypt, Mohammed Ali instead used the *tanẓīmāt* reforms to destroy the final vestiges of traditional Mamluk rulers and create an Egyptian monarchy.[9] In all these cases, the centralisation of state power led to the decline of traditional authorities in favour of a new class of bureaucrats and traders.

Western countries, especially France and England, were active parties in these transformations. The French and English forced the security covenant on the Tunisian bey, by, for example, sailing gunships into the bay of Tunis. They legitimised this covenant as a way to protect Jewish and Christian minorities. But, at the same time, it opened Tunisia up to European economic forces by severing the bey's legal hold over the national economy.[10] In Syria, the formalisation of religious groups brought tensions as each attempted to safeguard its position in an increasingly bureaucratic Ottoman state. It led groups to reach out to European powers: the Maronite Christians of Mount Lebanon (in today's Lebanon) built links with France, while the Druze from the same region built links with England. When tensions turned into a massacre in 1860, European powers, chief among which France, used the event as legitimation to send 12,000 troops to protect Maronite Christians in the region.[11] In short, the centralisation of state power occurred in unison with increased incursions from foreign states into Ottoman society and politics.

It can come as no surprise that in this context multiple thinkers discussed the position of Sunni Islam as the basis of a collective identity in opposition to a Western ascendency. Khair ad-Din al-Tunsi (1820–90), for example, became infamous for his treatise *The Surest Path*. In it, he argued for incorporating Western-style bureaucracies to strengthen Muslim societies – incorporating what works without losing one's own identity.[12] During his tenure as grand vizier to the Tunisian beylik, he implemented many of these views.[13] Jamal Ad-Din al-Afghani (1838–97), in turn, was sceptical of such an approach as it would dilute the religious identity and strength of the Islamic community. He argued instead for the importance of individual Muslims to return to their religious roots as the basis for personal growth, collective identity and public authority in response to Western power. Arguing for the empowerment of the Muslim world, he placed authority in the hands of a Muslim collective, taking authority away from the traditional *'ulamā'* and Islamic rulers.[14] A student of al-Afghani, Muhammad Abduh (1849–1905), was positioned somewhere in between these two approaches. He identified shared elements between Western and Sunni Islamic concepts to articulate authentic responses to European dominance. The term *maṣlaḥah* (interest), for example, mimics the notion of collective utility, *shūrá* (consultation) mimics parliamentary democracy and *ijmā'* (consensus) mimics public opinion.[15] Typical Sunni Islamic terms related to communal authority transformed into terms related to popular representation.

The innovations of al-Tunsi, al-Afghani and Abduh are relevant because they situated Sunni Islam in relation to emerging national identities and centralising state authorities. Each is an important religious reformer in their own right but together, even more so, they provided the first connections between Islam and emerging nation-states. With this, Sunni Islam turned from its traditional role of legitimating the authority of a ruler into a malleable, symbolic, discursive and institutional resource in social and political conflict. It is a transformation that was impossible without the creation of modern bureaucracies, national identities and Western incursions in the late Ottoman empire.[16]

In the decades after, the Ottoman empire continued its decline. In the Ottoman heartland, a young Ottoman, and later young Turk, nationalist movement emerged that constructed a national identity based on an Anatolian heritage – not on Sunni Islam.[17] Across the Arab world, people began to define themselves as Arabs, in clear opposition to their Ottoman rulers. It resulted in a successful Arab uprising against Turkish Ottoman rule, actively supported by European powers, and the establishment of the Arab Kingdom of Syria in 1919. Just one year later, in 1920, the French established a mandate in Syria and Lebanon in its stead, while the English established a mandate in Palestine, Transjordan and Mesopotamia (the latter turned into the Kingdom of Iraq). Arabs in the Middle East found themselves under control of the British and French in countries created by European powers.[18] In today's Türkiye, European powers sought to partition the remnants of the Ottoman empire. But, in this case, Turkish forces led by Mustapha Kemal successfully fought them off. Modern day Türkiye was established, as a secular state, in 1923. The caliphate was formally abolished in 1924.

State Interventions

Opposition to French and English mandate rule was widespread. Independence struggles provided the context in which several political movements emerged, for example Pan-Arabism, Arab Socialism and Islamism. Reflecting the centrality of nascent Arab states in attempts at postcolonial societal transformation, Islamist thinkers, such as Hassan al-Banna, Mustapha al-Siba'i and Taqi al-Din an-Nabhani, all in their owns ways, focused on the state in their efforts to strengthen the position of Islam in society.

The independence movements against French and English mandate rule strengthened national identities but also repositioned Islam in relation to Arab nations and states. In Tunisia, for example, a conflict erupted around the rights of Sunni Muslims to be buried in Muslim cemeteries after naturalising to French citizenship. Many argued that naturalising to the national identity of the colonial oppressor rendered one an apostate, losing the right to a Muslim burial.[19] The issue brought Sunni Islam to the centre of the nationalist struggle by providing an idiom that set Tunisian distinctness apart from French colonial rule. It meant that even the modernist Habib Bourguiba, one of the opposition's leaders, found it necessary to describe himself as the *Mujāhid al-Akbar* (the Supreme Combatant) and compare himself to Jamal Ad-Din al-Afghani.[20] In Syria, the French instead used religion to divide the Syrian kingdom into autonomous regions. They created an Alawi state around Latakia in the north-east, a Druze state in the south and Lebanon as a Christian majority state in the south-east. They divided the rest of Syria between the State of Aleppo in the north and a State of Damascus in the south. When Syrians rebelled against colonial rule in the Great Syrian Revolt in the mid-1920s, they did so around a Syrian nationalist identity: one of its aims was to create an independent and unified Syrian Arab state.[21] Devolution along religious identities became a hallmark of colonial interference.

When Arab states acquired their independence, most between the 1920s and 1950s, questions emerged about the relationship between newly independent states and the societies they governed. Various political movements provided their own answers to this question. First, a pan-Arab movement emerged that aimed to strengthen inter-Arab relations based on their shared Arab identity. At its most extreme, it abolished state boundaries to create a pan-Arab political union. The establishment of the Arab League in March 1945 is one outcome of this movement. Syria was one of its founding members, and Tunisia joined in 1958. Another example is the creation of the Unified Arab Republic, a union of Egypt and Syria, which lasted from 1958 to 1961.[22]

A second movement called for state-led transformation of Arab societies in name of progressive modernism and, often (Western-inspired) socialism. It gave birth to a plethora of socialist Arab parties and unions across the region. The Socialist Baath Party and the Arab Socialist Movement were founded, for example, in Syria in 1947 and 1950, respectively. In Tunisia, the Union Générale Tunisienne du Travail (UGTT) was founded in January 1946. The UGTT was part and parcel of the struggle for national independence and remains one of the most powerful Tunisian political agents today. Its leader, Farhat Hached, is still widely known among Tunisians for giving his life for union and independence activism.

A third movement aimed to guide Arab societies back to the strengths of an Islamic authenticity and reached out to nascent Arab states to do so. In this book, three individuals are important in this respect. First, Hassan al-Banna (1906–49) founded the Society of the Muslim Brothers (better known as the Muslim Brotherhood) in Ismailia, Egypt, in 1928. It aimed to rebuild Islam as a comprehensive way of life to reverse the moral decay of Muslim societies as caused by colonial influences. It called for struggle – both nonviolent and armed – to achieve this aim. The society started out as an Islamic *daʿwah*, or proselytisation, movement. As it grew, it increasingly interacted with the Egyptian state and turned into a formidable political actor. It had a tendency for political pragmatism, with Hassan al-Banna running for political office twice, in 1941 and 1945, though losing both times. As the party became more powerful, its pragmatism came under increasing strain. It created a secret apparatus to defend against state harassment, and the Prime Minister, Nokrashy Pasha, eventually dissolved the organisation. Nokrashy Pasha was subsequently assassinated in 1948. Hassan al-Banna met the same fate in 1949, turning him into a martyr for the movement.[23]

Second, Mustapha al-Siba'i (1915–64) established the Muslim Brotherhood in Syria and became its General Secretary between 1945 and 1961. He met Hassan al-Banna and joined the Muslim Brotherhood while studying at Al-Azhar in Cairo, one of the most important centres of Islamic learning in the Arab world. In *The Socialism of Islam*, published in 1959, al-Siba'i highlighted how social bonds in Islam were based on mutual assistance, cooperation and equality – demonstrating considerable overlap with socialism. He argued that Islam strengthened these notions by rendering them impervious to corruption and resilient to external aggression.[24] As his quote at the start of this chapter alludes to, it left the door open to interpreting Islam through the eyes of the public interests (*maṣlaḥah*) of a society.

Finally, Taqi al-Din an-Nabhani (1914–77), a religious scholar from Jerusalem, founded Hizb al-Tahrir (the Liberation Party) in 1958. He argued for a return to the Islamic way of life based on Islam's rational doctrine, or *ʿaqīdah*. It provided, he argued, the Muslim community with the intellectual power to resist colonial incursions. First, it did this by providing the basis for social bonds between people, surpassing bonds based on patriotism or nationalism. Second, it did this by providing the intellectual basis for a political ideology that went beyond capitalism and communism.[25] Taking these points together, Islam provided a superior basis for social cohesion and political ideology for the *ummah*, or Islamic community. But it still needed a unified executive power to be implemented. It followed that the intellectual repression of Muslims could only be reversed through the creation of an authentic form of government: an Islamic state.[26]

Al-Banna, al-Siba'i and an-Nabhani were all concerned with empowering Sunni Islam in society. Reflecting a general preoccupation with state-led social transformation during the 1940s, 1950s and 1960s, all three situated Islam in relation to executive power – through political pragmatism, socialist interventionism or Islamic authenticity – in pursuit of this aim. Connections between Islam, society and politics turned state-centric as a result.

Pan-Arab, socialist and Islamist movements intersected around the process of post-independence state formation. Egypt is a key example in this respect. In 1952, a coup d'état had deposed the king, turned the country into a republic and enabled the rise of Gamal Abdel Nasser to the presidency. After his ascent to power, Nasser constructed a political vision that fused pan-Arabism, socialism and Islamism into a unified ideological framework. In doing so, he drew on al-Siba'i's notion of socialism of Islam in combination with an emphasis on *walī al-amr*, or person in charge, to provide religious legitimation for his one person rule.[27] It was soon known as Nasserism. It inspired activists across the Arab world as a political ideology for modern Arab states that seemed distinctly Arab and challenged traditional social power structures while retaining an Islamic authenticity. Nasser used his executive power to enlarge the state while transforming society. He implemented land reforms in 1952 and 1961, expropriated British and French properties in 1956 and further nationalised businesses in 1960.[28] In 1958, Nasser created the Unified Arab Republic with Syria that lasted until 1961. He reformed al-Azhar and brought it in line with modern education. Nasser initially facilitated the reemergence of the Muslim Brotherhood – they supported his 1952 coup – but from 1954 onwards he had them rounded up, imprisoned, tortured and executed. Many fled the country. Nasser epitomised state-led social transformation based on pan-Arabism and socialism while giving it a veneer of Islamic legitimacy. In doing so, he enlarged the state, transformed society and silenced his critics.[29]

An alternative example is Saudi Arabia. Its roots go back to an alliance from 1744 between Muhammad bin Sa'ud, as political leader, and Muhammad bin Abd al-Wahhab (1703–92) as religious authority. Drawing on scholars such as Ibn Taymiyya and Ibn Qayyim, Abd al-Wahhab focused on the purification of Islam from, what he saw as, innovations (or *bid'ah*) of Sufism and Shiism, arguing for the restoration of the unity of faith (or *tawheed*). The Wahhabist religious scholars legitimated the rule of the Bin Sa'ud family in return for religious dominance over the population that they ruled. With Saudi Arabia, crucially, a state bureaucracy did not develop as it did during the Ottoman *tanẓīmāt* period. It meant that politics revolved around power struggles between various groups among the political and religious elites instead of attempts to control a state bureaucracy. When in the early 1930s the Arabian

American Oil Company, or Aramco, began to develop recently discovered oil fields, the resulting wealth was, initially, distributed through royal family networks – not through state institutions. There was little investment in public infrastructure.[30] Instead, in the case of Saudi Arabia, a reactive type of state enlargement happened: a ministry of finance was created in 1932 to manage the increase in wealth. A Saudi ministry of defence was established in 1944 because the US installed an army base near its oil installation in Dhahran. In 1953, a council of ministers was created, mostly as a framework to manage the distribution of power following the death of Ibn Saud. This council included ministries of the interior, education, agriculture, health, industry and commerce, but they came and went with changes in political fortunes. Development of public infrastructure fell to Aramco: it built schools, housing, airports, roads, educational centres and, eventually, also military bases – for example, the one in Dhahran – to protect oil sites. As a result, when an opposition movement emerged, such as a Nasserist one in the 1950s, it did so primarily within Aramco created institutions.[31] In a political regime that still mirrored a traditional relationship between ruler and subjects, legitimated by a class of Wahhabist religious scholars, institutions created by an American-controlled oil company provided the setting in which political movements appeared.

Revolutions

Two wars, six years apart, underlined the military, economic, political and international weakness of Arab states. Revolutionary challenges followed these defeats, and in the process, Islamists recast Islam as an alternative and challenge to existing states and their rulers. One of the most famous examples is that of Sayyid Qutb, who argued that religious ignorance, or *jāhilīyah*, was weakening Arab societies and regimes, necessitating the simultaneous overthrow of secular states and the Islamisation of society. In short, Islamism turned revolutionary.

In June 1967, in a matter of days, Israel's army destroyed the Egyptian, Syrian and Jordanian army – while occupying the Golan Heights in Syria, the West Bank from (Jordan controlled) Palestine and the Sinai Peninsula from Egypt. The war showed how diverging interests and distrust stood increasingly in the way of Arab cooperation, hampering a collective Arab response to Israel's onslaught.[32] It also showed that the stature of Nasser as pan-Arab leader had lost much of its allure – he would die three years later. In 1973, a second war started, with Egyptian and Syrian forces simultaneously attacking the Israeli occupied Sinai Peninsula and Golan Heights. Israel successfully countered the attack, while coordination between the Syrian and Egyptian armies soon faltered. Meanwhile, it set the Soviet Union, supporting Arab regimes, and the US, supporting Israel, against each other. It was the threat of outright war between the two that led, eventually, to a peace deal.[33]

The promise of unifying and empowering the Arab world, under the supervision of strong leaders such as Gamal Abdel Nasser, had proven divisive, illusionary and ineffective. Several socialist republics, such as Egypt and Syria, faced mounting public debt and struggling economies because of their statist policies, while other countries, especially in the Gulf region, turned increasingly wealthy. It led Nasser's successor, Anwar Sadat, to start a range of *infitāḥ* (liberalisation) policies in 1974, which gave more space to the Egyptian private sector. During the 1973 war, Saudi Arabia imposed an oil embargo on the US and other Western states for their support of Israel. It raised US awareness of the importance of safeguarding its control over oil reserves in the country.[34] The wars showed the extent that the US and Soviet Union had taken over from England and France in dictating political dynamics in the Arab world.

Where previously some Islamist activists, such as al-Siba'i, held hopes for nascent Arab states to enable the empowerment of religion, a new group emerged that was more critical. One of the most famous examples of this revolutionary turn was the Egyptian Muslim Brother Sayyid Qutb (1906–66). In his writings, he focused on *jāhilīyah* (religious ignorance) of contemporary society and Arab regimes. This religious ignorance not only weakened societies but also robbed political regimes of an authentic form of legitimacy. The solution was a movement that simultaneously aimed to overthrow secular states and Islamise society: it 'uses the methods of preaching and persuasion for reforming ideas and beliefs; and it uses physical power and jihad for abolishing the organisations and authorities of the *jāhilī* system'.[35] Qutb transformed al-Banna's focus on proselytisation to one of revolutionary mobilisation, aiming to establish God's sovereignty (*ḥākimīyah*) on earth.[36] The Egyptian authorities executed Qutb in 1966. Over the years, his political manifesto, *Milestones*, became the staple of revolutionary Islamist, and jihadist, activists across the world.[37]

Meanwhile, state repression and the influence of global capitalism, through oil wealth, resulted in increased migration flows. First, relations between Islamists and Arab rulers had soured. Nasser repressed the Muslim Brotherhood and controlled al-Azhar. In Tunisia, Bourguiba destroyed any vestiges of religious authority. In Syria, an Islamic field initially flourished but mostly because of state weakness. When, in the late 1970s, an Islamist challenge to Syrian ruler Hafez al-Assad did emerge, he had it ruthlessly repressed. Many of the Muslim Brothers that were exiled from Syria and Egypt left for Saudi Arabia. Second, a new wave of economic migrants joined these exiles following Egyptian and Syrian *infitah* policies and increasing Saudi wealth. Between 1973 and 1988, there was a tenfold increase in the migrant population in Saudi Arabia, with most migrants coming from Yemen, Jordan, Syria and Egypt.[38] Among these migrants were many Muslim Brothers.[39]

Saudi Arabia provided a context where an Islamist movement and transnational migration intersected. The growth of this Islamist diaspora happened at the same time as the Saudi regime faced a challenge from Nasser's socialist and Islamic-infused pan-Arabism: Nasserist movements emerged as opposition internally to the rule of the Saud family and externally as breakaway movements in Yemen. Crucially, the focus of Saudi's Wahhabist scholars on religious purity and their political quietism meant they provided very little in the way of countering the Nasserist challenge. As a solution, the Saudi regime gave the Muslim Brothers free rein to organise – especially in the emerging education sector – and articulate a more socially and politically activist combination of Muslim Brotherhood and Wahhabist thought. It turned into the basis of what later came to be known as *al-Ṣaḥwah al-Islāmīyah*, the Islamic Awakening.[40] A movement that combined the practical activism of Hassan al-Banna, the focus on *jāhilīyah* and *ḥākimīyah* of Sayyid Qutb and the preoccupation with religious purity and *tawheed* of Abdel-Wahhab. Some of the key thinkers in this respect are the Egyptian Muhammad Qutb – brother of Sa'id – and the Syrian Muhammad Surur Zayn al-ʿAbidin, a former Muslim Brother who moved to Saudi Arabia in 1964.[41]

The year 1979 was eventful for revolutionary movements across the world. In March, a People's Revolutionary Government was proclaimed in Grenada and in July the Sandinistas overthrew the Somoza regime in Nicaragua. It also proved a decisive year for Islamist revolutionary movements. In Iran, Ruhollah Khomeini (1900–89) and his followers took control of a popular uprising against Iran's Shah and established the Islamic Republic of Iran in April of that year. It sent shock waves throughout the world and galvanised Islamist movements.[42] In Saudi Arabia, 1979 saw the storming of the Kaaba in Mecca, the holiest place in Islam, by a messianic Islamist group led by Juhayman al-Otaybi. It resulted in a two-week stand off and eventual storming of the Kaaba, the complete destruction of the group and subsequent repression of the Muslim Brotherhood and its *al-Ṣaḥwah al-Islāmīyah*.[43] Going forward, other Gulf countries, such as Qatar and Kuwait, proved more welcoming to Muslim Brotherhood members, while Saudi Arabia used the export of Wahhabism as a counterweight to the global influence of the movement. That same year, a Soviet invasion of Afghanistan began that would see a popular resistance movement emerge around a jihadist collective identity. Thousands of activists travelled to Afghanistan to oppose the Soviet, communist invasion and build – with American and Saudi support – a global jihadist movement.[44] Last but not least, an Islamist activist assassinated Anwar Sadat, the President of Egypt, in 1981, after Sadat signed a US-brokered peace treaty with Israel (the Camp David Accords). Islamist movements found themselves at the centre of political upheaval in the Arab world – and beyond.[45]

Limits to Democracy

Between 1970 and 1990, Arab regimes further integrated into a liberal, capitalist world order while remaining fully autocratic. It led several individuals, such as Yusuf al-Qaradawi, Rashed Ghannouchi and Abdallah Azzam, to emphasise Islam as a source of individual morality, challenging – all in their own ways – the legitimacy of Arab rulers and their political regimes.

In North Africa, countries signed a series of multilateral agreements with the European Commission that brought their economies closer to the European market.[46] In the Gulf, the increase in oil prices, from the 1970s onward, created an influx of petrodollars and with it an increased dependence on the world market.[47] Following the end of the Cold War, the International Monetary Fund forced the last socialist Arab states to implement reforms that dismantled protectionist trade policies.[48] After a financial crisis, Syria passed a law to liberalise its economy in 1991. Figure 3.1 shows that Syrian state enlargement continued well into the 1980s but stalled in the 1990s and reversed in the early 2000s.[49] Political liberalisation accompanied these economic reforms. In 1977, for example, Morocco held its first parliamentary elections since 1964. In 1989, Tunisia held liberalised general elections and its first presidential elections in fourteen years.[50] Algeria, in 1990, had its first competitive local elections and parliamentary elections the year after. In Egypt, elections became gradually more open to opposition parties and independents from the 1980s onwards.[51]

It did not mean, though, that Arab states turned into proper capitalist democracies. Instead of heralding an age of liberalised economic and political regimes, integrating Arab states into a capitalist and liberal world order led to the transition of power structures from a centralised state to decentralised networks of political and economic elites. The influx of petrodollars in the Gulf,

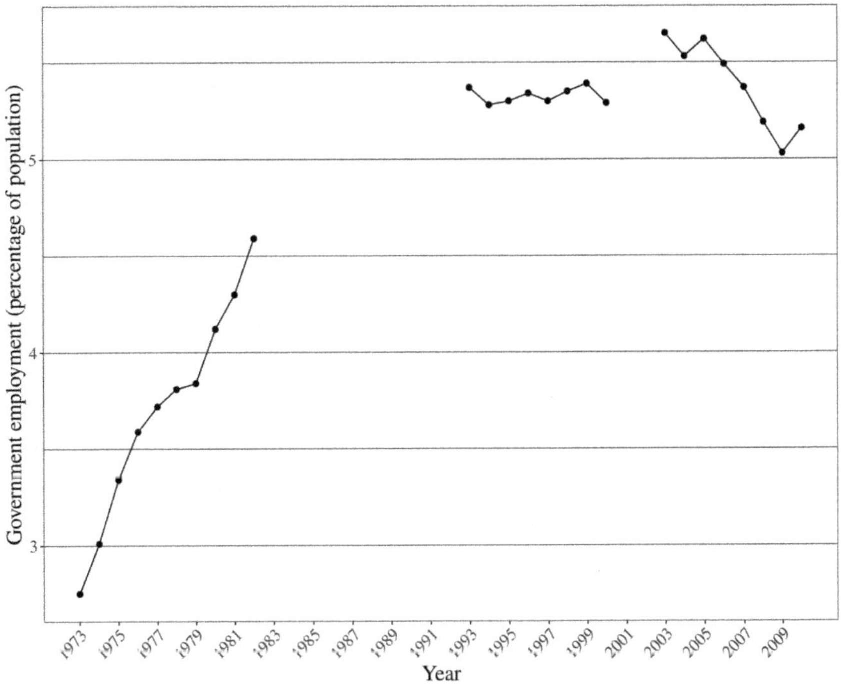

Figure 3.1 Government staff in Syria (as percentage of total population).
Source: Statistical Abstract Syria, 1977, 1998, 2011 and World Bank.

for example, led to the emergence of rentier states: wealth was distributed along patronage, family and clan relations. It created a web of dependency to political elites. In other Arab countries, political elites used their positions to act as gatekeepers to newly available economic resources. It was a form of institutionalised corruption, popularly known as *wāsṭah*, that helped stabilise autocratic regimes.[52] It can come as no surprise that political reforms proved empty. Despite the increased number of seats won by independent candidates and opposition parties in the Egyptian elections, for example, they never seriously challenged the ruling party. When the Tunisian Islamist Ennahda party was successful in the 1989 elections, the party was repressed, with many of its members incarcerated and its leader, Rached Ghannouchi, forced to go into exile in the UK.[53]

In this context, several Islamist thinkers moved away from a statist focus to one that revolved around individual morality – often referring to the notion of *al-Amr bi-al-Maʿrūf wa-al-Nahy ʿan al-Munkar*, or to enjoin what is right and forbid what is wrong – and its relation to political authority.[54] Yusuf al-Qaradawi (1926–2022), the former president of the International Union of Muslim Scholars, is an example of this trend.[55] He was an Egyptian Islamic scholar who became world famous through his TV show *Islam wa al-Hayat* (Islam and Life). He dealt at length with the question of how individual Islamic morality relates to state authority and the public good. In an extensive study of *zakāt*, or giving alms, he argues that, in theory, these are managed by an Islamic state. But he notes that Muslims should not give *zakāt* to contemporary Muslim governments as they 'suppress any Islamic voice and crush those who call for Islam'.[56] It is the individual Muslim's right to divest Islamic alms from a political regime. In a similar vein, he argued that a 'ruler; as viewed by Islam, is the representative of the community and thus its employee'. Hence, 'it is a basic right [of the community] to hold its representative accountable'.[57] In brief: Islam is compatible with democracy.

Rashed Ghannouchi (1941), the leader of the Tunisian Ennahda party, also emphasised the democratic character of Islamic thought. In the *Public Freedoms in the Islamic State,* written during imprisonment in the 1980s and published in 1993, he argued, in essence, that contemporary Arab states were colonial repressive entities that turned Muslims into servants of secular dictatorships.[58] He continued that an Islamic polity would instead nurture and build a democratic attitude. Implementing sharia through *shūrá* (consultation) among the *ummah* (Islamic community), he argued, breeds democratic attitudes because they are necessary for their proper functioning: sharia can only be implemented, and a ruler can only govern, through public consultation among equals. Islamic democracy negates secular autocracy.[59]

Finally, Abdallah Azzam (1941–89) used the notion of individual morality not to transform the relation of Islam to statist power but its relation to revolutionary activism. During the war in Afghanistan, he wrote *The Defence of Muslim Territories is The First Individual Duty*. In it, he argued that the jihad in Afghanistan was a *farḍ 'ayn*, or an individual duty. It meant that participation in this jihad was not only legitimate for inhabitants of the country under attack – but for all individual Muslims in the world.[60] He situated the notion of jihad, as a result, in relation to an Islamic community instead of a particular state. By relating it to individual morality, he turned jihad global. Putting his ideas into practice, he established a *maktab al-khidamāt* (bureau of services) to support individual Muslims wanting to participate in the Afghan jihad.[61]

With the further integration of Arab regimes into a liberalist and capitalist world order, ideas of human rights and individual representation became pervasive across the Arab world.[62] In this context, activists emphasised the relationship between individual morality and political legitimacy. They did so either by focusing on citizenship (see al-Qaradawi), democracy (Ghannouchi) or resistance (Azzam).

Universal Resistance

The Iraq war of 1990–1 and the Oslo Accords in 1993 inflamed tensions across the region. Together with the expanding reach of Arab news channels during the early 2000s, they nurtured a performative element in Islamist resistance movements aimed at a global audience, with the main example being Osama Bin Laden's al-Qaeda organisation.

The Iraq war started with Iraq's invasion of Kuwait and ended with the US and allies stationing troops in Saudi Arabia, liberating Kuwait and destroying Iraq's army. The deployment of non-Muslim military personnel in the country of Mecca and Medina, two of Islam's holiest places, became a fertile ground for challenging the weakness of contemporary Arab regimes. Subsequently, the signing of the Oslo accords in 1993, brokered by the US and Norway, forced the Palestinian Liberation Organisation to cease resistance against Israeli occupation in return for limited self-governance and the start of a peace process that might result in Palestinian statehood. When the promise of statehood proved empty, popular dissatisfaction turned into an uprising in the early 2000s.

During the same period, the global and Arab media landscape transformed. It had an immense impact on how these political developments reverberated across the Arab world. In November 1996, the Al Jazeera news channel was established in Qatar. In March 2003, Al Arabiya followed in Saudi Arabia, and in 2004 Alhurra started in the United States. These were three of many news channels that aimed at a global Arab-speaking audience, while projecting soft power from their respective nation-state backers – all vying to expand their influence over the region. Qatar's Al Jazeera, especially, turned into a dominant news channel throughout the 1990s and 2000s. Meanwhile, internet usage took off across the Arab world. In 1995, 0.01 per cent of the Arab population used the internet, ten years later this had risen to 8 per cent and in 2015 it was 42 per cent.[63] The combination of a pervasive spread of TV, petrodollars and increasing focus on individual morality and collective identity opened up the space for these Islamic scholars – the *'ulamā'* – to regain a position of authority as moral leaders in society.[64] Their rise was mirrored in the increased political influence of al-Azhar in Egypt[65] and an increasing global popularity of some TV savvy *'ulamā'*, such as the Egyptians Amr Khaled and Yusuf al-Qaradawi.[66]

The combination of a global audience and increasing military presence of the United States in the region introduced a performative element into Islamist, and especially jihadist, violence. The principal example of this transformation is the establishment of al-Qaeda and its leader Osama bin Laden (1957–2011). He supported Abdallah Azzam's *khidmāt al-'āmmah* during the Afghan jihad but returned to his native Saudi Arabia in 1989.[67] As Iraq invaded Kuwait, he fell foul with the Saudi regime because of his outspoken opposition to a US military presence in the country. In February 1998, he posted a fatwa stating that the US was occupying the Arabian Peninsula and the holiest places of Islam and was inflicting devastation on the Iraqi people, all with 'the aim [. . .] to serve the Jews' petty state and divert attention from its occupation of Jerusalem and murder of Muslims there'. He gave the fatwa 'to kill the Americans and their allies – civilians and military – is an individual duty (*farḍ 'ayn*) for every Muslim who can do it in any country in which it is possible to do it, in order to liberate the Al-Aqsa Mosque and the holy mosque [Mecca] from their grip'.[68] Six months later al-Qaeda hit the US embassies in Nairobi, Kenya, and Dar es Salaam, Tanzania, with near-simultaneous suicide bombs. A total of 224 people died, the vast majority of which were Kenyans and Tanzanians.

Some scholars describe the emergence of al-Qaeda as an attempt to integrate the near (local autocrats) and far enemy (the US and Israel) among jihadist movements.[69] Arguably, it also represented the adaptation of jihadism to the globalisation of media and communication. The culmination of this process was, of course, the attack on New York and Washington on 11 September 2001. The attack targeted the Twin Towers of the World Trade Centre in New York, the Pentagon and Capitol Hill in Washington: symbols of US global economic, military and political power, respectively. Three out of four targets were successfully hit, killing thousands of American civilians. It gave al-Qaeda its global media spectacle, which remains, arguably, unsurpassed to the present day.

Following the attacks, George Bush Jr declared a War on Terror which solidified the dominant role of the US in the Arab world and helped legitimise Islamism, and jihadism, as a global response to this presence.[70] The US and its allies attacked Afghanistan, ruled by the Islamist Taliban movement that had emerged after the Afghan war and was harbouring Osama Bin Laden and other senior al-Qaeda leaders. Later, in 2003, they attacked Iraq under the pretext of limiting the spread of weapons of mass destruction. Whatever the actual motive behind these attacks, they resulted in the presence of US and allied military troops in Afghanistan and Iraq and provided legitimacy for an Islamist uprising against these foreign occupations. Thousands of foreign jihadists travelled from around the world to Afghanistan and Iraq, drawn into a global war against Western, US-led dominance. Soon jihadist forums emerged across the web featuring clips of jihadist attacks on US troops, giving birth to a whole new genre of Islamist propaganda.

It was around this time, in December 2010, that a street vendor, Mohamed Bouazizi, set himself alight in the small Tunisian town of Sidi Bouzid, sparking a series of events that led to political transitions in Tunisia, Egypt and Libya as well as severe political crises in Oman, Yemen, Morocco, Jordan and Syria. It is at this point that this history chapter concludes.

This chapter provided a brief and selective genealogy of an Islamist movement until 2010. We observed how Islam turned into a symbolic, discursive and institutional resource during the decline of the Ottoman Empire. We then traced how activists, during the 1950s, used Islam to create a distinct type of social activism while turning to Arab states for their empowerment, how during the 1960s and 1970s, they used it to create a distinct type of revolutionary challenge to (Arab) states, how in the 1970s and 1980s, they drew on Islam to relate individual morality to political legitimacy through situating Islam in relation to citizenship, democracy and resistance, and how in the 1990s and 2000s, they used Islam to create a global, performative resistance movement. These are different ways of positioning Islam in relation to state power, social activism, national identities and collective violence. They cannot be seen in isolation from the context in which they emerged.

The next two chapters focus on the Tunisian transition and Syrian crisis, spanning the decade between 2011 and 2021. These episodes reshaped society and politics in the Arab world. They also transformed Islamism. As we will observe, the positions described in this chapter informed how activists situated Islam in relation to society and politics. At the same time, dynamics of these two episodes forced activists to find innovative ways of doing so. As we trace how an Islamist movement emerged, transformed and declined during these two episodes, we situate two specific occurrences of an Islamist movement in relation to the broader evolutionary history of Islamism that we explored in this chapter.

Notes

1. Siba'i, *al-Ishtirāqiya al-Islām*, 8.
2. Casanova, *Public Religions in the Modern World*; Asad, *Formations of the Secular: Christianity, Islam, Modernity*; Mahmood, *Politics of Piety: The Islamic Revival and the Feminist Subject*.
3. Volpi, *Political Islam Observed*.
4. White, *The Emergence of Minorities in the Middle East: The Politics of Community in French Mandate Syria*, 192.
5. Berkes, *The Development of Secularism in Turkey*; Hourani, 'Ottoman Reform And The Politics Of Notables', 102; Mardin, 'Religion and Secularism in Turkey'.

6. Hourani, 'Ottoman Reform and The Politics of Notables', 104.
7. Perkins, *A History of Modern Tunisia*.
8. Ibid.; Green, *The Tunisian Ulama 1873–1915: Social Structure and Response to Ideological Currents*.
9. Hourani, 'Ottoman Reform and The Politics of Notables'.
10. Perkins, *A History of Modern Tunisia*, ch. 1.
11. White, *The Emergence of Minorities in the Middle East: The Politics of Community in French Mandate Syria*.
12. Al-Tunisi, *The Surest Path: The Political Treatise of a Nineteenth-Century Muslim Statesman*.
13. See also Belkeziz, *The State in Contemporary Islamic Thought: A Historical Survey of the Major Muslim Political Thinkers of the Modern Era*, ch. 1.
14. Keddie, Nikki, *An Islamic Response to Imperialism: Political And Religious Writings of Sayyid Jamāl Ad-Dīn 'Al-Afghānī'*; al-Afghani, 'The Truth about the Neicheri Sect'.
15. Hourani, *Arabic Thought in the Liberal Age 1798–1939*, 144. See for an additional study on al-Afghani and Abduh, Belkeziz, *The State in Contemporary Islamic Thought: A Historical Survey of the Major Muslim Political Thinkers of the Modern Era*, ch. 2.
16. For an excellent overview of these developments across the region, see Hourani, *A History of the Arab Peoples*; Owen, *State, Power and Politics in the Making of the Modern Middle East*, ch. 1. For studies with a focus on Tunisia, see Anderson, *The State and Social Transformation in Tunisia and Libya, 1830–1980*; Green, *The Tunisian Ulama 1873–1915: Social Structure and Response to Ideological Currents*; Salem, *Habib Bourguiba, Islam, and the Creation of Tunisia*. For studies that focus on Syria, see White, *The Emergence of Minorities in the Middle East: The Politics of Community in French Mandate Syria*; Commins, *Islamic Reform: Politics and Social Change in Late Ottoman Syria*.
17. Heyd, *Foundations of Turkish Nationalism: The Life and Teachings of Ziya Gökalp*; Gökalp, *Turkish Nationalism and Western Civilization: Selected Essays*.
18. Hinnebusch, *Syria: Revolution From Above*, 15–25.
19. Lewis, 'Necropoles and Nationality: Land Rights, Burial Rites and the Development of Tunisian National Consciousness in the 1930s'; Barrie, 'The Contentious Politics of Nationalism and the Anti-Naturalization Campaign in Tunisia, 1932–1933'; Perkins, *A History of Modern Tunisia*, 97–98.
20. Salem, *Habib Bourguiba, Islam, and the Creation of Tunisia*, 103.

21. Batatu, *Syria's Peasantry, the Descendants of Its Lesser Rural Notables, and Their Politics*; Pierret, *Religion and State in Syria: The Sunni Ulama from Coup to Revolution*.
22. Hourani, *A History of the Arab Peoples*, 355–3; Salem, *Habib Bourguiba, Islam, and the Creation of Tunisia*, 103.
23. Mitchell, *The Society of the Muslim Brothers*; Euben and Qasim Zaman, *Princeton Readings in Islamist Thought: Texts and Contexts from Al-Banna to Bin Laden*, 49–55.
24. Tripp, 'Islam and The Moral Economy: The Challenge of Capitalism', 94; Siba'i, *al-Ishtirāqiya al-Islām*.
25. Pankhurst, *The Inevitable Caliphate?: A History Of the Struggle for Global Islamic Union, 1924 to the Present*, 93; an-Nabahani, *The System of Islam*, ch. 3.
26. Ibid., 46; Pankhurst, *The Inevitable Caliphate?: A History Of the Struggle for Global Islamic Union, 1924 to the Present*, 127–29.
27. Tripp, 'Islam and The Moral Economy: The Challenge of Capitalism', 99.
28. Ibid., 83.
29. For an excellent study on Islamic reactions to capitalism, see Tripp, 'Islam and the Moral Economy: The Challenge of Capitalism'. A general historical overview of this period is included in Hourani, *A History of the Arab Peoples*; Owen, *State, Power and Politics in the Making of the Modern Middle East*, ch. 2–3. For an excellent overview of various Islamist thinkers, including biographies to place activists in their historical contexts, see Euben and Zaman, *Princeton Readings in Islamist Thought: Texts and Contexts from Al-Banna to Bin Laden*. A classic study on the Muslim Brotherhood is Mitchell, *The Society of the Muslim Brothers*.
30. Lacroix, *Awakening Islam: Religious Dissent in Contemporary Saudi Arabia*, 8–13.
31. Salamé, 'Political Power and the Saudi State'; Lacroix, *Awakening Islam: Religious Dissent in Contemporary Saudi Arabia*.
32. Seale, *Asad: The Struggle for the Middle East*; Hourani, *A History of the Arab Peoples*.
33. Ibid., 416–23; Tripp, 'Islam and The Moral Economy: The Challenge of Capitalism'.
34. Hourani, *A History of the Arab Peoples*, 419–23.
35. Qutb, *Milestones*, 55.
36. See for an in-depth discussion of *jāhilīyah* and *ḥākimīyah*, Sayed Khatab, '"Hakimiyyah" and "Jahiliyyah" in the Thought of Sayyid Qutb'.

37. For an extensive biography see, Calvert, *Sayyid Qutb and the Origins of Radical Islamism*.
38. International Organization for Migration, 'Migration Data in Western Asia'.
39. Lacroix, *Awakening Islam: Religious Dissent in Contemporary Saudi Arabia*, 39–41.
40. For a detailed discussion of the developments of *al-Ṣaḥwah al-Islāmīyah* in Saudi Arabia, see Lacroix, *Awakening Islam: Religious Dissent in Contemporary Saudi Arabia*.
41. Ibid., 37–80.
42. See for in-depth discussion on the Iranian revolution: Abrahamian, *The Coup: 1953, The CIA, and The Roots of Modern U.S.-Iranian Relations*; Keddie and Richard, *Roots of Revolution: An Interpretive History of Modern Iran*; Kandil, *The Power Triangle: Military, Security, and Politics in Regime Change*.
43. Hegghammer and Lacroix, 'Rejectionist Islamism in Saudi Arabia: The Story of Juhayman Al-'utaybi Revisited'.
44. Roy, *Islam and Resistance in Afghanistan*.
45. For those interested, the following provide detailed discussions: van Dam, *The Struggle For Power in Syria: Politics and Society Under Asad and the Ba'th Party*; Seale, *Asad: The Struggle for the Middle East*; Perkins, *A History of Modern Tunisia*; Wolf, *Political Islam in Tunisia: The History of Ennahda*.
46. Cammett, *Globalization and Business Politics in Arab North Africa: A Comparative Perspective*.
47. Tripp, 'Islam and The Moral Economy: The Challenge of Capitalism', ch. 4.
48. Cammett, *Globalization and Business Politics in Arab North Africa: A Comparative Perspective*, 3.
49. In Syria, these reforms were further delayed because the discovery of oil in the late 1980s made the financial situation, for a brief period, less pressing. See Selvik, 'It's the Mentality, Stupid: Syria's Turn to the Private Sector', 43–44.
50. Perkins, *A History of Modern Tunisia*, 189–90.
51. Posusney, 'Multi-Party Elections in the Arab World: Institutional Engineering and Oppositional Strategies'.
52. Cunningham and Sarayrah, *Wasta: The Hidden Force in Middle Eastern Society*.
53. Wolf, *Political Islam in Tunisia: The History of Ennahda*; Tamimi, *Rachid Ghannouchi: A Democrat within Islamism*.
54. For a study on the development of this idea in Islamic thought, see Cook, *Commanding Right and Forbidding Wrong in Islamic Thought*.

55. Graf and Skovgaard-Petersen, *Global Mufti: The Phenomenon Of Yusuf Al-Qaradawi*.
56. al-Qaradāwī, *Fiqh Az-Zakat: A Comparative Study of Zakah, Regulations and Philosophy in the Light of the Quran and Sunnah (vol II)*, 126.
57. Euben and Qasim Zaman, *Princeton Readings in Islamist Thought: Texts and Contexts from Al-Banna to Bin Laden*, 235.
58. Ghannouchi, *Al-Ḥurrīyāt Al-'Āmmah Fī Al-Dawlah Al-Islāmīyah*.
59. Tamimi, *Rachid Ghannouchi: A Democrat within Islamism*, 93–102.
60. Hegghammer and Lacroix, 'Rejectionist Islamism in Saudi Arabia: The Story of Juhayman Al-'utaybi Revisited', 110.
61. Ibid., 112–13.
62. For more detailed information on this period, regarding Tunisia: Cammett, 'Business-Government Relations and Industrial Change: The Politics of Upgrading in Morocco and Tunisia'; regarding Syria: Perthes, *The Political Economy of Syria under Asad*.
63. World Bank, 'Individuals Using the Internet'.
64. For an excellent study on this process but focused on the Indian peninsula, see Qasim Zaman, *The Ulama in Contemporary Islam: Custodians of Change*.
65. Zeghal, 'Religion and Politics in Egypt: The Ulema of Al-Azhar, Radical Islam, and the State (1952–94)'.
66. Meijer, 'Introduction', 8.
67. Euben and Qasim Zaman, *Princeton Readings in Islamist Thought: Texts and Contexts from Al-Banna to Bin Laden*, 425–59; Cook, *Understanding Jihad*.
68. World Islamic Front, 'World Islamic Front Statement Urging Jihad Against Jews and Crusaders'.
69. Euben and Qasim Zaman, *Princeton Readings in Islamist Thought: Texts and Contexts from Al-Banna to Bin Laden*, 426.
70. CNN, 'Transcript of President Bush's Address'.

4

THE TUNISIAN TRANSITION

> It is just wonderful. You can have a beard without getting into trouble. At any prayer time, you can go to the mosque. You can just be Muslim, with no issue. It is such a huge difference. It is difficult to describe. You can finally be who you are. [. . .] We are also doing all kinds of activities: giving religious courses, providing charity and alms to the poor. During Ben Ali's reign, it was even forbidden to clean the mosque. They perceived it as activism under the banner of religion, which was not allowed. [Recently] we had an aid convoy to help the North. It is a little like the poor helping the poor, but it's just beautiful.[1]

The quote above is from Faisal, a young Tunisian activist, while talking to me at the Avenue Bourguiba in the centre of Tunis. It is telling, first, because of the diverse practices he describes as distinctly Islamic: wearing clothing, providing aid and organising social activities. He recasts these everyday practices as Islamic ones, as enactments of being Muslim and as an expression of being able to be who you are. A post-revolutionary coming out, so to speak, of being Muslim. Second, it is telling because he relates this individual transformation to participation in collective action, being active in aid and social initiatives. His personal transformation situates Faisal within an emerging Islamist movement.

This chapter narrates the rise, transformation and decline of an Islamist movement during the Tunisian transition. It spans the period from the departure of former autocrat Zine El Abidine Ben Ali to Saudi Arabia in January 2011 to Kais Saied's coup in July 2021. Over the course of a decade, activists established hundreds, if not thousands, of Islamic associations. Congregations replaced hundreds of imams, opening up Tunisian mosques to a diverse set of political movements. Salafists returned to public life as did Tunisian jihadists. Islamic political parties also reemerged, with the Ennahda Movement becoming a linchpin in struggles surrounding the drafting of a new constitution. These diverse agents were active in strengthening the position of Islam in society and politics, giving birth to an Islamist movement.

It was a movement that did not last. From 2014 onwards, the state closed numerous associations and barred many independent imams from preaching. In 2016, political pragmatism led Ennahda to distance itself from the Islamist label. Around this time, the internal cohesion of the movement had disappeared, leaving only individual activists. In 2019, there was a brief resurgence around a new populist party called the Dignity Coalition, but Kais Saied's coup brought this resurgence to a halt.

This is not the first study to tell the story of an Islamist movement during the Tunisian transition. Scholars such as Hamza Meddeb, Kasper Netterstrøm, Aaron Zelin, Monica Marks, Francesco Cavatorta and Fabio Merone have investigated different aspects of such a movement. Meddeb and Netterstrøm have detailed the struggles inside Ennahda as it embarked on a strategy of specialisation in formal politics,[2] while Zelin focused on the rise and fall of Ansar Charia as a jihadist organisation.[3] Marks, Cavatorta and Merone investigated the popularity, between 2011 and 2013, of jihadist and Salafist sheikhs among disenfranchised Tunisian youth.[4]

These scholars used ideology to distinguish movements and parties, which proved problematic in practice. Meddeb and Netterstrøm, for example, focused on the Ennahda Movement as an Islamist party and Zelin on Ansar Charia as a jihadist organisation. Marks, Cavatorta and Merone used (jihadi-) Salafism, and its various subdivisions, to distinguish a group of Tunisian sheikhs and movements. It often proved challenging to apply such categories in practice. As noted, Ennahda rebranded itself as a Muslim democratic party in 2016 to distance itself from the Islamist label. Many Salafists rejected this classification and instead called themselves simply proper Muslims.[5] Scholars described Ansar Charia as the principal jihadist organisation during the early years of the transition, but in practice, they were far more active in social activities and *da'wah* (proselytisation) than in organising collective violence, making the jihadist characterisation questionable. In addition, how scholars divided these movements differed between them. For instance, while Meddeb and Fahmi divided a Tunisian Salafist movement into a jihadi and scripturalist current, Monika Marks subdivided it into a jihadi, scientific and political one.[6] Many more examples of diverging categories exist.[7] Last but not least, the extent that the rank and file of these movements followed, or even knew, the ideologies of their organisations was often questionable.

I turn this issue on its head. The following is a study of the political impact of an Islamist movement based on what its participants did, instead of what ideologies they followed. I do not use ideologies to distinguish or subdivide an Islamist movement. Instead, I investigate how activists used Islam to make their practices distinct and, in the process, reshaped access to symbolic, institutional and material resources. It infused Islam with political significance. The struggle to define the legitimate ways of doing so drew activists together into an Islamist movement and situated them in relation to each other. In short, this is a study of how an Islamist movement, and its various currents, emerged from among the contentious interactions that comprised the Tunisian transition.

In the first section of this chapter, I describe how activists used Islam to enact distinct practices and, in doing so, infused religion with political significance. I observe how the creation of hundreds of Islamic associations provided a new autonomous space for social and political activism, how an increase in independent Islamic schools established an alternative educational field, how the provision of Islamic public services challenged the state and how the rise of Ennahda in Tunisian politics seemed to provide an avenue for political representation of, religiously conservative, citizens. Although there was no uniform way in which Islam informed charitable, educational and political practices, the act of using Islam to set them apart as somehow distinct was enough to reshape access to symbolic, institutional and material resources. It turned Islam political, Islamist, and turned religion itself into a contested resource.

In the second part of this chapter, I examine several conflicts that arose over how Islam could render practices distinct. These conflicts highlighted different positions that participants in an Islamist movement took in these struggles. For example, they distinguished the position of Ennahda from that of Hizb al-Tahrir and grassroots Islamist activists. Meanwhile, these conflicts drew them together as agents who had a stake in defining Islam as a distinct practice, inadvertently setting them apart as an – Islamist – movement during the Tunisian transition. In the final section, I trace how distinctly Islamic practices became increasingly rare by 2021, leading to the decline of the movement. Taken together, this chapter does not approach Islamism as an ideology that defined a movement. Instead, it views an Islamist movement as an emergent pattern of relational, contentious interactions.

Constructing Islamic Distinction

Zine El Abidine Ben Ali fled for Saudi Arabia on 14 January 2011. It left the Tunisian political regime and society in disarray and started an episode of social and political conflict around a transition toward democratic rule. During this episode, numerous activists used Islam to distinguish their practices, imbuing it with political significance. Activists established hundreds, if not thousands, of Islamic associations tilting Tunisian social activism toward charity and education while creating a subset of organisations that engaged in shared mobilisation in defence of Islam. The emergence of independent imams – imams that were appointed by their congregations rather than by the Ministry of Religious Affairs – provided a new autonomous space for social and political activism and fostered relationships to a new Islamic associational field. Establishing Islamic schools – either as private schools registered as associations or by restarting education at the Zaytuna Mosque – laid the basis for an alternative, Islamic, educational field that defied the state's control of education. Ansar Charia's provision of public services challenged the legitimacy of the Tunisian state. Finally, the rise of Ennahda in Tunisian politics provided a new, Islamic avenue for political representation. Let us discuss each in turn.

Establishing Islamic Associations

The Tunisian revolution led to a steep increase in the number of associations that activists established. Prior to the revolution, law 154 (from 1959) stipulated that associations needed approval from the Ministry of Interior to be established. It meant that the security services vetted each application. After January 2011, the Ministry of Interior ceased functioning and the political police was disbanded. Lacking any oversight, hundreds of new associations were registered in a few months. On 24 September 2011, through decree 88/2011, the government published a new law that allowed anyone older than sixteen years to establish an association as long as it did not have a political agenda.[8] (Political parties were subject to another law.) Data from the national registry of associations, the Centre for Information, Formation, Study and Documentation of Associations (IFEDA) shows that between 2006 and 2010 it added around 300 new entries per year. In 2011, as shown in Figure 4.1, this rose to 1,700 and in 2012 to over 3,000.[9] It was a tenfold increase over the course of two years.

Among these newly established associations was a group that related their activism to Islam. The exact number is impossible to establish because religion is not formally recognised as an associational category. Having said this, the rise of Islamic associations could be indirectly observed through, first, a

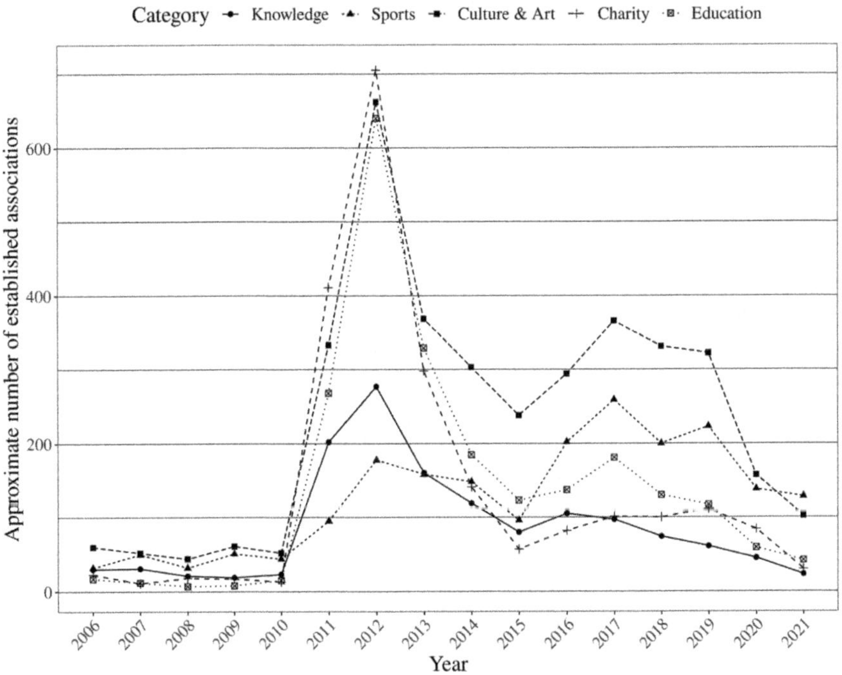

Figure 4.1 Approximate number of associations established in Tunisia in the top five categories of association between 2006 and 2021.
Source: IFEDA.

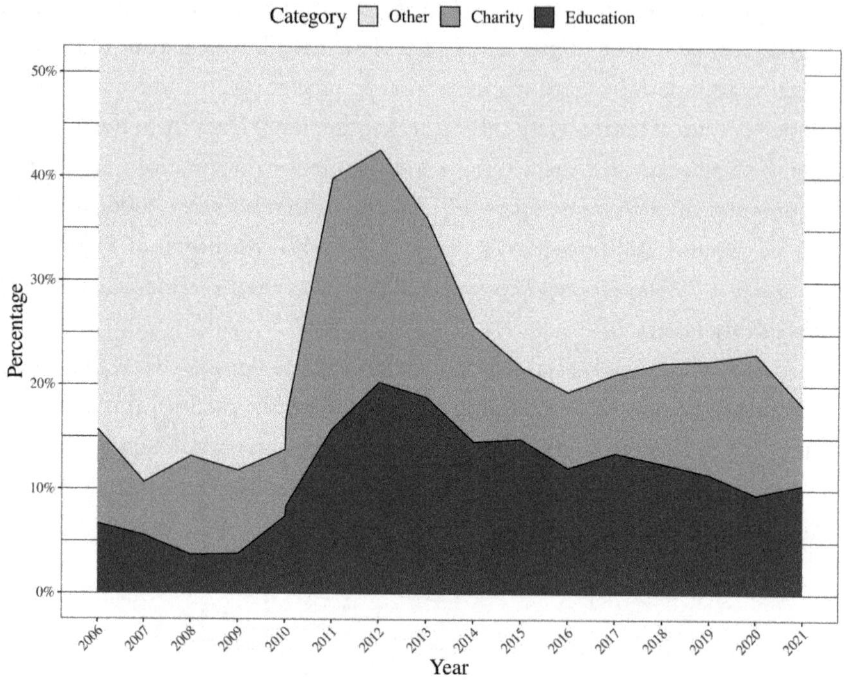

Figure 4.2 Approximate percentage of educational and social charity associations (out of total associations) established between 2006 and 2021 in Tunisia.
Source: IFEDA.

shift toward educational and charitable categories. Figure 4.2 shows a relative change in the type of associations that were founded. In both 2011 and 2012, the educational and charitable categories together made up approximately 40 per cent of the new entries. The year before this, they accounted for only 13 per cent. In less than two years, the relative share of educational and charitable entries tripled, while the overall number rose tenfold.

A likely cause of the relative rise is the number of Islamic associations that were being founded and their overrepresentation among charitable and educational associations.[10] A year after the revolution, a senior official in the Presidency of the Government noted that the largest group of new associations had been Islamic teaching and charitable ones.[11] In a study on Islamic charities, Ester Sigillò noted that Tunisian charitable associations 'trace their origins almost entirely from the Islamist movement'.[12] The statement reflected a broader recognition among scholars of the importance of education and charity in Islamic activism.[13] The numbers from the IFEDA indicate that between 2011 and 2013 activists established hundreds, if not thousands, of Islamic educational and charity associations. In the following years, as state repression returned, these categories of associations took the hardest fall.

Another way to observe this rise was through the numerous associations referencing Islam in their names, aims or self-descriptions. One notable example is the *Tunisian Association for Sharia Sciences* founded in 2011 by Noureddine Khadmi, an imam and religious scholar from Tunis. He established it to strengthen Islamic knowledge in Tunisian society.[14] Another example is the *Association for Proselytisation and Reform*, established by Habib Ellouze. He was a founder of the Ennahda party, member of its Shura Council and briefly led Ennahda in 1991 before being jailed for fifteen years by the Ben Ali regime.[15] Omar (a pseudonym) established a chain of Islamic private schools in and around the capital.[16] Registered as an Islamic educational association, its entry in the public registry states it aimed at 'cultivating a correct understanding of sharia sciences'.[17] Hamza (also a pseudonym), an activist from Sfax, helped establish a cultural and art association. It did not have any reference to religion in its formal description, stating only that it 'aimed to educate and train young people in cultural and arts fields'.[18] In contrast to this description, Hamza and his organisation were recognised as having an Islamic outlook: he himself became an imam in 2014, the organisation published statements in defence of Islamic sanctities and its members participated in protests calling for sharia to be included in the constitution.[19] These associations rendered themselves distinct by referencing Islam in their names, self-descriptions or through the activism of their members.

Islam set these associations apart from their non-Islamic counterparts. It rendered them distinct. Having said this, it was often challenging to identify a uniform influence of Islam on their activities. Some referenced religion explicitly in their goals, others did not. It did not help that many of them framed the content of their activities explicitly as being nondistinct. Aid given by charities was available to everyone, irrespective of their faith, gender, ethnicity or nationality. Directors of Islamic educational associations emphasised that they were open to all Tunisians and touted the quality of their education and interest in improving it, instead of their religious character.[20]

Having said this, the fact that they used Islam to set themselves apart from their non-Islamic counterparts was enough to turn these groups of Islamic associations into an indispensable resource for activism in name of defending Islam. Islamic associations published joint statements in support of religion at Tunisian universities, distributed petitions calling for sharia to be included in the constitution and organised protests denouncing repression of independent mosque imams – among many other related topics.[21] Activists referred to an 'Islamic civil society' that embodied, and was active in the defence of, the Islamic character of Tunisia.[22] We will return to these examples in more detail in the second section of this chapter.

Additionally, an Islamic distinction fostered relations between associations and a field of newly independent imams. Prior to the revolution, the Tunisian state appointed imams and provided them with a stipend. In the weeks following the revolution, many mosque congregations forced out their imams and replaced them with state-independent ones. Interviewees estimated that this happened in about 10, 30 or 50 per cent of the 3,500 mosques in the country.[23] Whatever the exact number, it created a large group of imams that were appointed without government oversight. Ridha Jaouadi is one example. He received his baccalaureate in literature in 1983 and his postgraduate studies in Islamic sciences from Zaytuna University in 1987. He became an imam soon after, only to be barred by the Ben Ali regime in 1991 and spending much of the next two decades teaching religious classes at primary and secondary schools.[24] His first post-revolutionary sermon was on 28 January 2011, and he became the Friday imam of the Lakhme Mosque in Sfax on 15 March.[25] Two other examples are Mohamed Afas and Ahmad Kharrat, both independent imams in Sfax (the former at the Grand Mosque in its old city). Abu Iyadh, a former jihadist who we will meet again later in this chapter, also preached at mosques. Khatib Idrissi, discussed at length in the introduction, had the wish to become Friday imam in his own mosque in Sidi Aoun.[26]

Relations between Islamic associations and independent imams emerged, for example, around the organisation of aid convoys. Faisal, in the quote at the start of this chapter, mentioned one example as early as 14 February 2011.[27] Lacking an explicit political agenda, these initiatives brought together associations, mosques and imams. In early 2012, Ridha Jaouadi's Lakhme

Mosque was involved in organising a convoy to Siliana, El Kef and Kasserine as was the Association for Imams and Sharia Sciences and the Tunisian Association of Mosque Imams.[28] Ridha Jaouadi ended up establishing the Lakhme Charitable Association a few months later. The association pledged that they were politically independent, would work together with any group in society and that they had a 'commitment to Islamic values in all the association's activities'.[29]

The rise of Islamic associations also fostered relations to the Ministry of Religious Affairs and Islamic political parties. The Ministry organised an aid convoy itself following requests from mosque congregations. According to people involved, it worked together with several associations to organise the trucks that went to these regions. One of them was Marhama, a charity established by Ennahda activists.[30] There were several other associations established with close ties to the Ennahda party. One additional example was the earlier mentioned Association for Proselytisation and Reform of Habib Ellouze, the prominent Ennahda politician.

Sometimes these relationships resulted from individuals holding multiple roles. Habib Ellouze was one example and another was Hamza, who managed culture and arts associations and became an imam. Noureddine Khadmi was imam at the al-Fateh Mosque in the centre of Tunis while also being the director at the Tunisian Association for Sharia Sciences. Ridha Jaouadi was the Friday imam at the Lakhme Mosque and the President of the Lakhme Charitable Association. In October that year he established a new labour union, the Tunisian Organisation for Work, as counterweight to the Tunisian General Labour Union (UGTT; see Figure 4.3).[31] It meant he was now not only an imam and director of a charitable association, he was also a union leader. In short, using Islam to establish a distinct type of association shifted activism toward charity and education, produced a pool of organisations that could be mobilised in defence of Islam and fostered relations to imams and mosques as well as to the Ministry of Religious Affairs and the Ennahda party.

Islamic Education

Another example related to educational practices, where an Islamic distinctness challenged established state control over education. Islamic nurseries

البديل عن اتّحاد الخراب
المنظمة التونسية للشغل
ORGANISATION TUNISIENNE DU TRAVAIL
O T T
«الاتحاد العام التّونسي للشّغل بقياداته الحاليّة
الأوْلى أن يُسَمَّى اِتحاد الإضراب والخراب.
و"المنظّمة التّونسيّة للشّغل" هي الوريث
الحقيقي للعمل النّقابي الصّادق لكلّ
من فرحات حشّاد و الشّيخ
الفاضل بن عاشور رحمهما الله.»
رضا الجوّادي إمام جامع اللّخمي بصفاقس

Figure 4.3 Facebook post by Ridha Jaouadi, September 2013. The post reads: 'The UGTT under its current leadership should better be known as the Union of Strikes and Ruin. The OTT is the true heir of honest union work from those like Farhat Hached and sheikh Ben Achour – God rest their souls.'

challenged the control of the Ministry of Women, Family and Children over early years childcare, private Islamic schools challenged the Association for Quranic Schools and Ministry of Employment and Training, and the Zaytuna Mosque challenged the Ministry of Education and Higher Education.

To start with the first example, numerous Islamic nurseries were established that provided preschool or after school childcare. They challenged established control of the Ministry of Women, Family and Children over preschool childcare. When I visited several of them, their directors were at pains to emphasise that the care they provided was qualitatively good and open to all Tunisians. Omar's school, for example, also included a nursery. He emphasised that they admitted everyone irrespective of faith or political affiliation. His school proved popular and expanded with branches across the country.[32] Another director, while giving a tour of several of his nurseries, asked if I could provide him with links to Western institutes to further improve their curriculum.[33] While they emphasised the quality of their care and curricula in relation to children's development, institutionally these nurseries placed themselves in relation to the Ministry of Religious Affairs or Social Affairs – not the Ministry of Women, Family and Children. They also set their own curricula. The latter Ministry did not know what went on in these nurseries. To make matters worse, from the viewpoint of the Ministry, was that relaxed funding rules meant organisations could freely receive foreign funding, potentially further undermining the control the Ministry had over early years education.[34] The creation of an alternative Islamic field of preschool childcare fostered a challenge to established state oversight.

Furthermore, there were many private Islamic schools founded that fell outside the established framework for state control of (religious) adult education. Following independence, during the 1950s President Habib Bourguiba (1903–2000) had brought together Islamic educational associations under one organisation that eventually evolved into the Association for Quranic Schools. It lay dormant until, around 2006, the government began allowing classes in the memorisation of the Quran. The Association was formally independent but presided over by an advisor to the president.[35] In addition, there was the Ministry of Employment and Training, providing oversight over adult education as part of its remit.

Many of the new private religious schools ignored this established institutional framework. Theoretically, they fell under the remit of the Ministry of Employment and Training, as they provided adult education, or under the Association for Quranic Schools, as an institute providing religious education. But as most registered as associations under the new law, they were subject to little to no government oversight and ignored both institutions. It meant that they set their own curriculum, set their own policies for hiring and firing teachers and found their own financial support. When I met Omar for the first time, he showed me around his school: apart from a nursery (ground floor), it provided classes for women (first floor) and men (second floor). The second floor had a camera, so they could live stream classes to the first floor. The top floor had a library with books donated by a Gulf organisation. He told me that they selected books in the library to fit Tunisian needs and perceptions.[36] His school was just one of many more that were established during this period.[37] Collectively, they undercut state control of adult religious education.

A particular example of newly established Islamic education related to the Zaytuna Mosque. As the oldest and most renowned mosque in Tunisia, it used to be an institute of learning somewhat akin to al-Azhar in Cairo. During the reforms of the 1950s, Bourguiba integrated these activities into regular primary and secondary education and spun it off into a Department for Sharia and Religious Studies at the University of Tunis.[38] Zaytuna turned into a regular mosque supervised by the Ministry of Religious Affairs.[39]

Following the revolution, Hussein Obeidi, a previously little-known religious scholar, became its Grand Imam. He aimed to empower the mosque as an autonomous centre of learning. In May 2012, Noureddine Khadmi, by then the Minister of Religious Affairs, together with the Ministers of Education and Higher Education, signed an agreement with Hussein Obeidi that recognised the Zaytuna Mosque as an independent, nonaffiliated Islamic educational institution and as an autonomous legal entity. Obeidi was elated, stating that the Zaytuna Mosque would return to train doctors, journalists and engineers. He also promised to claim back all property and endowments that were nationalised during the rule of Habib Bourguiba in the 1950s.[40] He argued these documents gave him the right to organise primary and secondary education at the mosque without interference from the Tunisian state.[41] The position of the relevant ministries was that the mosque might be independent but its teaching had to be accredited by them. It implied that the Zaytuna Mosque should follow ministerial requirements for its curricula. Despite these reservations, the Mosque began to provide classes independently. Figure 4.4 shows an announcement of these classes.

Finally, when visiting Zaytuna University (not to be confused with the Mosque) in October 2011, students decried the level of religious education. The problem was, they noted, that there was no depth to its religious curriculum because of years of state repression.[42] It was a sentiment shared by others interviewed. Zaytuna University was an outcome of Bourguiba's reforms of the Zaytuna Mosque: in 1987, Habib Bourguiba's successor, Zine El Abidine Ben Ali, transformed the Department for Sharia and Religious Studies at the University of Tunis into Zaytuna University. Established as a higher educational institution focused on religion, it described itself

Figure 4.4 Banner at Zaytuna Mosque. The banner reads: 'The Educational Committee of the Zaytuna Mosque invites you to the ceremony announcing the return of original Zaytuni education', 10 October 2012, Zaytuna Mosque, Tunis, Tunisia.

Source: author's archive.

as a successor to the Zaytuna Mosque but did not have any formal institutional relationship to it. Zaytuna University fell under the authority of the Ministry of Higher Education.[43] There were some students that argued that the solution to the poor level of religious education was to move the Zaytuna University to the Ministry of Religious Affairs.[44] In effect, it would recognise Zaytuna University as a religious institute providing higher education, instead of an institute of higher education focused on religion. Although this proposal never emerged as a serious challenge to the Ministry, it goes to show how rendering educational practices distinct has very real political consequences. The change would have empowered the Ministry of Religious Affairs as the executive representation of an alternative Islamic field of education.

In all these examples, individuals used Islam to render educational practices distinct. It fostered challenges to established state control over education. Islamic nurseries challenged the control of the Ministry of Women, Family and Children over early years childcare, private Islamic schools challenged the Association for Quranic Schools and the Ministry of Employment and Training, and the Zaytuna Mosque challenged the Ministry of Education and Higher Education.

Providing Services, Challenging Executive Power

A third example relates to the provision of social services and security. Abu Iyadh, a veteran of the Afghan jihad, set up an organisation, Ansar Charia, in May 2011. It aimed to guide people back to salvation through proselytisation and by providing a range of social services throughout Tunisia and, in doing so, challenged the legitimacy of the Tunisian state. Based on messages posted on their Facebook page, Aaron Zelin claims that, between November 2012 and August 2013, Ansar Charia organised over 800 activities throughout the country.[45] These initiatives went from helping Libyan refugees to repairing roads and cleaning streets.[46] They gave Ansar Charia a level of popularity in socioeconomically deprived areas because they organised services that the state failed to provide. In doing so, Ansar Charia challenged the legitimacy of the Tunisian state.

These initiatives differed in their extent and institutional organisation, but, with the Tunisian transition, never truly challenged the executive power of the Tunisian state. When I met with former political prisoners in Sidi Bouzid – all imprisoned for supposed jihadist activities – they told me that after the revolution they started Islamic classes and went out to provide knowledge to people and guide them back to religion. They had also proposed to provide security to the local market after there was some violence. Rather ruefully, they admitted that inhabitants had clearly and vocally rejected their proposal.[47] Although covered extensively in academic literature and with a number of initiatives might seem impressive, their impact – especially compared to the Syrian crisis – remained limited.[48]

The emergence of independent imams, such as Ridha Jaouadi, Mohamed Afas and hundreds of others, also challenged the power of the Tunisian state. The liberalisation of mosques implied a weakened control of the

Tunisian executive, especially the Ministry of Religious Affairs and Ministry of Interior, over Tunisian mosques and their imams. When Noureddine Khadmi became Minister of Religious Affairs in December 2011, one of his first priorities was to address the position of independent imams. Instead of trying to reclaim lost influence of the Ministry, he attempted to transform its position from a proactive one, with the Ministry assigning imams to mosques, to a reactive one recognising imams after they had been assigned by a congregation. At the beginning of January 2012, for example, the Ministry formally recognised Ridha Jaouadi's position as Friday imam at the Sfaxien Lakhme Mosque. Many other independent imams, at mosques throughout the country, also received formal recognition. It was around this time that Hussein Obeidi signed the agreement that recognised the autonomy of the Zaytuna Mosque. Finally, in June 2013, the Ministry of Religious Affairs formally recognised Khatib Idrissi's mosque, the one he built next to his house, as the Rahma Mosque in Sidi Aoun.[49] Khadmi facilitated the resurgence of an independent Islamic field by decreasing state involvement in religious affairs.

These policies were controversial from the start but also challenging to put into practice. How the Tunisian state should manage the religious field without controlling it quickly turned into a practical issue.[50] An advisor of Khadmi, responsible for religious speech in mosques, recalled that 'It was our struggle to develop and support religious speech, while retaining the freedom of imams'. Noting that in their view 'the issue was that imams are supposed to discuss any social issue, including politics, and do this based on religion alone. It implied that we, as state, could not control them'.[51] One strategy was to establish autonomous Islamic institutes that would mediate between the state and a religious field. One of Khadmi's first initiatives was a *Hayā Ahl al-Dhikr*, or Council of Religious Elders. It was composed of religious figures tasked to mediate conflicts about religious discourse between imams and the state and among imams themselves. He also tried to start a similar (but monthly) *Muntadá al-Wasaṭī*, or Forum of Moderation.[52] The attempt to decrease state involvement led to the creation of a new institutional layer between religion and state. These initiatives aimed to redefine the relationship between the Ministry of Religious Affairs and imams in the country. Neither initiative survived for long.

In both cases, distinctly Islamic service provision challenged the Tunisian state. Ansar Charia's provision of social services and security created an Islamic alternative to Tunisian public services. A second challenge came from the rise of independent imams. Here, their religious services were and remained Islamic but acquired legitimacy by being disassociated from state power. It challenged the pre-revolution hold of the Tunisian executive over the religious field and kindled attempts to redefine the role of the state in religious affairs.

Islam as Distinct Political Practice

Finally, during the Tunisian transition, there was no shortage of political parties that referenced Islam to render themselves distinct. Following the January 2011 revolution, an interim government was created that organised an election of a national constituent assembly (abbreviated as ANC after its French acronym). The ANC would draft a new constitution and organise the first democratic elections for a Tunisian assembly and president. In the run up to the ANC elections, numerous parties (re)appeared. Among these were several Islamic ones, such as the Ennahda Movement, Hizb al-Tahrir and the Reform Front.

Founded in 1989, during a brief period of political liberalisation, *Harakat Ennahda*, or the Ennahda Movement, never received formal recognition as a political party. Following the revolution, the party again applied, this time successfully.[53] As it resurfaced, it created offices throughout the country. It established its headquarters first at Rue d'Angleterre, close to Avenue Bourguiba, and later in the neighbourhood of Monplaisir. In an interview just before his return from exile, Rached Ghannouchi emphasised his support for a democratic transition and demanded that the former ruling party be dissolved, stating that it 'has become a symbol of corruption and oppression, and its survival reminds the Tunisian people of the painful past that they lived through'. He explicitly critiqued calls for an Islamic state made by protesters at several Tunisian embassies.[54] In their political programme for the October 2011 elections, Ennahda summarised their priorities:

> The power of Tunisia, her progressiveness, the protection and permanence of her independence, her sovereignty and her republican system; based on the

> separation between powers, the independence of the judiciary, democracy, (good) governance, equality between its citizens, economic growth, social development and the adherence to our Arab-Islamic national identity.[55]

In short, Ennahda's political programme was above all democratic and nationalist, with the notion of a shared Arab-Islamic authenticity as the sole religious reference.

Another example was Hizb al-Tahrir. They described themselves as a party based on Islam that aimed to establish a caliphate as means to foster an Islamic renaissance in society. Their electoral leaflet included a neat institutional outline of the caliphate to drive home the point.[56] In the left bottom of this outline, as shown in Figure 4.5, the legend divides the Islamic state into a governance (top), judicial (second from the top) and executive (third) branch. The bottom box in the legend refers to national and regional councils that represent citizens. The state is led by the caliph. Solid lines refer to relationships

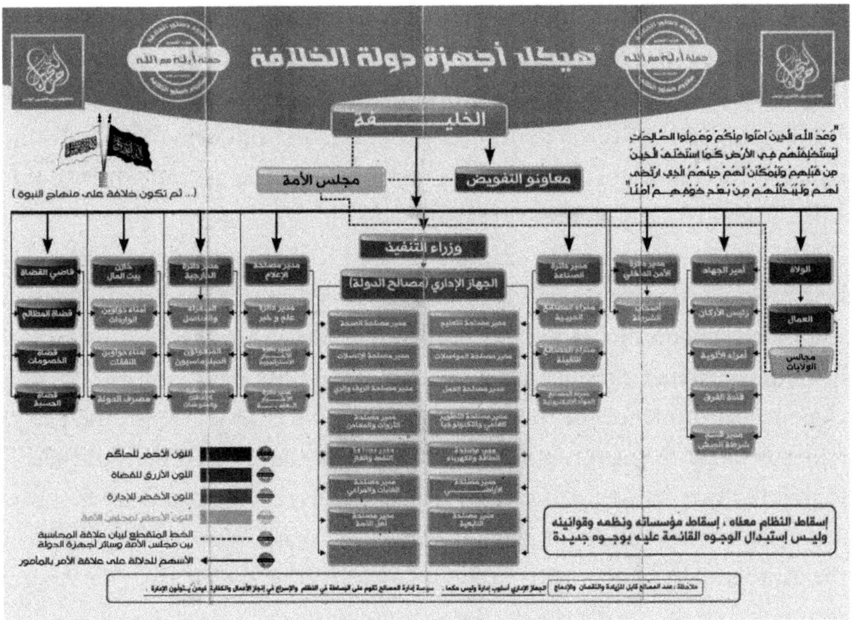

Figure 4.5 Overview of Hizb al-Tahrir's caliphate from a political leaflet received in 2011.

Source: author's archive.

between those giving and receiving commands, while the dotted lines refer to 'relationships of accountability between councils and state organisations'. It is up for debate what an actual Islamic state would look like were Hizb al-Tahrir to get the chance to implement one, but its focus on institutional separation in their state is striking. The party organised a public prayer at the central Avenue Bourguiba in Tunis in April 2011 to showcase their presence in Tunisian public life. A representative of the party explained to me they were the true representatives of Tunisian society and Islam, with other parties and movements – and above all Ennahda – being infiltrated by Western intelligence services.[57]

A third party is *Jabhat al-Iṣlāḥ*, or the Reform Front. Leaders of the Tunisian Islamic Front founded the party in 2011. The Front emerged in 1986 as an offshoot of the Movement for Islamic Tendency, the precursor of Ennahda, opposing their drive for institutionalisation.[58] Its manifesto stated they were a 'political party based on Islam, with its source in Quranic reformism, the Sunna and the method of the Prophet [*manhaj an-nabawi*]' and that they would 'work for the application of sharia rule in all parts of life, removing artificial boundaries resulting in the unity (*tawheed*) of the Islamic ummah'. They noted as their first aim the protection of the transition in the country and the principles of the revolution, with the second aim being the return of Islamic life to the country through the creation of an Islamic state that would apply sharia in society and nurture Islamic *da'wah*.[59]

Despite emphasising the example of the Prophet and religious unity in their political programme – which implies a rejection of the *madhāhib*, or established schools of Islamic jurisprudence and their religious authorities – their leaders stated they would also draw on traditional, Tunisian Maliki religious jurisprudence for their policies.[60] As with Hizb al-Tahrir, the party tried but failed to get formal recognition before the 23 October 2011 elections. Members subsequently ran (unsuccessfully) as independents.[61] Two other parties that called for the application of sharia were *Ḥizb al-Aṣālah* (the Authenticity Party) and *Ḥizb al-Raḥmah* (the Mercy Party).[62] Apart from Ennahda, none of these parties won any seats in any post-revolutionary election.

In brief, there was great diversity in how these parties used Islam to render their political practices distinct. Ennahda translated Islam into a particular type of political identity, Hizb al-Tahrir translated it into a specific type of political institution and the Reform Front used it as a normative framework for social interactions. It goes to show that even among Islamist parties that accepted political pluralism and democratic elections, the translation of Sunni Islam to distinct practices was immensely diverse. It is safe to assume that if, apart from Ennahda, any of these parties had won seats in the ANC, struggles would have emerged around the legitimate ways to represent Islam in the ANC and, eventually, Tunisian parliament. Instead, with the Tunisian transition, Ennahda proved by far the most popular party.

Challenging the Logic of Social Fields

In the above, we saw how activists used Islam to render associational, educational public service and political practices distinct and infuse it with political significance. We observed how activists established Islamic associations and shifted associational activism to charity and education. In addition, it created a subset of associations that engaged in shared mobilisation in defence of Islam and fostered relationships to imams and mosques. Also, we saw how activists enacted a distinct type of Islamic education through the creation of Islamic nurseries, independent religious education and starting education at the Zaytuna Mosque. In all examples – from nurseries to universities – practising a distinctly Islamic type of education challenged state control over education. Third, we saw that Abu Iyadh's Ansar Charia provided public services, challenging the legitimacy of the Tunisian state, while the rise of independent imams questioned the relationship between the executive and the Tunisian Islamic field. Finally, Islamic political parties reemerged and gained formal recognition, heralding hope for the representation of religion in Tunisian politics.

In these cases, Sunni Islam impacted collective action during the Tunisian transition. Not because it provided a set of particular political ideas, but because it kindled distinct initiatives related to associations, education, service provision and party politics that reshaped access to symbolic, institutional and material resources. Islam did not turn political because of the particular ideas it provided to activists, but because they used it to render practices distinct.

Taking Positions

When activists used Islam to distinguish their practices, Islam turned into something that mattered, a stake, in social and political conflict. This section illustrates how, as a result, social interactions became patterned by an Islamic distinction. First, a subset of agents were drawn together around Islam as a social and political stake. For instance, they published joint statements in defence of Islam, stood together in the face of threats to the independence of imams and mobilised to include sharia in the constitution. Second, distinct conflicts ensued among these agents, with activists arguing over how Islam could, and should, inform concrete, distinct practices in relation to education, party politics and governance. Unintentionally, these struggles set these activists apart from others during the Tunisian transition as having a stake in defending Islam in social and political conflicts. In the process, an internally diverse collective was forged that had persistent conflictual interactions with clearly defined external adversaries. In sum, these struggles constituted an Islamist movement.

By investigating the development of an Islamist movement as the emergence of a distinct pattern of contentious interactions, we describe its construction in relation to the broader historical and biographical context of the Tunisian transition. Participants' biographies – their upbringing, experiences in past conflicts and life histories – shaped the range of positions that activists took in conflict situations. Meanwhile, the context in which a movement arose constrained the scope and effectiveness of actions of its participants. As we will see, the development of an Islamist movement between 2012 and 2015 was very much shaped by individual and contextual histories.

In Defence of Tunisian Islam

Just weeks after the revolution, social tensions polarised. Following the murder of a Polish priest in February 2011, hundreds of people went onto the streets to defend the (secular) 'laique character' of the state and the pluralist nature of Tunisian society.[63] The protests turned into heated debates on the position of religion in a future Tunisia.[64] One activist noted she observed that some politicians 'and especially Islamists when they took power', argued that 'Tunisians are Arab Muslims and that's all'. She noted emphatically that this was not the case: 'There are, for instance, many Jewish Tunisian! Why are [Islamists] trying to impose the fact that Tunisians are just Arab Muslims?'[65]

Others instead took issue with what they saw as years of secularist inspired, top-down enforced, societal change under the previous Presidents Habib Bourguiba and Zine El Abidine Ben Ali. They now saw their chance to speak out and defend a Tunisian Arab and Islamic authenticity. In March 2011, a senior representative of Ennahda in Kairouan told me that 'when everyone shouts it just creates tensions. This is what happens with the secularist versus Islamist division'; he continued by saying that 'in the end, we all belong to the same Arab-Islamic background. Everyone accepts this, but for a small group of communists and lefties'.[66] There were multiple others that expressed similar views. Some noted, for instance, that secular Tunisians were out to get the Islamists after the revolution. And as they were in control of media, they were flooding the country with anti-Islam propaganda.[67] Others noted the dominance of a 'French *laique*' elite among university lecturers and professors, noting how they immediately repressed any new religious expressions at universities.[68]

This division emerged soon after the revolution and polarised quickly, but it was not new. A division between French inspired ideas of *laique* modernism (a state-enforced privatisation of religion in the name of modernisation) and ideas of pan-Arab and pan-Islamic national identities had been present in Tunisian society since the beginning of colonial influence. The three decades prior to the revolution had seen a constant back and forth between the regime and various expressions of Islamic activism, with periods of relative opening followed by sudden reversals and repression. It fostered, among one group in Tunisian society, the feeling that the secular character of the Tunisian nation and state was always under threat of a subversive Islamist movement. Among another group, it fostered a deep distrust of those in power, both politicians and civil servants, who they saw as using their powers without checks or balances to subjugate a domestic movement in name of defending Tunisian laicism.

Following the revolution, the bifurcation between a *laique* modernist and Islamic authenticity pole in Tunisian public debate polarised in a matter of months. At the University of Tunis, in March 2011, several students turned a classroom into a mosque. The Council of Professors reacted furiously to the action, and the mosque was subsequently closed.[69] In July 2011, thousands went onto the streets in Sfax in defence of Islam with banners stating 'God is our goal, the prophet our example and the Quran our constitution', 'Islam is our religion, and we do not accept its transgression', and as well as 'there is no God but God' banners. Ridha Jaouadi, with other imams, was involved in these protests.[70] In October that year, a protest turned violent in Sousse after a local university barred a Niqabi woman from registering.[71] That same month, the Nessma TV station, the largest private TV station in the country, aired the film Persepolis. It is an animated movie that depicts God, leading to protests at the TV station in Tunis. Some protesters set fire to the house of the owner of Nessma TV, Nabil Karoui.[72] In November 2011, another university protest emerged at the University of Manouba (on the outskirts of Tunis). Similar to the issue as the Sousse University, protesters opposed a decision to bar a young woman wearing the niqab from taking university exams.[73] At the Manouba University, these protests turned into a sit-in that lasted over two months.

Around these events, a new subset of individuals, associations and political parties positioned themselves. In relation to the Manouba protests there was, for example, a joint statement from Sfaxien associations, including Hamza's culture and arts association and the Sfaxien branch of Khadmi's Association for Sharia Sciences. It argued that the events at Manouba University showed that 'the struggle for the identity of our country is coming to a delicate stage' and critiqued the social polarisation, attacks on the 'authority of Islam' and limits placed on worship and public dress. The statement ended with the demand that 'universities respect the right of students to practise their worship, and safeguard the sanctity of neutrality of universities from ideological and political struggles' and noting their support for 'any initiative to provide prayers space to our people in every institute in the country'.[74]

Around the same time, Khatib al-Idrissi, Abu Iyadh and several other sheikhs reportedly created a council to channel the 'revolutionary enthusiasm' of the moment, bringing together sheikhs with an opposition to institutional politics and established religious authorities in the country.[75] All the while, the involvement of Abu Iyadh's Ansar Charia in the Manouba protests was actively discussed in Tunisian media.[76] The main Islamist party in the country, Ennahda, could not stay silent. In a statement from 6 December 2011,

Rached Ghannouchi and the Ennahda party leadership emphasised the right and freedom for students to dress as they wish, urged to keep universities away from 'ideological struggles' and critiqued those imposing their will on others in name of modernity or authenticity.[77]

The University of Manouba protest was one example of a conflict around which a subset of activists distinguished themselves. Another revolved around the drafting of the constitution. As campaigns for the elections of the ANC got underway in May 2011, the position of sharia in the future constitution had already become a contentious issue that drew activists together. 'Several Tunisian mosque imams' circulated a petition that demanded the constitution describe Tunisia as an Arab-Islamic state, that the president of the republic and the prime minister be Muslim, that no laws should be counter to the Quran and Sunna and that 'assaults on sanctities' should be criminalised.[78] On 17 March 2012, a protest occurred in Sfax that demanded 'the provision of sharia arbitration [*al-Tansīs 'alá Taḥkīm al-Sharī'ah*] in the constitution to ensure a good Islamic life that our people have been deprived of for many years'. The Sfaxien Association of Mosque Preachers and the Sfax Branch of the Tunisian Association for Mosque Imams organised the protest under the banner of 'The People want Sharia Rule'. The protest started – where else – at Ridha Jaouadi's Lakhme Mosque.[79] Hamza, our local activist from Sfax, remembers the protests well:

> It was Islamic civil society that organised these protests: there were many Islamic associations that decided on the title. In the end, this is what most Muslims want: the rule of sharia. It is not all these things [that people say] about killing and violence. It is the complete system . . . [for example] judges that apply sharia and other things.[80]

A week later the Tunisian Front for Islamic Associations organised a protest in Tunis, at the National Theatre at the heart of the Avenue Bourguiba, under the title of 'Victory for the Book of God'.[81] The Front had been established a few weeks before, and brought together around sixty Islamic associations from across the country. The first stated aim of the Front was to 'make Islamic sharia the one and only source for legislation in Tunisia'.[82] Between 2012 and the beginning of 2014, the Front published dozens of statements condemning transgressions of Tunisian sanctities, warning against a looming

Shia threat, disapproving the use of violence in protests, decrying state repression of protests and denouncing the barring of a conference of Ansar Charia in Kairouan.[83]

A third issue that drew these agents together was the defence of mosque autonomy. On 18 August 2014, several Islamic organisations staged a protest in the capital against the repression of imams and associations.[84] Figure 4.6 is a leaflet that was given to me, signed by the Association of Proselytisation and Reform, the Association for Sharia Sciences and other Sfaxien associations. It calls for an end to the supervision of mosques in name of mosque neutrality, an end to the muzzling of imams and an end to diminishing the role of the mosque in public affairs. These initiatives gathered pace as repression of independent imams increased at the start of 2015, following the inauguration of the Government of National Unity and the start of the tenure of Othman Battikh as Minister of Religious Affairs. Hamza, for example, was expelled from his imam position during this period.[85] On 2 July, Bashir bin Hussein, an infamous sheikh from Sousse, was dismissed from his mosque in

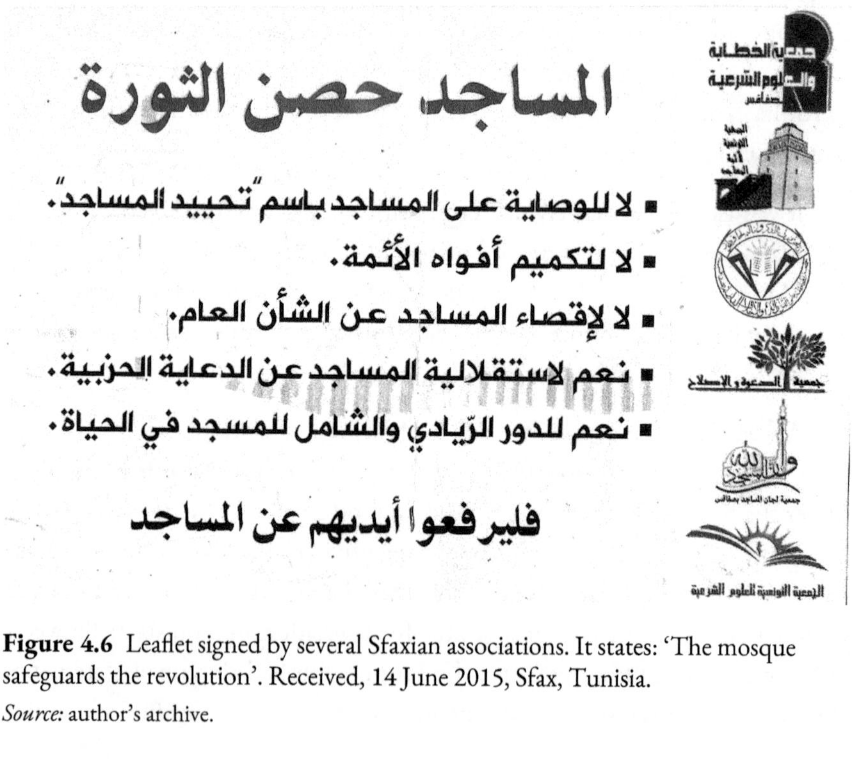

Figure 4.6 Leaflet signed by several Sfaxian associations. It states: 'The mosque safeguards the revolution'. Received, 14 June 2015, Sfax, Tunisia.
Source: author's archive.

response to a terrorist attack in the city.[86] The same happened to Mohamed Afas, imam at the Grand Mosque in Sfax, on 4 September.[87] And, finally, it was Ridha Jaouadi's turn on 15 September 2015.[88] Jaouadi's dismissal led to an immediate and furious reaction from fellow independent imams.[89] There were protests in Sfax opposing Jaouadi's eviction, and when the Ministry appointed a new imam at the Lakhme Mosque, this led to such an uproar that Battikh had the mosque closed for weeks.[90] Multiple government-appointed imams faced hostility and, sometimes, outright violence.[91]

Othman Battikh made clear why he would not come back from his decision, noting that the conduct of Ridha Jaouadi 'is haram in sharia and runs counter to the teachings in the Islamic faith that affirm that houses of God must be kept separate from all political and partisan influences and are for prayer and worship alone'. It was a thinly veiled reference to Article six in the 2014 constitution that stipulated that 'the state [. . .] ensures the neutrality of mosques and places of worship from partisan use'.[92] Ridha Jaouadi had his reply ready, noting that 'We [at the Lakhme Mosque] are also against partisanship at mosques, as stated in Article six of the constitution'.[93] When asked what the Friday sermons should be about, he continued:

> The Friday sermon is not a lesson in *fiqh* [Islamic jurisprudence] as some think. Instead, it is a political meeting in the complete understanding of Islam, that brings together Muslims with their imam every week to raise among them problems that Muslims and the people face. The imam presides over the work of reform in society and contributes to it. This is all in accordance with Article six of the constitution that prohibits partisan outreach and that provides the right to take on public, political and social affairs of the country.[94]

In short, following the revolution, a group of individuals and organisations came together in the name of defending Islam. We observed how Abu Iyadh, the leader of Ansar Charia, was reportedly involved in the protests at Manouba University that drew statements of support from Hamza's and Khadmi's associations, while Ennahda struck a far more critical tone. Idrissi Khatib joined a council with Abu Iyadh to channel 'revolutionary enthusiasm' around the same time. We also saw that, as the constitutional drafting process begun, Ridha Jaouadi and several associations mobilised to include sharia in the constitution. Associational activism nurtured, in the words of activists themselves, an 'Islamic civil society', embodied by the creation of distinctly Islamic umbrella organisations, such as the Tunisian Front of Islamic Associations. Omar, as we will see later on, was also involved in this mobilisation. Finally, the threat to the autonomy of imams, as state repression increased around 2015, drew together a wide variety of agents in denouncing acts of state overreach. These are a few examples of the many associations, imams and activists that were active in name of Islam. They show that as activists used Islam to render their practices distinct, it turned into a contested issue that drew a subset of agents together in name of defending religion in the country.

Continuity in Diversity

To get a better sense of those involved, and their differences, we need to briefly consider the genesis and evolution of Islamism in a country that was known for its secular progressiveness. Following the independence struggle, a fight ensued between two of its leaders, with Salah ben Youssef being more pan-Arab and pan-Islam inclined and Habib Bourguiba more French and modernist inclined. The fight proved crucial for the position of Islam in society: the demise of the former at the hands of the latter set the stage for a particular postcolonial development of Tunisian religion.[95] After Bourguiba signed the independence agreement with France in 1956, he destroyed any vestiges of the Youssefist challenge to his rule. Bourguiba portrayed Habus councils (that managed land held as religious endowments) as traitors, because they had sold land to the French, and he had their land nationalised. A policy to provide mass education to the population boosted attainment, and led to the closure of traditional Islamic schools.[96] Bourguiba further abolished sharia courts at the expense of a unified civil law modelled on the French *code civile*. Five years later, the position of Mufti of the Republic was created, a position that was directly responsible to the prime minister and served as a replacement for Zaytuna's authority on Islamic issues. Bourguiba detached religion from any social, bureaucratic or political power it had and placed it under direct state control. Tunisia then became known for its secular progressiveness and scepticism of pan-Arabism.

The image of Tunisia as a secular, or rather *laique*, country never quite reflected in reality. Despite its traditional religious authorities being severely weakened, already in the 1960s Tunisia saw the kindling of a domestic Islamist movement. Countering a perceived leftist threat to his rule, Habib Bourguiba had become more conciliatory toward religion. He changed, for example, the working hours during Ramadan to facilitate fasting, he limited the consumption of alcohol during Islamic holidays and he established the *Association pour la Sauvegarde du Coran*, or the Association to Safeguard the Quran, as an association for Islamic social activism.[97] In this context, several young Tunisians came together and created a loosely organised association – *al-Jamāʿah al-Islāmīyah*, or the Islamic Group – and started proselytising throughout the country.

Rached Ghannouchi, the later leader of the Ennahda party, was one of them. He came from a conservative family in Gabes and was strongly influenced by pan-Arabism during his youth. When he started university studies in the capital, he was so unnerved by the opposition between the Westernised character of Tunis and his traditional upbringing that he moved to the University of Cairo in Nasser's Egypt. The move turned out to be a complete failure. He was barred from the university within months. Additionally, Nasser's repression of the Egyptian Muslim Brotherhood appalled him. He subsequently chose to move to Damascus to study philosophy. It was here that he became increasingly influenced by Islamism. After he finished his studies in Damascus, he moved to Paris for his postgraduate studies, where he became involved with Dawa wa-Tabligh, an Islamist movement that is focused on proselytisation, rejecting institutionalisation and political activism.[98]

As Anne Wolf has described, on his return to Tunisia, the young Ghannouchi came into contact with Abdelfattah Mourou, a student of law at the University of Tunis, who was also a member of Dawa wa-Tabligh. They hit it off. Soon, together with another friend of Ghannouchi, Hmida Ennaifer, a leftist activist who had recently converted to Islamism, they started *al-Jamāʿah al-Islamıyah*. Their principal aim was proselytisation, reflecting their background in the Dawa wa-Tabligh movement, but with a focus on social change, reflecting their Arab nationalist and leftist influences. As a third influence, they would soon use the Muslim Brotherhood as an example to create an elaborate, layered recruitment structure that safeguarded their secret movement, while facilitating the onboarding of new recruits.[99]

Because the movement focused on proselytisation and social reform, it did not have clearly defined political aims. This changed, in the mid-1970s, as a new generation of *al-Jamāʿah al-Islāmīyah* members entered Tunisian universities and actively participated in political debates with leftist opposition groups. After one of these debates turned violent, students published a formal statement in 1977 in name of the *Mouvement de la Tendance Islamique* (MTI), or Movement of Islamic Tendency. They denounced the violence and articulated a more defined political position: opposing Bourguibist secularisation and his state Islam. An explicitly political organisation had emerged (the MTI), and it did so in direct interaction with Tunisian leftist student movements.[100]

The next two decades saw a constant see-sawing motion between repression and liberalisation, during which the MTI transformed and split, and various other movements established themselves. Being preoccupied with the political challenge by leftist opposition parties, Habib Bourguiba initially allowed political participation of the movement, with Ghannouchi and others publicly announcing their willingness to participation in democratic multiparty politics. When Bourguiba realised he had underestimated the strength of the MTI, he subsequently harshly repressed them. In 1981, the regime detained more than 100 activists, among which were Mourou and Ghannouchi. This first widespread repression of the party led to discussions about the correct strategies to interact with the regime. Some members argued for the necessity of keeping violence as option on the table, while others (among them Ghannouchi) argued for continuing attempts at political reconciliation.[101]

During this period, several other Islamist organisations and individuals emerged. For instance, Mohammad Khouja and Rafik Ouni established the Tunisian Islamic Front in 1987 after splitting from *al-Jamāʿah al-Islāmīyah* because they opposed the MTI's move towards institutionalisation. They would later, following the 2011 revolution, establish the *Jabhat al-Iṣlāḥ*, or the Reform Front.[102] Another was Hizb al-Tahrir. Originally established in Palestine in 1952, it opened a chapter in Tunisia in 1977. There were also Tunisians that travelled to Afghanistan in the late 1970s and 1980s to fight in the jihad. One example was Seifallah Ben Hassin, better known as Abu Iyadh al-Tunisi. While in Afghanistan he reportedly ended up creating the Tunisian Combat Group on instigation of al-Qaeda.[103] Also, an increasing number of Tunisians travelled to the Gulf as economic migrants. Some of them were influenced by Gulf scholars while residing there. One example is Idrissi Khatib, the Tunisian sheikh that I discussed in the introduction. He became one of the most well-known sheikhs advocating for a unity of faith that did not recognise Tunisian, Maliki religious traditions, schools of jurisprudence or authorities.

After Zine El Abidine Ben Ali staged a bloodless coup in 1987 against the ageing Habib Bourguiba, the political context made another see-saw motion. It nudged the MTI toward a transformation into the Ennahda party. Ben Ali initially allowed opposition parties to register and participate in elections. Encouraged by these developments, the MTI also applied for recognition as the Ennahda, or Renaissance, party, removing the religious reference in their name to comply with electoral laws. Ennahda members took part in the general elections of 1989 as independent candidates because the party had not received formal recognition yet. They won almost 15 per cent of the vote. The other opposition parties combined received only 5 per cent.[104] The reaction from the Ben Ali regime sent a clear message. It declined Ennahda's application and did not allow Ennahda candidates to take their parliamentary seats. Rashed Ghannouchi went into self-imposed exile in the UK soon after.[105] In the following two years, the regime destroyed much of Ennahda's domestic institutional structure: hundreds of its activists were arrested and tortured. Many others were caught up in the tide of repression. This was also the period, for example, that Ridha Jaouadi became an imam, in 1987, and was subsequently barred from preaching, in 1991.

Islamists faced severe repression from the Ben Ali regime, with scores of activists jailed, tortured and – also after their release – continuously being harassed by security forces. Many went into exile. Crucially, Ennahda exiles often left for European countries (France, Germany and Switzerland were popular) and rebuilt institutional structures there. Ghannouchi settled in the United Kingdom. Ennahda organised a major party congress in Germany in 1992 and exiled activists established Marhama, which would grow into a large charitable association, in the same country. Through these years, Ennahda became increasingly explicit in its acceptance of multiparty democracy and its rejection of violent forms of activism.[106]

The 11 September 2001 attacks further worsened the situation, fragmenting Tunisian Islamism. Following the 9/11 terrorist attacks, the US declared a global War on Terror which gave the Tunisian regime ample opportunity to repress dissent in name of national security. The government adopted a wide-ranging anti-terrorism and anti-money laundering law that had such a wide definition of terrorism that it could be applied to almost any form of dissent. In 2003, Türkiye extradited Abu Iyadh, the veteran of the Afghan jihad, to Tunisia – where he promptly received a prison sentence of forty-three years. In 2005, most of the 400 political prisoners in Tunisian prisons were suspected Islamists.[107] This was also the period in which the regime incarcerated Khatib Idrissi, who had returned from Saudi Arabia in 1994.[108]

But not all was quiet. Despite the repression, Islamists were still active. Ennahda activists slowly rebuilt an underground network. Activists later recalled the youth camps that were organised for children of imprisoned activists as one way in which the movement persisted.[109] In addition, there were youngsters that organised secret sound and video rooms to organise online classes with Saudi sheikhs. Omar did this for example with his university friends. Anecdotally, the use of virtual private networks to circumvent censorship became increasingly common among Tunisian internet users.[110] Jihadism also gained a foothold domestically. Between December 2006 and January 2007, the Tunis Court of First Instance sentenced thirty activists for an attempt to create a nationwide jihadist group to challenge the Ben Ali regime. The founders of the group had links to a Salafi-jihadist group in Algeria.[111]

Meanwhile, the regime opened up strictly regulated spaces for Islamic initiatives to bolster its religious credentials while sidelining independent Islamic activism. In 2007, an administrative tribunal annulled a degree from 1986 banning the wearing of the hijab in public institutions. A radio station, Radio Zaytuna, named after the Mosque, was created that focused on religious topics and aimed to provide a voice, in the words of its director, to traditional Tunisian pacifist Islam in response to the global threat of radicalism.[112] Finally, the regime allowed new religious schools to be established throughout the country. Officially founded under the Association for Quranic Schools, the activities and personnel of these schools were subject to checks by the Ministry of Interior. They were also only allowed to teach specific topics and were not allowed to publicise their activities or engage with mosques. Despite these constraints, they proved immensely popular.[113] Despite, or possibly because of, regime repression, Islamic activism was turning more diverse. There were Ennahda members active at home and abroad, Islamist youngsters who reached out to foreign sheikhs, a low-level jihadist insurgency occurred and interest in social Islamic activism blossomed.

Struggles around Islam as a Stake

Following the revolution, state control over the religious field collapsed. This provided mosques, their congregations and imams with a sudden and unexpected level of freedom. This freedom soon translated into conflicts between those who had held a stake in shaping the position of Islam during the Tunisian transition. Conflicts emerged between Ennahda, grassroots activists (such as Omar), the Tunisian Front for Islamic Associations, Khatib Idrissi, Abu Iyadh, Noureddine Khadmi and the Grand Imam of the Zaytuna Mosque, Hussein Obeidi. They revolved around the position of independent imams and their mosques, education at the Zaytuna Mosque and the inclusion of sharia in the constitution.

To start with the first example, several imams had links to Islamist organisations. In some mosques, imams took over with links to Ansar Charia;[114] others were members of Hizb al-Tahrir.[115] Some imams, such as Ridha Jaouadi, Mohamed Afas and Idrissi Khatib, did not have party affiliations, but all critically discussed social and political developments in their sermons. The diversity of these agents, and the power of the mosque as a space to address social and political issues, resulted in a struggle for control. The al-Fateh Mosque in the centre of Tunis, for example, where Noureddine Khadmi had been imam before becoming Minister of Religious Affairs, was taken over by Islamists who did not recognise Tunisian religious and state authorities. Sometimes these struggles turned into physical fights between congregations and those attempting to take over the pulpit.[116] In Sfax, activists changed the locks of the Grand Mosque in the old town – locking the imam out – and promptly changed the prayer time away from that set by the Tunisian Ministry of Religious Affairs, signalling a complete disassociation from state control. After three days, following fights in the mosque, popular outrage in the city, negotiations with the municipality and intervention by security forces, a consensus was reached on who should be the Friday imam.[117] Such scenes played out at mosques throughout the country.

Another, infamous, example is that of the Zaytuna Mosque. Its attempt to become an autonomous religious institute for education set off a string of contentious interactions between Hussein Obeidi as its the Grand Imam, government Ministries and the Ennahda party. Obeidi publicly vented his anger in reaction to attempts to curtail the power of the Mosque, stating that Ennahda declared war on Zaytuna to enable the spread of Wahhabism in the country. He also argued that the government of Mehdi Jomaa was implementing a colonial programme aimed at subjugating Tunisian religious authorities.[118] Many other activists also saw a stake in the conflict. A representative of the Tunisian Front of Islamic Associations told me that 'in the end everybody is in favour of restarting teaching at the Zaytuna Mosque, it is just that the USA and other foreign powers force Ennahda to keep Islam weak. So Ennahda is forced to block any teaching at the Zaytuna mosque for this reason'.[119] Omar had a somewhat different take:

> Every Muslim in Tunisia wants Zaytuna to return to the way it was. [. . .] But the struggle today between Ennahda and Zaytuna is not about the state, democracy or education. No, it is just because [Ennahda] wants to control the Mosque. [. . .] What is also striking is that the Minister of Religious Affairs [Noureddine Khadmi] before he became Minister, had an organisation: the Tunisian Association for Sharia Sciences. Many of its students now enrolled at the Zaytuna Mosque for classes. It started another struggle for control, but now from below.[120]

Whether true or not, there was little love lost between Omar and Noureddine Khadmi at this point in time; this statement is one more example that liberalising the religious field not only strengthened the position of Islam in public life – it also turned mosques into a contested space.

Another example of struggles among Islamists revolved around the drafting of the constitution. Ennahda won the elections of the ANC, in October 2011, with eighty-nine seats out of 217. It formed the Troika government with the Congress for the Republic, or CPR, and Ettakatol. The first is a centrist party led by Human Rights lawyer Moncef Marzouki, which became the second largest party with twenty-nine seats. The second is a social democratic party that received twenty-six seats. These results situated Ennahda as the most powerful party in the constitutional drafting process.

On 13 August 2012, a first draft of the new constitution leaked. The draft reflected the demands, tensions and conundrums around the position of Islam in the country. Article 1.4, for example, read that 'the state is the patron of religion', and it is 'the guarantor of freedom of belief and practice of religious rites, the protector of religious sanctities and the assurer of the neutrality of houses of worship from partisan propaganda'. Article 2.3 noted that 'The state shall guarantee the freedom of belief and the exercise of religious rites. The state shall also incriminate all acts of violation against any religious sanctities'. Article 2.28 stated that 'The state shall guarantee the protection of the rights of women and shall support the gains thereof as true partners to men in the building of the nation and as having a roll complementary thereto within the family'. And, finally, Article 4.46 dealt with the requirements for presidential candidates and was still undecided. Among the different opinions listed was that the candidate 'shall be Muslim', 'embrace Islam' or that it shall be 'a right entitled to all Tunisians' to be a candidate.[121] There were no reference to the Quran, hadith or sharia – nor would there be in the final version.

The leaked draft led to a public outcry. On the one hand, Article 2.28, defining women as complementary – not equal – to men, brought many to the streets in name of defending equality and the modern character of Tunisian society. Thousands flocked to Avenue Bourguiba to challenge this designation.[122] But it was not only secularist Tunisians that were up in arms. Omar explained that many younger activists, himself included, were getting fed up with Ennahda. As he explained in October 2012:

> So there was this massive protest in favour of sharia in the constitution [organised by the Tunisian Front for Islamic Associations]. Ennahda was like: we support you! I mean, they were at the protest! [Rached] Ghannouchi was there, Habib Ellouze was there. [. . .] Then they went to the ANC and presented their petition. Again, Ennahda told them: we support you, we also want sharia in the constitution. And then . . . Ennahda just pulled the rug out from underneath their feet.[123]

A leaked video around the same time shows Rashed Ghannouchi talking to activists, imploring them to take it easy on mobilisation. He tries to convince them that their position was just too weak:

> The Tunisian people want this [Islamic] religion. At the moment secular groups in this country, it is correct, do not make up the majority. But look at the press: until now it is in their hands. And the economy is in their hands, as is the Tunisian administration. [. . .] I say to our brothers concerning these issues, don't deceive yourselves with numbers when you go out [and protest] with a thousand, two thousand, ten thousand or twenty thousand. [. . .] The pillars of the state and its divisions are still in their hands. Take your time to change.[124]

The talk did not stand on its own. Omar confirmed there had been informal talks between Ennahda and grassroots Islamist activists on what to do, and what not to do.[125] A senior Ennahda representative stated that they tried to reach out, give knowledge and convince – with questionable results. Obviously annoyed, he remarked that they kept on being described as 'Islam light' by these activists.[126] Framed by detractors as proof that Ennahda was out to create an Islamic State in Tunisia, these interactions reflected Ennahda's strategy to reach out to, discuss with and, some would say, appease individuals such as Ridha Jaouadi, Omar and Hamza.

Through these internal struggles, participants of an Islamist movement situated themselves in relation to each other. Ennahda's approach of situating Islam as a source of Tunisian national identity translated into attempts to enshrine the protection of sanctities in the constitution and represent Islam through party politics. Several agents, such as Omar and the Tunisian Front for Islamic Associations, mobilised to include explicit references to sharia, representing Islam through codified law. Many among the grassroots activists initially perceived Ennahda to be a conduit to political resources that became accessible following the 2011 revolution. Instead, what they found was that Ennahda had its own approach to politics, shaped by a history of hope and betrayal at the hands of an authoritarian regime. It turned the party into a gatekeeper to political resources: engaging with, but keeping young activists away from legislative power. Ennahda's principal aim seemed to be its political survival and, directly related to this, the survival of a democratic transition that gave space for their party to be active.[127]

In response to pushback from activists, Ennahda seemed to try and redirect this activism into party politics. After Ghannouchi made clear that sharia would not be included in the constitution, in March 2012, the Troika government recognised the Reform Front as a political party. A few months later, in July, it recognised Hizb al-Tahrir.[128] The effectiveness of this strategy proved limited. Many grassroots activists around sheikhs such as Abu Iyadh and Idrissi Khatib deplored the fact that the Reform Front – with their political programme stating that they worked to implement sharia rule in all parts of life based on Islamic unity (*tawheed*) and the method of the Prophet (*manhaj an-nabawi*) – would submit itself to the fragmentation of party politics and national identities. But also, among sheikhs who opposed the Tunisian state and democratic politics, different positions appeared. Idrissi Khatib, for example, broke from the council he participated in with Abu Iyadh because of the latter's insistence on institutionalising activism. Using Islam to distinguish their practices during the Tunisian transition, these activists inadvertently positioned themselves in a struggle around the legitimate ways of doing so. Can, and should, this distinction be translated through Tunisian national identity, constitutional law, political representation, education and/or institutional activism – and if so, how? These activists all had different answers to these questions.

Ennahda: Differentiation versus Specialisation

As the constitutional drafting process got underway, tensions between grassroots activists and Ennahda emerged. But participation in politics also created tensions within Ennahda itself. It had been founded as a movement aimed at social activism and proselytisation and gradually institutionalised into a political movement and party. But a movement, building on a collective identity but very diverse in its makeup, is something different from a political party following a political programme with well-defined objectives. Participation in politics brought out tensions between the two. When asked, in October 2011, if Ennahda was a movement or a party, a regional Ennahda leader stated that:

> We already started discussing this topic in prison. [. . .] One of the most important topics that we face is about the relation between the party and movement. Do we keep a relation between the two? Or else: what do we do with the *da'wah* and more cultural movement?[129]

During the first post-revolution general conference of the Ennahda Movement, its ninth overall, held in July 2012, one of the discussion points was on whether the Ennahda Movement should remain a single organisation, divide itself into two sub-institutions or specialise in politics only. It was a question about prioritising religion as a distinction for their social and political activism, or subsuming to the logics of a Tunisian political and associational field. Various Ennahda members stated several camps had emerged around this question.[130] It was decided to postpone the discussion to the next general conference scheduled for 2016.

In the intervening years, the political context changed dramatically, forcing Ennahda to take increasingly pragmatist positions. It started out with the creation of Nidaa Tounes in June 2012. The principal founder and leader of Nidaa Tounes was the former Interim President Caid Essebsi. Another person involved was Nabil Karoui, a Tunisian media magnate and owner of the Nessma TV station that had aired the movie Persepolis in October 2011. The party brought together former members of President Habib Bourguiba's party (the Destourians), former members of the ruling party and trade union activists from the Tunisian UGTT.[131] Essebsi explicitly framed Nidaa Tounes as the political counterweight to Ennahda.[132]

Meanwhile, the constitutional drafting process progressed painfully slowly, while the opposition put increasing pressure on the Troika government. The ANC published multiple draft constitutions: one in December 2012, a second in April 2013 and a third in June 2013.[133] They resulted from slow moving, often acrimonious, debates.[134] The ANC had an original mandate of one year to draft a new constitution and organise elections. It extended the deadline repeatedly. Nidaa Tounes, the UGTT and others became increasingly vocal in voicing their discontent, while tensions along a *laique*–Islamist dichotomy continued to rise in society.

On the morning of 6 February 2013, these tensions exploded when Chokri Belaid, an ANC member for the leftist Democratic Patriots Party and outspoken critic of Ennahda, was assassinated. Government officials claimed the perpetrator had links to Abu Iyadh and Ansar Charia.[135] Bubakr Hakim, a veteran of the Iraqi jihad and involved in the attack, later explained that the aim was to create chaos in Tunisia and support 'our brothers in prison'. Chokri Belaid's work for the ANC made him one of the *'tawāghīt'* (tyrants) of the country, or so he explained, legitimising his killing.[136] If the aim was to create political and social chaos, the attack was successful. Violent street battles between anti-government protesters and the police followed. Protests in front of the seat of the ANC grew ever larger, calling for the Troika to be replaced by a technocrat government, while counter protests were organised that emphasised its popular, democratic legitimacy.[137]

In this context, the UGTT, on 18 June 2013, proposed a national reconciliation process that would spell the end of the Troika government by creating a technocrat government.[138] Although they initially opposed the initiative, Ennahda eventually gave in. The first reason was the 3 July coup in Egypt, in which Abdel Fattah El-Sisi took power and immediately repressed the Muslim Brotherhood and its sympathisers. The coup highlighted the continued existential risk to Ennahda, as an Islamist party, in Tunisia. Second, on 25 July, Mohamed Brahmi was assassinated. It was the third political assassination in less than a year. It sent shock waves throughout Tunisian politics and society and galvanised calls for the end to the Troika government. On 25 August, Rashed Ghannouchi appeared on Nessma TV, the station owned by Nabil Karoui, a founder of Nidaa Tounes, and stated that a transitional justice law, excluding former ruling party members from future political participation, would not be passed. He did this even though many Ennahda members and Ennahda's Shura Council supported the law. Rashed Ghannouchi was reaching out to Caid Essebsi to safeguard Ennahda's political future. Later that month, the two met for a personal *tête-à-tête* in Paris.[139] From then on, the political process started moving.

The final version of the constitution, adopted on 27 January 2014, reflected Ennahda's pragmatism. It did not contain an article describing women as complementary to men. Article 2.3, incriminating all acts of violation against religious sanctities, was also scrapped. Article 1.4, stipulating that the state is the assurer of neutrality of houses of worship, survived in a revised form as Article six. Regarding presidential candidates, the final constitution stated that 'every male and female voter who holds Tunisian nationality since birth, whose religion is Islam shall have the right to stand for election to the position of President of the Republic'.[140] Above all, the final draft reflected political compromises on a range of issues, including that of the position of Islam in the country.

Subsequent parliamentary elections severely weakened Ennahda's political power. The first since the departure of Ben Ali, they took place on 26 October 2014. The elections resulted in a win for Caid Essebsi's Nidaa Tounes with eighty-six out of 217 seats. Ennahda came second with sixty-nine seats.[141] Caid Essebsi himself won the presidential elections in December that year. Nidaa Tounes could form a government together with the Free Patriotic Union (sixteen seats) and Afek Tounes (eight seats), excluding Ennahda from political power. Instead, Essebsi reached out to Ghannouchi and invited Ennahda to join a government of national unity. One possible reason Essebsi invited Ennahda was that it created a strong government that incorporated possible polarising opposition while effectively pacifying it. It controlled 179 seats in parliament, leaving the opposition with only thirty-eight. Although Ennahda became part of the government, it only received one out of a total of twenty-seven ministries (the Ministry of Employment and Training).[142] It left Ennahda with very little influence on government policies.

The reason Ennahda participated in the government, despite only receiving one ministry, was clear. Following the social polarisation and Egyptian coup d'état, many in the party were acutely aware that the threat for widespread repression of the party was still present. It was better to take part in a government with Nidaa Tounes than end up in the opposition. The latter would leave the government with no party to check attempts to reconstruct a repressive state that could – and probably would – be used against it.[143] As Rashed Ghannouchi stated in response to why he supported the National Unity Government:

> Tunisia has not completely turned the page on tyranny and rigged elections and swearing allegiance to a dictator and depriving Tunisian nationals from their right to freedom of choice. Our goal is to ensure democracy triumphs over chaos and dreams of a coup d'état.[144]

Taking part in the National Unity Government reflected a continued sense of existential threat. Nadia Marzouki has argued it reflected Ennahda prioritising consensus over political representation.[145] While participating in the National Unity Government, Ennahda increasingly accommodated traditional elite groups. In 2015, for example, Ennahda

MPs supported a law to decrease import tax on alcohol. It was a move that was impossible to support based on the party's religious or social justice values. It also supported economic reforms recommended by the International Monetary Fund, such as cuts in fuel subsidies and increasing electricity and gas prices that ran counter the interests of its middle and working-class supporters.[146]

It was in this context that the tenth General Conference of Ennahda took place, during which they tried to resolve the tension between party politics and social activism. Following the Conference, in 25 May 2016, Ennahda published its final statement that included this passage:

> The conference confirms the strategic choice that the Ennahda Movement Party has become more than what some have used as a justification for considering it part of so-called 'political Islam'. This notion does not truly cover its current identity and does not reflect its future projects. Ennahda considers its activities to be part of a project of *ijtihad* [individual Islamic reasoning] that contributes to a broad movement of Muslim Democrats who reject the opposition between Islamic values and modernity. [. . .] Ennahda, as a political party, places itself at the forefront of safeguarding the democratic transition in our country.[147]

In effect, the conference resulted in a decision to situate Ennahda's activities solely in Tunisia's political field. In the party bylaws, Ennahda described the positive and negative experiences of having been in political power since 2012. They touted the former as the ability to support a democratic transition in Tunisia. They noted the latter as the inability to articulate clear views about social, political and economic problems; ambiguous positions regarding jihadism and Salafism and former regime elites; and a general lack of effective implementation of policy directives.[148] While acknowledging the holistic character of Islam as a source of social, economic and political transformation, the document stated that finding solutions to these negative experiences called for a strategy of prioritising professionalisation in order to increase effectiveness of implementing desired policies. It meant a strategy of *takhaṣṣuṣ*, or specialisation, in party politics.[149]

The decision had several concrete impacts on the political practices of Ennahda. One of which was an enforced distancing from associational activism. Despite a formal separation between the two, there were several associations presided by Ennahda politicians. The conference documents stated – in bold and extra large font – that 'associations may convergence with some political parties through their intellectual references [. . .] but autonomy from parties should be achieved in management and financing'.[150] A senior Ennahda representative explained that:

> When we specialised, we also asked everyone that presided over an association to resign from these positions. And the other way around: for people that remained active as presidents of associations to resign from the party. Obviously they can remain active within these organisations on individual grounds.[151]

Habib Ellouze's Association for Proselytisation and Reform is one example. Following Ennahda's political specialisation, he stepped down as president. Ellouze turned conspicuously quiet in public debate afterwards, but the organisation remained active. Meanwhile, these changes remained incomplete. The Ennahda representative quoted above remarked, for instance, that it was still 'very much a work in progress' and could not assess the number of individuals that were facing a choice between party membership and associational leadership.[152] Having said this, moving away from Islam as a unifying distinction for its activism had a profound impact on how access to political and associational resources could be combined. There was widespread opposition to the move among Ennahda's rank and file, but its leadership successfully safeguarded party discipline.[153]

Practising Islamist Movement

When activists used Islam to render their associational, educational, public service and political practices distinct, it created conflicts among Islamists about the legitimate and desirable ways to do so. The emergence of independent imams created a struggle around how to redefine the relationship between the state and Tunisian mosques, with some activists placing them completely outside the control of the Ministry of Religious Affairs. The Zaytuna Mosque provided an example where the creation of Islamic education triggered a struggle over institutional control over educational resources. The rise of Ennahda in Tunisian politics triggered a struggle about how to represent Islam in the constitution, reflecting the hope for political representation among grassroots activists. It led to acrimonious interactions about access to these newly accessible political resources during the constitutional drafting process. Internally, participation in politics led to a debate about the role of Islam as a unifying force between Ennahda's social activism and party politics. As previously noted, enacting a Sunni Islamic distinctness had direct, real world, implications for access to political, institutional and educational resources, laying the foundation for distinct social interactions between individuals with a stake in using Islam to access them.

All these individuals had their own biography in relation to a history of an Islamist movement. Rached Ghannouchi embodied the many political openings, subsequent repression, incarceration and exile that numerous Ennahda activists had lived through. Ridha Jaouadi was an example of those conservative Tunisians that had been caught up in the political turmoil of the early Ben Ali years. Abu Iyadh, in turn, was an archetypal jihadist with experience of institutional organisation among a global jihadist movement. Omar and Hamza, instead, were examples of the Islamist youngsters that had grown up in an age of repression and Islamising in a post-9/11 Tunisia. In contrast, Idrissi Khatib was one of many economic Gulf migrants that were shaped by Saudi Islam while residing there, emphasising a unity of Islam that challenged local particularities in Islamic authorities and jurisprudence, opposing institutionalised activism later in life. With each of these individuals, their prior experiences shaped the positions they took in these debates. We will discuss these positions in more detail in Chapter six.

In Chapter one, I defined a social movement, following Donatella della Porta and Mario Diani, as a social process through which agents share a distinct collective identity, engage in collective action, and construct enduring conflictual relations with clearly identified opponents.[154] Here, we observed a process through which a subset of agents came together around Islam as a stake, giving birth to a distinct Islamist collective engaged in defending Islam in Tunisian society and politics. Meanwhile, this process kindled particular patterns of social interactions among Islamist individuals and organisations, setting their activism apart as a type of collective action. In short, we observed the emergence of an Islamist movement.

The Decline of an Islamist Movement

The movement did not last. Following the assassination of Chokri Belaid on 6 February 2013 and Mohamed Brahmi on 25 July of that same year, Ansar Charia was designated as a terrorist organisation. Repression of the group, and anyone somehow deemed affiliated with it, immediately increased. Throughout late 2013 and early 2014, Tunisian security forces repressed the organisation with full force, leading to its demise. Abu Iyadh escaped to Libya where he died in June 2015. The demise of Ansar Charia did not spell the end of the use of violence by self-proclaimed jihadist groups. Instead, they fragmented, turned more clandestine and overtly violent against a wider range of targets. One group that became infamous was *Katibat Uqbah Bin Nafi* (KUBN). Although initially affiliated with al-Qaeda in the Islamic Maghreb, individuals affiliated to the Islamic State organisation (or ISIS) later took it over.[155] Although the groups' centre of activity was near the Libyan and Algerian borders, it had adherents throughout the country and especially among socio-economic disadvantaged neighbourhoods and regions.[156] On 18 March 2015, two gunmen attacked tourists at the Bardo National Museum in greater Tunis and killed twenty-two people. ISIS claimed responsibility for the attack, although Tunisian authorities pointed to KUBN as the perpetrators. A few months later, on 26 June 2015, a mass shooting occurred in a tourist resort in Sousse. Disguised as a tourist, a single gunman smuggled a Kalashnikov assault rifle into the Port El Kantaoui resort and subsequently killed thirty-eight tourists and wounded forty. These attacks did not stand on their own. In 2015 alone, ISIS carried out eleven attacks in Tunisia.[157]

The attacks bolstered the case for executive empowerment in name of national security. In response to the escalating threat, the government strengthened its anti-terrorism policies by adopting a counterterrorism and anti-money laundering Act on 7 August 2015. Although a long overdue law, the Act defined terrorism broadly and prescribed severe sentences. Among 'terrorist activities' it included – beyond murder and preparations for attacks on individuals with the aim to do bodily harm – accusations of apostacy, hate crimes based on race and religion, and causing intentional damage to the environment and property. The Act also created a National Commission to

Combat Terrorism to, among other tasks, improve communication between ministries and cooperate with international bodies around issues of national security.[158] 172 MPs voted in favour of the law, among which almost all Ennahda MPs.[159]

The Executive Strikes Back

A constant terrorist threat and calls for executive empowerment set the stage for subsequent social and political developments that ended up weakening an Islamist movement. On 29 January 2014, the technocrat government replaced the Troika government. Mehdi Jomaa, who had been Minister of Industry, became Prime Minister. Mounir Tlili, a professor of religion at Zaytuna University, replaced Nourredine Khadmi as Minister of Religious Affairs. They immediately set to work. One week after its inauguration, news emerged that the Ministry of Interior, Justice, Finance and Religious Affairs had met to discuss state governance of the Tunisian religious field. In March, Mehdi Jomaa stated in an interview that 'takfiri imams' controlled 149 mosques in the country and that the government was actively trying to place them back under state control.[160] The list of 149 mosques was not made publicly available. But the Zaytuna Mosque, with Hussein Obeidi as its Grand Imam, was on it.[161] Hussein Obeidi reacted that the project to neutralise mosques could not apply to the Zaytuna Mosque: the May 2012 agreement defined Zaytuna as an autonomous organisation and hence independent from the state, its ministries and their policies.[162] The government disagreed and tried, multiple times, to have Obeidi removed from his position – initially with little success.

Munir Tlili noted that several of the 149 imams on the list had given up control over their mosques voluntarily, while those that refused would receive a warning from the police not to show up for Friday prayers.[163] He also demanded the return of financial support given to preachers by the previous Minister of Religious Affairs, Noureddine Khadmi, and noted that he was working to reinstate preachers who had been unjustly removed from their positions.[164] Tlili publicly kept score on how state control of mosques progressed: in April 2014 he stated there were still 100 mosques beyond the control of the ministry. In May this number declined to ninety, in June to forty-nine, in August it was down to twenty-five and in November it was down to only four.[165] Despite these numbers being impossible to verify, the Tunisian state was clearly reasserting its control. It did not work out negatively for everyone: Hamza told me he became an imam under Tlili. He had passed an exam, and the Ministry subsequently appointed him to a mosque in Sfax. Jihadists had previously controlled the mosque, and after the state dismissed the Friday imam, it appointed him as its replacement.[166] He could not know that he would face the same fate as the previous imam when the next Minister of Religious Affairs, Othman Battikh, dismissed him. Hamza would be imam for little over a year.

At the beginning of 2015, The Ministry of Religious Affairs brought Obeidi of the Zaytuna Mosque to heel. A temporary internal commission of Zaytuna sheikhs aided the Ministry in these attempts by replacing Hussein Obeidi as the Grand Imam of the Mosque that January. Although Obeidi ignored the decision of the committee, it enabled the Ministry to argue that he did not represent Zaytuna, and hence the agreement signed between Obeidi and the Ministry in May 2012 did not apply.[167] Two months after, in March, a local court ruled that Obeidi had to leave the mosque – a ruling that was enforced by the police a few days later. With this, any discussion on Zaytuna's autonomy ceased. The May 2012 document was never mentioned again.

Mosques and their imams were not the only ones facing repression. Following an attack by armed men that killed more than a dozen soldiers close to the border of Algeria, 157 associations across Tunisia received notices in August 2014 via their regional governors to suspend their activities. The notices were issued at the Ministry of Interior and based on a 1979 law that gave governors the authority of oversight for associations in the name of public order and security. Each of these closures ran counter to the 2011 law on associations, which stipulated that associations could only be closed via a court order.[168] In Sfax alone, seven associations received notices; in the capital there were nine.[169] Hamza's association was one of them.[170] The same went for Omar's educational association:

> We received a notice ordering us to temporarily cease our activities. What temporarily meant was completely unclear: a month, two, three? The reason they gave was to 'safeguard public security'. We went to court to challenge the notice. [. . .] But it went nowhere. In the end, the real problem was

perception. People had the impression that there must be something wrong with the association. And so parents withdrew their children.[171]

Omar changed strategy as a result: 'Being active as an association was not working', he noted in 2016, 'so we registered our nursery at the Ministry of Women, the same with our primary school. We ended up implementing their curricula to the letter'. The only additional activity they provided compared with normal schools were optional classes in memorisation of the Quran. A few teachers at lower classes also gave some additional attention to social norms, based on Islam.[172] He remarked:

> So, my wife is the general manager [of the school]. And we, together, discuss [our educational strategies] all the time. We say, look, we wanted to do an Islamic project. And the aim and idea behind it was to provide an alternative [to existing education . . .]. But then, with repression, we keep on taking bits and pieces out: let's just only leave the Quran bit, let's just only leave that other bit . . . At the moment, we have to constantly retreat.[173]

In November that year, the General Commissioner of State Conflicts (an organisation somewhat similar to a public prosecutor) aimed to dissolve Ridha Jaouadi's Lakhme Charitable Association. The reason given was misappropriation of funds received from the Ministry of Employment and Training in 2012, when Ridha Jaouadi had pledged to get 1000 Tunisians back to work. In other words: corruption.[174] As he was about to hand over the reins to a new Minister for Religious Affairs in February 2015, Mounir Tlili reflected on his one-year tenure:

> Since the first meeting we had with him, Mehdi Jomaa, asked us: 'Are you ready to work for only one year?' He pointed out that we would do a 'soldier' year. The reforms needed to get Tunisia out of its bottleneck required sacrifice. We answered we were ready.[175]

In regard to Islamic activism, the one-year tenure of the Mehdi Jomaa government indeed made its mark. The government barred many independent imams from preaching, forced Islamic associations to cease their activities and, more generally, sent a chill through the Islamist movement. As a director of an Islamic nursery told me: 'They closed these 157 associations. All of them because of some kind of relation to Islam and without respecting the law. It was a message to Islamic civil society: you do not have the right to be active'.[176]

Data from IFEDA shows that the number of newly established associations, especially charitable and educational ones, dropped sharply around 2014 (see Figures 4.1 and 4.2 at the start of the chapter). Other associations, also those that did not face closure, became less active around this time. The Tunisian Front for Islamic Associations, for example, decreased its activities markedly around 2015.[177] Many of the founders and presidents of these organisations remained active but in an individual capacity only. For instance, Mukhtar Jabali, the President of the Tunisian Front for Islamic Associations, remained active online. One well-known activist imam noted to me that at the beginning of 2015 'there were really groups and organisation. But at the end of that year, hardly anything survived'. He continued to say that 'It's mostly individuals now. There is hardly any organisational structure'.[178] A director of a human rights organisation confirmed the observation:

> It does not matter how you organised. Even if you did if by the book: as an Islamist, you will always be repressed. If you organised as an association, the state will close it down. If you organised as a party [and control the government] they will organise a coup against you. See Egypt. [. . .] The only thing you have these days [in Islamic activism] are individuals here and there: there are no relations between them anymore. [. . .] The people of Ansar Charia that chose not to institutionalise are now laughing at us. And, frankly, they are right.[179]

Not all associations ended up moribund. The Tunisian branch of the International Union of Muslim Scholars remained active for example. It is an organisation created by Yusuf al-Qaradawi, a world-famous Sunni Islamic scholar, that is close to, but independent from, the Muslim Brotherhood. It opened a branch in Tunis in 2012 and in Sfax in March 2017.[180] The Marhama association also remained active. It is a well-known charity organisation that is presided by Mohsen Jandoubi, a member of Ennahda's Shura Council.[181] Ester Sigillò has noted the preoccupation of remaining associations with proving sound financial book-keeping, their strategy to cooperate with local authorities to identify recipients of aid and a tendency to underplay their religious distinction. All to avoid state repression.[182] Ennahda, as a political party, must have felt the same pressure. It was something that many outside the party acknowledged. Omar, for example, remarked in 2016:

> Ennahda is in a far tougher position than we are. We are an association and school; they are part of the state. They are pressured from everywhere: the intelligence services, the administration, from everywhere. The concessions Ennahda is making are very dangerous, but they result from the immense pressure Ennahda is experiencing. [. . .] I changed my opinion about Ennahda. It's true. It is because of personal experience. I saw what happened with our project.[183]

Finally, in March 2016, a representative of the local government confirmed that the last mosque outside of the control of the governorate in Sidi Bouzid, and one of the last ones in the whole country, was the Rahma Mosque of Khatib Idrissi in Sidi Aoun.[184] The main problem for enforcing state control was reportedly the fact that it stood on private land. They said the mosque was controlled by Salafists and jihadists.[185] Finally, in the summer of 2016 local authorities proved successful in also bringing this Mosque under state control.[186]

The Implications of Pragmatism

Regarding Ennahda, the choice to specialise in party politics transformed its political practices. As Hamza Meddeb has detailed, Ennahda first revised its policies for party membership. After the staggered cell-like structure that it had used to integrate prospective members under the threat of a repressive authoritarian regime, it turned to more conventional methods. Any individual could apply for party membership and was eligible for local level positions following a one-year probation period and national level positions after a two-year probation period. Anyone supporting Ennahda's political programme was, in principle, able to become a member, meaning that the party rendered religious (Sunni Muslim) or party (Ennahda) identity irrelevant. Second, to improve professional skills within the party, Ennahda recruited external professionals to train existing members and established an academy to train new recruits. The academy drew on external Tunisian and foreign experts.[187] A member of Ennahda's Shura Council remarked that:

> We tried to attract people who have skills [. . .] Some of them were in the RCD [Democratic Constitutional Rally], the ruling party under the dictatorship.

> It was also an attempt to say that we are not against these people, and we are open to people who served the former regime. We are against the oppressive system they served but not against these people.[188]

Despite its incomplete implementation, the strategy to specialise had a profound impact on the constitution of the party. The party was growing at an incredible pace. Maryam Ben Salem estimated that the party grew to 100,000 members in 2018 from around 10,000 in the 1990s.[189] During the Ben Ali era, the costs of party membership meant strong ideological attachment of members to the party. It also nurtured personal and familial links between party members.[190] Following the liberalisation of membership, a new generation of careerists emerged. These new members used party membership for building professional expertise, relations and skills. It created tensions with existing grassroots activists and old militants, especially with those who had served prison time under the previous regime.[191]

The choice for specialisation and its implementation reflected a pragmatic realisation among Ennahda leadership that many Tunisians who were formerly active within the ruling party had kept (or regained) crucial positions in ministries, unions and associations. To survive as a party, Ennahda needed to engage with these agents and draw on their expertise. It came as little surprise that in September 2017 Ennahda helped to pass a much reviled Reconciliation Act that Caid Essebsi originally introduced following the Bardo attacks in March 2015.[192] The Act stipulated that civil servants who did not personally benefit from their acts of corruption during the Ben Ali era – a distinction impossible to make in practice – were given amnesty, absolved from persecution and compensated for any fines they had already paid.[193] There were, again, serious misgivings about these political strategies among Ennahda's rank and file, but Ennahda leadership, again, was effective in maintaining party discipline.[194]

This changed with the eleventh general conference. Taking place every four years, a general conference should have occurred in 2020. As it was drawing closer, Rashed Ghannouchi made clear he wanted to run for a third term as president of the party. This went counter to a two-term limit set at the 2012 general conference. Widespread internal discontent to the move became public when an internal letter denouncing the move, signed by a hundred members of the party, leaked in September 2020. The single point made by the signatories and also reiterated in a second letter a few weeks later, was to urge Ghannouchi to abide by party bylaws and safeguard the democratic credentials of the party.[195] The party leadership responded with entrenchment. They denounced it as doing politics by media and likened Ghannouchi's position to that of a *za'im*, or great leader of the stature of Gamal Abdel Nasser, who stands above party bylaws.[196] Ennahda attempted to prioritise executive power over ideological clarity with its strategy of distancing itself from distinctly Islamic social and political practices. Instead, Ennahda became part of a broader collapse in Tunisian faith in democratic politics, as the importance of parliamentary democracy was hollowed out in favour of an executive empowerment – both inside and outside the party.

In Politicians We Distrust

The 2011 uprising demanded political change, but it was also driven by calls for improved economic growth and equality. Instead of growth and equality, the years since 2011 saw a stalling economy and retrenchment of economic and political elites. Figure 4.7 shows average yearly growth of income per capita combined with the inflation rate. Between 2001 and 2011, the growth of national income was similar to, or lower than, the inflation rate. Following the revolution, income growth stalled while inflation started rising. Between 2016 and 2018, the difference between the two increased at an alarming pace. The result was an acute fall in living standards for many Tunisians. Many felt the state was unable to provide proper public services, such as health, education and transport.[197] The economic collapse influenced popular perceptions of democracy. The 2018–19 wave of the Arab barometer, an opinion survey held every few years across twelve Arab countries, included the question 'what is the main characteristic of a democracy?'. Fifty-five per cent of respondents in Tunisia answered that a democratic country was one that 'ensured job opportunities for all'. It was the highest percentage with this answer across all countries taking part. Just 10 per cent answered 'free and fair elections'.[198]

Disillusionment in democratic politics provided a fertile ground for populism. When Tunisia started negotiations with the European Union to create a Deep and Comprehensive Free Trade Agreement in 2016, they soon stalled in the face of a widespread populist backlash.[199] The Tunisian General Labour

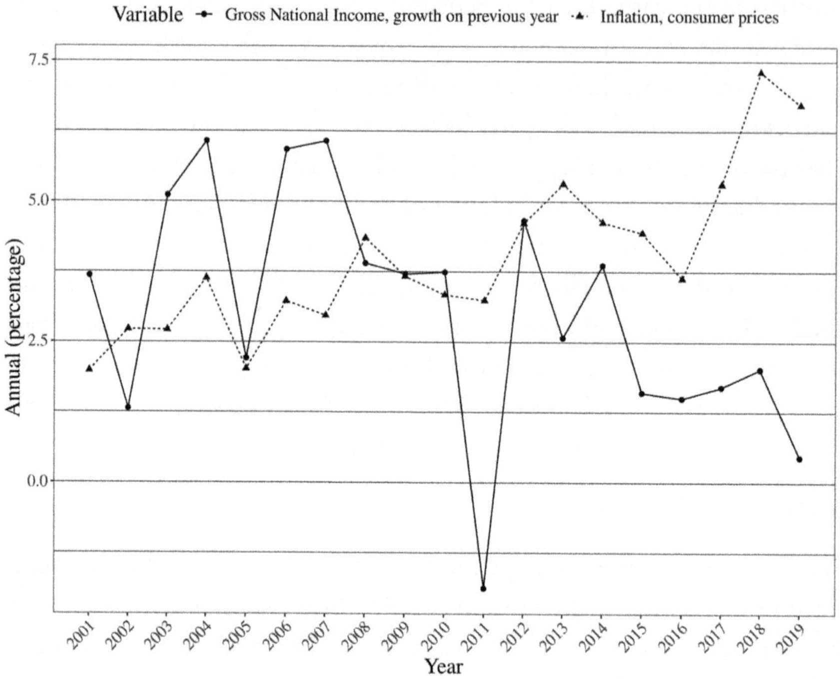

Figure 4.7 Gross national income growth and inflation of consumer products in Tunisia, 2000–19.
Source: World Bank.

Union, for example, decried the proposed liberalisations to Tunisia's economy.[200] Other groups, such as Hizb al-Tahrir, Ennahda grassroots activists, leftist activists and Arab nationalists, also became increasingly vocal in opposing foreign interference in Tunisia's economy, either focusing on the proposed EU agreement, austerity measures demanded by the International Monetary Fund or foreign companies allegedly appropriating natural resources.[201] This populist backlash eventually expanded from economic issues to include societal ones. In August 2017, Caid Essebsi created the Individual Freedoms and Equality Committee (in French abbreviated as the *Commission des Libertés Individuelles et de l'Égalité*, or Colibe) to address gender equality in inheritance, decriminalisation of homosexuality and the abolition of the death penalty. He did so on instigation of the EU parliament.[202] The final Colibe report argued for far-reaching reforms of these laws. The report, together with widespread positive coverage in foreign media, was met with a populist outcry. Many perceived the report and related media coverage as an attempt to alter Tunisian identity. The outcry spanned the political spectrum – from left to right, from secularist to Islamist – but shared a strong sense of national sovereignty, reflected in a particular Tunisian lifestyle and importance of the family unit that was under threat.[203]

Several populist parties emerged in the wake of these protests, for example the Free Destourian Party, Heart of Tunisia and the Dignity Coalition. The first was led by Abir Moussi, previously the assistant secretary-general responsible for women in the ruling party under Ben Ali. Although she was initially shunned from much of Tunisian public debate, her support for a strong presidential political system, critique of the 2014 constitution and constant attacks on Ennahda – which she described as a Muslim Brotherhood linked organisation that ought to be banned and have its activists imprisoned – found increasing resonance. Meanwhile, Abir Moussi described the 2011 revolution as having been instrumentalised by Hillary Clinton and the EU, refused to support results from the Colibe report and (although fluent in French) only spoke Arabic in interviews.[204] The second example was *Qalb Tounes*, or the Heart of Tunisia. Established in June 2019, the party was led by Nabil Karoui, the Tunisian media magnate who owned the Nessma TV station and was involved in the founding of Nidaa Tounes. He left the party in 2017 and gained popularity by framing himself – one of the richest men in the country – as the champion of the poor. He did this, for example, through a show in which he gave home appliances to those in need in peripheral regions in the country.[205]

Finally, there was *Itilaf al Karama*, or the Dignity Coalition. It was established in February 2019 and brought together former members from the Reform Front and the CPR, besides a range of other parties and independent individuals. Some of these organisations and individuals we have met before. Ridha Jaouadi and Mohamed Afas, the independent imams from Sfax, led the electoral list in Sfaxien districts 1 and 2, respectively. In addition, Saed Abid, the General Secretary of the Tunisian Organisation for Work, the union established by Ridha Jaouadi in October 2012, was a candidate for the party. Seifeddine Makhlouf, a well-known human rights lawyer who often defended individuals accused of jihadist activities, was its spokesperson.

During the electoral campaign for the 2019 elections, Ridha Jaouadi explained his candidacy:

> The Dignity Coalition is not a new party, rather it is a list of independent individuals [. . .] These individuals are not exact copies from one original, but variation on several themes: truth and justice, the persistence of faith, an Islamic-Arab identity, the sovereignty of the people, and their autonomy in their choices and their wealth.[206]

This is the context in which Tunisians went to their second presidential and parliamentary elections in late 2019: political paralysis, economic collapse, associational decline and rise of nationalist populist parties.[207] The results reflected the disillusionment among Tunisians with their established political class. The turnout was a mere 42 per cent, 27 per cent lower than in 2014. Ennahda won fifty-four seats out of the 217 in parliament. The only reason it came out as largest party was electoral fragmentation: none of the other lists received more than 20 per cent. The Heart of Tunisia Party, the Dignity Coalition and the Free Destourian Party all entered parliament for the first time. They received thirty-eight, twenty-one and seventeen seats respectively, becoming the second, third and fifth party in the parliament. The Democratic Current (twenty-two seats) was the only party represented in the previous parliament, apart from Ennahda, that made it among the largest five. Nidaa Tounes, which won eight-six seats in the 2014 elections, now won three.

The presidential runoff reflected the move towards conservative national populism. It pitted Nabil Karoui, the leader of the populist Heart of Tunisia party and owner of the Nessma TV channel, against Kais Saied, a relatively unknown constitutional law professor who had not run a formal campaign,[208] did not affiliate with any political party or list and ran on a vaguely framed programme that highlighted the primacy of legal accountability. While Karoui spent much of his campaign in jail on corruption charges, Tunisians increasingly described Kais Saied as RoboCop for his staccato speaking style, emphasising equality before the law and seemingly uncompromising stance to the corrupt Tunisian political class. Kais Saied won the final runoff with over 72 per cent.

Political instability marred the government.[209] All the while, Abir Moussi kept expressing her opinions on Ennahda and its role in Tunisia in no uncertain terms. In June 2020, she accused Ennahda of being connected to terrorism, and in September she argued that 'Ennahda is a party without Tunisian origin' because, she argued, it is part of an international Muslim Brotherhood organisation that is based in Türkiye and funded by Qatar.[210] All statements without basis in fact.[211] It did not help that to salvage their electoral campaign, Ennahda increasingly harked back to religion to secure votes, for example by arguing for a *zakāt* fund to address regional inequalities.[212] Moussi organised multiple protests in front of the Tunisian branch of the International Union of Muslim Scholars at the end of 2020, arguing the organisation encroached on Tunisian politics through their support of Islamist parties such as Ennahda and the Dignity Coalition. Ennahda strenuously denied these charges; while members of the Dignity Coalition stated they would now join the International Union of Muslim Scholars – just to make a point. All the while Abir Moussi continued with her attacks, arguing, for example, that the Muslim Brotherhood should be designated as a terrorist organisation, making anyone with contacts to the organisation subject to persecution under the 2015 anti-terrorism law.[213]

With Ennahda turning into a party that was primarily focused on holding onto executive power, the Dignity Coalition filled the void in a typical populist style. Mohamed Afas, of Sfax fame, made the following speech during a debate on women's rights in December 2020:

> They talk about women's freedom, and we see free access to women. What they call freedom, we call liberalisation – which means to be enslaved to fashion, the West, cravings and calls for immorality. [. . .] Women's gains for them is to have single mothers, bearing children outside marriage, the right to abortion and homosexuality. We tell them: they are just names you have given to things, for which God has given no authority. Single mothers were raped or are whores, procreation outside marriage is adultery, abortion is unlawful killing of oneself, and sexual freedom is fornication.[214]

In other words, the issues discussed in the Colibe report of June 2018, regarding women's freedom in Tunisia, are just a way to renew enslavement to the West and its culture. He implied that sovereignty is vested in authentic Muslim norms and values. Despite its fiery populist rhetoric, the Dignity Coalition adapted institutionally. In January 2021, Ridha Jaouadi published a statement that he would leave the Dignity Coalition and continue as an independent MP.

The reason was that the Dignity Coalition decided to reform and request recognition as a political party.[215] Ridha Jaouadi opposed this move towards institutionalised politics. The Coalition was formally recognised as a political party in May 2021.[216]

Political infighting, votes of no confidence, Ennahda instability, anti-Islamist and conservative politicians fanning the populist flames around the notion of Tunisian sovereignty: the 2019 elections did not improve the political process in the country. Meanwhile, the Tunisian economy collapsed. The GDP declined more than 9 per cent between 2019 and 2020,[217] the budget deficit increased to over 10 per cent of the GDP and unemployment rose to almost 18 per cent from 15 per cent.[218] And this was before the Covid-19 pandemic. In December 2020, Nabil Karoui was arrested – again – on corruption charges. It fed the popular image of the parliament being filled with corrupt politicians working only for their own benefit. Following their shared challenge to Kais Saied, both Ennahda and Dignity Coalition came out with statements of support for the multimillionaire media magnate.[219] The same multimillionaire media magnate who had aired Persepolis on his Nessma TV channel in October 2011, inciting violent protests in defence of Islam which ended up with protesters setting fire to Karoui's house.

The Executive Takes Over

The democratic process unravelled in the spring and summer of 2021. In February, a standoff between the President, Prime Minister and Speaker of the Assembly grid-locked the government.[220] Popular discontent with the political class continued to grow. Calls went around on social media to organise a protest in front of the seat of parliament on 13 June 2021, the date that Covid-19 lockdown measures were set to expire, to demand its dissolution and changes in the political regime. It was a request that the President was all too willing to grant. On 29 July, Kais Saied invoked Article 80 of the constitution. The article stated that 'in the event of imminent danger threatening the nation's institutions or the security or independence of the country [. . .] the President of the Republic may take any measure necessitated by the exceptional circumstance'. The constitution also noted that this had to be done in consultation with the Speaker of the Assembly and that the Speaker and MPs could test the state of emergency at the constitutional court.[221] Kais Saied used the article to take all executive power and assigned a new government and prime minister.[222] He did so without consultation or independent assessment by the constitutional court.

With the July 2021 coup d'état, I conclude the narrative of the Tunisian transition. In this chapter, I traced the rise, transformation and decline of an Islamist movement by focusing on the concrete practices of its participants. First, I observed how activists used Islam to enact distinct types of practices and, in doing so, politicised religion: the creation of new Islamic associations provided a new autonomous space for social and political activism; independent Islamic schools challenged state control of education; the provision of Islamic public services challenged state legitimacy; and the rise of Ennahda provided new avenues for political representation. Islam became political not because of the particular ideas it provided to activists, but because they used it to render associational, educational, executive and legislative practices distinct.

Second, I traced several conflicts that arose over how Islam could, and should, render practices distinct. State independent imams challenged established relationships between the state and Tunisian mosques; the Zaytuna Mosque provided an example where the creation of Islamic education triggered a struggle for institutional control over educational resources and the rise of Ennahda in Tunisian politics led to acrimonious interactions about access to political resources during the constitutional drafting process. Internally, participation in politics triggered a debate between Ennahda members about the role of Islam as a unifying force between social activism and party politics. Using Islam to render associational, educational, executive and legislative practices distinct created the foundation for distinct social interactions between individuals with a stake in using Islam to access related resources. It drew these activists together as participants in an Islamist movement.

The movement did not last. It declined from 2014 onwards, but some elements remained until the coup of 2021. The presidential power grab left Ennahda in crisis with more than a hundred of its politicians resigning from the party.[223] The new political regime arrested members from the Dignity Coalition, including Seifeddine Makhlouf and Mohamed Afes who faced trial in front of Tunisia's military court.[224] In the years that followed, repression escalated, with hundreds of activists and politicians, including Rached Ghannouchi and Habib Ellouze, facing trial. Following initial public elation, approval ratings for the President soon plummeted and anti-coup protests were organised. However, it seemed to have mattered little; as I write these final sentences, in July 2022, a new constitution has just been approved that gives almost unlimited powers to the president. The executive is back in control, and an Islamist movement is repressed – for now.

Notes

1. Interview with Faisal, 14 February 2011, Tunis, Tunisia.
2. Meddeb, *Ennahda's Uneasy Exit From Political Islam*; Netterstrøm, 'After the Arab Spring: The Islamists' Compromise in Tunisia'.
3. Zelin, *Your Sons Are at Your Service.*
4. Marks, 'Youth Politics and Tunisian Salafism: Understanding the Jihadi Current'; Merone and Cavatorta, 'Salafist Mouvance and Sheikh-Ism in the Tunisian Democratic Transition'.
5. Interview with Omar, 6 October 2011, greater Tunis, Tunisia. See also Merone, Blanc and Sigillò, 'The Evolution of Tunisian Salafism after the Revolution: From La Maddhabiyya to Salafi-Malikism', 456.
6. Fahmi and Meddeb, 'Market for Jihad: Radicalization in Tunisia', 5; Marks, 'Youth Politics and Tunisian Salafism: Understanding the Jihadi Current', 109.
7. See for instance Merone, Blanc, and Sigillò, 'The Evolution of Tunisian Salafism after the Revolution: From La Maddhabiyya to Salafi-Malikism'; Hamdi, *The Politicisation Of Islam: A Case Study Of Tunisia.*
8. Tunisian Republic, 'Décret-Loi N° 2011-88'.
9. These numbers are an approximation. Only data on associations with 'association' in their name was accessible, which was true for 22,824 of a total of 24,141 associations, or about 95 per cent. Original data from: http://www.ifeda.org.tn/ar/index.php, accessed 11 January 2022.
10. Interview with a representative of IFEDA, 9 November 2011, Tunis, Tunisia; director of an Islamic nursery, 18 July 2016, Sfax, Tunisia.
11. Interview with senior representative of the Presidency of the Government, 28 September 2012, Tunis, Tunisia.
12. Sigillò, 'Islamism and the Rise of Islamic Charities in Post-Revolutionary Tunisia: Claiming Political Islam through Other Means?', 812.
13. Singerman, 'The Networked World of Islamist Social Movements'; Clark, *Islam, Charity, and Activism: Middle Class Networks and Social Welfare in Egypt, Jordan and Yemen*; Selvik and Pierret, 'Limits to Upgrading Authoritarianism in Syria: Private Welfare, Islamic Charities, and the Rise of the Zayd Movement'.

14. See their website and description at https://chariaa.tn/.
15. Hamid and McCants, 'Islamists on Islamism Today: An Interview with Habib Ellouze of Tunisia's Ennahda Party'.
16. Interview with Omar, 2 October 2012, suburb of Tunis, Tunisia.
17. As per formal description of his association at the IFEDA records at http://www.ifeda.org.tn.
18. Ibid.
19. Interview with Hamza, 25 November 2015, Sfax, Tunisia.
20. Interview with Omar, 2 October 2012, suburb of Tunis, Tunisia; interview with director of a chain of Islamic private schools, 19 September 2012, greater Tunis, Tunisia.
21. Statement from Sfaxien Organisations. December 2011. The source is withheld for reasons of anonymity; Sfaxien Association of Mosque Preachers, "Arīḍah Ilá Kull Min Yuhammahu Al-Amr'.
22. Interview with Hamza, 25 November 2015, Sfax, Tunisia.
23. Interview with representative of local government, 16 March 2011, Ariana, Tunisia; interview with director of a chain of Islamic private schools, 19 September 2012, greater Tunis, Tunisia; interview with former advisor to Minister of Religious Affairs, 14 November 2015, Hay Tadamon, Tunisia. The number refers to mosques with a Friday imam. There were almost 5,000 mosques in total in Tunisia.
24. As noted in the CV he posted on his Facebook page, https://www.facebook.com/RidhaJaouadi.
25. Tunisie Islamique, 'Al-Khiṭbah Al-Ūwlá Lil-Shaykh Riḍā Al-Jawādī Ba'da 20 Sanah (2011/01/28)'; al-Ṭrābelsī, 'Masjid Al-Lakhmī Yustaqbal Al-Shaykh Riḍā Al-Jawādī Imāmā Jadīdan La-Hu'.
26. Interview with Khatib Idrissi, 6 April 2011, Sidi Ali Ben Aoun, Tunisia.
27. Interview with student and activist, 14 February 2011, Tunis, Tunisia.
28. al-Qaraqūrī, 'Masājid Ṣafāqis Tajammu' Tabaru'āt Lil-Manāṭiq Al-Mankūbah Balaghat Akthar Min 50 Ṭunā Min Al-Mawādd Al-Ghidhā'īyah Wa 50 Ṭunā Min Al-Malābis'.
29. Jaouadi, 'Al-Ḥamad Lillāh; 'Jam'īyat Al-Lakhmī Al-Khayrīyah Lil-Tanmiyah' Mawlūd Jadīd Li-Taḥqīq Al-Karāmah Al-Insānīyah'; al-Qasamṭīnī, 'Jam'īyat 'Al-Lakhmī' Al-Khayrīyah Lil-Tanmiyah Mawlūd Jam'yātī Jadīd Bi-Ṣafāqis'.
30. Interview with representative of local government in Tunis, 11 October 2012, Tunis, Tunisia; interview with senior civil servant at the Ministry of Religious

Affairs, 1 October 2012, Tunis, Tunisia; interview with senior representative of Marhama, 4 October 2012, Tunis, Tunisia.

31. Achahed, 'Amām Jāmi' Al-Lakhmī, Taḥta Nīrān Ittiḥād "al-Yasār" Wa "Nidā' Tūnis"'.
32. Interview at Omar's school, 6 October 2011, Greater Tunis, Tunisia.
33. Interview, and observations during tour, with director of a chain of Islamic private schools, 19 September 2012, Greater Tunis, Tunisia.
34. Ibid.
35. Interview with vice-President of an association for sharia sciences, 16 November 2011, Tunis, Tunisia.
36. Observations at Omar's school, 6 October 2011, Greater Tunis, Tunisia.
37. Interview, and observations during tour, with director of a chain of Islamic private schools, 19 September 2012, Greater Tunis, Tunisia; see also the data from the IFEDA noted above.
38. Donker and Netterstrøm, 'The Tunisian Revolution & Governance of Religion'; Salem, *Habib Bourguiba, Islam, and the Creation of Tunisia*; see also Bourguiba, *Ma vie, mon œuvre: 1938–1943*.
39. Interview with Vice-President of an association for sharia sciences, 16 November 2011, Tunis, Tunisia.
40. Babnet, 'Al-Shaykh Ḥusayn Al-'Ubaydī: Al-Imām Al-Mu'īn Min Al-Ḥukūmah Wa-Alladhī Sayu'tī Fī Ṣalāt Al-Jum'ah Sayuṭarid'.
41. Babnet, 'Nūr Al-Dīn Al-Khādimī: Ḥusayn Al-'Ubaydī Sayuwāṣl Imāmat Al-Muṣallīn Fī Jāmi' Al-Zaytūnah'.
42. Group interview with students from Zaytuna University, 20 October 2011, Tunis.
43. See their website of the university at: http://www.uz.rnu.tn/.
44. Group interview with students from Zaytuna University, 20 October 2011, Tunis.
45. Zelin, *Your Sons Are at Your Service*, 140.
46. Ibid., 145.
47. Group interview with three activists, 4 April 2011, Sidi Bouzzid, Tunisia.
48. See for example Merone and Cavatorta, 'Salafist Mouvance and Sheikh-Ism in the Tunisian Democratic Transition'; Al Jazeera, 'Salafist Group Clashes with Police in Tunisia'; Marks, 'Youth Politics and Tunisian Salafism: Understanding the Jihadi Current'; Merone, 'Analysing Revolutionary Islamism: Ansar Al-Sharia Tunisia according to Gramsci'; Zelin, *Your Sons Are at Your Service*, 145.

49. Tunisia Agence Presse, 'Bi-Sabab Al-Khaṭīb Al-Idrīsī: Wizārat Al-Shu'ūn Al-Dīnīyah Tlj' Ilá Al-Qaḍā' Lil-Naẓar Fī Masjid Khārij 'an Al-Sayṭarah'.
50. al-Kalbusi, 'Naḥnu ḍidda Al-Raqābah Al-Siyāsīyah Lil-Masājid Wa-'Alá Al-Khiṭāb Al-Dīnī an Yajma'u Al-Tūnisīyīn Lā an Yufarraqhum'.
51. Interview with a former adviser of Noureddine Khadmi, 14 November 2014, Tunis, Tunisia.
52. Ibid.
53. See for excellent recent studies on Ennahda: McCarthy, *Inside Tunisia's Al-Nahda: Between Politics and Preaching*; Wolf, *Political Islam in Tunisia: The History of Ennahda*.
54. Echorouk Online, 'Rāshid Al-Ghannūshī: Lastu Khomayniyā Wa Lan Akūn'.
55. The Ennahda Movement, 'Barnāmaj Al-Nahḍah: Min Ajl Tūnis Al-Ḥurrīyah Wa-Al-'Adālah Wa-Al-Tanmiyah', 7.
56. Hizb al-Tahrir Tūnis, 'Naḥwa Khilāfat 'alá Minhāj Al-Nubūwah'.
57. Interview with a representative of Hizb al-Tahrir, 22 July 2016, Sfax, Tunisia. See also Hizb al-Tahrir, 'Haykal Ajhizat Dawlat Al-Khilāfah'; Hizb al-Tahrir, 'Al-Mu'tamar Al-Ṣuḥufī Li-Ḥizb Al-Taḥrīr Tūnis Raghma Muḥāwalah Alghā'h'; Hizb al-Tahrir, 'Mashrū' Dustūr Dawlat Al-Khilāfah'.
58. Merone, Blanc and Sigillò, 'The Evolution of Tunisian Salafism after the Revolution: From La Maddhabiyya to Salafi-Malikism', 459.
59. The Reform Front, 'Barnāmaj Jabhat Al-Iṣlāḥ'.
60. Merone, Blanc and Sigillò, 'The Evolution of Tunisian Salafism after the Revolution: From La Maddhabiyya to Salafi-Malikism', 459.
61. Interview with the President and head of the political bureau of the Reform Front, 10 October 2012, Tunis.
62. Marks, 'Youth Politics and Tunisian Salafism: Understanding the Jihadi Current', 109–10.
63. al-'Uraysī, 'Tūnis: Muqatal Al-Qiss Al-Būlandī Yuthīr Makhāwif. . . Wa-Yu'ziz An'dām Al-Thiqah Bi-Al-Ḥukūmah'.
64. Ibid.; Fuller, 'Next Question for Tunisia: The Role of Islam in Politics'. Personal observations, 19 February 2011, Avenue Bourguiba, Tunisia.
65. Ibid. In addition, interview with Tunisian blogger, 19 March 2014, Tunis, Tunisia; interview with student activist, 17 March 2014, Tunis, Tunisia.
66. Interview with senior representative of Ennahda, 2 April 2011, Kairouan, Tunisia.
67. Interview with two young Ennahda activists, 16 March 2011, Tunis, Tunisia; interview with populist Islamist activist, 24 September 2012.
68. Discussion with university students, 28 March 2011, Carthage, Tunisia.

69. Observation at the University of Tunis, 5 March 2011, Tunis, Tunisia. Also, Council of Professors, 'Ḥawl Al-Istīlā' Ala Qā'a Tadrīs Bi-Da'wa Isti'amālha Baytan Li-L-Ṣalāa'.
70. SfaxTV, 'Al-Muẓāharah Al-Ghafīrah Jiddan Bi-Ṣafāqis 1 Juwiliyah'.
71. al-Chourouq, 'Sousse: I'itidā'alā Kātib 'Ām Kuliyat Al-Ādāb Rafḍ Tarsīm Ṭāliba Munaqiba'.
72. The Associated Press, 'Tunisia: Thousands Protest Film'; Dhūwāybiyah, '"Nismah" Tash'al Al-āḥtjājāt Qabla Ayyām Min Al-Intikhābāt'. Interview with Maryam, 26 October 2011, Tunis, Tunisia; interview with populist Islamist activist, 19 October 2011, Greater Tunis, Tunisia; interview with Ennahda youngsters, 8 November 2011, Tunis, Tunisia.
73. El-Khoury, 'Aṣwāt Al-Shabakah: Mā Alladhī Ḥaṣala Fī Jāmi'at Manūbah?'
74. Statement from Sfaxien Organisations. December 2011. The source is withheld for reasons of anonymity.
75. Merone, Blanc and Sigillò, 'The Evolution of Tunisian Salafism after the Revolution: From La Maddhabiyya to Salafi-Malikism', 462–63.
76. Greenberg, 'The Rise and Fall of Abu 'Iyadh: Reported Death Leaves Questions Unanswered'.
77. The Ennahda Movement, 'Ḥarakat al-Nahḍah Tunadad Bi-Āstidrāj al-Bilād Naḥwa al-Fawḍá'.
78. Sfaxien Association of Mosque Preachers, "Arīḍah Ilá Kull Min Yuhammahu Al-Amr'.
79. Sfaxien Association of Mosque Preachers, 'Al-Sha'b Yurīd Taḥkīm Shari' Allāh'.
80. Interview with Hamza, 25 November 2015, Sfax, Tunisia.
81. Tunisian Front for Islamic Associations, 'Nuṣrat Li-Kitāb Allāh'.
82. Tunisian Front for Islamic Associations, 'Bayān'. Also, interview with a director of a chain of Islamic schools, 19 September 2012, Greater Tunis, Tunisia.
83. Tunisian Front for Islamic Associations, 'Bayān Al-Jabhah Al-Tūnisīyah Al-Jam'īyāt Al-Islāmīyah: Ḥawla Khaṭar Al-Mudd Al-Shī'ī Bi-Tūnis Wa-Wājib Al-Taṣaddy La-Hu'; Tunisian Front for Islamic Associations, 'Bayān Al-Jabhah Al-Tūnisīyah Al-Jam'īyāt Al-Islāmīyah: Bi-Khuṣūṣ Tadnys Al-Muṣḥaf Al-Sharīf Wā-Al-ā'tidā' 'alá Muqadasātnā'; Tunisian Front for Islamic Associations, 'Bayān Al-Jabhah Al-Tūnisīyah Al-Jam'īyāt Al-Islāmīyah: Hawla Ba'ḍ Maẓāhir Al-Zulm Wa-Al-'Unf Fī Bilādunā'; Tunisian Front for Islamic Associations, 'Bayān Ḥawla Aḥdāth Al-Qayrawān Wa Ḥayy Al-Taḍāmun'.

84. Organisation Tunisienne du Travail, 'Al-Waqfah Al-Iḥtijājīyah Al-Silmīyah Bi-Sāḥat Al-Qaṣabah Bi-Al-'Āṣimah'.
85. Interview Hamza, 25 November 2015, Sfax, Tunisia.
86. African Manager, 'Wizārat Al-Shu'ūn Al-Dīnīyah: Riḍā Bilḥājj Kāna Y'm Al-Muṣallīn Fī Sūsah Dawwin Tarkhīṣ Qānūnī'.
87. African Manager, 'Tūnis - 'Azl Imāmyn Fī Ṣafāqis'.
88. Agence Tunis Afrique Press, 'Ṣafāqis .. Wizārat Al-Shu'ūn Al-Dīnīyah Tuqarriru I'fā' Riḍā Al-Jawādī Min Mahāmhā Ka'-Imām Bi-Jāmi' Al-Lakhmī'.
89. Babnet, 'Bashīr Ibn Ḥasan: Ḥasabnā Allāh Wa-Na'm Al-Wakīl Wa-Ana Lillāh Wa-an Ilayhi Rāja'ūn .. Tamma 'Azl Riḍā Al-Jawwādī'.
90. Būjnāḥ, 'Masīrat Ḥāshidah Bi-Ṣafāqis Munaddah Bi-Qarārāt 'Azl Al-A'immah'. Also, personal observations, 20 November 2015, Sfax, Tunisia.
91. al-Shābbī, 'Shahrān Sajanā Ma'a Ta'jīl Al-Tanfīdh Lil-Shaykh Ḥusayn Al-'Ubaydī'.
92. Agence Tunis Afrique Presse, "Uthmān Biṭṭīkh: Tawāṣul T'ṭīl Adā' Ṣalāt Al-Jum'ah Bi-Jāmi' Sīdī Al-Lakhmī Muḥarram Shar'an'. Also, interview with senior advisor to Othman Battikh, 18 November 2015, Tunis, Tunisia.
93. Addhamir, 'Qarārāt Al-Wizārah Hadadat Al-Silm Al-Īljtmā'ī Bi-Ṣafāqis'.
94. Ibid.
95. Perkins, *A History of Modern Tunisia*, ch. 3–4.
96. Hourani, *A History of the Arab Peoples*, 389–92; Perkins, *A History of Modern Tunisia*, 139.
97. Wolf, *Political Islam in Tunisia: The History of Ennahda*; see also Amal Mousa, *Bourguiba Wa Al-Masāla Al-Diniya*.
98. Wolf, *Political Islam in Tunisia: The History of Ennahda*, 33–35.
99. Ibid., 37.
100. Ibid., 27–52; Perkins, *A History of Modern Tunisia*, 165–7. Regarding the tensions between ideology and *da'wah*, see also Ghannūshī, *Min tajribat al-ḥarakah al-Islāmīyah fī Tūnis*.
101. Wolf, *Political Islam in Tunisia: The History of Ennahda*, 27–52; Perkins, *A History of Modern Tunisia*, 165–67.
102. Merone, Blanc, and Sigillò, 'The Evolution of Tunisian Salafism after the Revolution: From La Maddhabiyya to Salafi-Malikism'.
103. Greenberg, 'The Rise and Fall of Abu 'Iyadh: Reported Death Leaves Questions Unanswered'.
104. Wolf, *Political Islam in Tunisia: The History of Ennahda*; Tamimi, *Rachid Ghannouchi: A Democrat within Islamism*, 70.

105. Ibid., 67–72.
106. Wolf, *Political Islam in Tunisia: The History of Ennahda*, 87–95.
107. Human Rights Watch, 'Tunisia: Events of 2005'.
108. Interview with Khatib Idrissi, 6 April 2011, Sidi Ali Ben Aoun, Tunisia.
109. Interview with two Ennahda youth members, 16 March 2011, Tunis, Tunisia.
110. Interview with Omar, 2 October 2012, Tunis, Tunisia.
111. Wolf, *Political Islam in Tunisia: The History of Ennahda*, 125–28.
112. Ibid., 126–27.
113. Interview with director of a religious school, 3 March 2011, Greater Tunis. See also Souissi, 'Al-Katātīb Al-Qur'ānīyah Fī Salb Istrātījīyah Tūnis Li-Mukāfaḥat Al-Taṭarruf'.
114. Assabah News, 'Ba'da Ta'yīn Imām Jadīd Li-Masjad Fī Al-Jihah: Wālī Al-Qayrawān Yuwajjihu Tanbyhā Lil-Nāṭiq Al-Rasmī Bāsim Anṣār Al-Sharī'ah'.
115. According to a representative of Hizb al-Tahrir himself; interview with a representative of Hizb al-Tahrir, 22 July 2016, Sfax, Tunisia.
116. Interview Tunisian activist, 16 September 2012, Tunis, Tunisia.
117. Bujnāḥ, 'Intahat Azmat Al-Jāmi' Al-Kabīr: Lajnat Waqtiyah Lil-Ashrāf Alayhi . . . Wa-Al-Shaykh "'Abd Al-'Azīz Li-Wakīl" Khaṭīban Lil-Jāmi''.
118. Alchourouk, 'Ḥusayn Al-'Ubaydī: Al-Nahḍah A'lantu Al-Ḥarb 'Alá Al-Zaytūnah Wa-Al-Khādmī Sawwaq Lil-Wahābiyah'; Assabah News, 'Ḥusayn Al-'Ubaydī: Mahdī Jum'ah Amr Bi-Iqtiḥām Jāmi' Al-Zaytūnah . . . Wa-Mana'ī Min Ṣu'ūd Al-Minbar'.
119. Interview with senior representative of the Tunisian Front of Islamic associations, 4 October 2012, Tunis, Tunisia.
120. Interview with Omar, 2 October 2012, Greater Tunis, Tunisia.
121. Assemblée Nationale Constituante, 'Draft of the Constitution of the Republic of Tunisia'.
122. Loehr, 'Women, Media, Blasphemy, and the President: Four Constitutional Quarrels Explained'.
123. Interview with Omar, 2 October 2012, Greater Tunis, Tunisia.
124. Mizouri, 'Khaṭīr Jiddā Al-Fīdiyū Rāshid Al-Ghannūshī Ra'īs Ḥarakat Al-Nahḍah'. See also Marks, 'Tunisia's Ennahda: Rethinking Islamism in the Context of ISIS and the Egyptian Coup', 6.
125. Interview with Omar, 2 October 2012, Greater Tunis, Tunisia.
126. Interview with senior representative of Ennahda, 16 October 2011, Medenine, Tunisia.

127. Netterstrøm, 'After the Arab Spring: The Islamists' Compromise in Tunisia'.
128. Wolf, *Political Islam in Tunisia: The History of Ennahda*, 145–46.
129. Interview with senior representative of Ennahda, 16 October 2011, Medenine, Tunisia.
130. Interview with two Ennahda affiliated Islamic activists, 19 September 2012, Tunis, Tunisia; interview with a member of Ennahda's Shura Council, 8 October 2012, Tunis, Tunisia.
131. Antonakis-Nashif, 'Contested Transformation: Mobilized Publics in Tunisia between Compliance and Protest', 2.
132. Reuters, 'Al-Bājī Qāyid Al-Sebsy Y'alana Ta'sīs Ḥarakat "Nidā' Tūnis" Lil-Taṣady Li-Haymanah "Al-Nahḍah"'.
133. See Assemblée Nationale Constituante, 'Musawwadah Mushru' Al-Dustūr'; Assemblée Nationale Constituante, 'Mushru' Al-Dustūr'; Assemblée Nationale Constituante, 'Mushru' Al-Dustūr Al-Jumhūrīyah Al-Tūnisīyah'.
134. Zeghal, 'Constitutionalizing a Democratic Muslim State without Sharia: The Religious Establishment in the Tunisian 2014 Constitution'.
135. Zelin, *Your Sons Are at Your Service*, 174.
136. ISIS, 'Interview with Abū Muqātil At-Tūnusī', 59–60.
137. Gall, 'Protesters Press Tunisian Government to Resign, as Ruling Party Supporters Rally'.
138. Attounissia, 'Al-Naṣṣ Al-Kāmil Li-Mubādarat Al-Ittiḥād Al-'āmm Al-Tūnisī Lil-Shughl'. Also, interview with student unionist, 26 March 2014, Tunis, Tunisia.
139. Marks, 'Tunisia's Ennahda: Rethinking Islamism in the Context of ISIS and the Egyptian Coup'.
140. Tunisian Republic, 'Tunisian Constitution', Art. 74.
141. National Democratic Institute, 'Final Report, Legislative and Presidential Election', 28.
142. Grewal and Hamid, 'The Dark Side of Consensus in Tunisia: Lessons from 2015–2019'.
143. Ibid.
144. As quoted in Ben Younes, 'Tunisia: Ghannouchi Calls for National Unity Government'.
145. Marzouki, 'Tunisia's Rotten Compromise'.
146. Meddeb, *Ennahda's Uneasy Exit From Political Islam*. Also, interview with Islamist philosopher and Ennahda critic, 22 June 2015, Bizerte, Tunisia.

147. The Ennahda Movement, 'Al-Bayān Al-Khitāmī Lil-Mu'tamar Al-'Āmm Al-'Āshir Li-Ḥarakat Al-Nahḍah'.
148. The Ennahda Movement, 'Al-Lā'iḥah Al-Taqyīmīyah'.
149. The Ennahda Movement, 'Lā'iḥat Subul Idārat Al-Mashrū''; Ennahda could have chosen to split up into a political party and da'wah association (as, for example, multiple Muslim Brotherhood branches have done). It decided not to do so. See also Meddeb, *Ennahda's Uneasy Exit From Political Islam*.
150. The Ennahda Movement, 'Lā'iḥat Subul Idārat Al-Mashrū''.
151. Interview with senior representative of Ennahda, 20 July 2016, Sfax, Tunisia.
152. Ibid.
153. Meddeb, *Ennahda's Uneasy Exit From Political Islam*.
154. For this definition of a social movement, see Della Porta and Diani, *Social Movements: An Introduction*, 20.
155. Boukhars, *The Geographic Trajectory of Conflict and Militancy in Tunisia*; Zelin, *Your Sons Are at Your Service*, 239–42.
156. ICG, 'Jihadist Violence in Tunisia: The Urgent Need for a National Strategy'.
157. Zelin, *Your Sons Are at Your Service*, ch. 10.
158. Mersch, 'Tunisia's Ineffective Counterterrorism Law'; Tunisian Government, 'Al-Qānūn Al-Asāsī Raqm 26 Li-Sanat 2015 Tārīkh 7 Aghusṭus 2015 Bi-Sha'n Mukāfaḥat Al-Irhāb Wa-Man' Ghasl Al-Amwāl', sec. 6.
159. Data from https://www.albawsala.com/en/.
160. Bālṭayyib, 'Khāṣṣ: Yajma'u Wuzarā' Al-Dākhilīyah Wa-Al-'Adl Wa-Al-Shu'ūn Al-Dīnīyah .. Al-Yawm Ijtimā' ḥawla Al-Masājid'; Nessma TV, 'Mahdī Jum'ah: 149 Masjid Khārij 'an Al-Sayṭarah Wa-Barnāmjnā Wāḍiḥ Bi-Khuṣūṣ Taḥyīd Al-Masājid''.
161. Aljarida Attounissia, 'Ḥusayn Al-'Ubaydī: Jāmi' Al-Zaytūnah Ghayr Ma'nī Bi-Qarār Taḥyīd Al-Masājid'.
162. Hakaek Online, 'Ḥusayn Al-'Ubaydī: Jāmi' Al-Zaytūnah Ghayr Ma'nī Bi-Barnāmij Taḥyīd Al-Masājid'.
163. Assabah News, 'Wazīr Al-Shu'ūn Al-Dīnīyah: Hādhihi Ḥaqīqat 'lāqy Bi-Al-Nahḍah Wa-Bi-Al-Khādmī'.
164. Hakaek Online, 'Wazīr Al-Shu'ūn Al-Dīnīyah: Tūnis Dawlat Islāmīyah Wa-'alá Al-Jamī' Murā'āt Dhālika'.
165. Alchourouk, 'Taqlīṣ 'Adad Al-Masājid Al-Khārijah 'an Al-Sayṭarah Ilá Arba'ah'; Assabah News, 'Wazīr Al-Shu'ūn Al-Dīniyyah: 23 Masjidan Khārij Al-Sayṭarah'; Alchourouk, 'Wizārat Al-Shu'ūn Al-Dīnīyah Tastaraja' 100 Masjid Wa-Jāmi'';

Assabah News, 'Wazīr Al-Shu'ūn Al-Dīnīyah: Qurābat Al-90 Masjidan Māzālt Khārij Al-Sayṭarah'; Alchourouk, 'Wazīr Al-Shu'ūn Al-Dīnīyah: Tamma Istirajā' 49 Masjidan Min Jumlah 149 Wa-Qarīban Al-Sayṭarah 'Alá Al-Baqīyah'.

166. Interview with Hamza, 25 November 2015, Sfax, Tunisia.
167. Tuniscope, 'Ta'yīn Imām Khaṭīb Li-Khuṭbat Al-Jum'ah Fī Jāmi' Al-Zaytūnah Badalan 'an Ḥusayn Al-'Ubaydī'.
168. Human Rights Watch, 'Tunisia: Suspension of Associations Arbitrary'.
169. Bawajnāḥ, 'Ba'da īqāf 'Adad Min Al-Jam'īyāt 'an Al-Nashāṭ Bi-Wilāyat Ṣafāqis: Ghaḍab Wa-īstinkār Fī Ṣufūf Mumaththilīhā'; Aljarida Attounissia, 'Īqāf Nashāṭ 9 Jam'īyāt Fī Al-'Āṣimah'.
170. Interview Hamza, 25 November 2015, Sfax, Tunisia.
171. Interview with Omar, 6 May 2015, Greater Tunis, Tunisia.
172. Ibid.
173. Ibid.
174. African Manager, 'Qarār Bi-Ḥall Jam'īyat Al-Lakhmī Fī Ṣafāqis'. Regarding the original pledge see Shu'ūr, 'Ṣafāqis-Fī Ittifāqīyat Sharākat Bayna Wizārat Al-Tashghīl Wa-Jam'īyat Al-Lakhmī: Iḥdāth 1000 Mawaṭin Shughl Fī Aqall Min 'ām Bi-Al-Wilāyah'.
175. As quoted in al-Suhaylī, 'Munīr Al-Talīlī (Wazīr Al-Shu'ūn Al-Dīnīyah) L « Al-Tūnisīyah » Qarīban Ilḥāq Iṭārāt Al-Masājid Bi-Al-Waẓīfah Al-'Umūmīyah'.
176. Interview with director of an Islamic nursery, 18 July 2016, Sfax, Tunisia.
177. As assessed by activities promoted on its Facebook page, which was still active at the time of writing: https://www.facebook.com/front.national.des.associations.islamiques.
178. Interview with a Friday imam, 14 July 2015, Sfax, Tunisia.
179. Interview with director of a human rights association, 24 June 2015, Tunis, Tunisia.
180. See their Facebook pages at: https://www.facebook.com/AlathadAlalmyLlmaAlmslmynmktbTwns and https://www.facebook.com/608868095974774-الاتحاد-العالمي-لعلماء-المسلمين-فرع-تونس-مكتب-صفاقس respectively.
181. Dahmani, 'Tunisie: Partis Cherchent Mécènes'.
182. Sigillò, 'Islamism and the Rise of Islamic Charities in Post-Revolutionary Tunisia: Claiming Political Islam through Other Means?'
183. Interview with Omar, 6 May 2015, Greater Tunis, Tunisia.
184. al-Rizqī, 'Bi-Al-Asmā': Al-Masājid Al-Khārijah 'an Sayṭarat Wizārat Al-Shu'ūn Al-Dīniyyah'.

185. Tunisia Agence Presse, 'Bi-Sabab Al-Khaṭīb Al-Idrīsī: Wizārat Al-Shu'ūn Al-Dīnīyah Tlj' Ilá Al-Qaḍā' Lil-Naẓar Fī Masjid Khārij 'an Al-Sayṭarah'.
186. Tuniscope, 'Wazīr Al-Shu'ūn Al-Dīnīyah: Lā Tūjad Jawāmi' Khārij Sayṭarat Al-Wizārah Ḥāliyan'.
187. Meddeb, *Ennahda's Uneasy Exit From Political Islam*; Ben Salem, 'The Reconfiguration of Ennahda's Recruitment Strategy in Tunisia'.
188. Interview with a member of Ennahda's Shura Council, as cited in Meddeb, *Ennahda's Uneasy Exit From Political Islam*, 17.
189. Ben Salem, 'The Reconfiguration of Ennahda's Recruitment Strategy in Tunisia', 1.
190. Interview with Ennahda youth, 16 March 2011, Tunis, Tunisia.
191. Meddeb, *Ennahda's Uneasy Exit From Political Islam*.
192. The first time it was proposed, the law led to protest movement under the banner of *Manich Msamah* (I will not forgive). The movement brought together thousands in a protest campaign that lasted for two years. The bill was postponed but reintroduced in July 2016 and in May 2017. Each time it incited new protests. See Lincoln, 'Manich Msamah and the Face of Continued Protest in Tunisia'.
193. Guellali, 'New Reconciliation Law Threatens Tunisia's Democracy'.
194. Meddeb, *Ennahda's Uneasy Exit From Political Islam*.
195. Ennahda members, 'Naṣṣ Al-Risālah Al-Thāniyah Al-Muwajjahah Min 100 Qayyādī Min Ḥarakat Al-Nahḍah'; Sadiki, 'Intra-Party Democracy in Tunisia's Ennahda: Ghannouchi and the Pitfalls of 'Charismatic' Leadership'.
196. Ibid.
197. ICG, 'Avoiding a Populist Surge in Tunisia', 3–4.
198. The Economist, 'Kais Saied Plans to Transform Tunisia. It May Go Bust First'; Arab Barometer, 'Arab Barometer Wave V'.
199. Rudloff and Werenfels, 'EU-Tunisia DCFTA: Good Intentions Not Enough'.
200. Magnan, 'L'Europe Veut-Elle Imposer Un Accord de Libre-échange 'Complet' à La Tunisie?'
201. ICG, 'Avoiding a Populist Surge in Tunisia', 3–4.
202. See the European Parliament, 'European Parliament Resolution of 14 September 2016 on the EU Relations with Tunisia in the Current Regional Context'.
203. ICG, 'Avoiding a Populist Surge in Tunisia'.
204. Delmas, 'Tunisie: Abir Moussi Dans Les Pas Du Maréchal Sissi'; ICG, 'Avoiding a Populist Surge in Tunisia'.
205. Ibid.
206. Jaouadi, 'I'tilāf Al-Karāmah Laysa Ḥizbā Jadīdan'.

207. Nidaa Tounes collapsed during this period. As soon as Essebsi became President, and had to step down as leader of the party, leadership struggles and splits emerged. By December 2018, it had lost half its MPs. Caid Essebsi died on 25 July 2019, while still the President and aged 92.
208. Al Jazeera, 'Who Are the Main Candidates in Tunisia's Presidential Election?'
209. Allahoum, 'Tunisia's Political Wrangling Explained'.
210. As cited in Al-Ain Français, 'Tunisie: Ennahda fait allégeance à la Turquie et le Qatar et ne pas à la Tunisie, Selon Abir Moussi'.
211. Wolf, 'Snapshot – the Counterrevolution Gains Momentum in Tunisia: The Rise of Abir Moussi'.
212. F. K., 'Instance de la Zakat: Bochra Belhaj Hmida juge la proposition d'Ennahdha "inacceptable"'.
213. Redondo, 'Tunisian Abir Moussi Promotes Classifying the Muslim Brotherhood as a Terrorist Organization'.
214. Assemblée Des Représentants Du peuple, 'Muḥammad Al-'Afās'.
215. Radio Mosaique fm, 'Riḍā al-Jawādī Yustaqīl min I'tlāf al-Karāmah'.
216. S. H., 'La Coalition Al Karama obtient son visa et devient un parti'.
217. Institut National de la Statistique, 'Gross Domestic Product (GDP), Second Quarter 2021'.
218. Dridi, 'Tunisia Facing Increasing Poverty and Regional Inequalities'; World Bank, 'Overview'.
219. al-'Afās, 'Bayān'.
220. The New Arab, 'Tunisia PM Fires Five Ministers amid Growing Constitutional Crisis'.
221. Tunisian Republic, 'Tunisian Constitution'.
222. Volkmann, 'Tunisia: Kais Saied's Anti-Corruption War off to a Slow Start'.
223. Hakaek Online, 'Istiqālat Akthar Min 100 Qayyādī Min Al-Nahḍah (Wathā'iq)'.
224. See: https://www.facebook.com/Dr.MohamedAffes.

5

THE SYRIAN CRISIS

> This is not a sharia committee of only judges and a court, as most people normally expect, but our sharia committee has several branches. It has a civil and military court, an organisation for the [distribution of] electricity, gas and flour. Last but not least, we gave the oil refineries that we took from the regime to the Sharia Committee which now distributes its oil.[1]

In the quote above, Abu Muhammad al-Julani, leader of the Nusra Front, discusses public service provision in north Syria. He made the statement in July 2015 as Syrian rebel factions were fighting with ISIS, the Syrian regime, Kurdish rebels – and with each other – for control of north Syria. Al-Julani's statement is telling for making explicit the variety of services that were provided by this so-called Sharia Committee: it had a court, and utilities, food and oil were, according to him, distributed via this one organisation. This chapter shows how, in doing so, he positioned himself not only in competition with other rebel factions that provided services but also with other Islamist agents. He situated the Nusra Front, through their concrete practices, within a broader Islamist movement.

This chapter traces the rise, transformation and decline of an Islamist movement during the Syrian crisis. It begins in March 2011 with the start of a popular uprising against the regime of Bashar al-Assad and ends in 2020 when the front lines of its civil war stabilised. During these years, an armed insurgency overtook a nationalist uprising that demanded political accountability and democratic reforms. The insurgency resulted in a patchwork of rebel-controlled areas that, all in their own ways, were under constant strain. Everyday governance crumbled and had to be rebuilt, and lack of funding and the diverging interests of foreign patrons fragmented the insurgency. The rise of ISIS and its caliphate, foreign interventions and the fragmentation of rebel governance frustrated the creation of an alternative national political arena. All the while relentless and indiscriminate regime bombings never ceased. This made for a stark contrast with the Tunisian transition that, despite the influence of foreign powers, remained a relatively peaceful reform process of national politics and a state executive. The difference shaped the development of an Islamist movement.

The Syrian crisis was not about religion, sectarian identity or Islam. However, the number of organisations that described themselves as Islamist, Salafist or jihadist was testament to the fact that the crisis turned into a hotbed for Islamic activism. Numerous studies have appeared on the topic. For instance, Charles Lister published an excellent study on the development of jihadist groups – focusing on ISIS, the Nusra Front and Ahrar al-Sham – during the Syrian insurgency.[2] The same goes for Aron Lund and his multiple studies on specific Islamist and jihadist organisations.[3] Thomas Pierret traced the internal fragmentation of Salafist movements during the Syrian crisis and its relationship to the politics of foreign support.[4] In each of these studies, scholars used ideology to distinguish and subdivide an Islamist movement. Lund, for example, divides the Islamist movement during the Syrian crisis between a purist, Salafist strand and a pragmatist, Islamist one. Thomas Pierret focuses on a Salafist movement and subdivides it into a (global) jihadist, (politically engaged) Haraki and (state submissive) quietist current, linking each to specific parties (the Nusra Front, Syrian Islamic Liberation Front and Front for Authenticity and Development, respectively).[5]

The lack of consensus about these categorisations indicates the weak relationship between religion, ideology and concrete practices during the Syrian crisis. For instance, nearly every Islamist rebel group described itself as jihadist. Scholars often regarded the Muslim Brotherhood as a classic political Islamist organisation, despite its financial support for various Syrian jihadist factions. Tellingly, Thomas Pierret refers to Ahrar al-Sham as a 'jihadi lite' organisation for having foreign roots and supporters while remaining explicitly Syrian in its identity. This raises questions as to what extent jihadism is necessarily a global phenomenon.[6] Notably, a prominent member of a jihadist rebel faction stated that most of its rank and file were 'just conservative Muslims who, because of the situation, have drawn closer to their religion. As with the Tunisian transition, the extent that the rank and file of these movements followed, or even knew, the ideologies of their organisations was often questionable.[7] The same goes for the influence of religious ideologies on judicial practices. Rulings of jihadist-controlled sharia courts were, for example, so inconsistent that people would visit multiple courts until receiving a ruling that suited them.[8] The relationship between Islamic ideas and the concrete practices of Islamist groups during the Syrian crisis was weak.

Similar to the preceding chapter, I examine the political impact of an Islamist movement based on what its participants did, instead of what ideologies they followed. I do not reference ideologies to differentiate Islamist movements. Rather, I describe how activists used Islam to render public services, justice and governance distinct, reshaping access to symbolic, institutional and material resources. These practices infused Islam with political significance. I then show how the struggle to define the legitimate ways of rendering practices distinct drew activists together into an Islamist movement. In short, this chapter chronicles how an Islamist movement, and its various currents, emerged from among the contentious interactions that made up the Syrian crisis.

The first section examines how activists used Islam to render their practices distinct and, in doing so, imbued Islam with political relevance. For instance, by forming jihadist rebel groups, activists nurtured Islamic support networks and facilitated the influx of foreign fighters. Following the takeover of territory, sharia committees provided a distinct Islamic institutional framework for providing public services while sharia courts did so for the judiciary. In doing so, they reshaped access to judicial and governance resources while fostering a collapse between collective violence, service provision and judicial practices. Establishing Islamic emirates and an Islamic state allowed for full executive control over a territory. Using Islam to render practices distinct turned it political – Islamist – and transformed religion itself into a contested resource.

The second part of this chapter traces several conflicts that arose over how Islam could and should render practices distinct. These conflicts centred around control over sharia committees and courts, the codification of sharia law and the relationship between political authority and an Islamic collective identity. These conflicts brought together a wide range of agents that had a stake in defining Islam as a distinct practice, unintentionally setting them apart as a distinct, Islamist movement. Meanwhile, they highlighted different positions that Islamists took in these conflicts. The final section examines the decline of an Islamist movement. By 2020, foreign powers increasingly defined the dynamics of the Syrian crisis, leaving less space for local agents to enact distinct practices, resulting in the movement's decline.

Constructing an Islamic Distinction

On 6 March 2011, a group of youngsters wrote '*al-sha'b yurīd isqāṭ al-niẓām*' ('the people want the fall of the regime') on a wall in the southern city of Daraa. For copying what they had seen on television about Tunisia and Egypt, they were arrested. None of the boys was older than fifteen. Their arrest and treatment at the hands of the local security services enraged their families and others in the town. The regime harshly repressed protests, killing several. Their funerals turned into even larger protests. The Syrian uprising had started.[9]

In the subsequent months, as an armed insurgency appeared next to this uprising, rebels began to use religion to establish distinctly jihadist fighting factions. Sharia courts were founded that disrupted the judiciary field in rebel-held territories by offering an alternative judicial framework that did not rely on codified law or a body of professional lawyers and judges. Distinctly Islamic service providers, such as the sharia committees, challenged control over day-to-day governance. At its most extreme, as with ISIS's caliphate, it challenged governance far beyond the boundaries of the Syrian crisis. This section discusses each of these examples of distinctly Islamic practices.

Islam and the Syrian Uprising

But before I do so, let me highlight a false positive: the use of religion in the uprising without turning its practices distinct. From the start, religion was a part of the Syrian uprising, but it did not inform the demands or practices of an uprising that was shaped by, first and foremost, a nationalist and democratic movement. We see, for instance, that on 15 March 2011, during the first protests in Damascus, people chanted '*Allāh Sūriyā, ḥurrīyah uw bess*' ('God, Syria, freedom and that's it') besides repeating the slogan 'the people want the fall of the regime'.[10] During the first few weeks, protesters often repeated the chants, besides chanting '*Lā ilāh illā Allāh*' ('There is no God but God').[11] Protesters invoked religion as a discursive tactic to delegitimize Bashar's rule by implying that true sovereignty lies only with God – not with Bashar al-Assad and his regime. Activists often used mosques, and Friday prayers, as staging ground for protests. The al-Omari Mosque in Daraa turned into a central meeting point and makeshift hospital, for example, as did the Rahman mosque in Baniyas. Mosques were one of the few, if not only, places where people could congregate in large groups. One activist noted that, in a context that lacked organisational structures, they would 'go to the mosque, pray, and then people would just start shouting. That's how people found each other: ten, twenty, forty, eighty people . . . Then we started marching'.[12]

Meanwhile, the Syrian regime was at pains to describe the uprising as Islamist inspired and a foreign conspiracy. Bashar al-Assad, in a speech to the People's Assembly, stated on 30 March that Syria was being exposed to a foreign conspiracy to destabilise the country.[13] Bouthaina Shaaban, the political and media adviser to the President, described the protests as violent mobs, with armed youngsters attacking security forces and governance buildings in Daraa, Homs and Latakia in one day alone.[14] In April, the Interior Ministry charged that among these armed mobs were people calling for an armed insurrection in name of jihad with the aim to establish a Salafist state.[15] In the multisectarian context of a country like Syria (the country is home to various religious sects, from Twelver Shia to Greek Orthodox Christians), it spoke directly to the existential fear of many religious minorities and the need for regime protection against imminent Islamist rule. It legitimised brutal repression of the protests. Figure 5.1 shows the weekly number of casualties between March 2011 until July 2012, the period from the start of nonviolent protests until the outbreak of countrywide armed insurrection. From the very start, more than fifty people were killed per week. Quickly, at the beginning of April, this rises to more than a hundred. Three weeks later, in the week of Friday 23 April, it was over 300. Figure 5.1 also shows that worse – much worse – was still to come.

There is no evidence that jihadist movements were present in the early days of the uprising.[16] Protesters did not demand an Islamic state or sharia rule, and mosques provided the only physical space in which groups could congregate. Religion provided a discursive tool for an uprising that was nationalist and

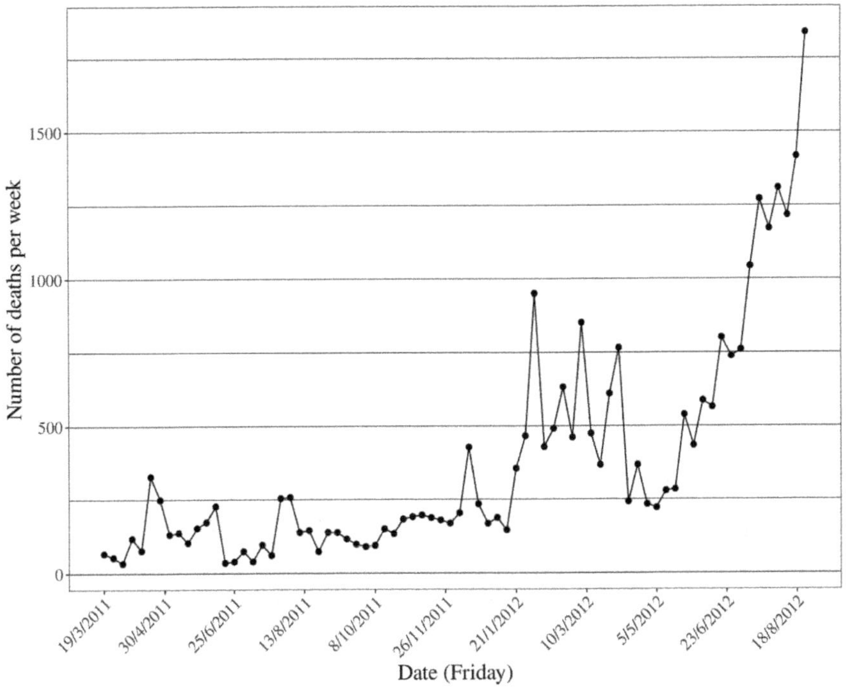

Figure 5.1 Casualties in the Syrian crisis, March 2011 to July 2012.
Source: syrianshuhada.com.

democratic: protesters demanded political change, freedom and accountability in name of human dignity. Meanwhile, a discourse around Islamism had, and still has, a political relevance because it bolsters the case for executive empowerment domestically and unilateralism internationally by shifting political discourse from issues of political representation and human rights to national security. The regime used the threat of Islamism to legitimate authoritarian and isolationist policies. Beyond the use as a discursive tool, Islam did not inform distinct types of protests, political demands, governance or other practices.

Using mosques as a staging ground for protests had an unintended consequence. It meant that sheikhs and imams rose to prominence in the uprising. Not because they represented Islam, but because they were representatives of the few available spaces where activists could organise themselves as a nationalist, democratic protest movement and where they could express their claims. Ratib, an activist imam from Daraa, was one example. He (and his extended family) had had problems with the Assad regime for years, and his mosque became an early focal point for protests. The Syrian regime was aware of the importance of imams as community leaders. Ratib recalls:

> The *mukhabarat* [intelligence services] came and talked to me before the sermon that March. They warned me I should call for calm. They did not tell me what to say specifically, apart from not mentioning the [arrested] children, but emphasised that my role as imam was to guard the social peace in Daraa. I did something else instead: I discussed the fact that life without freedom was no life at all.[17]

And he continues:

> [A few weeks later] I received some warnings in advance, that something was brewing. But nothing specific. Then, when I exited the mosque, I was shot. In my shoulder. I was stunned, just stood there in shock . . . and then I was shot a second time. I collapsed and was brought to someone's house where they operated on me. A regular hospital was not an option [because the regime would arrest me]. From that moment, I moved from house to house.[18]

But Ratib was not the only sheikh or imam to challenge the regime. Two individuals that will return in this chapter are Osama al-Rifai and Adnan al-Aroor. Osama al-Rifai is a famous Damascene sheikh who built up a powerful charitable movement after returning from exile in the 1990s. Two weeks into the uprising, he reflected on the regime's focus on national security as a response to the popular challenge to its legitimacy:

> One thing that [protesters] agitate against is corruption. Corruption has been present in this country from the moment it was created. It is present day and night. Officials know this perfectly well. Laws apply to the poor and hardworking. But the rich, they can just buy themselves out of anything, and are above the law. And any citizen knows this. Any official also knows this. [. . .] We can only truly live in security if this situation changes. It is the President, and officials of the state, that have the key to this change. If they make laws that respect the freedom and dignity of people, that end the emergency law and finish corruption – then, and only then, will we be able to say we are blessed with stability and security.[19]

Osama al-Rifai remained defiantly critical and was at one point, in August 2011, attacked in his mosque. He left Syria soon after.

Few knew Adnan al-Aroor before the uprising. A Saudi-based Syrian sheikh, he initially urged restraint in response to calls for protests. He suddenly changed his position as protests started and his patron, Saudi Arabia, came out in support of the uprising.[20] He subsequently became famous, almost overnight, for his outspoken support for the uprising in his speeches on TV and on YouTube.[21] There were reports of the apparent anti-Alawi and sectarian language underpinning al-Aroor's statements.[22] It was something he denied himself. When asked about al-Aroor, some interviewees enthusiastically discussed his broad appeal. They noted he had a huge impact not just on conservative Syrians but across society.

Not every imam or sheikh made the same choice as Ratib, Osama al-Rifai or Adnan al-Aroor. In many early interviews, Syrian activists vented their frustration with the sheikhs and imams who remained quiet or actively supported the regime.[23] They directed much of their scorn at Ahmad Hassoun, the Mufti of the Republic, who was widely regarded as an inferior religious scholar who was only assigned to his position for his regime support and strategic social position. Another, much more highly regarded, person was Ramadan al-Bouti. Regime opponents and supporters alike recognised him as a world-class religious scholar. But he always remained a staunch defender of the Syrian regime.[24] He was assassinated in March 2013.

Establishing Jihadist Rebel Groups

At the start of the Syrian crisis, there was no Islamist movement present within it. This changed as an armed insurgency developed next to the uprising. It meant that next to the decentralised network of nonviolent collective activism a fragmented amalgamation of various rebel factions appeared that needed constant funding and support. As we will see, using Islam to render oneself distinct as fighting group facilitated access to financial support, weapons and experienced fighters. It imbued Islam with acute political relevance as an armed insurgency increasingly dictated the dynamics of the Syrian crisis.[25]

From the very beginning, as a reaction to deadly regime repression, some activists questioned the use of a nonviolent protest repertoire.[26] There were instances of spontaneous use of live fire by small groups of protesters from March 2011 onwards.[27] On 6 June 2011, in Jisr al-Shughur, a town located south-west of Aleppo and close to the border of Türkiye, it initially seemed that a mass defection led to intra-army clashes.[28] It soon became clear that it was one of the first successful attempts by residents to ambush the army and subsequently ransack and attack all the government buildings in the town.[29] The regime's reaction meant to send a message. It surrounded the town, shelled it relentlessly and retook it a week later after heavy fighting. It was the first time that clashes at this scale had been reported. Despite the apparent failure of the exploit, Jisr al-Shughur proved an example for other groups across the country. Where violence among the opposition had been sporadic, it gradually became more widespread. From June 2011 onward, small militias to protect protesters emerged in various parts of the country. They were often created as informal groups in a neighbourhood, mosque or village and frequently included defected soldiers. Over time, these groups coalesced into more formalised organisations. The Khalid ibn al-Walid Brigade (established in Homs, July 2011) and the Farouq Brigades (Homs, October) are two early examples. On 11 November that year, Kataib Ahrar al-Sham (The Brigades of Freemen of the Levant) was established in Hama as was the Nur Ad-Din al-Zenki movement in the countryside of Aleppo around this time. These are four examples from among dozens, if not hundreds, of others.

As Yassin Kassab and al-Shami have described, the armed insurgency transformed the Syrian crisis.[30] Among others influences, it set the stage for the rise of jihadist groups that enacted a distinctly Islamic practice of collective violence. Several of their leaders had recently been released from regime custody. On 26 March 2011, for example, the regime released 260 inmates from its Sednaya prison. Located close to Damascus, it is infamous for housing political prisoners.[31] The released inmates included some Kurds, but many more had been incarcerated following their participation in a jihad against the US occupation of Iraq following its invasion of the country in 2003. At the end of May, the President announced a general amnesty that resulted in the release of hundreds of political prisoners. This time, the regime released many Syrian Muslim Brotherhood members.[32] It released more Islamists and jihadists in the spring and summer of 2011. Among those freed were Hussein Abdessalam (February), Hassan Aboud (March) and Zahran Alloush (June).[33] Few people knew these individuals at the time. All were jihadists who had travelled to Iraq. Hassan Aboud, who we will meet more often in this chapter, later recalled:

> They informed us that the procedure was about to finish and that the decision to release us was final. Before we left, one of the brothers stopped us. All around us were people from the military police. Despite this he said, "ok people: we are being released solely because it is God's will. Noone pressured us or made us submit to work for God's cause. We only submit to God. So now: let us get to work!"[34]

Hassan Aboud went on and established the Ahrar al-Sham Brigades, a precursor to what would become one of the most powerful Islamist rebel factions during the Syrian crisis. Hussein Abdessalam ended up establishing Fajr al-Islam, a powerful jihadist group in the Aleppo governorate that would later morph into Ahrar al-Sham. Zahran Alloush would establish the Army of Islam, for a long time the most powerful Islamist rebel faction in Eastern Ghouta in the south of Syria.

How these groups drew on Islam to construct a collective identity differed. One group, the Nusra Front, portrayed itself as a representative of a global jihadist movement coming to the aid of the Syrian uprising.[35] Ahrar al-Sham instead described itself as a local Syrian group with its roots in a global jihad. It claimed to be independent from any foreign organisation and did not receive any endorsement on al-Qaeda affiliated online forums.[36] The Tawheed Brigade, in contrast, situated itself as a local Islamist fighting group, being active in and around Aleppo. Institutionally, they also differed. The Nusra Front, for example, was organised as a tightly hierarchical organisation, whereas Ahrar al-Sham turned into a more decentralised rebel group.[37] Both these organisations had internal religious authorities, while the Tawheed Brigade delegated internal religious authority to Muhammad Ali al-Sabuni, a well-known Syrian religious scholar.[38]

To make matters more diffuse, Islamists worked together with other, non-Islamist rebels in temporary operation rooms to coordinate attacks, turning jihadists into an indispensable part of the insurgency. This was, for example, the case with the attack on the Taftanaz airbase (January 2013) in which Ahrar al-Sham, the Nusra Front, Suqour al-Sham and Free Syrian Army affiliated Farouq Brigades took part. The Nusra Front coordinated the attack on the Wadi al-Deif airbase between February 2013 and December 2014 in which Suqour al-Sham and the Idlib Military Council, both affiliated with the US-backed Supreme Military Council, also participated. Hassan Aboud noted that:

> The moment that a conflict becomes more organised, there is no choice but to transform and level up military efforts. [. . .] That is why we created joined operation rooms. In these operation rooms, we joined forces with the [Syrian nationalist] Free Syrian Army and with the Military Leadership [of the Supreme Military Council]. Just as we worked together with any other group.[39]

But references to Islam did set these groups apart from their non-Islamist counterparts. It provided them with a very particular, historically defined, set of resources. To start with, the leaders of these groups had experience with the Iraqi jihad, which provided them with organisational, funding and military skills as well as a wide network of others with similar experiences.[40] Hassan Aboud fought in Iraq and was incarcerated, together with numerous other jihadists, in Sednaya prison. Abu Jaber al-Sheikh had always remained in Syria, but facilitated jihadist travel to Iraq. He, too, was incarceration at Sednaya. Tellingly, it took Hassan Aboud a mere eight months from being released from Sednaya prison to declaring the founding of the Ahrar al-Sham Brigades.

With the Nusra Front, the relationship to Iraqi jihad was even clearer as it was established as a franchise of the Islamic State in Iraq. Ahmed Hussein al-Shar'a, better known by his *nom de guerre* Abu Muhammad al-Julani, was born in 1982 and grew up in the middle-class Damascus neighbourhood of Mezze. He travelled to Iraq in 2003 and gradually rose among the ranks of al-Qaeda jihadists active in the country. His ascent was paused when American forces incarcerated him in Camp Bucca between 2005 and 2008. But it gave the opportunity to network with other jihadists incarcerated there. When the Islamic State in Iraq (ISI) was established, he became a provincial leader.[41] He tells himself what happened next:

> [While at Camp Bucca] I had been talking with the leadership of the Islamic State in Iraq about plans after Iraq, and especially in relation to Syria, and her special place in the history of the Islamic ummah. So when the revolution started [. . .] there was an agreement, with the leadership of the Islamic

> State in Iraq, to enter Syria. [. . .] We made a plan and went to the country in August 2011, going with seven or eight men, many of whom were Syrians that remained [in Iraq].[42]

The result was the founding of *Jabhat al-Nusra l-il Ahl al-Sham*, or the Support Front for the Community of the Levant, more commonly referred to in English as the Nusra Front. Although a public secret, for all intents and purposes they were an offshoot of the Islamic State in Iraq. They published their first statement in January 2012, months after the start of the uprising.

Another resource that jihadists could draw on was experienced foreign fighters. Jihadist groups used Islam to describe themselves as being part of a global movement and hence drew in a large number of foreign fighters from all over the world. A report by Aaron Zelin, fellow at the Washington Institute for Near East Policy, estimated that from late 2011 to the beginning of December 2013, between 3,300 and 11,000 foreigners travelled to Syria to fight Bashar al-Assad's regime. They travelled from Europe, the Arab world, the Balkans and former Soviet countries. Although only approximately 20 per cent of those travelling stated a group affiliation, of those that did, the Nusra Front and, later, ISIS were the two main ones. Other groups that received foreign fighters were Ahrar al-Sham, Jaish al-Muhajireen wal-Ansar, Liwa al-Umma and the Sham al-Islam movement – all jihadist groups.[43]

This brings us to how an Islamic distinctness gave access to networks of foreign funding. With the Nusra Front, its sister organisation in Iraq, the ISI, reportedly initially contributed almost half of its budget to the new organisation.[44] Other jihadist groups found lucrative supporters in the Gulf, for instance in Kuwait. Elizabeth Dickinson detailed how its liberal laws regarding foreign donations turned it into a hub for fundraising. Much of this support drew on a network of sheikhs and charitable associations.[45] In one example, during the Ramadan of 2013, a group of Kuwaiti clerics, politicians and public figures 'participated in a collection "to prepare 12,000 jihadists for the sake of Allah"'.[46] Various groups, centred around leading sheikhs, would support particular jihadist groups. Shafi al-Ajmi, a member of the faculty at Kuwait University's College of Sharia and Islamic Studies, for example, supported Ahrar al-Sham. Mohammad Hayef al-Mutairi, a fundraiser and founder of Kuwait's Salafist Ummah Party, supported the Brigades of Liwa al-Islam and

Liwa al-Furqan. Dickinson reports that Ghanem al-Mutairi supported 'a Syrian affiliate of al-Qaeda', which seems to imply the Nusra Front.[47]

Unsurprisingly, numerous groups wanted a piece of these funding streams. Many of the newly established militias carried Islamic references in their names: the Farouq Brigades was named after Omar bin al-Khattab, a companion of the prophet, the Nour Ad-Din al-Zenki movement after a 12th-century emir of Aleppo and Damascus and the Khalid ibn al-Walid Battalion after a companion of Muhammad and successful military commander. Often, they were a marketing strategy to get access to private Gulf funders. Early on, activists acknowledged, for example, that opposition sheikhs were crucial in getting financial and material support to the Syrian uprising. One interviewee alleged rebel factions affiliated with the nationalist Free Syrian Army, the FSA, received far more support via individual sheikhs than via the FSA organisation.[48] When, in December 2012, 260 rebel commanders from across the Syrian crisis agreed – while actively supported by Saudi Arabia and the US – to the creation of a 30-member Supreme Military Council, jihadist groups were not invited. But one sheikh who was involved was no other than Adnan al-Aroor. Although his inclusion rendered the Supreme Military Council open to accusations of facilitating the rise of sectarianism, he also gave access to support from Saudi financiers.[49] The Khalid ibn al-Walid Battalion also had a subgroup named after Adnan al-Aroor – we can only guess why.[50]

Rendering their practices of collective violence distinctly Islamic, not only impacted access to foreign support and fighters, it also shaped their internal institutional structure. It necessitated an internal authority that provided a religious legitimation of their jihadist credentials. The Nusra Front, for example, had *al-qāḍī al-ʿāmm* (the supreme judge) to do this.[51] Ahrar al-Sham had a chief religious scholar with a similar role.[52] Most jihadist groups had internal sharia courts to adjudicate transgressions based on Islamic jurisprudence. The Tawheed Brigade was an exception, where religious authority was, initially, delegated to an external religious scholar. As clarified further below, the interpretations of sharia were flexible as most of these groups took a noncodified approach to Islamic law. Rulings, as a result, very much reflected the interests of rebel groups – not a fixed legal code. Having said this, the existence of religious judges, scholars and courts inside these groups meant they had additional positions of internal authority, based on Islam, that were not present in their non-Islamist counterparts.

One group that remained conspicuously quiet was the Syrian Muslim Brotherhood (SMB). They did attempt to acquire a foothold in the uprising, but were held back by their experiences of regime repression, internal fragmentation and lacking domestic footprint. Instead of having a background in the jihadist insurgency against the US invasion of Iraq, SMB members lived through a failed uprising against the Syrian regime during the 1970s and early 1980s. Reflecting experience of repression, they often worked covertly through existing associations and councils. For instance, they used a front organisation, the Civilian Protection Commission, to fund and influence nascent rebel groups.[53] Although formally independent, it was a public secret that it was initiated and funded by the SMB. But the support that the Muslim Brotherhood could provide paled compared with that given by other, often foreign, donors. To make matters worse, the SMB initially geared support toward Homs and Idlib, reflecting the power of its Homs branch inside the organisation. They only began to focus on Aleppo after they brought their Aleppo branch back into the fold in 2012. By then, Aleppo had turned into one of the main battle grounds of the insurgency and was already controlled by several other rebel groups. The Muslim Brotherhood never quite recovered.[54]

In summary, when an insurgency emerged, it meant that next to the decentralised network of the nonviolent uprising, a fragmented amalgamation of various rebel factions appeared that needed constant funding and support. An insurgency requires different (and far more) resources than a nonviolent uprising: weapons, ammunition, recruits, medical supplies, food. Using Islam to render oneself distinct as fighting group became crucial in efforts to access financial support, weapons and experienced fighters – all indispensable for an effective insurgency. It imbued Islam with acute political relevance as an armed insurgency increasingly dictated the dynamics of the Syrian crisis.

Sharia Courts and Committees

Another practice through which activists enacted an Islamic distinctness was the provision of public services and justice. It became an issue after rebels successfully took control over large parts of Syria. In July 2012, rebels launched an attack on Damascus and Aleppo. Although the attack on Damascus failed to dislodge the regime's hold of the capital, the attack on Aleppo resulted in rebel control of over half the city. From the Salah al-Din neighbourhood in the west, opposition control went counter clockwise to Sheikh Lutfi in the south, Tareeq al-Bab in the east and Sheikh Khedr and Sheikh Najjar in the north-east of the city. The centre itself, the military barracks to the east and the airport to its west remained in regime hands.

The attack on Aleppo and Damascus reflected wider successes of rebel factions. Figure 5.2 shows the approximate area controlled by the regime, opposition, ISIS and the Kurdish-led Syrian Democratic Forces between March 2011 and March 2022. In March 2012, the opposition controlled some areas in Homs and the countryside of Idlib as well as areas around al-Qusayr, a small town at the border of Lebanon. It made up a few per cent of Syrian territory. By March 2013, it had increased to almost 40 per cent. At this point, the opposition controlled much of the north, from Aleppo to Deir ez-Zor, areas in and around Saraqib, al-Bab and Azaz in the north-east, areas in Idlib's

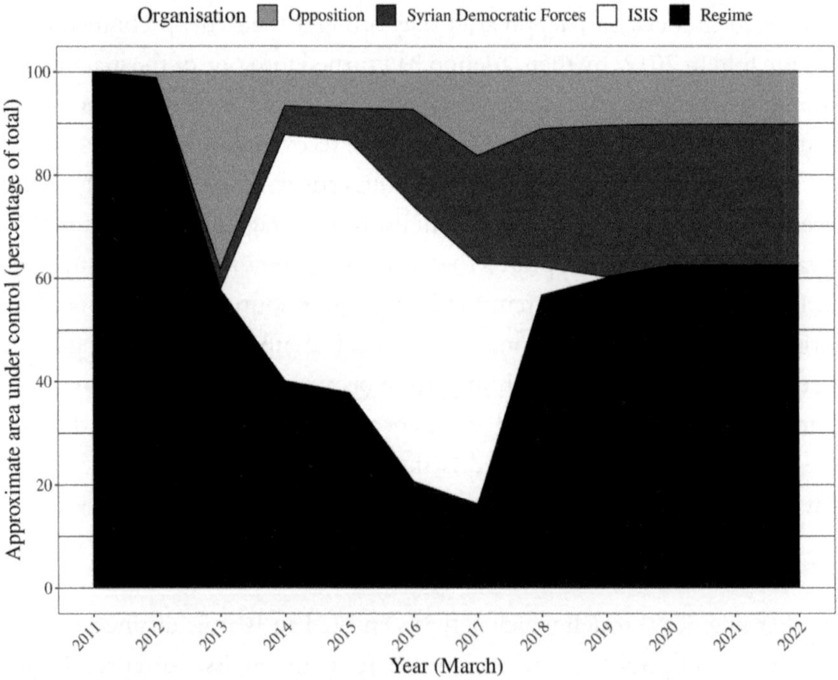

Figure 5.2 Approximate area of control, March 2011 to March 2022 (as percentage of Syrian territory).

Source: Syrian Network for Human Rights, 'On the 11th Anniversary of the Popular Uprising, 5'.

countryside, the Damascus suburb of Eastern Ghouta and areas in the south around Daraa.[55] It meant that rebel factions suddenly found themselves in control of territories in which millions of people lived.

Several problems arose after rebels took control of these areas: there were food shortages, for example, as well as endemic looting and a lack of security. The regime destroyed, or left empty, existing wheat silos that dotted the country, which were built to provide for a five-year strategic wheat supply. It led to bread shortages. With only a few functioning bakeries left in Aleppo, the price for a standard eight pack of pita-like flat bread rose from fifteen Syrian pounds (about fifteen pence) to over 200 (or nearly two British pounds).[56] In addition, rebel factions remained heavily dependent on unreliable private networks of funding. As a result, several groups grew increasingly dependent on resources taken from territories they secured. In the absence of independent police forces or functioning judiciary, and lacking any proper system of taxation or hierarchical military structures, it led to endemic corruption and looting. Other issues that arose were the collapse of rubbish removal and access to reliable internet, water and electricity. It did not help that rebel groups had not thought through what it meant to govern territory. A spokesperson of the Nour al-Din al-Zenki movement, one of the northern-based rebel factions taking part in the Aleppo attack, remarked frankly that:

> At the start we did not have a strategy. We created organisations when the need arose because of a specific practical issue. This was true of the courts, of the police. We needed service organisations because they were lacking [. . .] but in these days they always emerged in a pragmatic and dynamic way. One day we sat together and decided something, next day we tried to implement it. Of course all within the limits of the resources we had.[57]

Numerous initiatives and organisations emerged. People came together in neighbourhoods to clean roads and manage garbage collection. Also, many informal networks emerged to buy flour and propellants in Türkiye (or other accessible Syrian cities) and redistribute, or sell, them in Aleppo.[58] Some of these initiatives became more formalised as civil society organisations, such as the Muslim Youth Council[59] and the Ahali Halab Initiative.[60] Syrian Muslim Brotherhood members were involved in several of these initiatives.

One example is Tarif al-Sayed Issa, an exiled Syrian Muslim Brother, who returned, after more than thirty years, to his home country. He co-founded a humanitarian aid organisation, Sanabel al-Kheir, to distribute food and clothes across opposition-held countryside around Idlib.[61]

It is around the provision of public services that local councils and Sharia Committees, or *al-Hay'ah al-Shar'īyah*, were established. Sharia committees provided services in the framework of Sunni Islam: they had a court, prison and police force, and they organised the distribution of bread, provided water and electricity or did all of the preceding. The Sharia Committee in Aleppo described itself as representing 'the practical implementation of a comprehensive Islamic civilisation', stating that they created 'departments for the service of people and care for their interest, and is therefore active in all sectors of daily life'.[62] Figure 5.3 shows the entrance to the Sharia Committee in Aleppo. This chapter started with a quote from al-Julani, the leader of the Nusra Front, in which he told of the wide range of services that the Sharia Committee was providing: from a civil and military court to the distribution of electricity, gas, flour and oil. He boasted that the Sharia Committee distributed 100 tons of flour each day.[63] Multiple interviewees noted that the Sharia Committee

Figure 5.3 Screenshot, entrance to the Sharia Committee in Aleppo.
Source: Sharia Committee in Aleppo, 'Documentary on the Sharia Committee'.

during the first half of 2013 was far more effective than the Local Council. Marouan, a media activist from Aleppo, noted that:

> If you wanted to get married, you went to the board; if there was a conflict between people they had a judge. They had something for everything. The Local Council tried, but did not have the ability. [. . .] It is true that the Committee tried to control everything. But the thing was that they had a project. They had an ideology and structure, when nobody else had.[64]

These Sharia Committees were a distinctly Sunni Islamic response to the provision of services – including justice and security – in opposition-held territories.

Sharia committees stood in contrast to their civil counterparts: the local and district councils. In Aleppo, for example, a group of prominent doctors, engineers and entrepreneurs established the Transitional Council of Aleppo in August 2012. The idea was to act as a liaison between rebel and civilian groups. It had an elected council of 250 members, one for about every 20,000 inhabitants, that assigned a smaller group for executive governance.[65] Similar organisations emerged in Idlib, Deir ez-Zor and Deraa, as well as in other cities. These organisations quickly developed into a national governance structure. In November 2012, the National Coalition for Syrian Revolutionary and Opposition Forces was established, or the Syrian Opposition Coalition (SOC), for short.[66] It aimed to represent the Syrian population, with executive tasks delegated to a Syrian Interim Government (SIG), established in March 2013.[67] The SIG was the executive arm of the SOC and had Ministries of Interior, Finances, Local Administration, Health and Education among others.[68] The SOC elected the president, who proposed a team of ministers to the SOC for approval.[69]

Despite being positioned as Islamic alternatives to the SIG and local councils, a uniform influence of Islamic ideas on the services of sharia committees was challenging to distinguish. In Aleppo, it comprised offices for education, services, health, judiciary, grain and flour, fatwas and mosque affairs – with each of these offices having their designated specified tasks.[70] Apart from issuing fatwas, these offices closely resembled the type of services provided by the Local Council of Aleppo. They emphasised hiring employees on their professional abilities and highlighted that most of their employees did not affiliate with any rebel group.[71] That they felt the necessity to emphasise the effectiveness and independence of the services they provided goes to show that these services were assessed on their effectiveness, not on the extent that they implemented political change based on some kind of Islamist ideal.

We can make a similar observation in relation to the judiciary. Following the rebel takeover, courts ceased functioning, leading to endemic looting and corruption by rebel forces. As a solution, rebel groups established courts. The Tawheed Brigade, for example, established a Revolutionary Security Bureau (*Amn al-Thawrah*). It included a jail and court based on Syrian law, mostly run by defected lawyers.[72] The Transitional Council of Aleppo was another example that worked with civil courts,[73] as was the Free Judicial Council that controlled courts in the towns of Harem and Salqin to the west of Aleppo.

There were also Islamic alternatives. The Free Syrian Army, for example, initially depended on local sheikhs and sharia law to arbitrate conflicts that involved rebel fighters. Soon, sharia courts were established across towns and neighbourhoods in opposition-held territories.[74] These sharia courts set themselves apart from their civil counterparts by basing rulings on Islamic law, or sharia. Having said that, a consistent influence of Islam on their rulings was lacking. The sheikhs involved in the early FSA judiciary initiatives had been assigned because of their local social standing, not because of their credentials in Islamic law. They often had little knowledge of sharia. Many were teachers of religion at secondary schools prior to the uprising.[75] Courts related to sharia committees often based their fatwas and judgements on direct interpretations of the Quran and examples from the Prophet's life as recorded in the hadith, rejecting the *madhāhib*, or established schools of Islamic jurisprudence. But in the absence of an established legal framework, randomness characterised rulings, mixing custom with opinion, and a tendency to resolve civil disputes through reconciliation between parties. Often the political, clan and family affiliations of litigants influenced these reconciliation attempts.[76] Instead of religion, rulings reflected social dynamics. In addition, religious or civil, the effectiveness of courts depended on the extent that they could effectively run a jail and police units to enforce their decisions, which was often related to the extent that they were supported by one or more rebel factions. This meant rebel factions often influenced the adjudication of cases, leading to the proliferation of rebel specific courts. Some Syrians complained that 'it is almost the fashion to have your own courthouse now'.[77]

Sharia and civil courts did not differ because of the differences between Islamic and civil law but because of the institutional reforms that an Islamic distinction allowed. First, it transformed the basis on which judges were hired. Enab Baladi, an opposition newspaper, reported that there were initially professional lawyers working in the Sharia Committee in Aleppo, but they were gradually pushed out of the organisation. The remaining judges were not civil educated or professionally qualified lawyers or judges. Only a few were graduates from sharia colleges.[78] It left the door open to nonformalised hiring and firing practices. Individuals were appointed through a process of consultation between stakeholders, often including one or more rebel groups.

Second, an Islamic distinction fostered relations between rebel factions and courts. As most jihadist groups had an internal sharia court, they often assigned their own judges to external judicial positions. The Sharia Committee in Aleppo was, reportedly, initially proposed by the Tawheed Brigade for this very reason: it hoped to keep control over security, justice and service provision in Aleppo.[79] Its Shura Council had representatives from the rebel factions that created it. Its senior employees were affiliated to specific Islamist factions. Rebel factions directly supported specific committees and their courts. These factions provided individuals for their police and security forces. An Islamic distinctness facilitated this collapse of division between service providers, courts and military organisations.

The collapse of a division between services, judiciary and collective violence that an Islamic distinctness facilitated was increasingly reflected in internal transformations of jihadist groups. They went beyond a single focus on armed insurgency, situating themselves as comprehensive Islamist movements that were not only jihadist ventures but also strived for social and political change. Ahrar al-Sham is a case in point. In January 2013, the Ahrar al-Sham Brigades changed its name to the Ahrar al-Sham Movement. The name change reflected, Hassan Aboud later clarified, 'a transformation that was a move from work as a brigade, meaning military work, to work as a movement with the diverse activities that the latter involves. Military activities are only a particular element of the whole movement'.[80] They published a charter in which they described themselves as:

> A comprehensive Islamic reformist movement that is active to build an Islamic civilisational society in Syria. [. . .] The aims of the movement are,

first, the fall of the regime and provide security to our beloved Syrian lands. Second, to work to enable religion in the individual, society and state.[81]

From now on, a political bureau instead of a military leadership led the movement.[82] It created a coalition, the Syrian Islamic Front, that helped situate its activities as part of a broader *Mashrūʿ al-Ummah*, or the Project of the Ummah, in the uprising.[83] Online, under the banner of Project of the Ummah, it showcased humanitarian and social activities. It developed *daʿwah* centres and published propaganda clips in which it showcased its activities in education and distribution of food aid.[84] From a distinctly Islamic, jihadist fighting group, they turned into an organisation aimed at social and political change.

Summarised, Islamists founded sharia committees as Islamic counterparts to local councils and the Syrian Interim Government. The same applied to sharia courts, which were an Islamic alternative to civil courts. It was difficult to distinguish a particular influence of Islam on the services and adjudications of sharia committees and courts: services were assessed on their effectiveness not the extent that they implemented a type of Islam-inspired social change, and adjudications lacked consistency more generally. Instead, the fact that Islam was used to render these institutions distinct was enough to have an institutional impact: it transformed hiring practices in these organisations and led to a collapse of the division between service providers, courts and rebel factions. It nurtured a transformation of jihadist groups themselves, turning them from rebel factions to sociopolitical movements.

Enacting a Caliphate

Amid the chaos that was the Syrian crisis, in April 2013, ISIS emerged. They took the merging of collective violence, services and judiciary based on an Islamic distinction to a whole new level. A little over a year later, in June 2014, it declared itself to be a fully-fledged bureaucratic state. As they established their caliphate, ISIS emphasised its statist character. They implemented day-to-day governance, as explained by themselves, through several offices (or *dawāwīn*). Introduced as 'places for protecting rights', they aimed to maintain public interests and 'protect people's religion and security'. Organised as a decentralised state, comprising provinces (*wilayat*), each had offices for healthcare (*diwan al-sahah*), enforcing public norms (*diwan al-hisbah*), education (*diwan al-talim*), taxation (*diwan al-zakat*) and a dozen other services. Although the caliph was the highest executive authority, the size of the caliphate and the extent of its executive tasks, they explained, rendered it necessary to give authority to a delegated committee (*al-lajnah al-mufawaḊha*) comprising individuals that had know-how and were skilled, knowledgeable and 'upright'. All the offices and provinces referred matters of importance to the delegated committee – not the caliph.[85] Figure 5.4 is a summary of the structure of the caliphate as provided by ISIS.

ISIS practised a distinctly Islamic type of modern nation-state. As noted in Chapter 3, traditional caliphates represented the authority of a Muslim leader over a population (and as a result were multiethnic). In contrast, with ISIS, their Islamic state represented a specific, Sunni Muslim, community. It directly governed the daily affairs of their citizens through an extensive set of public services. Statements from ISIS emphasised good governance and executive expertise. The actual extent to which these offices functioned differed, but this does not change the fact that ISIS tried to implement the Islamic State as an executive organisation governing the daily affairs of its population in the name of representing Muslims worldwide. ISIS's caliphate was not groundbreaking because of its Islamic ideology but because it created a direct link

Figure 5.4 Screenshot, governance structure of the ISIS caliphate.
Source: Islamic State in Iraq and Syria, 'Structure of the Caliphate'.

between individual Islamic identity and a bureaucratic state. They practised a distinct Islamic type of modern nation-state, where every Muslim, in theory, was automatically a citizen. Basing its national identity on individual religiosity, it challenged the established post-Westphalian world order where national identities relate to bounded geographical areas.

With ISIS's caliphate, the above was not just theoretical. Several interviewees said that, around 2014 and 2015, ISIS brought security to the territories it controlled, ended endemic corruption and implemented a strict but evenly applied legal framework.[86] One interviewee described how ISIS attempted to implement a new educational policy, aiming to minimise public discontent:

> [After ISIS took over] first classes continued as if nothing happened. [. . .] The same curriculum just without [the Syrian regime's] Baathist topics. Then they offered an Islamic course to teachers. After that they came into classes to check the 'proper Islamic character' of education. And only ten days ago [end of October 2015] they introduced a complete ISIS curriculum. [. . .] But you do not have to send your children as they are not enforcing attendance – not yet at least.[87]

Without exception, they also described the extreme violence ISIS used. One activist noted that after he fled to Gaziantep, his extended family, who remained in Raqqa, received a visit from ISIS security. His family had argued that ISIS had a problem with him, not with his family. They subsequently left his family alone. He said that, despite their brutality, in this case ISIS showed a more civilised face than the regime of Bashar al-Assad.[88] Multiple interviewees narrated their interactions with one or more of the various caliphate offices and described them as efficient.[89] The bureaucratic character of ISIS' caliphate was also reflected in the multiple troves of bureaucratic documents found after the collapse of ISIS in Iraq and Syria.[90]

ISIS's caliphate was confined by a religious community, not a national one. In the uproar around its establishment, ISIS transformed into a global organisation. There were groups from Saudi Arabia, Yemen, Egypt, Libya and Algeria that gave a *bay'ah*, or pledge of allegiance, to the group. In a propaganda clip from late 2015, ISIS boasted that it comprised thirty-five *wilāyāt*, or provinces: nineteen in Iraq and Syria and sixteen outside.[91] The extent that they had effective executive power in these provinces is doubtful. Nonetheless, it indicates its global character.[92] It was undeniable that the organisation made an impression with the brutal murders of James Foley and Ali al-Sayyed in August 2014, Steven Sotloff in September and several others throughout that year and the next. It was also undeniable that they could stage attacks across the world. Examples are the Corinthia Hotel attack in Libya in January 2015, the Tunisian Bardo and Sousse attacks in March and June and the Paris attacks of November that same year. Finally, it was undeniable that with these attacks ISIS successfully picked a fight with global powers. In September 2014, to address a perceived threat to their own national securities, an international coalition led by the United States intervened. Supported by the Syrian Democratic Forces, a Kurdish-led coalition in North Syria, the international coalition attacked ISIS and Nusra Front targets.

Challenging the Logic of Social Fields

As during the Tunisian transition, we saw that Sunni Islam turned into a distinct type of practice. First, we observed how, with the start of an armed insurgency, rebels used religion to establish distinctly Islamist, or jihadist, fighting factions that facilitated access to distinct support networks and a global pool of jihadist foreign fighters. Additionally, sharia courts disrupted the judiciary field in rebel-held territories by offering an alternative judicial framework that did not rely on codified law or a body of professional lawyers and judges. Distinctly Islamic service providers, such as the sharia committees, challenged control over day-to-day governance and facilitated a collapse of the division between courts, service providers and collective violence. At its most extreme, as with ISIS's caliphate, it challenged governance far beyond the boundaries of the Syrian crisis.

In all these cases, Sunni Islam acquired political relevance. Not because it provided a particular set of political ideas but because it sparked distinct initiatives related to collective violence, public services, education and the judiciary that reshaped access to symbolic, institutional and material resources. The rendering of rebel groups as jihadist provided access to global support networks, while the establishment of sharia courts reshaped access to judicial resources. Bridging collective violence, services and judicial practices based on an Islamic distinction nurtured a transformation of jihadist rebel factions. Ultimately, practising a Sunni Islamic distinction had direct, real world implications for access to political, institutional and educational resources. Islam turned political, or Islamist, not because of the particular ideas it provided, but because it was used to render practices distinct.

Taking Positions

When activists used Islam to create distinct practices, they turned it into a social and political stake. In the following section we will observe how, as a result, social interactions during the Syrian crisis became patterned along an Islamic distinction. We will see, first, how jihadists organised distinct types of rebel coalitions and published joint declarations denouncing civil governance organisations. Second, we observe how Islamists fought among themselves for control over sharia courts and committees, territorial control and, above all, the political representation of an Islamic community. These were conflicts to define how Islam could, and should, be translated into concrete distinctive practices in fields such as the judiciary, service provision and governance. These struggles set them apart during the Syrian crisis as belonging to an Islamist movement.

As noted in the previous chapter, by investigating contentious interactions around Islam as a social and political stake, we describe the construction of an Islamist movement in the broader historical and biographical context of the Syrian crisis. Their upbringings, experiences in past conflicts and life histories shaped the range of positions that activists took in conflict situations. Meanwhile, the Syrian context constrained the scope and effectiveness of their actions. As we will see, the development of an Islamist movement was very much shaped by the individual and contextual histories of the Syrian crisis.

Organising Collective Violence

A group of Islamist factions were becoming more powerful in the Syrian crisis – fast. The Nusra Front and Ahrar al-Sham would prove to be two among the most powerful and long-lasting throughout the crisis. But there were several others: Suqour al-Sham and Liwa al-Ummah in the Idlib region, the Ansar Brigade in Homs, the Tawheed Brigade and the Fajr al-Islam Movement in Aleppo are examples.[93] Most of these groups started out as local brigades, with the Nusra Front being one of the more important exceptions. Many became part, through unions and mergers, of nationwide rebel organisations. An Islamic distinctness increasingly shaped this consolidation of the organisation of collective violence.

One example was the formation of the Syrian Islamic Liberation Front in September 2012 that was announced by some of the most powerful rebel groups at the time: Suqour al-Sham in Idlib, the Farouq Battalions in Homs and the Tawheed Brigade in Aleppo. They described it as 'a front with an Islamic reference'.[94] The leadership of these factions, in contrast to Ahrar al-Sham and the Nusra Front, was not dominated by veterans of jihadist struggles. The military leader of the Tawheed Brigade, Abdul Qader Saleh, was a local merchant from Marea who, after completing his time as army conscript, had travelled to Jordan, Türkiye and Bangladesh to proselytise with the Dawa wa-Tabligh (an apolitical movement focused on proselytisation) before returning to Syria to start a family.[95] Both Suqour al-Sham and the Tawheed Brigade had received support from the Syrian Muslim Brotherhood controlled Civilian Protection Commission while also aligning themselves with the Supreme Military Council. The latter was a, US and Saudi Arabia initiated, effort to coordinate the organisation of collective violence of the insurgency.[96] Last but not least, despite its Islamist references, the Tawheed Brigade initially did not have an internal religious authority and took religious guidance from Muhammad Ali al-Sabuni, the president of the League of Syrian Ulema, an independent organisation.[97]

A second initiative was the Syrian Islamic Front. Announced in December 2012, it brought together eleven Islamist rebel factions. The dominant one was the Ahrar al-Sham Brigades; other notable factions that participated were Liwa al-Haqq, the Fajr al-Islamiya Movement, and the Ansar al-Sham Brigades.[98] They described themselves as a 'comprehensive Islamic reform front' that worked to defeat the Assad regime, build an Islamic civilisational society governed by Islamic Sharia and to foster Islam among its people and society.[99] They received much of their support from Kuwaiti donors. Ahrar al-Sham would soon reform from a brigade into a movement and use this description word-by-word as their own.[100]

When, in November 2013, the dominant factions of the Syrian Islamic Liberation Front and Syrian Islamic Front merged into the Islamic Front, it reflected both the ascendency of Ahrar al-Sham as a powerful jihadist faction and a further hardening of the Islamic distinction among the Syrian insurgency. In a context in which sectarian tensions were becoming increasingly pervasive, they explicitly rejected the notion of a secular state and full democracy and emphasised emphasised the supremacy of sharia. They never worked with the Supreme Military Council.[101] This hardening also reflected in joint statements from jihadist groups. On 24 September 2013, the Nusra Front, Ahrar al-Sham, the Tawheed Brigade and nine other groups declared they were comprehensive – civil and military – movements working within an 'Islamic frame' that only recognised sharia as a source of legislature. They denounced the SIG and SOC as foreign bodies that did not represent the domestic uprising.[102] The statement was met with an international outcry, and several groups distanced themselves from it in the days after. But it was the first time that these jihadist groups presented themselves together as a distinct collective against civil governance organisations.[103]

The creation of the Syrian Revolutionaries Front, on 9 December 2013, can be seen as part of this development: it was the consolidation of rebel factions supported by the US and Saudi Arabia, acting as counterweight to the growing influence of the Islamic Front, Ahrar al-Sham and the Nusra Front. Created by Jamal Maarouf, a well-known nationalist rebel leader, it had strong ties to the Supreme Military Council and its financial backer, Saudi Arabia. It also adopted a discourse challenging many of the non-Saudi supported rebel groups. Several jihadist factions soon perceived the Syrian Revolutionaries Front as a direct threat.[104] Describing it as a puppet of Saudi Arabia and Western regimes, within months the Nusra Front attacked their positions in the Idlib region.

As an Islamist movement shaped the dynamics of the Syrian insurgency, sharia courts rose in prominence as an accepted framework for conflict resolution between rebel groups. Because jihadist groups had internal religious authorities – such as sharia courts and councils with Islamic judges and sheikhs – they proved instrumental for arbitration and resolution of inter-Islamist conflicts. An infamous example is the (failed) religious court proposed by al-Zawahiri to arbitrate between the Nusra Front and ISIS.[105] Another is the sharia court proposed in September 2014 by the Islamic Front to mediate between the Nusra Front and the Syrian Revolutionaries Front.[106] Following the takeover of Idlib in 2015, the Nusra Front proposed a shared sharia court among the most powerful rebel groups.[107] In these cases, Islamist factions used religion as the basis for arbitration among participants of an armed insurgency. It was testament to the power of jihadist rebel factions among the Syrian insurgency.

A History of Syrian Islamic Activism

The development of an armed insurgency gives a first glimpse of the agents that had a stake in defining distinctly Islamic practices: Syrian Islamic scholars, Hassan Aboud of Ahrar al-Sham, al-Julani of the Nusra Front and the Muslim Brotherhood are a few examples. We cannot understand the positions these agents took without taking the history of the Syrian state and its political regime into account. Let us take a step back and briefly consider this history. We start with the 1963 coup d'état that brought the socialist Baath party to power and the 1970 'corrective movement' in which its Minister of Defence, Hafez al-Assad, outmanoeuvred, and neutralised, his rivals in the party. The rise of Hafez al-Assad would prove crucial in the development of an Islamist movement in Syria. An Alawi from the town of Qardaha, he embodied the ascendency of Alawi religious minorities in the Syrian army and political power.[108] Hafez stabilised his rule through informal relations (or *'aṣabīyah*) to his own tribe and extended family.[109] It meant that the Syrian regime under Hafez al-Assad had all the usual state institutions (a president, government, parliament, security services and an army) but that real power became vested in an informal network around the President that had particular regional, familial and sectarian characteristics.[110]

The Baath regime of Hafez al-Assad clashed with an Islamist movement in the mid-1970s. It set the stage for the emergence of organisations and individuals as we know them today. Starting out as an urban-based uprising, the Syrian Muslim Brotherhood (SMB) and continuously evolving, ill-defined offshoots became increasingly central to its development.[111] One infamous example was a young Muslim Brotherhood activist from Hama, Marwan Hadid, who became active in an armed group called the Fighting Vanguard. He drew directly on Sayyid Qutb's revolutionary approach but placed it in the sectarian Syrian context by framing their uprising as a jihad against an Alawi, apostate regime.[112] Countering this sectarian language, others in the SMB instead emphasised an aim for a democratic and multifaith Syria.[113] As a result, the uprising not only challenged the Syrian regime but also laid bare the internal schisms inside the SMB. The organisation fractured along a Damascene and Aleppine branch on one side, favouring more pragmatic and liberal political strategies, and on the other side, a Homs and Hama branch, favouring more radical activism. The uprising climaxed in February 1982 in the city of Hama. Jihadist fighters provoked the army (although accounts differ) into a violent response. The army ended up shelling civilian quarters and shooting whole families, even after they had pacified the town.[114]

Islamists found themselves chased out of the country and scattered across the Arab world and Europe. Tarif al-Sayed Issa, a Muslim Brotherhood member, took part in protests in his home town, Idlib, and received military training. Following his exile, after years of wandering the region, he ended up settling in Sweden.[115] In 1981, Osama al-Rifai, the eldest son of Karim al-Rifai, a well-known Syrian sheikh, fled to Saudi Arabia.[116] So did Adnan al-Aroor, an unknown sheikh from Hama, in 1982. During the 1990s, slowly but steadily, the regime released activists and allowed exiles to return. Osama al-Rifai returned to Syria in the late 1990s. Meanwhile, several religious sheikhs who had supported the regime, chief among them being Ramadan al-Bouti and Ahmad Kuftaro, acquired powerful positions. Al-Bouti became the dean of the Faculty of Sharia at the University of Damascus between 1977 and 1983 and kept prominent academic and religious positions throughout his life. Ahmed Kuftaro became Grand Mufti of Syria, and his religious school in the capital became one of the largest in the country.[117] Following his death, he was succeeded by another regime supporting sheikh: Ahmad Hassoun.

In June 2000, Bashar al-Assad succeeded his father as president. The first decade of his rule reshaped the position of the above groups in relation to the regime. First, Bashar's ascent seemed to herald a more liberal era with increased civil and political freedoms. Technocrats took over in government, protectionist policies were reformed and opportunities were created for new private enterprises. For instance, Syriatel was founded in 2000 and became one of the largest mobile phone and internet providers in the country. Political salons started across the capital in which opposition figures openly discussed social, economic and political issues.[118] Encouraged by these reforms, the Syrian Muslim Brotherhood, with its more liberal Aleppo branch in power, engaged with reemerging opposition movements and emphasised its own democratic outlook. In a charter from 2004, they reiterated their support for democratic elections and Syrian Nationalism.[119] A more liberal Syria seemed possible.

When domestic opposition figures demanded substantial political reforms, the regime backtracked on its liberalisations, had all the political salons closed and activists jailed.[120] The liberalised economic field ended up mirroring the power structures of the political regime. Syriatel, as one example, was owned by Rami Makhlouf, the maternal cousin of Bashar al-Assad, reflecting the economic power of several families with close ties to the regime. The episode also impacted the Muslim Brotherhood internally: its political strategies having failed, the Aleppo branch and its leader Ali Bayanuni were sidelined within the SMB, in favour of the Homs/Hama branch.[121]

Meanwhile, following the 2003 Iraq invasion, some in the American administration mentioned Syria as a subsequent target for democratisation. The Syrian regime reacted by allowing youngsters to travel to Iraq and fight a jihad there. With the SMB destroyed domestically, these youngsters had few, if any, links to the organisation or opposition sheikhs. One imam in Aleppo, Abu Qaqa, became infamous for his fiery speeches railing against the US occupation and calling for a jihad against them. Buses full of youngsters travelled straight from Syrian cities to Iraq to fight American and allied forces.[122] Hassan Aboud (who ended up establishing Ahrar al-Sham) was one of them. The same went for Abu Muhammad al-Julani and Abu Muhammad al-Adnani: the former became the leader of the Nusra Front, the latter its spokesperson. Hashem al-Sheikh, who became the leader of Ahrar al-Sham after Hassan Aboud was killed, never left Syria but facilitated jihadist's travels to Iraq.[123] After 2005, when many of the jihadists returned, the regime immediately incarcerated them at a prison in Sednaya, a town close to the capital Damascus. In July 2008, frustrated with their treatment and incarceration, prisoners in Sednaya rose up, took their guards hostage and took control of the prison. The regime violently repressed the uprising, killing dozens of inmates and hostages.[124]

It was not the only crisis the regime faced. In 2005 Rafiq Hariri was assassinated. He was a Lebanese construction tycoon, turned Prime Minister, who returned from Saudi Arabia to Lebanon after the Lebanese Civil War

(1975–90). The reconstruction of war-ravaged Lebanon proved to be a hugely lucrative market, and the Syrian regime supported Hariri's position as he proved proficient in opening up corrupt construction deals to Syrian, regime-linked elites. Just before his assassination, he had turned more critical of his Syrian patrons. Hezbollah, the powerful Shia Lebanese party, was implicated in the assassination. It highlighted how relations between Iran, Hezbollah and the Syrian regime had strengthened through years of international political isolation. For instance, Syria supported Hezbollah by shipping Iranian weapons to South Lebanon, increasing their importance as a negotiation partner, while gaining legitimacy as one of the last Arab countries continuing armed opposition to Israel.[125]

Finally, to stave off civil unrest that these crises might create, the regime allowed various Islamic social initiatives. After his return from exile, Osama al-Rifai built a popular charity movement in Damascus, the Zayd movement.[126] The Qubaysiyat, an Islamic women's movement led by Munira al-Qubaysi (1933–2022), took over an increasing number of Islamic schools in and around Damascus.[127] During this period, the number of students in Islamic schools increased rapidly (see Figure 5.5).[128] While at pains to situate themselves as nonpolitical agents, several of these sheikhs were engaged with the regime to further, and safeguard, their social and educational activities.[129] It turned them into a crucial element in Syrian state–society relations.

Remnants of a splintered Muslim Brotherhood, powerful Islamic charity movements and incarcerated jihadists in Sednaya prison were agents that were not so much the product of particular Islamist ideas but of particular historical trajectories. The Syrian Muslim Brotherhood emerged from a field of associational organising following independence, but was infused with a jihadist element through the uprising of the 1970s. Together with the exile of many of its members, it nurtured its internal fragmentation. Meanwhile, the field of post-independent associational organising also gave birth to powerful charitable movements and Sunni sheikhs who engaged with the Syrian regime to safeguard and expand their social initiatives. And, more recently, the Syrian regime allowed youngsters to organise and travel to Iraq to fight in a jihad there. In the process they gained experience with a global jihadist movement. It is these trajectories that gave birth to the agents that we saw as having a stake in defining the position of Islam in the Syrian crisis. They found themselves in a context

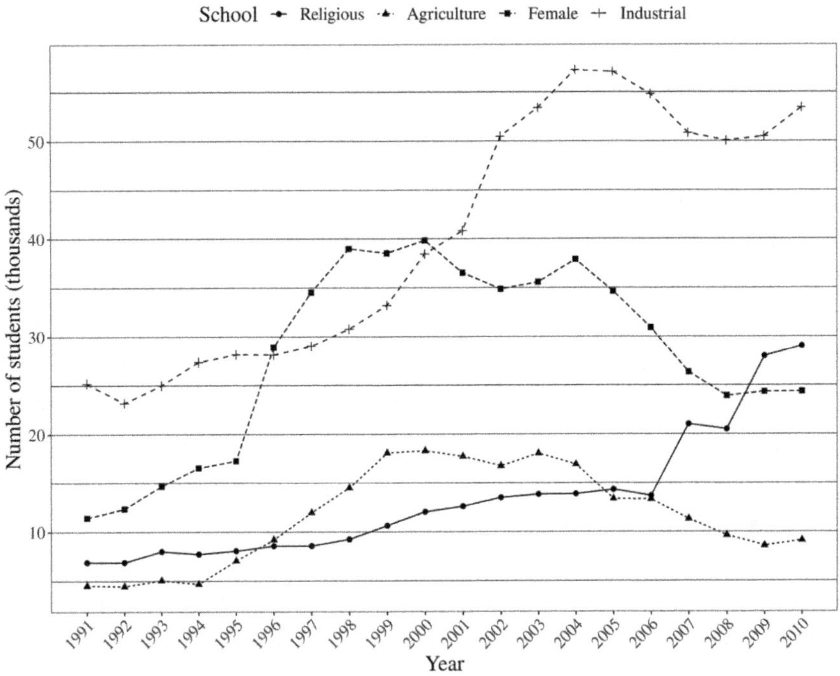

Figure 5.5 School attendance in Syria per school type.
Source: Statistical Abstract Syria, 2011.

shaped by regional forces: Iran was increasingly supporting the Syrian regime, Syria's relationship to Lebanon was being reformed and Syria had become involved in the Iraqi civil war and agitated the United States and its allies.

The War of Courts

As Islam turned into something that mattered in the Syrian crisis, conflicts emerged between those agents that had a stake in its use to render practices distinct. Islamists fought among themselves, for example, for control over sharia courts, sharia committees and, above all, the political representation of an Islamic community. They pitted individuals, such as Osama al-Rifai, Hassan Aboud, al-Julani and al-Adnani, and organisations, such as the Syrian Islamic Council, Ahrar al-Sham, the Nusra Front, the SMB and ISIS, against each other. These conflicts brought this diverse set of agents together into an Islamist movement.

As rebels established sharia courts as alternatives to a civil judiciary, any semblance of a unified legal system in Aleppo (and rebel held territories more widely) collapsed. As a response to the resulting judicial chaos, in October 2012, several rebel factions established the Integrated Judicial Council of Aleppo (IJCA). It aimed to unify legal systems among the opposition by unifying the assignment of judges, providing a unified code of law and integrating courts into a single institutional structure. The council itself comprised ten *shar'īyīn* (religious legal scholars), seven lawyers and three judges.[130] Courts linked to the council consisted of one lawyer and two sheikhs that were hired based on their legal, professional knowledge.[131] As a code of law, it eventually adopted the Unified Arab Penal Code, providing a legal framework aiming to incorporate both sharia and Arab law. At its inception, numerous rebel factions in Aleppo signed a declaration in its support.[132] Exceptions were Ahrar al-Sham and the Nusra Front, which did not recognise the IJCA as it drew on the Unified Arab Penal Code; they argued that Islamic law could not be codified nor combined with secular law. The Syrian Interim Government (SIG) aligned with the IJCA as judiciary in North Syria. It paid salaries and provided financial support for its services.[133]

This attempt to unify the judiciary in Aleppo only led to more conflict. In February 2013, the Sharia Committee in Aleppo used its police force to attack the offices of the IJCA and took many of its lawyers and other employees to a base of the Nusra Front – reportedly for refusing to hand over newly refurbished offices.[134] The Nusra Front released the employees after several hours. Subsequent attempts to resolve their differences through an adjudication committee were, apparently, ignored by the Sharia Committee.[135] In November 2013, another attack followed when the Fastaqim Union, one of the many rebel factions active in Aleppo, attacked the IJCA offices and effectively ended its work.[136] A similar struggle occurred in September 2012 between a sharia committee and the IJCA in al-Bab, north of Aleppo.[137] It did not help that the SIG provided little actual support throughout this period: the IJCA complained they had received only 5 per cent of requested funds.[138]

With the insurrection and its rebel groups increasingly defining the dynamics of the Syrian crisis, the sheikhs and *'ulamā'* that supported the nationalist, and democratic, uprising – such as Usama al-Rifai – were left increasingly sidelined. It showed in a lack of influence over sharia committees and courts. Tellingly, in a December 2013 interview, Osama al-Rifai, the Syrian imam from Damascus who fled to Türkiye, complained that:

> We are in touch with the larger sharia committees [inside Syria]. We have shared projects with them about Islamic knowledge and religious rulings. But how is it possible to engage with every sharia committee [and its courts] in the country? Almost every small town with between four and five thousand inhabitants established a sharia committee. It is impossible to keep up with all their religious rulings.[139]

He lamented that many who fought in name of Islam became arrogant when wielding the power of a gun. Osama al-Rifai might have argued it was because of arrogance that these fighters strayed from an established body of religious knowledge, but it is safe to state that it was not out of arrogance but in the effort to control a judiciary field that these struggles for control over sharia rulings emerged. Al-Rifai continued that he and the scholars of the Association of Syrian *'Ulamā'* would not stand idly by. Despite describing himself as a nonpolitical, religious agent, he made clear they would act to defend Syrian religion from these, in his view, corrupting influences.[140]

To regain influence in a Syrian religious field, in April 2014 several prominent Syrian *ulamā'* established the Syrian Islamic Council (SIC). The council intended to unify religious authority in rebel held territories, drawing on sharia 'following the approach of the Qur'an and Sunnah for the Syrian people'[141] and provide a counterweight to non-Syrian Salafist movements in the country.[142] Osama al-Rifai was one of its founders. Ratib, the sheikh from Daraa, became a senior member of the organisation. Meanwhile, a former senior representative of the Syrian Muslim Brotherhood argued that the group had instigated and supported the founding of the SIC.[143] It was impossible to verify this claim, but it is safe to state that it was an attempt by the sidelined *ulamā'* to regain influence over how religion was used in the Syrian uprising and insurgency. Osama al-Rifai, who became the President of the SIC, emphasised its domestic reach at its inauguration in Istanbul, Türkiye:

> The Syrian Islamic Council is a group that incorporates all the *'ulamā'* associations and sharia committees on our beloved Syrian land. To provide

the services that they can provide to the Syrian people. There are just a few smaller sharia committees that the executive council could not reach.[144]

Another scholar present at the meeting, Abd al-Karim Bakkar, toned down this claim by clarifying that the council represented forty sharia committees at its inception and that the 'largest military factions [were] represented in the council'.[145] The aim to unify religious authority implied that the SIC was an effort to separate religious authority from the politics of rebel infighting. Reflecting this attempt, it soon supported the implementation of the Unified Arab Penal Code. It was the same code the IJCA had previously followed in Aleppo. By implementing a codified legal framework, it took away authority from individual Islamic judges and scholars to freely interpret sharia and create fatwas as they saw fit. Even though the council presented itself as a nonpolitical umbrella organisation for sharia committees, this was very much a political programme. Ahrar al-Sham initially joined the Council but pulled out ten days later after Ayman Abu al-Tut, the chief religious scholar of Ahrar al-Sham, failed to be elected into its executive board. Without direct influence, Ahrar al-Sham expected the Council to end up challenging its own internal religious authorities. It was something they did not allow to happen. Zahran Alloush, whose Army of Islam also initially participated, decried that the SIC was not more outspoken about the threat of Alawites and Shias, using derogative sectarian terms while doing so.[146] The Nusra Front never even considered taking part. The extent that the SIC impacted the dynamics of the Syrian crisis was questionable. For now, at least.

The War of Committees

Besides a struggle for control over courts, a battle over sharia committees occurred. In Aleppo, for example, power was divided among multiple rebel groups that each had control over certain neighbourhoods. This fragmented power structure led, initially at least, to inter-jihadist cooperation in establishing the Sharia Committee. The four most powerful jihadist factions in Aleppo at the time – Suqur al-Sham, the Nusra Front, Ahrar al-Sham and the Tawheed Brigade – founded it in December 2012.[147] This cooperation soon turned to competition as rebel groups vied for control over the city. As the Nusra Front turned into one of the most powerful groups at the start of

2013, it quickly strengthened its hold over the Committee. A sheikh affiliated with the Nusra Front, for example, led the Judicial Office; the same was true for the Office of Public Service Provision.[148] It rendered the Sharia Committee effectively the judicial and executive arm of the Nusra Front in Aleppo and, more widely, North Syria.[149]

Similar struggles for control played out when the Committee expanded to al-Firdous, al-Sukari, Hraytan, al-Bab, Azaz and Anadan and when new committees were established in the countryside of Idlib, in Binnish, Bab al-Hawa and Sarmada. Ahrar al-Sham, for example, took control of the Sharia Committee in Binnish. The same held for many other, smaller sharia committees in the Idlib countryside. Although they presented themselves as independent and supported by a coalition of rebel factions, sharia committees were increasingly controlled by one particular rebel group – with Ahrar al-Sham or the Nusra Front being most often in charge.[150]

There were similar conflicts in many, if not all, rebel-controlled areas. In each case, they reflected local crises dynamics. Eastern Ghouta, just east of the capital Damascus, found itself under siege early on. It led to a dynamic where one jihadist rebel faction, the Army of Islam under Sednaya alumnus Zahran Alloush, turned hegemonic. The Army of Islam placed its religious legal scholars in the Sharia Committee and took control. At the same time, a strong civil local council, providing crucial services, kept its independence for a long time against the Army of Islam dominated Sharia Committee.[151] In Armanaz, a conflict between the sharia committee and local council ended up with an agreement that the former would only deal with military affairs.[152]

Following the takeover of Raqqa, in March 2013, rebel groups were instead enjoying the fruits of controlling a provincial capital and all its resources. Ahrar al-Sham took over a public hospital and the central bank, the Nusra Front took over the governorate building and the Ahfad Rusul Brigades, a smaller local jihadist group, made the old train station their headquarters.[153] Numerous families, according to a member of the former local council of Raqqa, flocked to the various rebel factions in search of security – which meant that their size and power increased rapidly.[154] Here, the rebel factions involved (the Nusra Front, Ahrar al-Sham and the Ahfad Rusul Brigades) did not create a strong sharia committee. There seems to have been little incentive to do so.

Ahl Al-Ḥall Wa-Al-ʿaqd

Struggles to control distinctly Islamic services, judicial and governance practices were turning increasingly central to the developments of the Syrian crisis. They were about to become more central still. Abu Bakr al-Bagdadi, the leader of the Islamic State in Iraq, had become increasingly agitated about the autonomy and strength of the Nusra Front in the Syrian crisis. He received backchannel information – from, among others, Abu Muhammad al-Adnani, the Nusra Front's spokesperson – that noted al-Julani was turning increasingly pragmatic and independent in his policies.[155] On 8 April 2013, al-Baghdadi published a speech in which he made the, previously secret, relationship between the Nusra Front and the Islamic State in Iraq public, and clarified that they sent al-Julani to establish a jihadist organisation in the Syrian battlefield.[156] He continued:

> The Nusra Front is but an extension of the Islamic State in Iraq and is part of it. [. . .] As such, trusting God, we declare we cancel the names 'the Islamic State in Iraq' and 'the Nusra Front'. We unify them under the name of 'The Islamic State in Iraq and Syria'.[157]

It was the creation of ISIS. Al-Julani was not amused. The next day he declared that al-Baghdadi had not consulted him on the decision, and he had to hear it from the news. He stated that with this lack of informed consent, the establishment of the organisation was illegitimate.[158] He continued:

> I respond to the call of al-Baghdadi [with . . .] a renewed pledge of allegiance from the members of the Nusra Front and their General Official to the sheikh of jihad Ayman al-Zawahiri [of al-Qaeda]. The banner of the Front will remain as it is and nothing will change.[159]

In short, al-Julani confirmed his role as Syrian representative of a global jihad and al-Qaeda while taking away legitimacy of Baghdadi's state project. Ayman al-Zawahiri (1951–2022) himself soon entered the conflict by ordering the two organisations to remain separate entities aimed at Iraq and Syria, respectively.[160] Al-Baghdadi ignored the statements. Marouan described what happened next:

> Most of Nusra's fighters in Aleppo went straight to ISIS. Little was left of the Nusra Front. In the end it meant that Aleppo was emptying, and that ISIS could take over numerous neighbourhoods [. . .]. They did not create a sharia committee or something similar. They were the state. A state with dedicated offices for x, y or z. It was clear the situation was untenable, but the remaining rebel factions had trouble opposing ISIS. They had appropriated the jihadist identity, which made it challenging to fight them.[161]

As ISIS aggressively expanded its influence on the Syrian battlefield, it came into conflict with an ever-increasing number of rebel factions. A sharia court was proposed to adjudicate between ISIS and other jihadist groups, but ISIS never showed up. Representatives of ISIS noted that as they were the institutional representation of Islam, it was impossible to subject oneself to a sharia court that was not part of its own state structure.[162] After ISIS tortured and killed a popular leader of Ahrar al-Sham at the end of 2013, multiple rebel factions created an alliance, the Army of Mujahideen, which successfully challenged the group. ISIS retreated from Aleppo on 2 March 2014 and from Idlib and the Latakia provinces on 16 March.[163] The attack on ISIS could not hide the fact that rebel factions lost much of their control over Syrian territory. As shown in graph 5.2 at the start of this chapter, in March 2013 they controlled almost 40 per cent of Syrian territory; a year later this was down to approximately 10 per cent – much of it because of ISIS takeovers.

The rise of ISIS directly resulted from Islamist infighting – between the Nusra Front and the Islamic State in Iraq – about representing a global jihadist movement in a localised, national insurgency. This tension, and related fights, further escalated with the declaration of the founding of an Islamic caliphate. On Friday 27 June 2014, al-Adnani (previously the spokesperson of the Nusra Front) published a speech in his new role as the spokesperson of the Islamic State in Iraq and Sham. Titled 'the Promise of Allah', he narrated that generations of Muslims 'were drowning in oceans of disgrace' but that 'the time has come for the ummah of Muhammad to wake up from its sleep' and that 'the sun of jihad has risen', now that 'the flag of the Islamic State, the flag of unity, rises and flutters and covers the land from Aleppo to Diyala'.[164] There was but one obligation, he stated, that remained unfulfilled: the creation of a caliphate.

And now that ISIS had the 'essentials necessary for a caliphate', it would be 'sinful if they do not establish' it. He continued:

> The Islamic State – represented by *ahl al-ḥall wa-al-ʿaqd*, comprising its senior figures, leaders, and the Shura Council – resolved to announce the establishment of the Islamic caliphate and the appointment of a caliph for Muslims, and the pledge of allegiance to the sheikh al-Baghdadi. He has accepted the *bay'ah* [pledge of allegiance]. Thus, he is the imam and caliph for Muslims everywhere. The 'Iraq and Sham' in the name of the Islamic State is henceforth removed from all official deliberations and communications, and the official name is the Islamic State from the date of this declaration.[165]

The notion of *ahl al-ḥall wa-al-ʿaqd*, or 'those that loosen and bind' denotes the individuals qualified to appoint and depose a caliph. They represent the authority of the Sunni community as they pledged allegiance to al-Baghdadi.[166] Al-Adnani made clear in no uncertain terms what this implied:

> We clarify to Muslims that with this declaration of a caliphate, it is incumbent upon all Muslims to pledge allegiance to the caliph Ibrahim [al-Baghdadi] and support him. The expansion of the caliphate's authority and arrival of its troops to their areas renders the legality of all emirates, groups, states, and organisations, null and void.[167]

The statement was a direct challenge to al-Qaeda, the Nusra Front, Ahrar al-Sham and other jihadist groups. It sent shock waves through the Syrian opposition and across the world. The reply from al-Julani did not take long. Without mentioning the group by name, he declared on 11 July that the Nusra Front was establishing emirates in various parts of Syria, to apply *ḥudūd* laws, safeguard the rights of Muslims and protect their dignity and sanctities in Syria. Instead of implementing an Islamic State based on a global Sunni Islamic identity, the Nusra Front implemented localised governance in name of a global jihadist movement – al-Qaeda – to serve the Syrian people.[168]

In August, a reply from al-Qaeda followed. Rather hopefully titled *An End to the Discussion on the Caliphate*, it first attacked the declaration of a caliphate for lacking religious legitimacy. There was no transparency on who was consulted prior to the declaration, and only those close to the group had been involved. Whatever way you interpreted the notion of *ahl al-ḥall wa-al-ʿaqd*, it did not conform with how ISIS used it.[169] Second, the statement attacked ISIS for the level of its executive power. When considering the Taliban in Afghanistan and Ansar al-Sharia in Yemen, there was no basis to claim that ISIS represented the overarching executive body that legitimated the declaration of a global caliphate.[170] In a subsequent rebuttal, a senior ISIS scholar argued these requirements rendered the establishment of a caliphate impossible: it was not possible to find a consensus among the *ahl al-ḥall wa-al-ʿaqd* globally. This also did not happen in Muhammad's time. One can only find consensus, he argued, among those already under your control.[171]

Ahrar al-Sham could not sit idly by and let the fight between the Nusra Front and ISIS define the dynamics of jihadism in the country. Less than two weeks after al-Julani's emirate declaration, the group sent out a statement that 'Any declaration of creating a caliphate, emirate or government on Syrian land was not the choice of the Syrian people and not a decision of the *ahl al-ḥall wa-al-ʿaqd*. These decisions are void and carry no authority'. They argued that these statements would only help empower the regime's position in the Syrian crisis.[172] Barely two months later, on 9 September 2014, an explosion hit a top level, secret meeting of Ahrar al-Sham. It decimated its leadership. Hassan Aboud was among those killed. The cause of the explosion remains unknown, but many suspect either ISIS or the Nusra Front.[173]

The SIC and its religious scholars also did not stay quiet. In a lengthy statement, they outlined that the only community that ISIS's *ahl al-ḥall wa-al-ʿaqd* could represent was that of the areas under their control. In other words, the boundaries of ISIS's monopoly of violence defined the Muslim community providing religious legitimacy to their global caliphate. Scholars of the SIC were not buying it: 'How can a pledge of allegiance by the *ahl al-ḥall wa-al-ʿaqd* represent the will of the Muslim community when that community itself was created through oppression and force?'[174] That there were numerous scholars opposing the announcement of a caliphate was testament to its illegitimacy. 'The announced "Islamic State" only represents itself. In reality, it is a transgressive unjust group that does not represent the ummah and contradicts reliable and trustworthy *ʿulamāʾ* of the ummah. It is a waste of the blessed jihad in Syria'.[175]

The struggle around the notion of *ahl al-ḥall wa-al-ʿaqd* revolved around a question of representation. On what basis did a central authority represent a population? It is one of the most basic questions in the development of nation-states: how to construct and maintain the hyphen between the collective identity of a nation and the centralised authority of a state? ISIS's caliphate brought up a question of the role of Islam in constructing and maintaining this hyphen. ISIS itself, reflecting their global revolutionary zeal, maintained there was no problem: Islam superseded any earthly political authority and collective identities and would, therefore, neatly and completely overlap in their Islamic State. Others, from the Nusra Front to the Syrian *ulamāʾ*, vehemently objected. It provided a topic around which a distinct set of agents – those that had a stake in defining the relationship between Islam and collective identity – set themselves apart from others during the Syrian crisis.

Reforming Sharia Courts and Committees

In Aleppo, the defection of many of Nusra's rank and file to ISIS left the rebel group, and the Sharia Committee, weakened. To make matters worse, when several rebel groups created, at the start of 2014, the anti-ISIS Army of Mujahideen, it did not include the Nusra Front. The coalition drove ISIS out of Aleppo and subsequently reformed the weakened Sharia Committee into a Supreme Islamic Court. Apart from its judiciary arm, they placed all its services under the control of the local council. But the local council lacked the support of one or more rebel factions. The Nusra Front tried to save what it could. It spun off the Office of Public Service Provision of the Sharia Committee into an independent organisation: the General Management of Services.[176] Despite being weakened, it began a steady campaign of taking over buildings and equipment that were crucial to service provision and placing them under its control. For instance, the water and electricity booster station in the Bab al-Nairab neighbourhood and Suleiman al-Halabi would for years be under their control.[177] Also, the only vehicle for repairing electricity cables in the city would for a long time be in the hands of the General Management of Services – not the local council.[178] It turned into a simmering proxy war over the provision of services in the city.

In addition, following al-Julani's declaration of establishing an emirate in July 2014, the Nusra Front established a new sharia court system, the *Dar al-Qadaa* or House of Judges, in the Idlib province.[179] These courts were an alternative to other sharia courts and challenged their authority. In Maarat al-Numan, the sharia court was taken over by force, and in other towns they were subject to overt or covert attempts at subjugation. The Dar al-Qadaa courts began handing out increasingly invasive rulings, ordering the closure of cafés for example. It also ordered the closure of civil police stations in Hraytan in north Aleppo (because of their affiliations to 'foreign factions'), dissolution of several local councils and the arrest of rival rebel leaders from, for example, the Syrian Revolutionaries Movement (October 2014) and the Hazzm Movement (March 2015).[180] It ended with the Nusra Front attacking and eventually destroying these two groups.

In this context, and following the September 2014 explosion that killed much of its leadership, Ahrar al-Sham attempted to position itself as a moderate jihadist agent and distance itself from ISIS and the Nusra Front. Within twenty-four hours after the explosion, its Shura Council assigned Abu Jaber al-Sheikh as General Leader of the group. Another alumnus of the Sednaya prison, the regime detained him in 2005 for facilitating jihadist's travel to Iraq. The regime released him in 2011. He had risen through the ranks of Ahrar al-Sham and was the head of its Shura Council prior to the explosion. In the following year, as Ahmad Abazeid, a Syrian researcher, has detailed, the movement transformed its articulation of being a jihadist movement in the Syrian uprising. From being a campaign around the *Mashrū' al-Ummah*, or the Project of the Ummah, Ahrar al-Sham went to one revolving around the title of *Thawrat al-Sha'b,* or the People's Revolution. It highlighted a shift toward positioning the movement as a moderate, nationalist alternative to transnational jihadist groups such as the Nusra Front and ISIS.[181]

In March 2015, the Nusra Front, Ahrar al-Sham, Faylaq al-Sham and several other groups joined forces in a coalition named Jaish al-Fateh, or Army of Conquest. The coalition was, reportedly, supported by Saudi Arabia and Qatar – who had earlier been at loggerheads – and was created with the aim of conquering Idlib and the surrounding regions.[182] With rebel factions increasing pressure on the city throughout 2014, the Army of Conquest proved successful after a lightning offensive.[183] It was only the second regional capital, after Raqqa, that was captured by rebel forces. Tarif al-Sayed Issa, the Muslim Brother who had lived in exile in Sweden and founded the Sanabil al-Kheir association on his return to the region in 2011, was there:

> When I realised that there would be an operation to liberate Idlib city, I changed roles. I began working with an armed group in the Army of Conquest called Faylaq al-Sham, which contains some people from the Muslim Brotherhood. They made me field commander of a small unit. I had already received military training in the 1980s, when the Muslim Brotherhood first rose up against Hafez al-Assad. Now, I took a short refresher course in a training camp that had been established before the Idlib operation.[184]

The attack did not stop there. In the months after, Jisr al-Shughur, a town to the south of Idlib, was also captured as well as several other regions and towns in the area. With support of Jordan, a new front opened in the south of the country. It threatened regime control of Daraa. As rebel forces expanded their area of control around Idlib, they opened up the coastal region – the heartland of the Syrian regime – to attack from rebel forces. It seemed the regime was close to exhaustion and had trouble replenishing its ranks.[185] Increasing coordination between Islamist rebel factions and their patrons – Türkiye, Saudi Arabia and Qatar – seemed to have its impact.

The rebel offensive had several unintended, negative consequences. First, the attack resulted in control of areas with many religious minorities. Some rebel factions, and especially the Nusra Front, became increasingly aggressive toward these groups. Rebels laid siege to the Shia majority towns of Kafraya and Fu'ah, for example, and the Nusra Front killed dozens of Druze in the town of Qalb Loze (apparently after an altercation about the confiscation of a house by the group). Second, with some of the heartland of regime support under threat, Russia intervened in September 2015. Although officially to support the fight against terrorism, it was soon clear that most attacks were targeting various rebel factions fighting the Assad regime. Finally, it showed how the Nusra Front embedded itself within the Syrian uprising. The Nusra Front, designated a terrorist organisation by the US and affiliated with al-Qaeda, was working together within the Army of Conquest with a wide range of rebel factions, including those supported by Qatar and Saudi Arabia. Having had the experience of losing weapons donated to the now defunct Supreme Military

Council to Ahrar al-Sham (and subsequently the Nusra Front) it led to intense pressure from the US and EU to control arms supplies. Aid to rebel factions decreased while they were coming under attack from Russia.

Despite these setbacks, Idlib needed to be governed. As had been the case in other cities, rebel factions established their own executive organisations. There was the Civil Service Administration of the Army of Conquest, the General Administration of Services of the Nusra Front and the Committee of Service Administration of Ahrar al-Sham. This was besides the local council and SIG related civil society organisations.[186] There were also numerous charitable organisations active in Idlib. One of these organisations was Sanabil al-Kheir: the organisation co-founded by Tarif al-Sayed Issa. He rejoined the association following the liberation of his hometown Idlib.[187]

In Aleppo, meanwhile, attempts to unify courts continued. In July 2015, the Supreme Judicial Council was established which, according to themselves, controlled approximately 90 per cent of sharia courts in Aleppo and its countryside: all courts except those that were controlled by Ahrar al-Sham and the Nusra Front. The court applied the Unified Arab Penal Code to rein in the fragmented character of judicial rulings.[188] Several FSA-affiliated rebel factions, for example Nour al-Din al-Zenki, supported it. Eventually the Supreme Islamic Court in Aleppo, the remnant of the Sharia Committee in Aleppo, merged with the Supreme Judicial Council in September 2016.[189] With the provision of services, a simmering proxy war continued. The local council accused the General Management of Services of selectively providing services, refusing cooperation with the council and leaving whole neighbourhoods – literally – in the dark.[190] The General Management answered that it was at least trying but was severely constrained by circumstances in the city.[191] With increasing Russian bombardments and as the rebel lines collapsed around Aleppo in November 2016, this enduring conflict stopped in its tracks as any form of normality (which the regime had already heavily degraded through the constant use of barrel bombs on the city) collapsed during the final regime assault on rebel-held neighbourhoods.

Practising Islamist Movement

When rebels gained control of several territories across Syria, conflicts ensued over how to provide services, administer justice and govern these territories. It led to conflicts among those with vested interests in the use of Islam to render these practices distinct. The establishment of distinctly Islamic sharia courts, for example, triggered a struggle for control over this alternative judicial field, especially around the use of Unified Arab Law. The creation of sharia committees, in turn, meant the establishment of an alternative institutional framework for public service provision besides that of the SIG and local councils. It provoked a struggle between jihadist rebel groups, notably between the Nusra Front and Ahrar al-Sham, for control over these organisations. Finally, the involvement of Islamist rebel groups in local governance sparked a debate around the relationship between an Islamic collective identity and executive power – for example around the notion of *ahl al-ḥall wa-al-ʿaqd*. These inter-Islamist conflicts involved individuals such as Osama al-Rifai, Abdul Qader Saleh, Hassan Aboud, al-Julani, al-Adnani and organisations such as the Syrian Islamic Council, Ahrar al-Sham, the Nusra Front, the SMB and ISIS. Using Islam to render practices distinct brought them together into what we now can identify as an Islamist movement.

These individuals all had their own personal experiences in relation to such a movement. Osama al-Rifai had been exiled in the 1980s and returned to Syria to set up a large charitable movement. Abdul Qader Saleh had been involved with Dawa wa-Tabligh. Tarif al-Sayed Issa participated as a Muslim Brotherhood member in the domestic uprising of the 1980s, finding himself in exile for the three decades after that. Hassan Aboud, al-Julani and al-Adnani had experience with the jihadist uprising against the US invasion of Iraq, with the former returning to Syria in 2005 and being incarcerated at Sednaya. Al-Julani and al-Adnani remained in Iraq and rose through the ranks of the Islamic State in Iraq. In each case, the positions they took was informed by their prior experiences. We will discuss these positions, and related biographies, in more detail in Chapter six.

The Decline of an Islamist Movement

As with the Tunisian transition, an Islamist movement did not last. On 10 December 2017, Muhamad Ahmad al-Sheikh, previously the president of the Idlib University, sent out a communique as the President of the newly established Syrian Salvation Government. It read:

> Statement No.1: To the Syrian Interim Government. We warn you to close all your remaining offices in the liberated areas, and evacuate all your individual assets – and do this within seventy-two hours of this statement.[192]

To understand what the Salvation Government was, why al-Sheikh sent this communique and what it meant for an Islamist movement during the Syrian crisis, we need to consider the political developments in opposition-held territories from 2016 onward. With decreasing foreign support and under Russian attack, rebel forces had several setbacks. Zabadani, a city north-west of Damascus and close to the border of Lebanon, surrendered to the regime in September 2015. The rebel-held neighbourhoods of Aleppo fell to the regime in December 2016. In both cases, rebel fighters, activists and many inhabitants were bussed to Idlib in the framework of their negotiated surrender. Despite the territory under control of ISIS diminishing sharply between March 2016 and March 2018 (see Figure 5.2 at the start of this chapter), this did not translate into an increase in rebel-held territory: it was the US backed, and Kurdish led, Syrian Democratic Forces and the Syrian regime that profited most.

The changing fortunes of rebel factions had several knock-on effects on the influence of foreign powers in the crisis. Fearing a spillover of Kurdish fighters into its territory, Türkiye invaded Syria in August 2016 and created a security zone north of Aleppo, running from Azaz in the north to al-Bab in the south and Jarabulus in the east. Türkiye led the invasion, with support from multiple Syrian rebel factions. It meant that Türkiye became a fourth country, next to the US, Iran and Russia, with a sizable military presence in the country. Meanwhile, the politics of the Syrian opposition turned poisonous. A Homs activist turned SIG representative noted that:

> There was a meeting at the beginning of 2015 in Cairo that was heavily supported by Russia and in which they invited a subset of members from the Syrian Opposition Coalition [SOC] . The meeting resulted in a split between a Russia and non-Russia backed opposition in the Coalition. Russia began to label parts of the Coalition and Free Syrian Army as terrorists. [. . .] How can you work in such a situation? I used to say I loved the democratic character of the Coalition. We would fight about issues in a meeting, and all go for a coffee afterwards. I do not dare do this anymore. I would fear for my life.[193]

The year after, the Homs activist ceased their political activism. To make matters worse, the SOC as a whole lost its influence in international mediation initiatives. A UN-backed peace process did not produce any tangible results and was widely critiqued for providing the regime with political legitimacy without the impetus to accept any meaningful concessions. In December 2016, Russia, Türkiye and Iran started an alternative diplomatic track aimed at ceasing hostilities in the conflict. It excluded demands for a political transformation of the Syrian regime and did not engage with the Syrian opposition.[194] With Türkiye supporting, and controlling, rebel factions and Iran and Russia supporting the government, the Astana talks, as they came to be known, were successful in establishing so-called de-escalation zones in Idlib, Eastern Ghouta, South Damascus and Homs in May 2017.[195]

In practice, it meant that Syrian rebel and opposition groups lost the ability to define the dynamics of the uprising. Türkiye invaded again, in 2018, establishing outposts in the Idlib region. It invaded a third time, in October 2019, when it gained control of an area in North Syria running from Tel Abyad to Ras al-Ayn. Out of the four original de-escalation zones, only Idlib remained after 2018. Regime forces overran Eastern Ghouta, South Damascus and Homs with impunity and, as with the fall of Aleppo and Zabadani, many were bussed to Idlib.[196] The security zones that Türkiye created not only meant an increased level of protection for Türkiye from Kurdish troops, they also meant increased protection for Syrian rebels from regime attacks. In return, Türkiye increasingly controlled the Syrian opposition. It helped create a so-called Syrian National Army that they funded, trained and provided with military support. Most rebel groups in North Syria were integrated into this army. It placed rebel factions in a military command structure of legions and brigades. It also increased support and control over local councils in areas north and west of Aleppo. Sharia courts and committees were placed under the SIC. It gave the SIC enormous clout, but within the political lines set by Türkiye.[197] Taken together, the Syrian crisis lost much of its internal dynamism, being increasingly shaped by the interactions between foreign powers that controlled warring parties on the ground.

Dynamics of Dependence

In this context, the Nusra Front went through two institutional transformations in quick succession. The first, in July 2016, occurred when it changed its name to *Jabhat Fatah al-Sham*, or the Front for the Conquest of the Levant. As made explicit by al-Julani in its founding statement, the name change signalled a disengagement from the global jihadist movement. Al-Julani started the statement by thanking al-Qaeda and al-Zawahiri for their support for the Syrian uprising, noting that 'their noble stance will be recorded in the annals of history'. He then continued:

> We, of the central command of the Nusra Front, in accordance with [. . .] our obligations in serving the people of al-Sham and their jihad [. . . will fulfil] the requests of the people of al-Sham to expose the deceptions of the international community, the leaders of the US and Russia, in their relentless bombardments and displacement of the Muslim masses of al-Sham under the pretence of targeting the Nusra Front, an al-Qaeda affiliate. For the aforementioned reasons, we declare the complete cancellation of all operations under the name of the Nusra Front and the formation of a new group operating under the name of Jabhat Fatah al-Sham.[198]

The creation of Jabhat Fatah al-Sham signalled a break from al-Qaeda as a pragmatic answer to changing circumstances in the Syrian crisis. But the split was far from uncontested among the religious and military leadership of the Nusra Front, with multiple senior leaders breaking away. In September 2016, a letter from al-Zawahiri denounced the creation of Jabhat Fatah al-Sham and in effect demanded the re-establishment of the Nusra Front.[199]

Al-Julani, though, had other plans. Less than six months later, in January 2017, a new organisation was announced: Hayat Tahrir al-Sham (HTS). It resulted from a merger between several rebel factions, including, first and foremost, Jabhat Fatah al-Sham and Nour al-Din al-Zenki (a rebel group that was especially powerful to the north and west of Aleppo) besides several other groups. Ahrar al-Sham had also been involved in the talks for its creation. Some among its most senior leaders, for example Abu Jaber al-Sheikh, were in favour of joining the new organisation. In the end, though, the merger was rejected in a vote among Ahrar al-Sham's leadership.[200] But the person reading out the statement was no other than Abu Jaber al-Sheikh, the now former senior member, and former leader, of Ahrar al-Sham:

> Hayat Tahrir al-Sham is an independent entity, it does not represent any of the previously existing factions. She is a new stage in the blessed revolution [. . .] Hayat Tahrir al-Sham asks everyone active on the Syrian stage to unify under one entity and one leadership for the military and political effort to attain the aim of the revolution to bring down the criminal regime.[201]

Instead of unilaterally deciding that they represented a global Muslim community (as ISIS had done) or a global jihadist movement (as with al-Qaeda and the Nusra Front), HTS decided they were the sole representation of the Syrian insurgency. The inclusive language of the founding statement could not hide the fact that instead of unifying Islamist rebel factions under its flag, the creation of HTS placed the nascent organisation in direct competition with Ahrar al-Sham for control over the Idlib region. It was a competition that soon spiralled out of control. In July 2017, HTS overran the Bab al-Hawa crossing, controlled by Ahrar al-Sham, and attacked its positions in Idlib city. Appalled by these attacks, Nour al-Din al-Zenki left HTS and began to cooperate with Ahrar al-Sham.[202]

It became clear that the creation of HTS was an attempt by the Nusra Front to appease foreign powers that had battered it in the name of fighting terrorism, while rendering itself indispensable to the uprising by strengthening its dominance within it. The exit of Nour al-Din al-Zenki initially created a relatively stable dual power structure in the Idlib region. But following the US retreat and the Turkish second attack on North Syria in December 2018, HTS took its chance and attacked Ahrar al-Sham and Nour al-Din al-Zenki with full force. Despite sharia courts mediating conflicts and numerous statements calling for unity among opposition ranks – when HTS could not become hegemonic through peaceful means, it would do so through more violent ones.[203] Around 2019, it became the hegemon of the Idlib province. Ahrar al-Sham and Nour al-Din al-Zenki only kept a presence to the north of Aleppo.

Enforcing Pragmatism

The dominance of HTS among Syrian rebel groups in the Idlib region stood in stark contrast with the severely constrained broader context in which they found themselves. It faced a severe lack of resources and a military situation shaped, and increasingly controlled, by Türkiye.[204] It constrained the extent that it could implement governance initiatives on the ground. What HTS did instead was to facilitate an existing governance initiative from independent agents and use its coercive capabilities to render this initiative hegemonic in Idlib while controlling its internal composition.

This is where the Syrian Salvation Government came in. It started with a Civil Administration Initiative, facilitated by HTS, in August 2017. It was held by urban elites, academics and individuals engaged in previous social initiatives in the region and aimed to provide a coherent governance structure in Idlib. What bound these agents together was a sense of exclusion from the SIG, other rebel factions domestically and deception within opposition politics.[205] These were people that prioritised stability and security, echoing the pragmatism of the de-escalation zone in which they were active. The Civil Administration Initiative acted as the constituent body for the Syrian Salvation Government. In November 2017, it appointed Muhammad al-Sheikh, the former President of Idlib University, as its President.[206] It did not have a political programme.[207] Its ministers and president were elected by a General Shura Council that was meant to be a general representation of citizens living in the territory that the Salvation Government controlled. Many argued that in reality HTS controlled the General Shura Council and, with it, the Syrian Salvation Government.[208]

Following its creation, the Salvation Government implemented its dominance in Idlib governance through cooperation, negotiation and enforcement. It was a process that was impossible without the support of HTS. The local Chamber of Commerce willingly gave several of its prerogatives to the Ministry of Economy. HTS placed its directorates for the camps and displaced persons under the Ministry of Humanitarian Affairs. Local councils in regions controlled by HTS were placed under the Salvation Government. Some councils were placed under its control by force, as happened with the Local Council of Idlib. Councils in regions controlled by other rebel factions, and especially those with stronger local councils, remained autonomous for longer. After January 2019, following the complete takeover of Idlib by HTS, the Salvation Government demanded all local councils recognise it as sole authority. Eventually all councils were integrated into the Salvation Government's governance structure.[209]

A similar process occurred in the judiciary field. All courts run by rebel factions, either through negotiations or force, were placed under the Salvation Government and its Ministry of Justice. In March 2019, a High Council of Fatwa was established, which regulated fatwas created by scholars active in the Idlib region. It intentionally included a wide range of, mostly Syrian, religious scholars and based its fatwas on deliberations and consensus. A close ally of al-Julani presided over the council, and it aimed to be a check on the influence of foreign sheikhs. As he noted himself in this respect, 'There is now a general order that everyone must accept'.[210] As was the case with service provision, HTS forcefully imposed a unified structure onto the judiciary through the Salvation Government.

The End of an Islamic Distinction

The Salvation Government did not have the resources to implement a distinct type of educational, judicial, economic or social programme. It controlled the distribution of water and electricity and levied a tax on these utilities. It also controlled the Bab al-Hawa crossing and attempted to implement a levy on international aid convoys but had to backtrack after widespread protests against the policy.[211] To attract some level of investment, it opened up its markets to exclusive trade agreements with Turkish firms.[212] Together, though, it did not amount to sufficient financial resources to implement effective governance in the areas it controlled. It meant it could not implement any type of distinct policies.

As a result, the Salvation Government had limited executive power. International NGOs and their local partners took over the tasks of the Health Ministry. The Ministry of Education only paid salaries of its administrative staff. It did not set a curriculum, nor did it have teachers on its payroll. The Qatar Foundation financed a UN-endorsed curriculum for preparatory and secondary levels, while it was the Syrian Interim Government – not the Salvation Government – that issued diplomas. It relied on volunteers and secondary organisations to maintain school buildings.[213] Regarding the religious sphere, the Minister of Religious Affairs stated in 2020 that they were running 1,200 mosques with around 6,000 people working in them, which made it 'simply impossible for us to replace them'.[214] They did not impose constraints on the content of sermons. In Idlib city, forty out of forty-six mosques were run by the same staff as before the Salvation Government took over.[215]

The pragmatic governance practices of the Salvation Government echo changes that occurred inside HTS regarding religious authority. They maintained their aversion to codified sharia law, but sharia scholars drew increasingly on local legal traditions. Before, HTS sharia scholars opposed references to local Syrian traditions of religious jurisprudence (the *madhāhib*). After 2017, they rehabilitated the idea of these traditional schools of jurisprudence. Abu Abdullah al-Shami, head of HTS' religious council, noted that 'sharia remains our reference. But there are conditions for its application' and 'we are always trying to anchor in the movement the idea of relying on the *madhāhib* because it is a way of getting closer to people'.[216] HTS followed the Shafi'i approach of jurisprudence because it was the dominant approach in Syria. Rehabilitating these locally dominant traditional schools of jurisprudence had the effect of further delegitimising foreign sheikhs and empowering more local ones and hence further distancing HTS from al-Qaeda and global jihadism.[217]

These changes were far from uncontested. Representatives of HTS acknowledged, for instance, that many among their rank and file did not support the ideological changes and that several middle-ranking commanders had resisted them. As HTS turned away from global jihadism, several elite members – mostly those with close ties to al-Qaeda – left or were expelled: Talha Abu Shuaib was expelled because he did not respect 'the policies of the group'; the same happened to Abu al-Yaqdhan al-Masri because he did not abide 'publicly by the framework set by HTS through its leadership and sharia council'.[218] On 27 February 2018, Hurras ad-Din emerged as an organisation that brought together many of these former HTS leaders. It explicitly did not accept the Russian and Turkish presence in Syria and presented itself as al-Qaeda's representation in the Syrian battlefield.[219]

In response to these challenges, HTS leadership increased internal control over the organisation and initially contained, and eventually repressed, Hurras ad-Din. It started by banning the use of *takfir*, or excommunication, by any other than its sharia council – which subsequently ceased using it. It forced all fatwas and rulings to be vetted by the sharia council before publication. Regarding Hurras al-Din, HTS initially targeted its military commanders, personnel and resources, leaving the group starved for cash, weapons and fighting power. They effectively sidelined the group.[220] In March 2020, in the framework of the Russia–Türkiye peace deal, Turkish troops flooded the Idlib region. Hurras ad-Din opposed the incursion, threatened Turkish troops and with it the legitimacy of HTS. The latter did not hesitate and destroyed any remaining positions of Hurras ad-Din. It all led an anonymous Syrian al-Qaeda scholar to compare al-Julani to Kadyrov, the Chechen jihadist leader and his son who sold out to their Russian patrons.[221] HTS forced any vestiges of al-Qaeda and representations of global jihadism underground.

Taken together, Islam ceased to be the source of a distinct pattern of social interactions during the Syrian crisis. To the north of Aleppo, opposition groups and rebel factions were effectively controlled by Türkiye. In and around Idlib, a local hegemon had emerged – al-Julani and HTS – that lacked the ability to implement distinct practices in a judiciary, services, governance, collective violence and the religious field. A distinct Islamist movement during the Syrian crisis had collapsed.

With this, I conclude my narrative of the Syrian crisis. In this chapter, I first observed how activists established jihadist rebel groups and, in doing so, nurtured distinctly Islamic support networks and facilitated the influx of foreign fighters. Following the takeover of territory, sharia committees provided a distinctly Islamic institutional framework for providing public services, and created new avenues to control trade, gas and electricity networks. Meanwhile, sharia courts provided a new, distinctly Islamic judicial framework in these territories, offering access to the resources of an alternative judicial field. The establishment of an Islamic state, and emirates, gave full control over a territory and its resources. Using Islam to render practices distinct turned it political – Islamist – and transformed religion itself into a contested resource.

Second, I traced several conflicts over how Islam could, and should, render practices distinct. They revolve around control over sharia committees and courts, the codification of sharia law and the relationship between political authority and an Islamic collective identity. These conflicts brought together a wide range of agents that had a stake in defining Islam as a distinct practice, inadvertently setting them apart as a distinct Islamist movement.

Finally, I chronicled the decline of this movement. The peace agreement between Türkiye and Russia froze the front lines. It also further disempowered HTS, in the Idlib region, and Ahrar al-Sham and others in the north. Although most of these groups and their leaders still referred to the crisis as a jihad, the distinct influence of Sunni Islam on the dynamics of the crisis became harder to distinguish. The Syrian crisis lost much of its autonomous dynamics, and with it, Sunni Islam lost its distinctiveness as a social and political stake in the crisis.

Notes

1. Mansour, 'Abū Muḥammad Al-Jawlānī Amīr Jabhat Al-Nuṣrah'.
2. Lister, *The Syrian Jihad: Al-Qaeda, the Islamic State and the Evolution of an Insurgency*.
3. Lund, 'Politics of the Islamic Front'; Lund, 'Syria's Salafi Insurgents: The Rise of the Syrian Islamic Front'; Lund, 'The Jihadi Spiral'.
4. Pierret, 'Salafis at War in Syria: Logics of Fragmentation and Realignment'.
5. Ibid.; Lund, 'The Jihadi Spiral'.
6. Pierret, 'Salafis at War in Syria: Logics of Fragmentation and Realignment', 142.
7. Lund, 'Politics of the Islamic Front', pt. II.
8. Al-Akhbar, 'Al-Hay'ah Al-Shar'īyah Fī Ḥalab: al-Istibdād Mutadathran bi-'Abā'h al-Dīn'.
9. France 24, 'Suqūṭ Qatlá Khilāl Muẓāharāt Fī Dar'ā Wa-Īshtbākāt Ma'a Qūwāt Al-Amn Fī Mudun Ukhrá'.
10. France 24, "Asharāt Al-Sūrīyīn Yulabūn Da'wat Lltẓāhr Min Ajl Al-Taghyīr Wa-Al-Ḥurrīyah'.
11. Misbar Syria, 'Al-Thawrah Al-Sūrīyah Jum'ah Al-'Azzah Jāmi' Al-Rifā'ī 25 Ādhār'.
12. Interview with a Syrian journalist, 25 August 2011, Istanbul, Türkiye.
13. France 24, 'Al-Asad Ya'ud Bi-Ī'ḥbāṭ 'Mu'āmarah' Tata'araḍ La-Hā Al-Bilād Wy'kd Min Jadīd 'Alá Iṣlāḥāt Mu'Alanah Sābiqan'.
14. SANA, 'Majmū'ah Musallaḥah Taḥtal Asṭaḥ Ba'ḍ Al-Abniyah Fī Madīnat Al-Lādhiqīyah'.
15. Al Jazeera, 'Gunfire in Locked-down Syrian City'; Lister, *The Syrian Jihad: Al-Qaeda, the Islamic State and the Evolution of an Insurgency*, 54.
16. It was also strenuously denied by multiple interviewees. Interview with a Syrian journalist, 25 August 2011, Istanbul, Türkiye; Skype interview with senior

Kurdish activist, 4 September 2011; interview with Istanbul-based Syrian activist, 24 September 2011, Istanbul, Türkiye.

17. Interview with Ratib, 27 September 2011, Istanbul, Türkiye.
18. Ibid.
19. al-Rifai, 'Al-Shaykh Usāmah Al-Rifāʿī Khuṭbat Al-Naṣīḥah Fī Jumʿah Al-ʿAzzah 25 3 2011'.
20. Pierret, 'Salafis at War in Syria: Logics of Fragmentation and Realignment'.
21. See his YouTube channel at: http://www.youtube.com/user/adnanalarour. See also Rosen, 'Islamism and the Syrian Uprising'.
22. Sarkis, 'Hasserfüllte Milizennamen'.
23. Interview with activist sheikh from Jisr al-Shughur, 26 August 2012, Reyhanlı, Türkiye; interview with former aid to Ahmad Hassoun, 11 September 2012, Istanbul, Türkiye.
24. Carnegie Endowment, 'Profiles of Syrian Sunni Clerics in the Uprising'.
25. Donker, 'Between Rebellion and Uprising Intersecting Networks and Discursive Strategies in Rebel Controlled Syria'.
26. Shadid, 'Disparate Factions from Streets Fuel New Opposition in Syria'.
27. Slackman and Stack, 'Syria Tense as Protesters Mourn Their Dead'.
28. Stack, 'Syria, Claiming Heavy Toll in Town, Hints at Retaliation'.
29. Landis, 'What Happened at Jisr Al-Shagour?'
30. Yassin-Kassab and Al-Shami, *Burning Country: Syrians in Revolution and War*.
31. France 24, 'Al-Sulṭāt Taṭlaq Sarrāḥ 260 Muʿataqlā Siyāsīyan Baynahum Islāmiyūn Wa-'Akrād'. See also Syrian Human Rights Committee, 'New Massacre in Sednaya Military Prison'.
32. France 24, 'Al-Asad Yaṣduru 'Afwan 'Āman Wa-Al-Muʿāraḍah Taṣafahu Bi-'Ghayr Kāf'.
33. Al Jazeera, 'Fīlm Aḥrār Al-Shām'; al-'Awdāt, 'Zahrān 'Allūsh Alladhī Aṭlaq Al-Asad Sarāḥhu Li-Ibtida' 'Askarat Al-Thawrah'.
34. Al Jazeera, 'Fīlm Aḥrār Al-Shām'.
35. al-Julani, 'Jabhat Al-Nuṣrah Taḥmil 'alá 'Ātqhā an Takūn Silāḥ Hādhihi Al-Ummah'.
36. Pierret, 'Salafis at War in Syria: Logics of Fragmentation and Realignment', 142.
37. Lister, *The Syrian Jihad: Al-Qaeda, the Islamic State and the Evolution of an Insurgency*, 103–5.
38. Pierret, 'Salafis at War in Syria: Logics of Fragmentation and Realignment', 145.
39. Allouni, 'Ḥassān 'Abbūd .. Ḥarakat Al-Shām Al-Islāmīyah'.
40. Hegghammer, 'Syria's Foreign Fighters'.

41. Baladi News, 'Baʿda Sanawāt Min Al-Ghumūḍ .. Maṣdar Yakshif Li-Baladī Nīwz Huwīyah 'Abū Muḥammad Al-Jawlānī"; Al Jazeera, 'Abū Muḥammad Al-Jawlānī .. Zaʿīm Jabhat Fatḥ Al-Shām'.
42. Mansour, 'Abū Muḥammad Al-Jawlānī Amīr Jabhat Al-Nuṣrah'.
43. Zelin, 'Up to 11,000 Foreign Fighters in Syria; Steep Rise among Western Europeans'. Although their use was not exclusive to jihadist rebel groups, the number of foreign fighters among non-Islamist groups was far smaller. For instance, later on in the crisis, the fight against ISIS and creation of Rojava drew in foreign fighters to the People's Protection Units, the military arm of the Kurdish Democratic Union Party in Syria. Estimated between 1 and 400 fighters, their numbers never came close to those fighting in name of an Islamist jihad. See Leduc, 'Far Left on the Front Lines: The Westerners Joining the Kurds' Fight in Syria'.
44. Lister, *The Syrian Jihad: Al-Qaeda, the Islamic State and the Evolution of an Insurgency*, 58.
45. Dickinson, 'Playing with Fire: Why Private Gulf Financing for Syria's Extremist Rebels Risks Igniting Sectarian Conflict at Home', 7–9.
46. Ibid., 13.
47. Ibid., 14.
48. Interview with activist sheikh from Jisr al-Shughur, 26 August 2012, Reyhanlı, Türkiye.
49. O'Bagy, 'The Free Syrian Army'; MacFarquhar and Saad, 'Rebel Groups in Syria Make Framework for Military'; Dickinson, 'Playing with Fire: Why Private Gulf Financing for Syria's Extremist Rebels Risks Igniting Sectarian Conflict at Home'.
50. See Sarkis, 'Hasserfüllte Milizennamen'.
51. Lister, *The Syrian Jihad: Al-Qaeda, the Islamic State and the Evolution of an Insurgency*, 104.
52. Abazeid, 'Aḥrār Al-Shām Baʿda 'Ām Ṭawīl'.
53. Lund, 'Struggling to Adapt: The Muslim Brotherhood in a New Syria'.
54. Ibid.
55. Interview with representatives of local council in Ghouta, 17 October 2016, Gaziantep, Türkiye.
56. al-Halabi, 'Ḥalab .. Tahjīr Mumanhaj LIṭāqāt Al-Shabābīyah'; MacFarquhar, 'A Bread Shortage Is the First Big Test of Transitional Council in Aleppo'; Ciro Martínez and Eng, 'Struggling to Perform the State: The Politics of Bread in the Syrian Civil War'.

57. Interview with a representative of the Nour al-Din al-Zenki rebel faction. 24 October 2016, Gaziantep, Türkiye.
58. Interview with a media activist related to the Fastaqim Union. 21 October 2016, Gaziantep, Türkiye.
59. As on their Facebook page: www.facebook.com/MuslimYouthCommittee/.
60. Khalaf, Ramadan and Stolleis, 'Activism in Difficult Times Civil Society Groups in Syria 2011–2014'.
61. Lund, 'Going Home: An Interview with Tarif Al-Sayyed Issa'.
62. Hadath Media Center, 'Taqrīr Mufaṣṣal 'an Al-Hay'ah Al-Shar'īyah Fī Ḥalab'.
63. As said during an interview with Ahmad Mansour Al Jazeera, 'Abū Muḥammad Al-Jawlānī .. Za'īm Jabhat Fatḥ Al-Shām'.
64. Interview with Marouan, 21 October 2016, Gaziantep, Türkiye.
65. MacFarquhar, 'A Bread Shortage Is the First Big Test of Transitional Council in Aleppo'.
66. Lund, 'Syrian Jihadism'. Interview with a member of the SIG, 29 October 2015, Gaziantep, Türkiye.
67. See website of the Syrian Interim Government: https://www.syriaig.net/ar/home and the Syrian Opposition Coalition: https://www.etilaf.org/.
68. Syrian Interim Government, 'al-Ahdāf wa-al-Haykalīyah'.
69. Interview with a member of the SIG, 29 October 2015, Gaziantep, Türkiye.
70. Hamdan, 'Al-Hay'ah Al-Shar'īyah Bi-Ḥalab .. Adwār Muta'addidah'. See also Hadath Media Center, 'Taqrīr Mufaṣṣal 'an Al-Hay'ah Al-Shar'īyah Fī Ḥalab'.
71. Ibid.
72. Baczko, Dorronsoro and Quesnay, 'Building a Syrian State in Time of Civil War', 11.
73. MacFarquhar, 'A Bread Shortage Is the First Big Test of Transitional Council in Aleppo'.
74. Baczko, Dorronsoro and Quesnay, 'Building a Syrian State in Time of Civil War'.
75. Ibid. Interestingly, the authors of this report also observed that some sheikhs who acted as judges in sharia courts still received a regime salary for their previous jobs as religion teachers well into 2013.
76. Al-Akhbar, 'Al-Hay'ah Al-Shar'īyah Fī Ḥalab: al-Istibdād Mutadathran bi-'Abā'h al-Dīn'.
77. As quoted in Macfarquhar, 'A Battle for Syria, One Court at a Time'.

78. Schwab, 'Insurgent Courts in Civil Wars: The Three Pathways of (trans) formation in Today's Syria (2012–2017)'; Enab Baladi, 'Qaḍā' Sūriyā Al-Muḥarrarah .. Thalāth Marji'īyāt Tunadhir Bi-Taqsīm Al-Bilād'.
79. Schwab, 'Insurgent Courts in Civil Wars: The Three Pathways of (trans)formation in Today's Syria (2012–2017)'.
80. Al Jazeera, 'Fīlm Aḥrār Al-Shām'.
81. As quoted in Ibid.
82. Abazeid, 'Aḥrār Al-Shām Ba'da 'Ām Ṭawīl', 20.
83. Al Jazeera, 'Fīlm Aḥrār Al-Shām'; Syrian Islamic Front, 'Mīthāq Al-Jabhah Al-Islāmīyah Al-Sūrīyah'.
84. Ahrar al-Sham, 'Jānib Min Al-Nashāṭ Al-Thaqāfī Wa-Al-Da'awī Fī Ḥalab'; Ahrar al-Sham, 'Preparation of Faith and Education for Children in Aleppo'. This was also confirmed by an activist from the movement. Interview with junior Ahrar al-Sham activist, 2 March 2015, Istanbul, Türkiye.
85. Islamic State in Iraq and Syria, 'Structure of the Caliphate'.
86. Interview with teacher from Ghouta, 12 March 2015, Istanbul, Türkiye.
87. Interview with a physician from Raqqa, 3 November 2015, Gaziantep, Türkiye.
88. Ibid.
89. Interview with an aid worker from Raqqa, 31 October 2016, Gaziantep, Türkiye.
90. Callimachi, 'The ISIS Files: When Terrorists Run City Hall'; Malik, 'The Isis Papers: Behind 'Death Cult' Image Lies a Methodical Bureaucracy'.
91. Islamic State in Iraq and Syria, 'Structure of the Caliphate'.
92. Bunzel, 'From Paper State to Caliphate: The Ideology of the Islamic State', 42.
93. Lund, 'Syrian Jihadism', 23–45.
94. Syrian Islamic Liberation Front, 'Min Naḥnu?'
95. Pierret, 'Salafis at War in Syria: Logics of Fragmentation and Realignment', 145; Chivers, 'A Rebel Commander in Syria Holds the Reins of War'.
96. Kuwaiti donors, such as Ahrar al-Sham supporting Shafi al-Ajmi, accused it of being an effort to sideline non-Saudi aligned rebel factions. It led to public feuding between Adnan al-Aroor, a Saudi-based sheikh who supported the Supreme Military Council, and al-Ajmi. See Pierret, 'Salafis at War in Syria: Logics of Fragmentation and Realignment'. Lund, 'Politics of the Islamic Front', pt. II.
97. Pierret, 'Salafis at War in Syria: Logics of Fragmentation and Realignment'.
98. Lund, 'Syria's Salafi Insurgents: The Rise of the Syrian Islamic Front'.
99. Syrian Islamic Front, 'Mīthāq Al-Jabhah Al-Islāmīyah Al-Sūrīyah'.
100. As quoted in Al Jazeera, 'Fīlm Aḥrār Al-Shām'.

101. Lund, 'Politics of the Islamic Front', pt. IV.
102. Multiple rebel factions, 'Bayān Raqm 1: Ḥawla Al-I'tilāf Wa-Al-Ḥukūmah Al-Muftaraḍah'.
103. Hubbard and Gordon, 'Key Syrian Rebel Groups Abandon Exile Leaders'; Lund, 'Islamist Groups Declare Opposition to National Coalition and US Strategy'.
104. Lister, *The Syrian Jihad: Al-Qaeda, the Islamic State and the Evolution of an Insurgency*, 177.
105. al-Sayf, 'Al-Raṣāṣah L'bṭāl Maqāl Al-Khulāṣah'.
106. Lister, *The Syrian Jihad: Al-Qaeda, the Islamic State and the Evolution of an Insurgency*, 288.
107. Abazeid, 'Aḥrār Al-Shām Ba'da 'Ām Ṭawīl', 28–30.
108. Batatu, *Syria's Peasantry, the Descendants of Its Lesser Rural Notables, and Their Politics*, 158–60.
109. Hinnebusch, *Syria: Revolution From Above*; van Dam, *The Struggle For Power in Syria: Politics and Society Under Asad and the Ba'th Party*.
110. Kelidar, 'Religion and State in Syria', 17; Zisser, 'Appearance and Reality: Syria's Decisionmaking Structure'; Salih, 'The Syrian Shabiha and Their State – Statehood & Participation'.
111. abd-Allah, *The Islamic Struggle in Syria*.
112. Lobmayer, *Opposition Und Widerstand in Syrien*, 199.
113. abd-Allah, *The Islamic Struggle in Syria*.
114. Seale, *Asad: The Struggle for the Middle East*, 333; Lobmayer, *Opposition Und Widerstand in Syrien*, 325–27, fn 152; see also Ziadeh, *Al-Islām Al-Siyāsī Fī Sūriyā*.
115. Multiple authors, 'al-Mawqi' al-Ta'rīfī bi-al-Shahīd Ṭarīf al-Sayyid 'Īsá'.
116. Orient.net, 'Ba'da Antkhābh Muftiyan 'Āman li-Sūriyā .. Min Huwa al-Shaykh Usāmah al-Rifā'ī?'.
117. Böttcher, *Syrische Religionspolitik Unter Asad (Syrian Religious Politics under Al-Assad)*; Pierret, *Religion and State in Syria: The Sunni Ulama from Coup to Revolution*.
118. Perthes, *Syria under Bashar al-Asad: Modernisation and the Limits of Change*.
119. The Syrian Muslim Brotherhood, 'Mukhtaṣar: Al-Mashrū' Al-Siyāsī Li-Sūriah Al-Mustaqbal'.
120. International Crisis Group, 'Syria Under Bashar (I): Foreign Policy Challenges'; International Crisis Group, 'Syria Under Bashar (II): Domestic Policy

Challenges'; della Porta et al., *Social Movements and Civil War: When Protests for Democratization Fail*, ch. 3.

121. International Crisis Group, 'Syria Under Bashar (II): Domestic Policy Challenges'; Lund, 'Struggling to Adapt: The Muslim Brotherhood in a New Syria'.
122. Moubayed, 'Syria's Abu Al-Qaqa: Authentic Jihadist or Imposter?'
123. Al Jazeera, 'Fīlm Aḥrār Al-Shām'.
124. Syrian Human Rights Committee, 'New Massacre in Sednaya Military Prison'.
125. Leenders, *Spoils of Truce: Corruption and State-Building in Postwar Lebanon*.
126. Selvik and Pierret, 'Limits to Upgrading Authoritarianism in Syria: Private Welfare, Islamic Charities, and the Rise of the Zayd Movement'.
127. Hamidi, 'Dimashq Tasmaḥu Li-Al-Qubaysiyāt Bi-Nashāṭ 'Alanī'; Hamidi, 'They Wear the Dark Blue Veil and Have a Wide Network for Teaching and Influence . . . "The Misses of Al-Qubaysiyat" Are the Entrepreneurs in Syria for Involvement of Women in the "Islamic Da'wa" . . . With the Consent of the Authorities'.
128. Conversation with a former activist in the Qubaysi movement, 16 August 2012, Istanbul, Türkiye.
129. Donker, 'Islamic Social Movements and the Syrian Authoritarian Regime'.
130. Al Jazeera, 'Al-Sulṭah Al-Qaḍā'īyah Bi-Nak'hat Al-Thawrah Fī Ḥalab'.
131. Integrated Judicial Council of Aleppo, 'Bayān Tashkīl Majlis Al-Qaḍā' Al-Muwaḥḥad Bi-Ḥalab'.
132. Schwab, 'Insurgent Courts in Civil Wars: The Three Pathways of (trans) formation in Today's Syria (2012–2017)'; Enab Baladi, 'Qaḍā' Sūriyā Al-Muḥarrarah .. Thalāth Marji'īyāt Tunadhir Bi-Taqsīm Al-Bilād'.
133. Baczko, Dorronsoro and Quesnay, 'Building a Syrian State in Time of Civil War'.
134. Macfarquhar, 'A Battle for Syria, One Court at a Time'.
135. Integrated Judicial Council of Aleppo, 'Bayān Mushtarak Ṣādir 'an Majlis Al-Qaḍā' Al-Muwaḥḥad Bi-Ḥalab Wa-Muḥāmū Ḥalab Al-Aḥrār'.
136. Enab Baladi, 'Qaḍā' Sūriyā Al-Muḥarrarah .. Thalāth Marji'īyāt Tunadhir Bi-Taqsīm Al-Bilād'.
137. Baczko, Dorronsoro and Quesnay, 'Building a Syrian State in Time of Civil War', 6.
138. Al Jazeera, 'Al-Sulṭah Al-Qaḍā'īyah Bi-Nak'hat Al-Thawrah Fī Ḥalab'.
139. Sharbajī, 'Ḥiwār Khāṣṣ Ma'a Al-Shaykh Usāmah Al-Rifā'ī .. Ra'īs Rābiṭat 'Ulamā' Al-Shām'.
140. Skype interview with Syrian journalist, 28 October 2015.

141. Syrian Islamic Council, 'Bayān Ta'sīs Al-Majlis Al-Islāmī Al-Sūrī'; Pierret, 'The Syrian Islamic Council'.
142. Interview with representative of Syrian Islamic Council, 6 November 2015, Istanbul, Türkiye.
143. Interview with former SMB politician, 3 November 2015, Gaziantep, Türkiye.
144. Syrian Islamic Council, 'Bayān Ta'sīs Al-Majlis Al-Islāmī Al-Sūrī'.
145. Ibid.
146. Interview with representative of Syrian Islamic Council, 6 November 2015, Istanbul, Türkiye; Pierret, 'The Syrian Islamic Council'; Pierret, 'The Struggle for Religious Authority in Syria'.
147. Hadath Media Center, 'Taqrīr Mufaṣṣal 'an Al-Hay'ah Al-Shar'īyah Fī Ḥalab'; Hamdan, 'Al-Hay'ah Al-Shar'īyah Bi-Ḥalab .. Adwār Muta'addidah'.
148. Al-Akhbar, 'Al-Hay'ah Al-Shar'īyah Fī Ḥalab: al-Istibdād Mutadathran bi-'Abā'h al-Dīn'.
149. Enab Baladi, 'Qaḍā' Sūriyā Al-Muḥarrarah .. Thalāth Marji'īyāt Tunadhir Bi-Taqsīm Al-Bilād'.
150. Ibid.
151. Schwab, 'Insurgent Courts in Civil Wars: The Three Pathways of (trans) formation in Today's Syria (2012–2017)'; Enab Baladi, 'Qaḍā' Sūriyā Al-Muḥarrarah .. Thalāth Marji'īyāt Tunadhir Bi-Taqsīm Al-Bilād'.
152. Interview with a member of the SIG, 29 October 2015, Gaziantep, Türkiye.
153. al-Attar, 'Al-Raqqah: 'An Wāqi' Al-Katā'ib Al-'Askarīyah, Wa-Idārat Al-Madīnah Al-Muḥarrarah, Wa-Al-Thawarāt Al-Lāḥiqah'.
154. Interview with a Syrian aid worker from Raqqa, 31 October 2016, Gaziantep, Türkiye.
155. Bunzel, 'From Paper State to Caliphate: The Ideology of the Islamic State'.
156. al-Baghdadi, 'Wa-Bashir Al-Mu'minīn', 7.
157. Ibid., 8.
158. al-Julani, 'Tafrīgh Kalimah Al-Shaykh Abī Muḥammad Al-Jawlānī Al-Mas'ūl Al-'Āmm Li-Jabhat Al-Nuṣrah-Al-Manārah Al-Bayḍā' Li-Mujāhdī Al-Shām'.
159. Ibid.
160. Bunzel, 'From Paper State to Caliphate: The Ideology of the Islamic State', 25.
161. Interview with Marouan, 21 October 2016, Gaziantep, Türkiye.
162. al-Sayf, 'Al-Raṣāṣah L'bṭāl Maqāl Al-Khulāṣah'.
163. Army of Mujahideen, 'Akādhīb Tanẓīm 'Al-'Irāq Wa-Al-Shām' Wa-Al-Mut'aṣbīn La-Hā'; Enab Baladi, 'Ba'da Taslīmhā Ṭabiban Maqtūlan Ilá Ḥarakat Aḥrār Al-Shām'.

164. Al-Adnani, 'This Is the Promise of Allah', 4.
165. Ibid., 5.
166. See Bunzel, 'From Paper State to Caliphate: The Ideology of the Islamic State', 18.
167. Al-Adnani, 'This Is the Promise of Allah', 5.
168. Enab Baladi, 'Al-Jawlānī Yakshif 'an Nafsihi Amāma Muqātlī Ḥalab Wa-Yubashir Bi-'Imārat Islāmīyah'; al-Julani, 'Bayān'.
169. Muhajir, 'Al-Khulāṣah Fī Munāqashah I'lān Al-Khilāfah', 10–11.
170. Muhajir, 'Al-Khulāṣah Fī Munāqashah I'lān Al-Khilāfah'.
171. al-Sayf, 'Al-Raṣāṣah L'bṭāl Maqāl Al-Khulāṣah', 5.
172. Islamic Front, 'Bayān'; as provided in Abazeid, 'Aḥrār Al-Shām Ba'da 'Ām Ṭawīl'.
173. Al Jazeera, 'Fīlm Aḥrār Al-Shām'; Abazeid, 'Aḥrār Al-Shām Ba'da 'Ām Ṭawīl'.
174. Syrian Islamic Council, 'Dirāsah Da'āwá Al-Khilāfah Al-Islāmīyah'.
175. Ibid.
176. Al Jazeera, 'Taḥaddiyāt Tuwājihu Al-Idārah Al-'Āmmah Lil-Khidmāt Bi-Ḥalab'.
177. General Management of Services in Aleppo, 'Khurūj Maḥaṭṭat Miyāh 'an Al-Khidmah'; The General Management of Services, 'Statement on the Status Quo of Suleiman Al Halabi Water Station'.
178. Interview with Marouan, 21 October 2016, Gaziantep, Türkiye.
179. Enab Baladi, 'Qaḍā' Sūriyā Al-Muḥarrarah .. Thalāth Marji'īyāt Tunadhir Bi-Taqsīm Al-Bilād'.
180. Lister, 'Profiling Jabhat Al-Nusra'; Dār Al-Qaḍā' fī Ḥrītān, 'Ta'mīm', 28 December 2014; Dār Al-Qaḍā' fī Ḥrītān, 'Ta'mīm', 7 January 2015; for these and more statements see Al-Tamimi, 'Archive of Jabhat Al-Nusra Dar Al-Qaḍa Documents'.
181. Abazeid, 'Aḥrār Al-Shām Ba'da 'Ām Ṭawīl'.
182. Ignatius, 'A New Cooperation on Syria'.
183. Lund, 'Syrian Rebels Capture Idlib'.
184. Lund, 'Going Home: An Interview with Tarif Al-Sayyed Issa'.
185. EIU, 'Russia Launches Air Attacks in Syria'.
186. Al Dassouky, 'The Role of Jihadi Movements in Syrian Local Governance'.
187. Lund, 'Going Home: An Interview with Tarif Al-Sayyed Issa'.
188. SMART News Agency, 'Majlis Al-Qaḍā' Al-A'lá, Waḥdunā Mu'aẓẓam Maḥākim Ḥalab Wa-Rīfihā Bi-'Istithnā' Maḥākim Al-Nuṣrah Wa-Al-'Aḥrār'.
189. Schwab, 'Insurgent Courts in Civil Wars: The Three Pathways of (trans)formation in Today's Syria (2012–2017)', 814.

190. Local Council of Aleppo City, 'Bayān Min Al-Majlis Al-Maḥallī Li-Madīnat Ḥalab'.
191. General Management of Services in Aleppo, 'Radan 'Alá Bayān 'Al-Majlis Al-Maḥallī Li-Madīnat Ḥalab' Ḥawla Taghdhiyat Aḥyā' Al-Zabdiyah Wa-Al-'Anṣārī Al-Sharqī Bi-Al-Tayār Al-Kahrabā'ī'.
192. Syrian Salvation Government, 'Indhār'.
193. Interview with a member of the SIG, 29 October 2015, Gaziantep, Türkiye.
194. Dalay, 'From Astana to Sochi: How De-Escalation Allowed Assad to Return to War'.
195. Al Jazeera, 'Final de-Escalation Zones Agreed on in Astana'.
196. Al Nofal and Hamou, 'Astana Talks Placed Three de-Escalation Zones under Government Control. Is Idlib Next?'
197. In 2021, the Syrian Interim Government appointed Osama al-Rifai as Mufti of the Republic. See Orient.net, 'Ba'da Antkhābh Muftiyan 'Āman li-Sūriyā .. Min Huwa al-Shaykh Usāmah al-Rifā'ī?'
198. al-Julani, 'Jabhat Fatḥ Al-Shām I'lān Tashkīl'.
199. Lister, 'How Al-Qaida Lost Control of Its Syrian Affiliate: The Inside Story'.
200. Drevon and Haenni, 'How Global Jihad Relocalises and Where It Leads. The Case of HTS, the Former AQ Franchise in Syria', 3.
201. al-Sheikh, 'I'lān Tashkīl Hay'at Taḥrīr Al-Shām'.
202. Newlee, 'Hay'at Tahrir Al-Sham (HTS)'.
203. Enab Baladi, 'Mādhā warā' al-Muwājahāt Bayna 'Taḥrīr al-Shām' wa 'al-Jabhah al-Waṭanīyah' bi-rīf Idlib?'; Enab Baladi, 'Tafāṣīl Alāqttāl bayna 'Taḥrīr al-Shām' wa 'al-Jabhah al-Waṭanīyah' Gharbī Idlib'.
204. Drevon and Haenni, 'How Global Jihad Relocalises and Where It Leads. The Case of HTS, the Former AQ Franchise in Syria'.
205. Ibid., 5.
206. Orient TV, 'Al-Duktūr Muḥammad Al-Shaykh Ra'īs Ḥukūmat Al-Inqādh Al-Sūria - Liqā' Khāṣṣ'.
207. See their website: https://syriansg.org/.
208. Drevon and Haenni, 'How Global Jihad Relocalises and Where It Leads. The Case of HTS, the Former AQ Franchise in Syria', n. 22; Enab Baladi, 'Salvation Government Elects New Shura Council President'.
209. Drevon and Haenni, 'How Global Jihad Relocalises and Where It Leads. The Case of HTS, the Former AQ Franchise in Syria'.
210. Ibid., 12–13.

211. Enab Baladi, 'Abū Muḥammad al-Jawlānī Yuẓhiru mjddan .. Rasā'il Siyāsīyah 'abra Barīd al-Iqtiṣād'.
212. See for example Syrian Salvation Government, 'Nashr I'lān Tijārīyah Ḥaṣrīyah – Dogus'; Syrian Salvation Government, 'Nashr I'lān Tijārīyah Ḥaṣrīyah – Bifa'.
213. Drevon and Haenni, 'How Global Jihad Relocalises and Where It Leads. The Case of HTS, the Former AQ Franchise in Syria', 7–8.
214. As cited in Drevon and Haenni, 'How Global Jihad Relocalises and Where It Leads. The Case of HTS, the Former AQ Franchise in Syria'.
215. Ibid., 18.
216. As cited in Ibid., 14–15.
217. Ibid., 16.
218. Drevon and Haenni, 'How Global Jihad Relocalises and Where It Leads. The Case of HTS, the Former AQ Franchise in Syria'.
219. Lister, 'How Al-Qaida Lost Control of Its Syrian Affiliate: The Inside Story'.
220. Ibid.
221. Ajjoub, 'Reading Kadyrov in Al-Sham: 'Adnan Hadid on Chechnya, Syria, and Al-Qaida's Strategic Failure'.

6

COMPARING DISTINCT PRACTICES

> To understand the practices of [agents . . .] entails understanding that they are the result of a meeting of two histories: a history of the position they occupy and the history of their dispositions. Although position helps to shape dispositions, the latter, in so far as they are the product of independent conditions, have an existence and efficacy of their own and can help to shape positions. [It makes the] confrontation between positions and dispositions [. . .] continuous [and] uncertain.[1]

This chapter compares the life cycle of an Islamist movement during the Tunisian transition and Syrian crisis. It argues for a focus on situational distinctness to further comparative analyses of political Islam and social movements. The relational positions that activists take in struggles to define distinctly Islamic practices can be used to compare, across conflict episodes, the social process that is an Islamist movement. The chapter can be read on its own, but it builds extensively on the analysis in Chapters four and five that traced the emergence, transformation and decline of an Islamist movement during the Tunisian transition and Syrian crisis.

The preceding chapters acknowledged the situational and contingent character of relations between politics and religion. Scholars such as Muhammad Qasim Zaman, Charles Tripp and Sarah Tobin have convincingly shown how boundaries between these concepts are constantly being renegotiated and fought over.[2] Supporting these accounts, we observed how, during the Tunisian transition, the Ennahda Movement fought with grassroots activists about the way to represent an Islamic character of Tunisian identity in the constitution. During the Syrian crisis, there were struggles over the extent that Islamic law should be codified in rebel courts and, around the rise of ISIS and its caliphate, how national identity should relate to an Islamic one in the legitimation of political rule. In tracing these conflicts, we observed that the translation of notions such as *caliphate*, *sharia*, *tawheed* (unity of faith), *manhaj an-nabawi* (method of the prophet and his companions), *ahl al-ḥall wa-al-ʿaqd* ('those that loosen and bind', denoting the individuals qualified to appoint and depose a caliph) into the concrete practices of Islamists varied between agents and contexts. Relations between these religious notions and concrete social and political practices were subject to constant conflict and challenge.

These chapters also mirrored recent relational approaches in social movement studies. Scholars such as Charles Tilly, Sidney Tarrow, Doug McAdam, Neil Fligstein and James Jasper analyse social movements not as substantive entities but as dynamic processes, observing the formation and transformation of social fields and placing interactions between agents at the centre of their analyses.[3] In Chapters four and five, we observed an Islamist movement as an emergent phenomenon around the enactment of Islam as a stake in social and political conflict. An Islamist movement did not exist as a substantive entity – with a collective identity and sociopolitical behaviour structured by its ideological characteristics – but emerged as a distinct pattern of social interactions between individual activists. During the Tunisian transition, activists published joint statements in defence of Islam, mobilised to include sharia in the constitution and fought for control over mosques. During the Syrian crisis, distinctly Islamist rebel factions were founded, jihadists fought for control over sharia committees and polarised debates took places around the legitimacy of ISIS's declaration of an Islamic State. These conflicts set a subset of activists apart for having a stake in controlling the use of Islam to render practices distinct. It gave birth to an Islamist movement. This a movement emerged from the conflictual interactions of the Tunisian transition and Syrian crisis – it did not, and could not, exist in isolation from them.

Both the constructivist approach to political Islam and the relational approach to social movements are challenging to use in comparative analyses. With the former, the phenomenon of political Islam collapses under the pressure of situational contingency. It becomes difficult to speak of a coherent Islamist movement if constructions between politics and religion vary across time and space. The object of study disappears. With relational approaches in studies on social movements, there is an issue with situating relational interactions (either conceptualised as mechanisms, fields or strategic interactions) in a broader conceptual, empirical or historical context. It makes comparative analysis challenging.[4]

In this chapter, I apply the contentious practices approach as described in Chapter two and argue for a focus on situational distinctness to enable a comparative analysis of Islamist movements, comparing the positions that individual Islamists take when situating their distinct practices in relation to particular contexts. Such an approach enables, first, a comparison of relational positions taken by participants to situate Islam as a stake in relation to the Tunisian transition and Syrian crisis. It allows for a comparative analysis of a social movement that goes beyond the confines of a single conflict episode. Second, it enables a comparative analysis of different currents within a single Islamist movement. A focus on situational distinctness can be used to divide struggles around Islam as a stake into multiple, more specific issues. As we will see below, this means we can situate an occurrence of an Islamist movement not only in relation to a conflict episode but also in relation to the general genealogy of Islamism.

The chapter is structured into three parts. I first describe three ideal-typical relational positions that activists can use to situate distinct practices in a particular context. They are homology, heterology and analogy. These relational positions are simplified to the extreme, reflecting standard logics of engagement, challenge and disengagement, but are used to highlight how relational positions have their own genealogy – their own historical and biographical roots – in an Islamist movement that goes beyond the boundaries of a particular conflict episode. Relational positions show how Islam, as a distinct stake, endures across episodes of conflict despite being subjected to the temporal and spatial forces that ought to tear it apart into situational particularisms.

Second, using these ideal-typical relational positions, I provide a comparative analysis of an Islamist movement during the Tunisian transition and Syrian crisis. First, I establish the existence of an Islamist movement during both episodes. Subsequently, I compare its impact on these episodes and, briefly, explore various Islamist currents. Finally, based on this comparative analysis, I discuss some possible scenarios for its future development.

I conclude with a few preliminary thoughts on the causal mechanisms that explain the evolution of an Islamist movement across multiple conflict episodes. The section highlights the imperfect reproduction of relational positions across episodes as a source of social variation and innovation. Meanwhile, it argues that internal conflicts around Islam as a stake act as a mechanism of social, contentious selection of relational positions. It is theorised that these two mechanisms, together, constitute the social process that is an Islamist movement. These mechanisms highlight how social movements comprise a contentious process to reproduce and select the legitimate ways to render practices distinct.

Positions of Distinction

Relational positions are the logics that individual activists use to situate an Islamic distinction in relation to other social fields. In order to describe such positions, I draw on Bourdieu, using terms borrowed from biology: homology, heterology and analogy.[5] They are ideal-types and act as a heuristic device to describe how Islamists situate Islam through their distinct practices in conflict episodes. In doing so, they reflect individual dispositions of activists and the hierarchical structures of the contexts in which they are active. Let me discuss each in turn.

Homology

I use homology to refer to a position where an Islamic distinctness is practised through the established rules of an external field. This logic could be observed, for instance, when Islamists established associations and registered them with the relevant state bodies. These associations were, during the Tunisian transition, formally indistinguishable from their non-Islamist counterparts. Their Islamic distinctness was practised through an emphasis on (religious) education and charity or in the description of their aims and identity. This also happened, for example, when Islamists established parties within an existing political context. They became political parties like any other, except that their political programmes were, in one way or another, inspired by Islam. The Tunisian Ennahda party and the Syrian Muslim Brotherhood were examples, but so were the Reform Front and Hizb al-Tahrir during the Tunisian transition. A similar homological position is reflected in attempts to equate national and Islamic collective identities: discourse, for example, around an Arab-Islamic source to a Tunisian nationalism or the particularity of Syrian Islam. It is important to note that the actual social activities, political policies and nationalist discourses that these activists practised in the name of Islam was immensely diverse.

What binds these positions together is not the content of their social, political or discursive practices. Rather, it is their shared homological position, or semblance, between an Islamist movement and the fields in which participants are active. Such a position does not imply that an Islamic distinctness does not transform these fields: it opens these fields to new participants – new politicians in the case of Ennahda, social activists in the case of Islamic associations and teachers in case of religious schools – bringing with them new individual dispositions and new avenues for accessing resources. It inadvertently reshapes established norms and structural hierarchies of these social fields.

Homological positions are part of the discursive and institutional resources of an Islamist movement, as well as reflecting the individual dispositions of many of its participants. There is a large body of Islamist discourse, around notions such as *maṣlaḥah*, *shūrá* and *ijmāʿ*, that legitimates homological positions as well as Islamic political parties, schools, charities and associations that comprise its institutional expression. They provide the discursive and institutional resources needed to practise such positions. Meanwhile, the lived experiences of several Islamist leaders and activists, such as Rached Ghannouchi and Tarif al-Sayed Issa, inculcate homological dispositions.

The position reflects a discursive history of attempts to bridge Western political notions with Sunni Islamic ones. Muhammad Abduh (1849–1905), for example, bridged notions such *maṣlaḥah* (interest) to utility, *shūrá* (consultation) to parliamentary democracy and *ijmāʿ* (consensus) to public opinion. Mustapha al-Siba'i's (1915–64), the General Secretary of the Syrian Muslim Brotherhood, highlighted in *Socialism of Islam* the overlap between Islam and socialism, arguing that the former strengthened notions of the latter. While doing so, he intentionally mixed the notion of Islamic schools of jurisprudence (the *madhāhib*) and the civil notion of political programme (*barnāmij*).[6] In the *Public Freedoms in the Islamic State,* Rached Ghannouchi (1941), the leader of the Ennahda party, argued that an Islamic polity would nurture and build a democratic attitude through *shura* (consultation) among the *ummah* (Islamic community),[7] equating democracy and Islam while opposing secular autocracies. These individuals situated Islam as homological to Western political concepts, such as socialism and democracy.

These positions are not only practised discursively. Hassan al-Banna (1906–49), the Egyptian founder of the Muslim Brotherhood, ran for political office twice, in 1941 and 1945 – though he lost both times. The Syrian Muslim Brotherhood participated in elections in 1949, 1954 and 1961, though they remained a small party compared with those that represented large landowning elites. The party itself was established as a unification of several Islamic associations that had been established in the preceding decade. In Tunisia, the Ennahda party emerged as an explicit attempt to take part in the 1989 democratic elections. The name Ennahda (or Renaissance) itself results from removing religious references from its name in order to comply with electoral laws. All these are examples of homological positions: situating an Islamic distinctness as resembling the institutional structures of an existing (in this case political) field.

Homological positions reflect in the life histories of several of the activists discussed in this book. For instance, the life of Rached Ghannouchi, the leader of the Ennahda party, has to a large extent revolved around the effort to articulate and enact homological positions of Islamic distinctness. He began to emphasise the democratic character of the movement while in exile in Europe in the 1990s and, following the revolution of 2011, actively sought to resemble other political parties to ensure Ennahda's political survival. It led to the party rebranding itself as Muslim Democrat. Another example, from the Syrian crisis, is Tarif al-Sayed Issa. As a member of the Syrian Muslim Brotherhood, he lived through the violent uprisings of the 1970s and 1980s and ended up in exile in Sweden. It gave him personal experience with political activism, a democratic regime and armed insurgency. During the crisis, he started out as a member of a Syrian opposition body in Istanbul, went on to found a charity association and distribute aid in North Syria and ended up being a jihadist attacking Idlib. He shifted positions in light of a changing context, continuously resembling the general dynamics of the crisis and embedding himself among them.

In summary, homological positions are part of the resources and dispositions that make up an Islamist movement. They practise an Islamic distinctness while resembling the rules of established fields, opening up these fields to new participants, reshaping structured hierarchies and inculcating new dispositions. They are the outcome of a discursive and institutional history of an Islamist movement and the biographies of its participants.

Heterology

I use heterology to describe a position where an Islamic distinctness is enacted in a way that directly challenges established rules of an existing field. An example of this position is Ansar Charia, which during the Tunisian transition provided social services across the country. In doing so, they did not register themselves and acted as an alternative to, and challenged the legitimacy of, the Tunisian state. During the Syrian crisis, sharia committees provided an alternative institutional framework to the civil local councils for the provision of public services. The same applied to sharia courts, such as the Nusra Front's *Dar al-Qadaa*, or House of Judges, and the use of noncodified approaches to sharia in sharia courts: both challenged the power of a civil judicial field in rebel-controlled territories. Last but not least, ISIS's caliphate provided an alternative bureaucratic state structure that challenged established norms of international relations between nation-states. These are a few of the examples that were discussed in this book, where activists used Islam to create distinct associations, courts, service providers and governance organisations that directly challenged existing associational, judicial, service and governance fields.

As with homological positions, heterology is present among the structural resources of an Islamist movement, as well as the individual dispositions of its participants. Notions such as *jāhilīyah*, or religious ignorance, *ḥākimīyah*, or God's sovereignty on earth, and *farḍ ʿayn*, or individual duty, are instantaneously recognisable as discursive notions enabling such positions. The Nusra front, al-Qaeda and ISIS as well as their global support networks, provide their institutional resources. Meanwhile, the embodied biographies of the likes of Abu Iyadh, Hassan Aboud and Abu Muhammad al-Julani – all well-known jihadists – inculcated individual dispositions towards heterological positions. Together, they provide the resources and dispositions for practising heterology.

There are many historical examples of heterological positions taken by Islamists. The position reflects, for instance, in Sayyid Qutb's (1906–66) notion of *jāhilīyah* (religious ignorance) and *ḥākimīyah* (God's sovereignty on earth) as revolutionary, jihadist, challenges to the political and executive authority of Arab states.[8] Abdallah Azzam (1941–89) is a later example. He situated the notion of jihad in relation to an Islamic community instead of a particular state by arguing that a jihad was a *farḍ 'ayn*, or an individual duty, turning heterological positions global. Putting his ideas into practice, he established a *maktab al-khidamāt* (bureau of services) to support individual Muslims wanting to take part in the Afghan jihad of 1979–89. A few years later, it would be Osama bin Laden (1957–2011) who, in the context of US forces being stationed in Saudi Arabia to attack Saddam Hussein's Iraq, published a statement that argued explicitly that the killing of Americans and their allies was an individual duty (*farḍ 'ayn*).[9] Soon al-Qaeda would become infamous for a string of attacks on Western targets, culminating in the attacks on Washington and New York on 11 September 2001. In the process, al-Qaeda emerged as a global jihadist organisation challenging the authority of Arab leaders, Israel and Western governments.

We saw this history reflected in several individual life stories of participants of an Islamist movement during the Tunisian transition and Syrian crisis. Abu Iyadh, for instance, was a Tunisian who travelled to Afghanistan in the 1990s where he reportedly worked with al-Qaeda and was tasked with creating the jihadist Tunisian Combat Group. In 2003, Türkiye extradited him to Tunisia, where he received a forty-three-year prison sentence. Following the revolution, he founded Ansar Charia. Hassan Aboud travelled to Iraq in 2003 to join a jihad against the US invasion. So did Abu Muhammad al-Julani. The former would return to Syria and was incarcerated at the infamous Sednaya prison. After his release in 2011, he ended up establishing the Ahrar al-Sham Brigades that morphed into one of the most powerful jihadist organisations during the Syrian crisis. Abu Muhammad al-Julani instead remained in Iraq, was incarcerated by the Americans in Camp Bucca and used the opportunity to network among the leadership of al-Qaeda (and later the Islamic State in Iraq). Following his release, he soon moved up its ranks.

Following the start of the crisis, he travelled to Syria with the explicit task of establishing their presence among its nascent armed insurgency – the result was the Nusra Front.

It is safe to state that these individual life histories shaped dispositions towards positions of heterology: using Islam to enact distinct practices that challenge existing social and political fields. These activists were part of a history that produced global jihadist organisations, such as al-Qaeda and ISIS, numerous local ones, such as the Tunisian Combat Group and Ahrar al-Sham, transnational support networks of jihadist sheikhs and a pool of experienced jihadist fighters. Heterological positions are present in an Islamist movement as distinct discursive and institutional resources, as well as among the dispositions of its participants. This both reflects and enables practices of Islamist heterology.

Analogy

Finally, I use analogy as the inverse of both homology and heterology. Whereas heterology referred to the use of Islam to challenge existing fields, analogy refers to its use to create alternative ones. Instead of engagement with fields through homology, it implies disengagement: instead of participating in existing fields, it means the creation of new ones. It implies not just autonomy but isolation of an Islamic field from other existing social fields. Building your own mosque, on your own land, and becoming the imam there and teaching sharia sciences, as was done by Khatib Idrissi, is an example of such an approach.[10] Tellingly, Khatib Idrissi split from Abu Iyadh because the latter created Ansar Charia as an organisation for their activism. The position also reflects in political quietism: positioning Islam as a distinct social field that provides legitimacy to a political ruler – a ruler that provides it with a high degree of autonomy in return. Adnan al-Aroor, for example, is a Saudi-based Syrian sheikh who argued against rising up in the weeks prior to the uprising but completely changed his position as the uprising started and Saudi Arabia came out to support the challenge to Bashar al-Assad's rule. His position moved from quietism to activism given it did not oppose his political patrons.

An analogical position is reflected in a preoccupation for the safeguarding of an Islamic creed (or *'aqīdah*) and the purity of religion (in name of a unity of faith, or *tawheed*), rejecting established schools of Islamic jurisprudence (the *madhāhib*) and opposing religious innovations (or *bid'ah*). These terms act as a signifier for attempts to construct an Islamic field that is autonomous from the worldly affairs of political, educational, judicial and other social and political fields, in the name of a return to an authentic, real Islam.[11] This autonomy is, often, partial – sometimes it is an outright farce. Analogical positions are often taken by activists who engage in educational and charitable activism, rendering their analogical position partial. Sometimes, they are taken in tacit support for a ruling regime (for example with Saudi Wahhabist scholars), giving them immense political clout. More often, the fact that activists reference a restoration of a true Islam challenges established hierarchies of an Islamist movement, altering their internal dynamics and their external impacts.

One historical figure who should be mentioned in relation to this position is Muhammad bin Abd al-Wahhab (1703–92) who, drawing on scholars such as Ibn Taymiyya and Ibn Qayyim, articulated a distinctly analogical position around the notion of *tawheed*. Crucially, in this case, he created an alliance with Muhammad bin Sa'ud where the latter acted as a political leader and the former as a religious authority of what would become Saudi Arabia. Although by far not the only Islamist current taking analogical positions, the particular political quietist character of these analogical positions taken by subsequent Wahhabist scholars would have an important impact on activism during the Tunisian transition and Syrian crisis.

The life histories of several individuals discussed in Chapters four and five mirrored an analogical lineage in an Islamist movement. Idrissi Khatib, for example, emigrated to Saudi Arabia in 1985 for work. While there, he became influenced by Wahhabist scholars. On his return to Tunisia in 1994 he became a leading voice among a Tunisian Islamist movement, advocating noninstitutionalised, quietist social activism. Adnan al-Aroor fled Hama, Syria, in 1982 during the Islamist uprising against Hafez al-Assad, the father of current Syrian president Bashar al-Assad. He settled in Saudi Arabia. A final example is the Tunisian activist Omar, who started secret video rooms in the early 2000s to listen and learn from Gulf sheikhs. In almost complete isolation, he never left Tunisia and was one of the many youngsters being influenced by these Gulf sheikhs.

These resources and dispositions are practised through analogical positions. They reflect in the existence of a body of Islamist sheikhs who distance their activism from existing social and political fields because they provide tacit support to a political regime, as with Wahhabism, or because they perceive social and political interactions to somehow corrupt an Islamic distinction. Together with the biographies that inculcate analogical dispositions, it provides Islamist analogy with a distinct history and biography.

Relational Positions Compared

The existence of an Islamist movement can be empirically observed: an Islamist movement is constituted by the distinction that separates relational, contentious interactions between those with a stake in shaping the use of Islam to render practices distinct and those who do not. The conflicts between Ennahda and grassroots activists around the inclusion of sharia in the constitution, fights for control over mosques and struggles around resuming education at the Zaytuna Mosque were all examples of distinct conflicts between activists with a stake in shaping the position of Islam in Tunisian society and politics. During the Syrian crisis, such distinct patterns were reflected in conflicts between Ahrar al-Sham and the Nusra Front to control a judiciary field in rebel-controlled territories and fights around *ahl al-ḥall wa-al-ʿaqd* to define the relationship between an Islamic community and political authority. These struggles brought together a subset of activists into a collective movement. It seems reasonable to label these movements as Islamist ones because they revolved around using Islam to render practices distinct, turned Islam into a social and political stake and ended up imbuing Islamic faith with political relevance.

It is different with the notion of relational positions. They are a heuristic device, an ideal-type to help make sense of the conflicts that draw an Islamist movement together. Relational positions cannot be used to characterise Islamist organisations or individuals. It might be tempting, for instance, to describe the Syrian Muslim Brotherhood or the Tunisian Ennahda Movement as homological organisations. The problem is that it does not conform to empirical reality. The Syrian Muslim Brotherhood is fractured along different wings, with the Hama/Homs wing traditionally being of more heterological inclination than the Aleppo/Damascus one, while the Ennahda Movement also had its fair share of relational struggles between members who advocated for armed, heterological activism and those more inclined to take pragmatic, homological actions. During the transition, debates emerged between those who advocated for pure homology in a political field, implying professional specialisation, and those that advocated for retaining a coherent social-political movement based on Islam. Islamist organisations are too internally diverse to be described by a single positional label. They are better described as sites of struggle – as social fields themselves – in which a group of agents interact and struggle for dominance.

The same applies to individual activists. A single individual can, and does, interact with multiple social fields, often taking different, seemingly contradictory, positions. Ridha Jaouadi, for instance, was an independent imam who established a charitable association and labour union during the early years of the Tunisian transition and later became a member of parliament for the Dignity Coalition. It seems to imply a rather homological approach to Islamist activism. Meanwhile, he directly challenged the Minister of Religious Affairs on the extent that he could discuss politics as an imam, his charity was closed because it did not comply with financial regulations and he left the Dignity Coalition when it applied for formal status as a political party, arguing that he opposed formal political institutionalisation. All far more analogical positions. Omar created a private school as an association, complying with relevant regulations while challenging the authority of the Ministry of Women, Family and Children. It goes to show that the positions that activists take are shaped as much by their biographies (and the resulting individual dispositions) as the context in which they are active (and the structured resources that come with it). The exact position that activists take in relation to a particular event is unknowable until the moment it has been enacted. Individuals, as well as organisations, cannot be characterised in advance by a type of relational position – only practices can.

This brings us to an important observation: an Islamist movement is a field that comprises numerous subfields (such as organisations, institutions, congregations) that all have their own Islam-related stakes and regulative principles. It means that an Islamist movement, on closer inspection, falls apart into subfields until you get to the level of individual activists. An Islamist movement is not subdivided along different homological, heterological or analogical positions or along a Salafist, jihadist or quietist current. Rather, it is subdivided along further conflicts to define the relevance of Islamist resources, dispositions, organisations and individuals in shaping social and political practices.

Comparing Episodes

The observation that an Islamist movement is a field itself, comprising numerous subfields, shapes how we can compare occurrences across conflict episodes. It implies we compare processes instead of substantive entities. The result is a comparative analysis of the process through which Islam turned into a stake, rendering its social interactions distinct from the broader social dynamics of a conflict episode. Comparing an Islamist movement during the Tunisian transition and Syrian crisis, for example, results in tracing the process through which Islam turned into a distinct social and political stake and patterned contentious interactions that made up these episodes of social and political conflict.

In Chapter four, for example, we observed how in the weeks and months after the Tunisian revolution, Islam turned into a social and political stake and brought together a subset of agents in a set of distinct, and often contentious, social interactions. These were individuals such as Rached Ghannouchi and Habib Ellouze, both Ennahda politicians, Hussein Obeidi, the Grand Imam of the Zaytuna Mosque, Abu Iyadh, veteran jihadist and founder of Ansar Charia, Ridha Jaouadi and Idrissi Khatib, both independent imams and Omar, a grassroots activist who established a chain of Islamic schools. These individuals took very different positions when enacting distinctly Islamic practices. An Islamist movement started out as diverse and lacking a clear hierarchy.

As the Tunisian transition progressed, homological positions turned increasingly hegemonic. Reflecting its political clout, Ennahda's emphasis on pragmatism and preoccupation with retaining political power became dominant. This was especially the case after 2013 and 2014, when repression of Islamic associations and schools increased. Other positions, practised by Obeidi, Abu Iyadh, Khatib and Omar, were sidelined. Obeidi was rendered irrelevant as he was sacked as Grand Imam of the Zaytuna Mosque, Jaouadi was barred from preaching, Idrissi Khatib's mosque was closed – as was Omar's school and association. Some activists left Tunisia altogether (Abu Iyadh left for Libya where he was killed in 2015 and many other youngsters who took a similar position left for Syria to fight in the jihad there). Ennahda's pragmatic Islamist homologies turned dominant. It meant that when, in 2016, Ennahda rejected its Islamist credentials out of political pragmatism and from then on solely focused on party politics, an Islamist movement in the Tunisian transition collapsed. A brief populist Islamist resurgence by the Dignity Coalition during the 2019 elections could do little about this.[12]

During the Syrian crisis, an Islamist movement rose in unison with the emergence of an armed insurgency next to a nonviolent, nationalist and democratic uprising. We observed in Chapter five that when Islam turned into a social and political stake, it drew together a subset of agents. Some examples were: Osama al-Rifai and Ratib, a famous Syrian religious scholar and imam from Daraa, respectively, and both members of the Syrian Islamic Council; Hassan Aboud as the leader of Ahrar al-Sham; Abu Muhammad al-Julani as the founder and leader of the Nusra Front and later Hayat Tahrir al-Sham; Abu Muhammad al-Adnani as spokesperson of the Nusra Front and later ISIS; and Tarif al-Sayed Issa as veteran Syrian Muslim Brotherhood member who returned from exile after the start of the uprising. Also in this case, these individuals took very different positions when rendering their practices distinctly Islamic.

Throughout the first few years of the Syrian crisis, a heterological, jihadist position against civil authority became increasingly dominant. Several early Islamist factions, such as the Tawheed Brigade, referred to an external religious authority, embedding themselves in established social and religious fields. Later, groups that created their own internal religious authorities – as internal sharia councils and courts – became more powerful. Examples are Ahrar al-Sham and the Nusra Front. Later still, ISIS's Islamic State created a state bureaucracy that was subservient to a religious authority. Becoming ever more powerful, these organisations ended up sidelining the nonviolent uprising and the traditional religious authority of the Syrian *'ulamā'* (religious scholars). As rebel groups took control over various territories, it meant that heterological positions in relation to governance, judiciary and public services turned dominant. They created a plethora of distinctly Islamic governance organisations, courts and service providers that directly challenged governance organisations created by civil opposition groups. In doing so, they enabled the attachment of Sunni Islam to global and local collective identities, increasing sectarian tensions. It also opened up a conflict about how to relate Sunni Islamic collective identity and authorities to the concrete localised development of the Syrian crisis.[13]

As the insurgency fractured along local and global conflict dynamics, so did these initiatives. An Islamist movement turned increasingly away from a national focus. It turned both localised and globalised as the Syrian uprising fractured because of foreign incursions, with the rise of ISIS as its culmination. Eventually, foreign interventions and internal infighting created the context in which a local hegemon – al-Julani of Hayat Tahrir al-Sham – could emerge, while a Turkish intervention empowered the traditional *'ulamā'*, such as al-Rifai and Ratib and their Syrian Islamic Council. Both were severely constrained by a lack of resources and inability to shape the dynamics of the conflict. Hassan Aboud and much of Ahrar al-Sham's leadership were assassinated in 2014, Abu Muhammad al-Adnani was killed in 2016 and Tarif al-Sayed Issa was murdered in 2018. The Syrian crisis had lost much of its autonomous dynamics and with it an Islamist movement declined.

In the briefest of terms, an Islamist movement during the Tunisian transition increasingly revolved around the conflict to define how to practise homology in relation to a political field. It reflected the relatively stable, nationally defined character of social fields during the Tunisian transition. During the Syrian crisis, an Islamist movement revolved increasingly around the struggle to define heterological Islamist practices. It mirrored, and nurtured, the instability and fragmentation of social fields during the crisis. These different impacts emerged at the intersection of, the historically defined, structural contexts of the Tunisian transition and Syrian crisis and the, biographically defined, individual dispositions of activists involved.

Comparing Currents

The observation that an Islamist movement is a field itself, comprising numerous subfields, also shapes how we compare currents within a single Islamist movement. It implies that an Islamist movement is subdivided along lineages of internal conflicts to define Islamic distinctness, not along particular relational positions or ideological characteristics. Its subdivisions are descriptions of distinct social processes, not ideological structures. Following this approach, it is possible to, for example, distinguish between a political and jihadist current in an Islamist movement.

Political Islamists can refer to those activists who are involved in a conflict to define the legitimate ways to situate an Islamic distinctness in relation to party politics. Participants in this conflict are, for example, the Syrian Muslim Brotherhood and the Tunisian Ennahda. Another group is the Tunisian Reform Front, which advocated for a unity of faith and advocated for mirroring the prophet's life – while institutionalising as a political party. The Tunisian branch of Hizb al-Tahrir, arguing they would create an Islamic State when gaining a parliamentary majority, is another example. Engagement with a political field brings up questions among Islamists of how to relate to popular and religious legitimacy while participating in party politics. These agents take very different relational positions in regard to this issue but are set apart as a current in an Islamist movement because they interact as political parties a in democratic political field.

Jihadist Islamists can refer to those agents that practise an Islamic type of organised collective violence. It detaches the practice from the monopoly of violence of existing nation-states. This means that jihadist Islamists are engaged in a struggle about how to relate the global practice of jihadist collective violence to national identities and local governance initiatives. The tensions between the Nusra Front and the Islamic State in Iraq, revolving around the extent that al-Julani embedded his organisation in the local dynamics of the Syrian insurgency, is an example. It led to the creation of ISIS: a fully-fledged bureaucratic organisation representing the global Muslim community that was detached from the aspirations of the Syrian uprising and insurgency. Again, it is possible to take very different positions in relation to this struggle.

In both cases, these currents exist because a particular stake emerged within the Islamist movement – political legitimacy and collective violence – that gave birth to a distinct historical and biographical lineage and to distinct subtypes of structural resources and individual dispositions. It is possible to distinguish other currents. Quietist Islamists can refer to those Islamists who are brought together around the struggle to practise (non)political activism: publicly situating themselves as nonpolitical while actively trying to transform societies and providing legitimacy to established political regimes. Wahhabist Islamists can be those Islamists who engage in a struggle to situate a political allegiance to Saudi rulers in relation to local dynamics of an Islamist movement. The designations of currents are flexible as stakes within an Islamist movement as it emerges, transforms and declines. With it, currents rise and fall.

Future Scenarios

This brings us to the impacts of the two case studies on future developments of an Islamist movement. The scenarios I describe are nothing more than informed guesses, but in doing so, I outline the logic through which a contentious practices approach (CPA) can articulate scenarios of future change. It is a predication of evolutionary transformation: what currents are present and which ones are likely to find social and political niches in which they will thrive?

First, the Tunisian transition and Syrian crisis made certain struggles dominant while marginalising others. It is likely that the struggle around relating Islam to party politics becomes more marginal. In both episodes, attempts to translate Islam into a distinct type of party politics failed. The Syrian Muslim Brotherhood was sidelined in an, increasingly powerless, Syrian Interim Government. Under pressure of political pragmatism, the Tunisian Ennahda distanced itself from an Islamist label altogether. Direct, revolutionary challenges to states are also likely to remain marginal. In both case studies, an Islamist movement was not present during the initial uprising. ISIS built an alternative Islamic nation-state, instead of trying to take over an existing one. During the Tunisian transition, it was the state executive that provided the most formidable opponent to an Islamist movement. The civil character of state bureaucracies seems so entrenched that it will be able to resist any Islamist challenge. Third, al-Qaeda's approach of creating local franchises of a global jihadist struggle imploded with Julani's takeover in Syria and ISIS emergence. Instead, what seems to have won out is the struggle to create local governance in name of a global state. In short, the way that the Tunisian transition and Syrian crisis worked out seems to have empowered struggles around the legitimate ways to implement local governance in name of a global Sunni Islamic nation-state within an Islamist movement.

The second question that the CPA implies is whether there will be sociopolitical niches that provide a breeding ground for such struggles. Failing and weak states, where social services, justice and security are imploding, would seem to provide fertile contexts for such approaches to be enacted. It implies a transformation of jihadist movements from being focused on collective violence (al-Qaeda) to state building (ISIS) to increasingly focused on malleable local instances of service provision – including justice and violence – but whereas these previously happened in name of emirates, it is likely they will increasingly happen in name of a transnational Islamic State. It can be expected that it will lead to constant splits and reunifications of subgroups around the ways to do so in practice. It would mean that one of the central questions of our time – how to situate local identities and national states in relation to a globalising world – will transpose into the Islamist movement.

Mechanisms of Distinction

In both the Syrian crisis and Tunisian transition, an Islamist movement emerged, transformed and declined. Meanwhile, these two rather different occurrences can be considered part of a single broader Islamist movement. For instance, the relational positions described above, and their lineages, applied to both because they shared a historical and biographical genealogy. Activists in both movements knew about, or even had first-hand experiences with, Egyptian Muslim Brotherhood activism, the Saudi Islamic Awakening and the jihadist uprising against the US invasion of Iraq, to name a few examples. It meant that activists could, and did, travel between episodes of social conflict while practising distinctly Islamic types of practices. Activists travelled from Tunisia to fight in the Syrian crisis, the International Union of Muslim Scholars (of Yusuf al-Qaradawi) was active in both episodes and ISIS and al-Qaeda established a presence in both Tunisia and Syria. Despite emerging in relation to a particular episode of social and political conflict, these Islamist movements are related through the histories and biographies of a global Islamist movement.

In Chapter two, I noted that a social movement is subjected to temporal and spatial forces that create tensions between structural positionality and individual dispositions. On the one hand, the uniqueness of individual experiences is always at odds with the history of the context in which activists find themselves. On the other hand, the geographic spread of a movement creates tensions between the distinctness of movement practices and the diversity of accepted norms and fields in which they are active. How is it possible that an Islamist movement keeps its cohesion despite being subjected to such diverse forces across time and space? In the following section, I propose two causal mechanisms that can explain this variety and endurance: reproductive innovation and contentious selection. These two mechanisms relate individual dispositions (and their biographies) to contextual resources (and their histories) and, at their intersection, make up a relational process that is a social movement.

Reproductive Innovation

With reproductive innovation, I refer to the transfer of relational positions between contentious episodes. Reproduction of these positions builds on the spatial and temporal distance between the internalisation and enactment of individual dispositions. In simpler terms, a practice is reproduced when an individual gains an experience in one situation and practises it in another. This can be because individuals physically move from one to another (for example jihadists in the Syrian crisis with lived experiences from the Iraqi uprising) or through indirect exposure (for example through sound rooms in which Omar and his friends received classes from Saudi sheikhs). Such reproductions are never exact carbon copies and are always imperfect because they are shaped by individual aptitude, biography and experiences. It implies they are the source of social variation. I give two examples of such variation related to individuals that were discussed earlier in this chapter, but Chapters four and five provide more examples.

Compare Hassan Aboud (the late leader of Ahrar al-Sham) with Abu Muhammad al-Julani (the leader of the Nusra Front) and their transfer of heterological positions. Although both fought for, and internalised, similar practices in the Iraqi jihadist uprising of 2003–4, Hassan Aboud's experience with these practices differed from that of Abu Muhammad al-Julani. The former returned to Syria in 2005, and on his return was incarcerated in Sednaya by the Syrian regime. He was released after the uprising started. The latter remained in Iraq, where the Americans incarcerated him for several years. When they found themselves in the Syrian crisis, these experiences shaped how they constructed distinctly Islamist ways of articulating Islamic collective identity: Hassan Aboud practised a Syrian jihadist identity and Al-Julani situated his Nusra Front as a representative of a global jihadist community that came to the aid of a localised struggle against an apostate ruler. These two leaders approached the construction of a jihadist community in different ways. This difference cannot be explained without taking their different biographical experiences into account.

Another example is the Tunisian Rached Ghannouchi and the transformation of *al-Jamāʿah al-Islāmīyah*, or the Islamic Group. Ghannouchi briefly studied in Egypt and observed the repression of the Muslim Brotherhood first hand. As he was barred from the University of Cairo, he moved to Damascus to study philosophy, where he converted his political allegiance from pan-Arabism to Islamism. After he finished his studies in Damascus, he moved for his postgraduate studies to Paris, where he became involved with the Dawa wa-Tabligh, an Islamist movement that is strongly focused on proselytisation, rejecting institutionalisation and political activism. When Ghannouchi co-founded *al-Jamāʿah al-Islāmīyah*, their principal aim was proselytisation – reflecting a background in the Dawa wa-Tabligh movement – but with a focus on social change – reflecting an Arab nationalist and leftist influence. They used the Muslim Brotherhood as an institutional example to create an elaborate, layered recruitment structure that safeguarded their secret movement, while facilitating the onboarding of new recruits. In short, *al-Jamāʿah al-Islāmīyah* reflected knowledge of the Muslim Brotherhood and experience with Dawa wa-Tabligh activism but translated into a particular Tunisian context.

These are two examples of reproducing practices from one context to another. Both these examples show the importance of individual biography in this process. It implies that the reproduction of practices is unique: it varies from one individual to the next.

Contentious Selection

With contentious selection, I refer to the struggles to define the legitimate principles along which practices are rendered distinct. These struggles limit the range of legitimate positions in a social movement. They are specific to a conflict episode. The conflict around including sharia in the constitution during the Tunisian constitutional drafting process is one example. Another example is the struggle for independent education at the Zaytuna Mosque and the repression of Ansar Charia's activities after the assassination of two Tunisian politicians. During the Syrian crisis, the fight for control over sharia courts is an example, as is the struggle to define the *ahl al-ḥall wa-al-ʿaqd*, or the representation of a Muslim community that has the authority to assign and depose a caliph. These are struggles to control Sunni Islam as symbolic, social and economic resource in relation to a conflict episode.

These struggles are distinct to, and form the basis of, an Islamist movement during a conflict episode. During the Tunisian transition, we observed how an Islamist movement started out as diverse and turned homological under Ennahda's dominance. Nonhomological positions, practised by Obeidi, Abu Iyadh, Khatib and Omar, were sidelined. During the Syrian crisis, an Islamist movement emerged in unison with an armed insurgency, challenging Bashar al-Assad's regime through violent means. With many participants taking their experiences from the Iraqi insurgency, this Islamist movement became dominated by a heterological, jihadist position against civil authority, sidelining, among others, the traditional religious authority of the Syrian *'ulamā'*.

Islamist movements during the Tunisian transition and Syrian crisis had their own dynamics, with different relational positions becoming dominant in each episode. They emerged around conflicts to select the legitimate ways to render social and political practices distinctly Islamic. It is with this lens that we compared an Islamist movement between the two episodes of social and political conflict.

Social Movement

Together, the two mechanisms of reproductive innovation and contentious selection combine in a process of evolution of distinct practices across time and space. Individuals reproduce practices from one contentious episode to another, and hence they diverge. Within each episode there are struggles to define the legitimate ways of constructing distinctly Islamic types of contentious practices, and hence practices converge. The transfer of distinct practices is shaped by individual biographies, turning into reproductive innovation. The struggle to define legitimate principles of distinct practices is shaped by contextual history, turning into contentious selection.

Combined, these two mechanisms make up the evolution of distinctly Sunni Islamic practices between contentious episodes across time and space. The above theorisation echoes Bourdieu's remark that to understand the practices of agents, we need to understand that 'they are the result of a meeting of two histories: a history of the position they occupy and the history of their dispositions'.[14] Each has their own type of social reproduction and variation – as they build on a different relations between time, action and actor – and hence the 'confrontation between positions and dispositions' is one that is an enduring part of social life. Together, they form the mechanisms through which a social and political stake, in this case Sunni Islam, evolves across contentious episodes and gains an enduring character. In short, these two mechanisms make up the process of an Islamist movement. They define its impact on the Tunisian transition and Syrian crisis – and beyond.

Notes

1. Bourdieu, *The Field of Cultural Production: Essays on Art and Literature*, 61.
2. Qasim Zaman, *The Ulama in Contemporary Islam: Custodians of Change*; Tripp, 'Islam and The Moral Economy: The Challenge of Capitalism'; Tobin, *Everyday Piety: Islam and Economy in Jordan*.
3. McAdam, Tilly and Tarrow, *Dynamics of Contention*; Fligstein and McAdam, 'Toward a General Theory of Strategic Action Fields'; Jasper, 'A Strategic Approach to Collective Action: Looking for Agency in Social-Movement Choices'.
4. For a detailed discussion of these issues, see Chapter two, *Relational Approaches in Social Movement Studies*.
5. For his use of Homology, see Bourdieu, 'Symbolic Power', 81; Bourdieu, *The State Nobility: Elite Schools in the Field of Power*, 270–1.
6. Siba'i, *al-Ishtirāqiya al-Islām*, 8.
7. Ghannouchi, *Al-Ḥurrīyāt Al-ʿĀmmah Fī Al-Dawlah Al-Islāmīyah*.
8. Qutb, *Milestones*.
9. World Islamic Front, 'World Islamic Front Statement Urging Jihad Against Jews and Crusaders'.
10. Interview with Khatib Idriss, 4 April 2011, Sidi Ali Ben Aoun, Tunisia.
11. See Chapter three, *State Interventions*; *Revolutions*.
12. See Chapter four for a more detailed discussion of these developments.
13. See Chapter five for a more detailed discussion of these developments.
14. Bourdieu, *The Field of Cultural Production: Essays on Art and Literature*, 61.

7

CONCLUSIONS

I started this book by narrating a visit to Khatib Idrissi. He is a sheikh who lives in Sidi Ali Ben Aoun, a small town in the inland of Tunisia. Khatib Idrissi was incarcerated during the regime of Ben Ali between 2006 and 2009 and became active again following the January 2011 revolution. When I visited him, in April 2011, he had resumed teaching classes in memorisation of the Quran, Islamic exegesis, creed and jurisprudence. He was also building a mosque next to his house. When finished, he would use it to teach sharia sciences. Every weekend he travelled with a small group of students around the country to give speeches and lessons at local mosques.[1] I started with the story of Khatib Idrissi because he exemplified the topic of this book: the impact of an Islamist movement on the Tunisian transition and Syrian crisis.

Throughout this book, I came back to Khatib Idrissi a few more times. The Ministry of Religious Affairs, in June 2013, formally recognised his mosque as the Rahma Mosque. Despite this formal recognition, the mosque kept its autonomy. The Ministry did not assign its Friday and weekly imams and did not pay a stipend to them. In the following years, as the Ministry of Religious Affairs increasingly enforced control over the hiring and firing of imams, the Rahma Mosque turned into one of the last bastions of resistance. The Ministry described it as harbouring Salafist and jihadist activists but could not bring the Mosque under its supervision because it was built on private land. Eventually, though, during the summer of 2016, the Ministry prevailed.

The story of Khatib Idrissi reflected the emergence and decline of an Islamist movement during the Tunisian transition. As narrated in Chapter four, immediately following the revolution, activists established hundreds of Islamic associations, Islamists were released from prison, mosque congregations replaced imams and Islamic political parties were rebuilt. As a result, an Islamist movement emerged. When, in the following years, an empowered state executive increasingly challenged the Tunisian transition, this movement declined. An Islamist movement also emerged – and declined – during the Syrian crisis, as chronicled in Chapter five, mirroring the development of an armed insurgency that had developed next to a nonviolent uprising challenging the regime of Bashar al-Assad. Both case studies approached an Islamist movement not as a substantive phenomenon defined by a particular ideology but as a distinct pattern of relational interactions that emerged around Islam as social and political stake.

Three Propositions

What is the impact of Islamist movements on post-2011 Arab activism? Drawing on the analytical approach described in Chapter two, the historical narrative of Chapter three, the empirical data provided in Chapters four and five and the comparative analysis of Chapter six, I propose the following.

The Impact of Islamist Movements is Relationally Practised

Sunni Islam impacts collective action during episodes of social and political conflict not because of the particular ideas it provides but because activists use it to render practices distinct. For instance, during the Tunisian transition we observed that, in a wave of associational organising following the 2011 revolution, Tunisian activists established numerous Islamic associations aimed at charitable activism, education, knowledge and social reform. Activists also enacted a distinct type of Islamic education through the creation of Islamic nurseries, independent religious adult education, developing classes at mosques and fighting for the educational autonomy of the, historically powerful, Zaytuna Mosque. During the Syrian crisis, rebels used Islam to establish distinctly jihadist fighting factions. Following the takeover of large parts of Syrian territory, sharia courts disrupted the judiciary field, and Islamic service providers, such as the sharia committees, disrupted day-to-day governance.

During the Tunisian transition, Abu Iyadh, a veteran of the Afghan jihad, established Ansar Charia as an organisation to provide services and police public behaviour. Last but not least, ISIS's caliphate enacted a modern nation-state that represented a global Sunni Muslim community. In these examples, activists positioned Islam in relation to associational activism, education, executive power, collective violence, judiciary and legislature by using Islam to render their practices in these fields distinct.

Because activists used it to render their practices distinct, Sunni Islam impacted collective action. The establishment of hundreds of Islamic associations produced a subset of associations that engaged in shared mobilisation in defence of Islam and fostered relationships to imams and mosques. The emergence of independent imams – imams that were appointed by their congregations, rather than by the Ministry of Religious Affairs – provided a new and autonomous space for collective action. Private Islamic schools created an alternative, Islamic educational field challenging the control of the Ministry of Women, Family and Children and the Ministry of Education. The electoral victory of the Ennahda Movement in the 2011 elections gave hope for political representation of religiously conservative Tunisians who had previously faced regime repression. Rendering rebel groups jihadist facilitated access to global support networks. Establishing sharia courts upended control over judicial resources. The same applied to the day-to-day governance of public service provision by creating sharia committees. In all these cases, practising a Sunni Islamic distinctness had very real implications for access to political, institutional and educational resources. Sunni Islam impacted collective action because activists used it to disrupt established power hierarchies in associational, educational, executive and legislative fields by creating distinctly Islamic alternatives to their established practices.

Islamist Movements Comprise a Two-fold Struggle to Define their Impact

When Islamists enact distinctly Islamic educational, charitable, public service, governance or legislative practices, it brings them into conflict with other non-Islamist agents in related fields. With the provision of services, for example, Islamists found either ministries (during the Tunisian transition) or local councils and the Interim Government (during the Syrian crisis) against them. In conflicts over building a mosque at the University of Tunis, the Council of

Professors stood their ground against mobilised students. Eventually, jihadist rebel groups faced off with civil groups in the Syrian civil war. In each case, the enactment of distinctly Islamic practices challenged the position of established agents in related fields. It had an external impact. It led to sustained conflictual interactions between Islamist and non-Islamist agents.

Concurrently, when Islamists enact these practices, they were, inadvertently, also caught up in internal struggles about the legitimate ways in which practices can be rendered Islamic. Ennahda's approach of situating Islam as a source of Tunisian national identity translated into attempts to enshrine the protection of sanctities in the Tunisian constitution and represent Islam through party politics. Several agents, such as Omar and the Tunisian Front for Islamic Associations, mobilised to include explicit references to sharia, aiming to represent Islam through codified law instead. Meanwhile, grassroots activists around sheikhs such as Abu Iyadh and Idrissi Khatib argued that the aims of the Reform Front – a party legalised in 2012 during the Ennahda-led Troika government – to implement sharia rule in all parts of life, based on Islamic unity (*tawheed*) and the method of the Prophet (*manhaj an-nabawi*), were not compatible with the fragmentation of party politics and national identities. But among these sheikhs who opposed the Tunisian state and democratic politics also different positions appeared. Idrissi Khatib initially participated in a joint council with Abu Iyadh, for example, but left because of the latter's insistence on institutionalising activism.

As noted before, the enactment of a Sunni Islamic distinctness had direct, real world implications for access to political, institutional and educational resources. In doing so, it laid the basis for distinct social interactions between a subset of agents that had a stake in using Islam to access these resources. It gave birth to a distinct pattern of social interactions between individuals such as Ghannouchi, Ellouze (both Ennahda politicians), Abu Iyadh (leader of Ansar Charia), Jaouadi (an independent imam), Obeidi (Grand Imam of the Zaytuna Mosque) and Omar and Hamza (both grassroots activists). As a result, these individuals were brought together as participants of an Islamist movement during the Tunisian transition.

During the Syrian crisis, the creation of distinctly Islamic sharia courts set off a struggle over judicial authority. It kindled a struggle around the extent that Islamic law should, or should not, be codified. The establishment of sharia committees, in turn, meant the creation of an alternative institutional framework for public service provision. It triggered a struggle among jihadist rebel groups, especially between the Nusra Front and Ahrar al-Sham, for control over these organisations. The involvement of Islamist rebel groups in local governance kindled struggles around the relationship between an Islamic collective identity and executive power. The split between the Nusra Front and ISIS revolved around this issue. It subsequently led to a polarised debate around the notion of *ahl al-ḥall wa-al-ʿaqd* and diverging strategies of bridging a jihadist collective identity to that of the Syrian uprising. These inter-Islamist conflicts involved the Syrian Islamic Council, Ahrar al-Sham, the Nusra Front, ISIS and many other groups. They pitted individuals such as al-Rifai (of the Syrian Islamic Council), Aboud (Ahrar al-Sham), al-Julani (the Nusra Front), al-Adnani (ISIS), Ratib (the local sheikh from Daraa) and Issa (a Muslim Brotherhood member) against each other. As with the Tunisian transition, it brought them together as participants in an Islamist movement, but this time in relation to the Syrian crisis.

Impact of an Islamist Movement is Historically and Biographically Situated

Experiences during prior conflicts shapes how activists use Islam to render practices distinct during contemporary ones. With Rached Ghannouchi, it is safe to assume that the experiences of political struggles in the 1980s, incarceration and his subsequent exile in Europe shaped his tendency for pragmatic consensus, or what we can call a homological position, during the Tunisian transition. The more adversarial, or rather heterological, positions taken by Islamist rebel groups during Syrian crisis need to be understood in light of their experiences with the jihadist insurgency against the US invasion of Iraq and subsequent incarceration at the Sednaya prison close to Damascus. The split between the Nusra Front and ISIS cannot be understood without taking into account the transformation of al-Qaeda into the Islamic State in Iraq. Idrissi Khatib's isolationist, or analogical, approach relates to his emigration to Saudi Arabia in the 1980s and exposure to Wahhabist scholarship. This is also true for Omar and his experiences of learning from Gulf sheikhs in his secret sound rooms. Every time, the positions that agents took reflected their embodied experiences.

Inversely, the use of Islam to render practices distinct is situated in a historical context. When an individual takes a position in a conflict around

Islamic education, sharia in the constitution, sharia courts or governance, their actions are constraint by a, historically contingent, structural context of an educational, judicial legislative or governance field. The historical strength, despite years of autocratic rule, of Tunisian associations, student movements and labour unions created a context that fostered institutionalisation of social activism, while a history of state-led, top-down privatisation of religion forced a strong secularist versus Islamic bifurcation onto the dynamics of the Tunisian transition. In the case of the Syrian crisis, a history of a brutal crackdown of an uprising in the 1980s led to a large group of exiled sheikhs living in Europe and the Gulf. Bashar al-Assad's use of jihadists against US forces in Iraq nurtured a Syrian element among jihadist movements in the region. Domestically, the regime played on sectarian fears to act as protector of minorities which historically frustrated the development of a strong relationship between a national identity and state authority. It meant that when the Syrian crisis started, sectarian fears legitimated a brutal crackdown, while jihadists were readily available to Islamise an armed insurgency. In combination, it meant that when an armed insurgency appeared, the Syrian crisis soon developed into a protracted civil war in which jihadist factions had an outsized influence.

It implies that an Islamist movement results from the meeting of two histories. First, it results from the biographies of its participants and, second, of the history of the context in which a movement emerges. When, for instance, Ghannouchi squared off with grassroots activists around including sharia in the Tunisian constitution, it was the meeting of a biography of 1980s activism and subsequent exile with youth who had become accustomed to Islamism through informal underground online education during the early 2000s. This happened in relation to a political transition that became polarised along a bifurcation between a *laique* and Islamist social pole. It gave Ennahda – and Ghannouchi – access to political resources while being forced into pragmatism, while the sudden liberalisation of society and politics gave young grassroots activists the sense they could, finally, have a meaningful impact. They were fighting to shape the position of Islam during the Tunisian transition in the image of their embodied past.

The same applies to the Syrian crisis. When Osama al-Rifai, Hassan Aboud, al-Julani and al-Adnani fought to define the meaning of *ahl al-ḥall wa-al-ʿaqd*, their positions could not be understood without considering their experiences of exile in Saudi Arabia, insurgency in Iraq and incarceration at Sednaya prison. Meanwhile, the dynamics of their interactions – and the conflict around *ahl al-ḥall wa-al-ʿaqd* itself – could only emerge because of the state collapse and sectarian tension that enabled the rise of ISIS. In short, the impact of an Islamist movement during conflict episodes can only be understood if we approach it as the meeting of two histories: a history of participants' dispositions and the history of the structural context, and its positions, in which they find themselves.

The Contentious Practices Approach Assessed

In this book, I argued that scholars should focus on what people do, instead of what they think, when investigating the impact of Islamist movements on conflict episodes. The notion of distinct practices is a useful tool to do this. I finish this book with a brief discussion of three potential contributions that the concept of distinct practices can make to studies on social movements and political Islam.

First, the concept of distinct practices emphasises the importance of contextual history and individual biography in the study of social, and Islamist, movements. During the last two decades there have been numerous studies on social movements – and quite a few on Islamist movements – that applied a relational, interactionist analysis.[2] These studies revolved around the notion of causal mechanisms, strategic action fields or strategic interactions. They highlighted the interactive, dynamic character of social movements. What they proved less good at is situating these social mechanisms among a broader set of social processes, or a particular strategic action field among others, that make up the broader historical and biographical context in which relational interactions occur.[3]

Distinct practices instead provides a meso-level analysis of how social movements develop at the intersection of biography and history. It does this by analysing how a stake is being situated, by rendering it distinct, in relation to other social fields. Chapter six provided a taxonomy of relational positions taken by Islamists. Each position described a particular relational logic – of homology, heterology and analogy – that used Islam to render practices distinct. These relational positions all had their own genealogies, situating them in relation to a history of an Islamist movement, referencing the likes of Hassan al-Banna, Sayyid Qutb, Rached Ghannouchi, Abdallah Azzam and Osama bin Laden. These genealogies also situated these positions in relation to the contexts in which they emerged: from post-independence state reforms, to the revolutions of the 1970s, aborted democratisations of the 1990s and global identitarian conflict of the 2000s.

As individual activists practised homological, heterological or analogical positions in inter-Islamist struggles during the Tunisian transition and Syrian crisis, they enacted an embodied history of an Islamist movement. The relational positions described in Chapter six emerge at the intersection of individual dispositions – and biographies – and the contexts in which they are practised – and their history. This meso-level intersection is the source of social conflict, change and movement.

Second, the notion of distinct practices helps position Islamist movements in relation to local, regional and global conflicts. It goes beyond the, still prevalent, focus on either global or national movements in studies on social movements. Doing so, it moves social movements and political Islam away from being defined by polities, towards an approach that defines them in relation to conflict. The dominance of the political process approach and the concept of political opportunity structures in studies on social movements has led to a near monopoly of analyses that define social movements along the polity with which they interact. Studies focus on social movements' interactions with particular nation-states or as movements active at a global stage – with al-Qaeda being the primary example of what scholars describe as a transnational or global social movement.[4] The same applies, to some extent, to studies on political Islam and Islamism, with scholars dividing Islamist organisations along their national or global character.[5] The problem is that these fixed categorisations do not conform to empirical reality. Ansar Charia was created to transform Tunisian society and state, while its founder – Abu Iyadh – was a veteran of the global jihad. As state repression increased, he had no trouble embedding himself back into transnational Islamist movements. The same applied to many of its lower-level activists who had no trouble with switching – and travelling – from localised Tunisian projects to fighting in name of a global jihad in Syria. During the Syrian crisis, the Nusra Front, as one example, started out as the representation of global jihad in the Syrian crisis and ended up as the local hegemon around Idlib city. Islamism is not defined by polities: it is shaped by conflict dynamics. These dynamics, more often than not, straddle local, national and global contexts.

This study went beyond a focus on either nation-states or global politics. The case studies, for example, were two conflict episodes, rather than national polities. Although both these episodes started out challenging a particular state, only the Tunisian transition kept a national character throughout. The Syrian crisis instead gained an increasing localised and international dynamic. It meant that the narrative in Chapter five focused mostly on North-West Syria. Another example is the taxonomy of positions presented in the comparative analysis of Chapter six. It is a taxonomy that applies to other social conflicts irrespective of their local, national or transnational character. I traced the trajectories of an Islamist movement, for example, through the creation of local service provision in Aleppo and the drafting of a national constitution in Tunisia. I could map how local rebel groups (such as the Tawheed Brigade), national opposition bodies (such as the Syrian Islamic Council) and transnational organisations (the Nusra Front, ISIS) interacted. Distinct practices provide a conceptual lens through which Islamist movements can be analysed in relation to episodes of conflicts, instead of in relation to particular polities.

Third, the CPA, and distinct practices, makes the case for social movements and political Islam as a distinct empirical phenomenon of analytical interest. During the past twenty years, social movement studies have seen a relational turn: the *Dynamics of Contention*, *Theory of Fields* and *Getting Your Way* are examples. This focus on relational interactions has rendered the concept of social movements increasingly irrelevant. The *Dynamics of Contention*, for example, revolves around the concept of contentious episodes. Contentious episodes include social movements, but also civil war, strike waves and other forms of transgressive contention.[6] The *Theory of Fields* foregrounds the struggles around institutionalising governance of social fields, not the emergence, transformation or decline of social movements.[7] Similarly, *Getting Your Way* focuses on individual, micro-level interactions in so-called arenas of social interaction. These arenas can be, to give a few examples, social movements, the state, electoral politics, political parties or revolution.[8] The same applies to Islamism and political Islam. As relational, constructivist approaches became more dominant, scholars increasingly questioned the usefulness of the concept of political Islam altogether.[9]

The notion of distinct practices reads the politics of Islamism through its concrete material and dispositional impacts. Using Sunni Islam to render practices distinct is to infuse it with political significance. It results in alternative educational spheres and challenges to the authority of established executive authority and frameworks for funding and organising collective, jihadist violence. It turns Sunni Islam into a social and political stake around which an Islamist movement emerges. The notion of distinct practices highlights the material and dispositional impacts of rendering practices distinct. It saves the concept of Islamism from voluntarism – which would render the meaning of political Islam empty – and situates its political relevance in relation to contextual histories and individual biographies.

In doing so, distinct practices also makes the case for taking the phenomenon of social movements seriously. It acknowledges the enduring character of relational struggles to situate a particular stake in relation to education, politics, governance, service provision, knowledge production, collective violence or any other social field. As a result, stakes morph as they diversify through the mechanisms of reproductive innovation and contentious selection. It means that distinct practices tilt research into an evolutionary analysis of collective contentious action: tracing genealogies, theorising mechanisms and outlining future scenarios of conflicts around transforming, in this case Sunni Islam, as a stake in conflict episodes. It is a process that is empirically distinct from other transgressive types of contention that relate to particular polities, such as revolutions and civil wars, that are confined geographically and temporally. Instead, this process is defined by its enduring, and evolving, contentious interactions across time and space. It is, in short, a social movement.

Finally, taking everything together – and at its most fundamental level – distinct practices highlights the importance of how relational connections between time, action and agents are constructed. Social movements can be seen as efforts to create similarities – or rather homologies in Bourdieusian language – between individual embodied experiences and the realities of structural positions.[10] Such similarities are forever elusive. The resulting tensions, between biography and history, are what gives birth to eventful conflicts and sociopolitical transformations. Seen through the lens of distinct practices, social movements are, simply, the expression of contemporary struggles to define the future relevance of an embodied past – and Islamist movements are one of its most polarising examples today.

Notes

1. Interview with Khatib Idriss, 4 April 2011, Sidi Ali Ben Aoun, Tunisia.
2. For instance Tuğal, "Transforming Everyday Life: Islamism and Social Movement Theory"; Bayat, *Making Islam Democratic: Social Movements and the Post-Islamist Turn*; Alimi, Bosi and Demetriou, *The Dynamics of Radicalization: A Relational And Comparative Perspective*.
3. See Chapter two for a more detailed discussion.
4. For instance, Brachman, *Global Jihadism: Theory and Practice*.
5. See for example Volpi and Stein, 'Islamism and the State after the Arab Uprisings: Between People Power and State Power'.
6. McAdam, Tilly and Tarrow, *Dynamics of Contention*, 7–8.
7. Fligstein and McAdam, *A Theory of Fields*, ch. 1.
8. Jasper, *Getting Your Way: Strategic Dilemmas in the Real World*, 176–77.
9. Volpi, *Political Islam Observed*.
10. Bourdieu, *Practical Reason: On the Theory of Action*.

REFERENCES

Abazeid, Ahmad. 'Aḥrār Al-Shām Ba'da 'Ām Ṭawīl'. Istanbul: Omran for Strategic Studies, September 30, 2015.

abd-Allah. *The Islamic Struggle in Syria*. Jakarta: Mizan Press, 1982.

Abrahamian, Ervand. *The Coup: 1953, The CIA, and The Roots of Modern U.S.-Iranian Relations*. New York: The New Press, 2013.

Abu-Lughod, Lila. 'Do Muslim Women Really Need Saving? Anthropological Reflections on Cultural Relativism and Its Others'. *American Anthropologist* 104, no. 3 (September 2002): 783–90.

Achahed. 'Amām Jāmi' Al-Lakhmī, Taḥta Nīrān Ittiḥād "al-Yasār" Wa "Nidā' Tūnis"', December 8, 2012. http://www.turess.com/achahed/5851.

Addhamir. 'Qarārāt Al-Wizārah Hadadat Al-Silm Al-Īljtmā'ī Bi-Ṣafāqis', October 28, 2015.

'Afās, Muḥammad al-. 'Bayān', December 25, 2020. https://www.facebook.com/1555171278120159/photos/a.1886898138280803/2505756973061580/.

Afghani, Jamal Al-Din al-. 'The Truth about the Neicheri Sect'. In *An Islamic Response to Imperialism: Political and Religious Writings of Sayyid Jamāl Ad-Dīn 'Al-Afghānī'*, edited by Nikki Keddie, 101–9. Berkeley: University of California Press, [1880–1] 1983.

AFP. 'Tunisia Revolution: 129 Died, 634 Injured, Official Count Shows', March 20, 2021. https://english.alarabiya.net/News/north-africa/2021/03/20/Tunisia-revolution-129-died-634-injured-official-count-shows.

African Manager. 'Qarār Bi-Ḥall Jam'īyat Al-Lakhmī Fī Ṣafāqis', November 30, 2014. http://www.turess.com/africanmanager/36913.

———. 'Tūnis - 'Azl Imāmyn Fī Ṣafāqis', September 4, 2015. http://www.turess.com/africanmanager/303662.

———. 'Wizārat Al-Shu'ūn Al-Dīnīyah: Riḍā Bilḥājj Kāna Y'm Al-Muṣallīn Fī Sūsah Dawwin Tarkhīṣ Qānūnī', July 2, 2015. http://www.turess.com/africanmanager/45710.

Agence Tunis Afrique Press. 'Ṣafāqis .. Wizārat Al-Shu'ūn Al-Dīnīyah Tuqarriru I'fā' Riḍā Al-Jawādī Min Mahāmhā Ka'-Imām Bi-Jāmi' Al-Lakhmī', September 15, 2015. http://www.turess.com/assabahnews/109895.

———. "Uthmān Biṭṭīkh: Tawāṣul T'ṭīl Adā' Ṣalāt Al-Jum'ah Bi-Jāmi' Sīdī Al-Lakhmī Muḥarram Shar'an'. *Turess.com*, November 8, 2015. http://www.turess.com/assabahnews/112711.

Ahrar al-Sham. 'Jānib Min Al-Nashāṭ Al-Thaqāfī Wa-Al-Da'awī Fī Ḥalab', March 11, 2013. http://www.youtube.com/watch?v=EUM0jWp1doE.

———. 'Preparation of Faith and Education for Children in Aleppo', September 14, 2013. https://www.youtube.com/watch?v=aqtWCLgsNkE.

Ajjoub, Orwa. 'Reading Kadyrov in Al-Sham: 'Adnan Hadid on Chechnya, Syria, and Al-Qaida's Strategic Failure', January 21, 2021. https://www.jihadica.com/reading-kadyrov-in-al-sham/.

Al-Adnani, Abu Muhammad. 'This Is the Promise of Allah', June 19, 2014.

Al-Ain Français. 'Tunisie: Ennahda fait allégeance à la Turquie et le Qatar et ne pas à la Tunisie, Selon Abir Moussi', September 24, 2020. https://fr.al-ain.com/article/ennahda-pledges-allegiance-to-turkey-and-qatar-and-not-to-tunisia-says-abir-moussi.

Al-Akhbar. 'Al-Hay'ah Al-Shar'īyah Fī Ḥalab: al-Istibdād Mutadathran bi-'Abā'h al-Dīn', October 28, 2013. https://al-akhbar.com/Syria/62580.

Alchourouk. 'Ḥusayn Al-'Ubaydī: Al-Nahḍah A'lantu Al-Ḥarb 'Alá Al-Zaytūnah Wa-Al-Khādmī Sawwaq Lil-Wahābiyah', March 24, 2014. https://www.turess.com/alchourouk/1043855.

———. 'Taqlīṣ 'Adad Al-Masājid Al-Khārijah 'an Al-Sayṭarah Ilá Arba'ah', November 16, 2014. https://www.turess.com/alchourouk/1078819.

———. 'Wazīr Al-Shu'ūn Al-Dīnīyah: Tamma Istirajā' 49 Masjidan Min Jumlah 149 Wa-Qarīban Al-Sayṭarah 'Alá Al-Baqīyah', April, 17 2014. https://www.turess.com/alchourouk/1047399.

———. 'Wizārat Al-Shu'ūn Al-Dīnīyah Tastaraja' 100 Masjid Wa-Jāmi'', June 16, 2014. https://www.turess.com/alchourouk/1056838.

al-Chourouq. 'Sousse: I'itidā'alā Kātib 'Ām Kuliyat Al-Ādāb Rafḍ Tarsīm Ṭāliba Munaqiba', 2011.

Al Dassouky, Ayman. 'The Role of Jihadi Movements in Syrian Local Governance', July 14, 2017. https://omranstudies.org/publications/papers/download/54_e74f67124c695167a5c6994f9a3b6fa9.html.

Alimi, Eitan Y., Lorenzo Bosi, and Chares Demetriou. *The Dynamics of Radicalization: A Relational and Comparative Perspective*. Oxford: Oxford University Press, 2015.

Aljarida Attounissia. 'Ḥusayn Al-'Ubaydī: Jāmi' Al-Zaytūnah Ghayr Ma'nī Bi-Qarār Taḥyīd Al-Masājid', March 13, 2014. http://www.turess.com/aljarida/29686.

———. 'Īqāf Nashāṭ 9 Jam'īyāt Fī Al-'Āṣimah', August 12, 2014. https://www.turess.com/aljarida/34983.

Al Jazeera. 'Abū Muḥammad Al-Jawlānī .. Za'īm Jabhat Fatḥ Al-Shām', July 26, 2015. https://www.aljazeera.net/encyclopedia/icons/2015/7/26/أبو-محمد-الجولاني.

———. 'Al-Sulṭah Al-Qaḍā'īyah Bi-Nak'hat Al-Thawrah Fī Ḥalab', January 3, 2013. https://www.aljazeera.net/news/reportsandinterviews/2013/1/4/السلطة-القضائية-بنكهة-الثورة-في-حلب.

———. 'Fīlm Aḥrār Al-Shām', March 3, 2016. https://www.youtube.com/watch?v=_lydv7dr6qE.

———. 'Final de-Escalation Zones Agreed on in Astana', September 15, 2017. https://www.aljazeera.com/news/2017/9/15/final-de-escalation-zones-agreed-on-in-astana.

———. 'Gunfire in Locked-down Syrian City'. *Al Jazeera*, April 19, 2011. https://www.aljazeera.com/news/2011/4/19/gunfire-in-locked-down-syrian-city.

———. 'Salafist Group Clashes with Police in Tunisia', May 20, 2013. https://www.aljazeera.com/news/2013/5/20/salafist-group-clashes-with-police-in-tunisia.

———. 'Taḥaddiyāt Tuwājihu Al-Idārah Al-'Āmmah Lil-Khidmāt Bi-Ḥalab', March 31, 2014. http://www.aljazeera.net/home/Getpage/f6451603-4dff-4ca1-9c10-122741d17432/94419031-7575-4a28-8739-98b9c531509a.

———. 'Who Are the Main Candidates in Tunisia's Presidential Election?', September 15, 2019. https://www.aljazeera.com/news/2019/9/15/who-are-the-main-candidates-in-tunisias-presidential-election.

al-Kalbusi. 'Naḥnu ḍidda Al-Raqābah Al-Siyāsīyah Lil-Masājid Wa-'Alá Al-Khiṭāb Al-Dīnī an Yajma'u Al-Tūnisīyīn Lā an Yufarraqhum', July 7, 2013. http://www.turess.com/assabah/92155.

Allahoum, Ramy. 'Tunisia's Political Wrangling Explained'. *Al Jazeera*, July 20, 2020. https://www.aljazeera.com/news/2020/7/20/tunisias-political-wrangling-explained-in-600-words.

Allani, Alaya. 'The Islamists in Tunisia between Confrontation and Participation: 1980–2008'. *The Journal of North African Studies* 14, no. 2 (June 2009): 257–72.

Allouni, Tayseer. 'Ḥassān 'Abbūd .. Ḥarakat Al-Shām Al-Islāmīyah', June 9, 2013. https://www.youtube.com/watch?v=vEFRdEPeE74.

Al Nofal, Walid and Ammar Hamou. 'Astana Talks Placed Three de-Escalation Zones under Government Control. Is Idlib Next?', August 18, 2019. https://syriadirect.org/astana-talks-placed-three-de-escalation-zones-under-government-control-is-idlib-next-timeline/.

al-Qaradāwī. *Fiqh Az-Zakat: A Comparative Study of Zakah, Regulations and Philosophy in the Light of the Quran and Sunnah (vol II)*. Jeddah: Scientific Publishing Centre, King Abdulaziz University, 1999.

al-Rifai. 'Al-Shaykh Usāmah Al-Rifā'ī Khuṭbat Al-Naṣīḥah Fī Jum'ah Al-'Azzah 25 3 2011', July 27, 2011. https://www.youtube.com/watch?v=UpwoNLZ5vr4.

Al-Tamimi, A. J. 'Archive of Jabhat Al-Nusra Dar Al-Qaḍa Documents', 2015. http://www.aymennjawad.org/2015/03/archive-of-jabhat-al-nusra-dar-al-qaa-documents.

Al-Tunisi, Leon Carl (trans), Khayr Al-Din; Brown. *The Surest Path: The Political Treatise of a Nineteenth-Century Muslim Statesman*. Cambridge, MA: Harvard University Press, 1967.

Ancelovici, Marcos. 'Bourdieu in Movement: Toward a Field Theory of Contentious Politics'. *Social Movement Studies* 20, no. 2 (March 4, 2021): 155–73.

Anderson, Lisa. *The State and Social Transformation in Tunisia and Libya, 1830–1980*. Princeton: Princeton University Press, 2014.

Antonakis-Nashif, Anna. 'Contested Transformation: Mobilized Publics in Tunisia between Compliance and Protest'. *Mediterranean Politics* 21, no. 1 (January 2, 2016): 128–49.

Arab Barometer. 'Arab Barometer Wave V', 2019. https://www.arabbarometer.org/surveys/arab-barometer-wave-v.

Arat, Yesim. *Rethinking Islam and Liberal Democracy: Islamist Women in Turkish Politics*. Albany: SUNY Press, 2012.

Army of Mujahideen. 'Akādhīb Tanẓīm 'Al-'Irāq Wa-Al-Shām' Wa-Al-Mut'aṣbīn La-Hā', January 4, 2014. http://orient-news.net/index.php?part=news_show&id=7030.

Asad, Talal. *Formations of the Secular: Christianity, Islam, Modernity*. Stanford: Stanford University Press, 2003.

Assabah News. 'Ba'da Ta'yīn Imām Jadīd Li-Masjad Fī Al-Jihah: Wālī Al-Qayrawān Yuwajjihu Tanbyhā Lil-Nāṭiq Al-Rasmī Bāsim Anṣār Al-Sharī'ah', June 19, 2013. http://www.turess.com/assabahnews/23912.

———. 'Ḥusayn Al-'Ubaydī: Mahdī Jum'ah Amr Bi-Iqtiḥām Jāmi' Al-Zaytūnah ... Wa-Mana'ī Min Ṣu'ūd Al-Minbar', June 27, 2014. https://www.turess.com/assabahnews/87799.

———. 'Wazīr Al-Shu'ūn Al-Dīnīyah: Hādhihi Ḥaqīqat 'lāqy Bi-Al-Nahḍah Wa-Bi-Al-Khādmī', March 4, 2014. https://www.turess.com/assabahnews/82243.

———. 'Wazīr Al-Shu'ūn Al-Dīnīyah: Qurābat Al-90 Masjidan Māzālt Khārij Al-Sayṭarah', May 3, 2014. https://www.turess.com/assabahnews/85122.

———. 'Wazīr Al-Shu'ūn Al-Dīniyyah: 23 Masjidan Khārij Al-Sayṭarah', September 20, 2014. https://www.turess.com/assabahnews/91573.

Assemblée Des Représentants Du peuple. 'Muḥammad Al-'Afās', December 3, 2020. https://www.youtube.com/watch?v=W2KCU4M_8hA.

Assemblée Nationale Constituante. 'Draft of the Constitution of the Republic of Tunisia', August 14, 2012. https://constitutionnet.org/sites/default/files/draft_constitution-english.pdf.

———. 'Musawwadah Mushru' Al-Dustūr', December 14, 2012. http://majles.marsad.tn/uploads/documents/constitution_tunisie_ar_2012_12_14.pdf.

———. 'Mushru' Al-Dustūr', April 22, 2013. https://anc.majles.marsad.tn/uploads/documents/constitution_tunisie_ar_2013_04_22.pdf.

———. 'Mushru' Al-Dustūr Al-Jumhūrīyah Al-Tūnisīyah', June 1, 2013. https://anc.majles.marsad.tn/uploads/documents/constitution_tunisie_ar_2013_06_01.pdf.

The Associated Press. 'Tunisia: Thousands Protest Film', October 15, 2011. https://www.nytimes.com/2011/10/15/world/africa/in-tunisia-thousands-protest-film.html.

Attar, Muhammad al-. 'Al-Raqqah: 'An Wāqi' Al-Katā'ib Al-'Askarīyah, Wa-Idārat Al-Madīnah Al-Muḥarrarah, Wa-Al-Thawarāt Al-Lāḥiqah'. مجموعة الجمهورية للدراسات, August 2013.

Attounissia. 'Al-Naṣṣ Al-Kāmil Li-Mubādarat Al-Ittiḥād Al-'āmm Al-Tūnisī Lil-Shughl', August 22, 2013. http://www.turess.com/attounissia/98605.

'Awdāt, Bāsil al-. 'Zahrān 'Allūsh Alladhī Aṭlaq Al-Asad Sarāḥhu Li-Ibtida' 'Askarat Al-Thawrah', February 28, 2015. https://web.archive.org/web/20151227034441/http://www.alarab.co.uk/m/?id=46295.

A., Z. "Tunisie: Le Prédicateur Salafiste Jihadiste Al-Khatib Al-Idrissi Arrêté et Relâché', March 3, 2015. http://www.kapitalis.com/societe/27932-tunisie-le-predicateur-salafiste-jihadiste-al-khatib-al-idrissi-arrete-et-relache.html.

Babnet. 'al-Khaṭīb al-Idrīsī yanfī I'tiqālhu." *Babnet*, October 25, 2013. https://www.babnet.net/rttdetail-73431.asp.

———. 'Al-Shaykh Ḥusayn Al-'Ubaydī: Al-Imām Al-Mu'īn Min Al-Ḥukūmah Wa-Alladhī Sayu'tī Fī Ṣalāt Al-Jum'ah Sayuṭarid', August 9, 2012. https://www.babnet.net/cadredetail-52945.asp.

———. 'Bashīr Ibn Ḥasan: Ḥasabnā Allāh Wa-Na'm Al-Wakīl Wa-Ana Lillāh Wa-an Ilayhi Rāja'ūn.. Tamma 'Azl Riḍā Al-Jawwādī', September 15, 2015. https://www.turess.com/babnet/111919.

———. 'Nūr Al-Dīn Al-Khādimī: Ḥusayn Al-'Ubaydī Sayuwāṣl Imāmat Al-Muṣallīn Fī Jāmi' Al-Zaytūnah', June 21, 2012. http://www.turess.com/babnet/50976.

Baczko, Adam, Gilles Dorronsoro and Arthur Quesnay. 'Building a Syrian State in Time of Civil War'. Washington DC: Carnegie Endowment for International Peace, 2013. http://carnegieendowment.org/files/syrian_state.pdf.

———. *Civil War in Syria: Mobilization and Competing Social Orders*. Cambridge: Cambridge University Press, 2018.

Baghdadi, Abu Bakr al-. 'Wa-Bashir Al-Mu'minīn', April 9, 2013.

Baladi News. 'Ba'da Sanawāt Min Al-Ghumūḍ .. Maṣdar Yakshif Li-Baladī Nīwz Huwīyah 'Abū Muḥammad Al-Jawlānī', June 1, 2020. https://baladi-news.com/ar/articles/61201/بعد-سنوات-من-الغموض..-مصدر-يكشف-لبلدي-نيوز-هوية-"أبو-محمد-الجولاني."

Bālṭayyib, Nūr-Al-Dīn. 'Khāṣṣ: Yajma'u Wuzarā' Al-Dākhilīyah Wa-Al-'Adl Wa-Al-Shu'ūn Al-Dīnīyah .. Al-Yawm Ijtimā' ḥawla Al-Masājid'. تورس, February 5, 2014. http://www.turess.com/alchourouk/1037234.

Banerjee, Sikata. 'Armed Masculinity, Hindu Nationalism and Female Political Participation in India: Heroic Mothers, Chaste Wives and Celibate Warrior s'. *International Feminist Journal of Politics* 8, no. 1 (2006): 62–83.

Barrie, Christopher. 'The Contentious Politics of Nationalism and the Anti-Naturalization Campaign in Tunisia, 1932-1933'. *Nations and Nationalism* 23, no. 4 (2017): 707–25.

Batatu, Hanna. *Syria's Peasantry, the Descendants of Its Lesser Rural Notables, and Their Politics*. Princeton: Princeton University Press, 1999.

Bawajnāḥ, Fatḥī. 'Ba'da īqāf 'Adad Min Al-Jam'īyāt 'an Al-Nashāṭ Bi-Wilāyat Ṣafāqis: Ghaḍab Wa-īstinkār Fī Ṣufūf Mumaththilīhā', August 10, 2014. http://www.turess.com/attounissia/131667.

Bayat, Asef. *Making Islam Democratic: Social Movements and the Post-Islamist Turn*. Stanford: Stanford University Press, 2007.

BBC News. 'Uttar Pradesh: India's Muslim Victims of Hate Crimes Live in Fear'. *BBC*, February 21, 2022. https://www.bbc.co.uk/news/world-asia-india-60225543.

Belkeziz, Abdelilah. *The State in Contemporary Islamic Thought: A Historical Survey of the Major Muslim Political Thinkers of the Modern Era*. Edited by Markaz Dirasat Al-Wahdah al-Arabiyah. London; New York: I. B. Tauris, 2009.

Benford, Robert D. 'An Insider's Critique of the Social Movement Framing Perspective'. *Sociological Inquiry* 67, no. 4 (October 1997): 409–30.

Benford, Robert D., and David A. Snow. 'Framing Processes and Social Movements: An Overview and Assessment'. *Annual Review of Sociology* 26, no. 1 (2000): 611–39.

Ben Salem. 'The Reconfiguration of Ennahdha's Recruitment Strategy in Tunisia'. *Issue Brief* 4 (2018). https://scholarship.rice.edu/bitstream/handle/1911/102750/bi-brief-043018-cme-carnegie-tunisia4.pdf.

Ben Younes, Kamal. 'Tunisia: Ghannouchi Calls for National Unity Government', October 31, 2014. https://eng-archive.aawsat.com/k-benyounes2/news-middle-east/tunisia-ghannouchi-calls-for-national-unity-government.

Berkes, Niyazi. *The Development of Secularism in Turkey*. Routledge, 1998.

Böttcher, Annabelle. *Syrische Religionspolitik Unter Asad (Syrian Religious Politics under Al-Assad)*. Freiburg: Arnold Bergstraesser Institut, 1998.

Bottero, Wendy, and Nick Crossley. 'Worlds, Fields and Networks: Becker, Bourdieu and the Structures of Social Relations'. *Cultural Sociology* 5, no. 1 (March 2011): 99–119.

Boukhars, Anouar. *The Geographic Trajectory of Conflict and Militancy in Tunisia*. JSTOR, 2017.

Bourdieu, Pierre. *Distinction: A Social Critique of the Judgement of Taste*. Cambridge, MA, Harvard University Press, 1984.

———. *The Field of Cultural Production: Essays on Art and Literature*. New York: Columbia University Press, 1993.

———. 'The Field of Cultural Production, or: The Economic World Reversed'. *Poetics* 12, no. 4 (November 1, 1983): 311–56.

———. 'Genèse et Structure Du Champ Religieux'. *Revue Française de Sociologie* 12, no. 3 (1971): 295–334.

———. 'Genesis and Structure of the Religious Field'. *Comparative Social Research* 13, no. 1 (1991): 1–44.

———. *Practical Reason: On the Theory of Action*. Stanford: Stanford University Press, 1998.

———. *The Rules of Art: Genesis and Structure of the Literary Field*. Stanford: Stanford University Press, 1996.

———. *The State Nobility: Elite Schools in the Field of Power*. 1st ed. Stanford: Stanford University Press, 1998.

———. 'Symbolic Power'. *Critique of Anthropology* 4, no. 13–14 (January 1, 1979): 77–85.

Bourdieu, Pierre and Loïc J. D. Wacquant. *An Invitation to Reflexive Sociology*. Chicago: University of Chicago Press, 1992.

Bourguiba, Habib. *Ma vie, mon œuvre: 1938–1943*. Paris: Plon, 1986.

Brachman, Jarret M. *Global Jihadism: Theory and Practice*. Abingdon: Routledge, 2008.

Bujnāḥ, Fatḥī. 'Intahat Azmat Al-Jāmi' Al-Kabīr: Lajnat Waqtiyah Lil-Ashrāf Alayhi . . . Wa-Al-Shaykh "Abd Al-'Azīz Li-Wakīl' Khaṭīban Lil-Jāmi'", July 7, 2012. https://www.turess.com/attounissia/63597.

Būjnāḥ, Fatḥī. 'Masīrat Ḥāshidah Bi-Ṣafāqis Munaddah Bi-Qarārāt 'Azl Al-A'immah', October 19, 2015. https://www.turess.com/attounissia/160357.

Bunzel, Cole. 'From Paper State to Caliphate: The Ideology of the Islamic State'. The Brookings Project on U.S. Relations with the Islamic World, 2015.

Callimachi, Rukmini. 'The ISIS Files: When Terrorists Run City Hall'. *The New York Times*. April 5, 2018. https://www.nytimes.com/interactive/2018/04/04/world/middleeast/isis-documents-mosul-iraq.html.

Calvert, John. *Sayyid Qutb and the Origins of Radical Islamism*. New York: Columbia University Press, 2010.

Cammett, Melani. 'Business-Government Relations and Industrial Change: The Politics of Upgrading in Morocco and Tunisia'. *World Development* 35, no. 11 (1994): 1889–1903.

———. *Globalization and Business Politics in Arab North Africa: A Comparative Perspective*. Cambridge: Cambridge University Press, 2007.

Carnegie Endowment. 'Profiles of Syrian Sunni Clerics in the Uprising', March 25, 2013. carnegieendowment.org/2013/03/25/profiles-of-syrian-sunni-clerics-in-up rising.

Casanova, José. *Public Religions in the Modern World*. Chicago: University of Chicago Press, 1994.

Casas, Angélica M. 'One Mother's Mission to Ban 'Vulgar' Books'. *BBC*, April 1, 2022. https://www.bbc.co.uk/news/av/world-us-canada-60947937.

Castells, Manuel. *Networks of Outrage and Hope: Social Movements in the Internet Age*. Hoboken: John Wiley & Sons, 2015.

Chacko, Priya. 'The Right Turn in India: Authoritarianism, Populism and Neoliberalisation'. *Journal of Contemporary Asia* 48, no. 4 (August 8, 2018): 541–65.

Chivers, C. J. 'A Rebel Commander in Syria Holds the Reins of War'. *The New York Times*. February 2, 2013. https://www.nytimes.com/2013/02/02/world/middleeast/the-saturday-profile-hajji-marea-a-rebel-commander-in-syria-holds-reins-of-war.html.

Chomiak, Laryssa, and John P. Entelis. 'The Making of North Africa's Intifadas'. *Middle East Report* 41 (2011). http://www.merip.org/mer/mer259/making-north-africas-intifadas.

Ciro Martínez, José, and Brent Eng. 'Struggling to Perform the State: The Politics of Bread in the Syrian Civil War'. *International Political Sociology* 11, no. 2 (January 9, 2017): 130–47.

Clark, Janine A. *Islam, Charity, and Activism: Middle Class Networks and Social Welfare in Egypt, Jordan and Yemen*. Bloomington: Indiana University Press, 2004.

CNN. 'Transcript of President Bush's Address', September 21, 2001. http://edition.cnn.com/2001/US/09/20/gen.bush.transcript/.

Commins, David Dean. *Islamic Reform: Politics and Social Change in Late Ottoman Syria*. Oxford; New York: Oxford University Press, 1990.

Cook, David. *Understanding Jihad*. Berkeley: University of California Press, 2015.

Cook, Michael. *Commanding Right and Forbidding Wrong in Islamic Thought*. Cambridge: Cambridge University Press, 2001.

Council of Professors. 'Ḥawl Al-Istīlā' Ala Qā'a Tadrīs Bi-Da'wa Isti'amālha Baytan Li-L-Ṣalāa', 2011.

Crossley, Nick. *Making Sense of Social Movements*. Buckingham; Philadelphia: Open University Press, 2002.

Cunningham, Robert, and Yasin Sarayrah. *Wasta: The Hidden Force in Middle Eastern Society*. Westport: Preager, 1993.

Dahmani, Frida. 'Tunisie: Partis Cherchent Mécènes', February 6, 2014. https://www.jeuneafrique.com/134673/politique/tunisie-partis-cherchent-m-c-nes/.

Dalay, Galip. 'From Astana to Sochi: How De-Escalation Allowed Assad to Return to War', February 20, 2018. http://www.middleeasteye.net/opinion/astana-sochi-how-de-escalation-allowed-assad-return-war.

Dār Al-Qaḍā' fī Ḥrītān. 'Ta'mīm', December 28, 2014. https://twitter.com/ajaltamimi/status/549213257588695040.

———. 'Ta'mīm', January 7, 2015. https://justpaste.it/policeshutdownnusra.

Della Porta, Donatella, and Mario Diani. *Social Movements: An Introduction*. Oxford: Blackwell Publishing, 2006.

Delmas, Benoît. 'Tunisie: Abir Moussi Dans Les Pas Du Maréchal Sissi', September 11, 2019. https://www.lepoint.fr/afrique/tunisie-abir-moussi-dans-les-pas-du-marechal-sissi-11-09-2019-2335097_3826.php.

Dhūwāybiyah, Muná. "Nismah' Tash'al Al-āḥtjājāt Qabla Ayyām Min Al-Intikhābāt', October 17, 2011. http://www.france24.com/ar/20111017-nessma-tv-broadcasting-persepolis-ignited-tunisian-islamist-salafist-protesters.

Diani, Mario. 'Networks and Social Movements: A Research Programme'. *Social Movements and Networks: Relational Approaches to Collective Action*, 2003, 299–319.

Dianteill, Erwan. 'Pierre Bourdieu and the Sociology of Religion: A Central and Peripheral Concern'. *Theory and Society* 32, no. 5/6 (2003): 529–49.

Dickinson, Elizabeth. 'Playing with Fire: Why Private Gulf Financing for Syria's Extremist Rebels Risks Igniting Sectarian Conflict at Home'. *The Brookings Project on US Relations with the Islamic*, December 6, 2013. https://www.brookings.edu/research/playing-with-fire-why-private-gulf-financing-for-syrias-extremist-rebels-risks-igniting-sectarian-conflict-at-home/.

Dochuk, Darren. *From Bible Belt to Sunbelt: Plain-Folk Religion, Grassroots Politics, and the Rise of Evangelical Conservatism*. 1st ed. New York: W.W. Norton, 2011.

Donker, Teije Hidde. 'Between Rebellion and Uprising Intersecting Networks and Discursive Strategies in Rebel Controlled Syria'. *Social Movement Studies* 18, no. 1 (January 2, 2019): 17–35.

———. 'Islamic Social Movements and the Syrian Authoritarian Regime: Shifting Patterns of Shifting Patterns of Control and Accommodation'. In *Middle East Authoritarianisms: Governance, Contestation, and Regime Resilience in Syria and Iran*, edited by Steven Heydemann and Reinoud Leenders, 107–24. Stanford: Stanford University Press, 2013.

Donker, Teije Hidde, and Kasper Ly Netterstrøm. 'The Tunisian Revolution & Governance of Religion'. *Middle East Critique*, 2017. https://www.tandfonline.com/doi/abs/10.1080/19436149.2017.1285469.

Drevon, Jerome. 'Embracing Salafi Jihadism in Egypt and Mobilizing in the Syrian Jihad'. *Middle East Critique* 25, no. 4 (October 1, 2016): 321–39.

Drevon, Jerome, and Patrick Haenni. 'How Global Jihad Relocalises and Where It Leads. The Case of HTS, the Former AQ Franchise in Syria'. European University Institute, January 1, 2021. http://dx.doi.org/10.2139/ssrn.3796931.

Dridi, Manel. 'Tunisia Facing Increasing Poverty and Regional Inequalities'. Washington, DC: Carnegie Endowment for International Peace, October 26, 2021. https://carnegieendowment.org/sada/85654.

Echorouk Online. 'Rāshid Al-Ghannūshī: Lastu Khomayniyā Wa Lan Akūn', January 22, 2011. https://www.echoroukonline.com/راشد-الغنوشي-لست-خمينيا-ولن-أكون.

The Economist. 'Kais Saied Plans to Transform Tunisia. It May Go Bust First', September 30, 2021. https://www.economist.com/middle-east-and-africa/2021/10/02/kais-saied-plans-to-transform-tunisia-it-may-go-bust-first.

EIU. 'Russia Launches Air Attacks in Syria', October 1, 2015. http://country.eiu.com/article.aspx?articleid=1123554496&Country=Syria&topic=Politics.

Eligür, Banu. *The Mobilization of Political Islam in Turkey*. Cambridge: Cambridge University Press, 2010.

El-Khoury, Tatiana. 'Aṣwāt Al-Shabakah: Mā Alladhī Ḥaṣala Fī Jāmiʿat Manūbah?' France24/Youtube, December 1, 2011. https://www.youtube.com/watch?v=Mtduk8xGVUc.

Emirbayer, Mustafa. 'Manifesto for a Relational Sociology'. *The American Journal of Sociology* 103, no. 2 (1997): 281–317.

Enab Baladi. 'Abū Muḥammad al-Jawlānī Yuẓhiru mjddan .. Rasā'il Siyāsīyah 'abra Barīd al-Iqtiṣād'. عنب بلدي, January 12, 2022. https://www.enabbaladi.net/archives/538823.

———. 'Al-Jawlānī Yakshif 'an Nafsihi Amāma Muqātlī Ḥalab Wa-Yubashir Bi-'Imārat Islāmīyah', July 14, 2014. http://www.enabbaladi.org/archives/18136.

———. 'Baʿda Taslīmhā Ṭabiban Maqtūlan Ilá Ḥarakat Aḥrār Al-Shām', January 6, 2014. http://www.enabbaladi.net/archives/14712.

———. 'Mādhā warā' al-Muwājahāt Bayna 'Taḥrīr al-Shām' wa 'al-Jabhah al-Waṭanīyah' bi-rīf Idlib?' عنب بلدي, December 4, 2018. https://enabbaladi.net/archives/267590.

———. 'Qaḍā' Sūriyā Al-Muḥarrarah .. Thalāth Marjiʿīyāt Tunadhir Bi-Taqsīm Al-Bilād', December 20, 2015. https://www.enabbaladi.net/archives/57254.

———. 'Salvation Government Elects New Shura Council President', April 24, 2020. https://syrianobserver.com/news/57603/salvation-government-elects-new-shura-council-president.html.

———. 'Tafāṣīl Alāqttāl bayna 'Taḥrīr al-Shām' wa 'al-Jabhah al-Waṭanīyah' Gharbī Idlib', December 4, 2018. https://enabbaladi.net/archives/267556.

Ennahda members. 'Naṣṣ Al-Risālah Al-Thāniyah Al-Muwajjahah Min 100 Qayyādī Min Ḥarakat Al-Nahḍah', October 14, 2020. https://www.facebook.com/alhadath.Tunis/photos/a.2364423100509102/2899483380336402/.

The Ennahda Movement. 'Al-Bayān Al-Khitāmī Lil-Mu'tamar Al-'Āmm Al-'Āshir Li-Ḥarakat Al-Nahḍah', 2016.

———. 'Al-Lā'iḥah Al-Taqyīmīyah', February 2018. https://web.archive.org/web/20180210002529/http://www.ennahdha.tn/اللائحة-التقييمية.

———. 'Barnāmaj Al-Nahḍah: Min Ajl Tūnis Al-Ḥurrīyah Wa-Al-'Adālah Wa-Al-Tanmiyah', September 2011.

———. 'Ḥarakat al-Nahḍah Tunadad Bi-Āstidrāj al-Bilād Naḥwa al-Fawḍá', December 6, 2011. http://www.ennahdha.tn/حركة-النهضة-تندد-باستدراج-البلاد-نحو-الفوضى-.

———. 'Lā'iḥat Subul Idārat Al-Mashrū'', February 2018. web.archive.org/web/20180214111543/http://www.ennahdha.tn/لائحة-سبل-إدارة-المشروع.

Eryani, Fadhl, and Nizar Habash. 'Automatic Romanization of Arabic Bibliographic Records'. In *Proceedings of the Sixth Arabic Natural Language Processing Workshop*, 213–18. https://aclanthology.org/volumes/2021.wanlp-1/.

Euben, Roxanne Leslie, and Muhammad Qasim Zaman. *Princeton Readings in Islamist Thought: Texts and Contexts from Al-Banna to Bin Laden*. Princeton: Princeton University Press, 2009.

European Parliament. 'European Parliament Resolution of 14 September 2016 on the EU Relations with Tunisia in the Current Regional Context', September 14, 2016. https://op.europa.eu/en/publication-detail/-/publication/30d02743-6ed4-11e8-9483-01aa75ed71a1.

Fahmi, Georges, and Hamza Meddeb. 'Market for Jihad: Radicalization in Tunisia'. https://carnegieendowment.org, 2015. https://carnegieendowment.org/files/Brief_CMEC_55_Fahmi_and_Meddeb.pdf.

F. K. 'Instance de la Zakat: Bochra Belhaj Hmida juge la proposition d'Ennahdha "inacceptable"', September 29, 2019. https://www.realites.com.tn/2019/09/instance-de-la-zakat-bochra-belhaj-hmida-juge-la-proposition-dennahdha-inacceptable/.

Fligstein, Neil. *The Architecture of Markets: An Economic Sociology of Twenty-First-Century Capitalist Societies*. Princeton: Princeton University Press, 2002.

Fligstein, Neil, and Doug McAdam. *A Theory of Fields*. Oxford; New York: Oxford University Press, 2012.

———. 'Toward a General Theory of Strategic Action Fields'. *Sociological Theory* 29, no. 1 (March 2011): 1–26.

France 24. 'Al-Asad Yaṣduru 'Afwan 'Āman Wa-Al-Mu'āraḍah Taṣafahu Bi-"Ghayr Kāf"', May 31, 2011. http://www.france24.com/ar/20110531-syria-politics-unrest-amnesty-bashar-alassad.

———. 'Al-Asad Ya'ud Bi-Ī'ḥbāṭ 'Mu'āmarah' Tata'araḍ La-Hā Al-Bilād Wy'kd Min Jadīd 'Alá Iṣlāḥāt Mu'Alanah Sābiqan', March 30, 2011. http://www.france24.com/ar/20110330-syria-president-bechar-assad-political-cahnge-speech-parliament-clashes-popular-deraa-arabic-demonstrations.

———. 'Al-Sulṭāt Taṭlaq Sarrāḥ 260 Mu'ataqlā Siyāsīyan Baynahum Islāmiyūn Wa-'Akrād', March 26, 2011. http://www.france24.com/ar/20110326-syria-protest-prisoners-260-authorities-release-islamists.

———. "Asharāt Al-Sūrīyīn Yulabūn Da'wat Lltẓāhr Min Ajl Al-Taghyīr Wa-Al-Ḥurrīyah', March 15, 2011. www.france24.com/ar/20110315-syria-demonstrations-change-freedom-bashar-alassad-facebook.

———. 'Suqūṭ Qatlá Khilāl Muẓāharāt Fī Dar'ā Wa-Īshtbākāt Ma'a Qūwāt Al-Amn Fī Mudun Ukhrá', March 18, 2011. http://www.france24.com/ar/20110318-syria-damascus-police-mosque-friday-pray-demonstration-unrest.

Friedland, Roger. 'The Endless Fields of Pierre Bourdieu'. *Organization* 16, no. 6 (November 2009): 887–917.

Fuller, Thomas. 'Next Question for Tunisia: The Role of Islam in Politics'. *The New York Times*. February 20, 2011. https://www.nytimes.com/2011/02/21/world/africa/21tunisia.html.

Furseth, Inger. 'Religion In the Works of Habermas, Bourdieu, and Foucault'. In *The Oxford Handbook of the Sociology of Religion*, edited by Peter B. Clarke. Oxford: Oxford University Press, 2011.

Gall, Carlotta. 'Protesters Press Tunisian Government to Resign, as Ruling Party Supporters Rally', July 29, 2013. https://www.nytimes.com/2013/07/29/world/africa/protesters-press-tunisian-government-to-resign-as-ruling-party-supporters-rally.html.

The General Management of Services. 'Statement on the Status Quo of Suleiman Al Halabi Water Station', November 29, 2016.

General Management of Services in Aleppo. 'Khurūj Maḥaṭṭat Miyāh 'an Al-Khidmah', April 29, 2016. https://www.facebook.com/edara3amah/photos/a.1532636220332449.1073741828.1525290301067041/1685072271755509/?type=3&theater.

———. 'Radan 'Alá Bayān 'Al-Majlis Al-Maḥallī Li-Madīnat Ḥalab' Ḥawla Taghdhiyat Aḥyā' Al-Zabdiyah Wa-Al-'Anṣārī Al-Sharqī Bi-Al-Tayār Al-Kahrabā'ī', May 10, 2016. https://www.facebook.com/edara3amah/photos/a.1532636220332449.1073741828.1525290301067041/1688838811378855/?type=3&theater.

Gerges, Fawaz A. 'ISIS and the Third Wave of Jihadism'. *Current History; Philadelphia* 113, no. 767 (December 2014): 339–43.

Ghannouchi, Rached. *Al-Ḥurrīyāt Al-'Āmmah Fī Al-Dawlah Al-Islāmīyah*. Markaz al-Dirāsāt al-Wahda al-Arabiya, 1993.

Ghannūshī, Rāshid. *Min tajribat al-ḥarakah al-Islāmīyah fī Tūnis*. al-Markaz al-Maghāribī lil-Buḥūth wa-al-Tarjamah, 2001.

Giugni, Marco, Ruud Koopmans, Florence Passy and Paul Statham. 'Institutional and Discursive Opportunities for Extreme-Right Mobilization in Five Countries'. *Mobilization: An International Quarterly* 10, no. 1 (February 2006): 145–62.

Gökalp, Ziya. *Turkish Nationalism and Western Civilization: Selected Essays*. London: Allen and Unwin, 1959.

Goldstone, Jack A. 'More Social Movements or Fewer? Beyond Political Opportunity Structures to Relational Fields'. *Theory and Society* 33, no. 3 (2004): 333?365.

Gorski, Philip S. 'Bourdieusian Theory and Historical Analysis: Maps, Mechanisms, and Methods'. *Bourdieu and Historical Analysis*, 2013, 327–67.

Gorski, Philip S., and Ateş Altınordu. 'After Secularization?' *Annual Review of Sociology* 34, no. 1 (2008): 55–85.

Gorski, Philip, John Torpey, Jonathan VanAntwerpen and David Kyuman Kim. *The Post-Secular in Question: Religion in Contemporary Society*. New York: NYU Press, 2012.

Graf, Bettina, and Jakob Skovgaard-Petersen, eds. *Global Mufti: The Phenomenon of Yusuf Al-Qaradawi*. London: Hurst, 2009.

Green, Arnold H. *The Tunisian Ulama 1873–1915: Social Structure and Response to Ideological Currents*. Leiden: Brill, 1978.

Greenberg, Nathaniel. 'The Rise and Fall of Abu 'Iyadh: Reported Death Leaves Questions Unanswered'. Jadaliyya, 2015. https://www.jadaliyya.com/Details/32287.

Grewal, Sharan, and Shadi Hamid. 'The Dark Side of Consensus in Tunisia: Lessons from 2015-2019'. *Foreign Policy at Brookings*, no. 1 (2020). https://www.brookings.edu/wp-content/uploads/2020/01/FP_20200131_tunisia_consensus_grewal_hamid.pdf.

Guellali, Amna. 'New Reconciliation Law Threatens Tunisia's Democracy'. *Human Rights Watch* 2 (October 2, 2017). https://www.hrw.org/news/2017/10/02/new-reconciliation-law-threatens-tunisias-democracy.

Gunning, Jeroen. *Hamas in Politics: Democracy, Religion, Violence*. New York: Columbia University Press, 2008.

Gunning, Jeroen and Ilan Zvi Baron. *Why Occupy a Square?: People, Protests and Movements in the Egyptian Revolution*. Oxford: Oxford University Press, 2014.

Hadath Media Center. 'Taqrīr Mufaṣṣal 'an Al-Hay'ah Al-Shar'īyah Fī Ḥalab', May 2013. https://www.youtube.com/watch?v=MVeCnztP4BM.

Hafez, Mohammed M. 'A Political Process Explanation of GIA Violence in Algeria'. In *Islamic Activism: A Social Movement Theory Approach*, 37–60. Bloomington: Indiana University Press, 2004.

Hakaek Online. 'Ḥusayn Al-'Ubaydī: Jāmi' Al-Zaytūnah Ghayr Ma'nī Bi-Barnāmij Taḥyīd Al-Masājid', March 14, 2014. http://www.turess.com/hakaek/57706.

———. 'Istiqālat Akthar Min 100 Qayyādī Min Al-Nahḍah (Wathā'iq)', September 25, 2021. https://www.hakaekonline.com/article/134368/استقالة-أكثر-من-100-قيادي-من-النهضة-وثائق.

———. 'Wazīr Al-Shu'ūn Al-Dīnīyah: Tūnis Dawlat Islāmīyah Wa-'alá Al-Jamī' Murā'āt Dhālika', March 9, 2014. https://www.turess.com/hakaek/57484.

Halabi, Huna al-. 'Ḥalab .. Tahjīr Mumanhaj Lltāqāt Al-Shabābīyah', June 8, 2014. http://www.enabbaladi.net/archives/17567.

Hamdan, Hassan. 'Al-Hay'ah Al-Shar'īyah Bi-Ḥalab .. Adwār Muta'addidah', June 2013. http://www.aljazeera.net/home/Getpage/f6451603-4dff-4ca1-9c10-122741d17432/ac66c6e0-e28b-41fd-aa64-f9914b34b246.

Hamdi, Mohamed Elhachmi. *The Politicisation of Islam: A Case Study of Tunisia*. Boulder: Westview Press, 1998.

Hamid, Shadi, and William McCants. 'Islamists on Islamism Today: An Interview with Habib Ellouze of Tunisia's Ennahda Party', May 25, 2017. https://www.brookings.edu/blog/markaz/2017/05/25/islamists-on-islamism-today-an-interview-with-habib-ellouze-of-tunisias-ennahda-party/.

Hamidi, Ibrahim. 'Dimashq Tasmaḥu Li-Al-Qubaysiyāt Bi-Nashāṭ 'Alanī'. الحياة (al-Hayat), May 2006.

———. 'They Wear the Dark Blue Veil and Have a Wide Network for Teaching and Influence . . . 'The Misses of Al-Qubaysiyat' Are the Entrepreneurs in Syria for Involvement of Women in the 'Islamic Da'wa' . . . With the Consent of the Authorities', May 2006.

Haykel, Bernard. 'On the Nature of Salafi Thought and Action'. In *Global Salafism: Islam's New Religious Movement*, edited by Roel Meijer, 33–57. New York: Columbia University Press, 2009.

Hegghammer, T. 'Syria's Foreign Fighters'. 2013. https://ffi-publikasjoner.archive.knowledgearc.net/bitstream/handle/20.500.12242/727/1078289.pdf.

———. *Jihad in Saudi Arabia: Violence and Pan-Islamism since 1979*. 1st ed. Cambridge: Cambridge University Press, 2010.

———. 'Jihadi-Salafis or Revolutionaries? On Religion and Politics in the Study of Militant Islamism'. In *Global Salafism: Islam's New Religious Movement*, edited by Roel Meijer. New York: Columbia University Press, 2009.

Hegghammer, Thomas, and Stéphane Lacroix. 'Rejectionist Islamism in Saudi Arabia: The Story of Juhayman Al-'utaybi Revisited'. *International Journal of Middle East Studies* 39, no. 1 (February 2007): 103–22.

Heyd, Uriel. *Foundations of Turkish Nationalism: The Life and Teachings of Ziya Gökalp*. London: Luzac and Harvill Press, 1950.

Hinnebusch, Raymond A. *Syria: Revolution from Above*. 1st ed. London: Routledge, 2001.

Hizb al-Tahrir. 'Al-Mu'tamar Al-Ṣuḥufī Li-Ḥizb Al-Taḥrīr Tūnis Raghma Muḥāwalah Alghā'h'. *YouTube.com*, October 20, 2011. www.youtube.com/watch?v=YifvZkjIScQ.

———. 'Haykal Ajhizat Dawlat Al-Khilāfah', n.d.

———. 'Mashrū' Dustūr Dawlat Al-Khilāfah', n.d.

Hizb al-Tahrir Tūnis. 'Naḥwa Khilāfat 'alá Minhāj Al-Nubūwah', 2014.

Hjellbrekke, Johs, Brigitte Le Roux, Olav Korsnes, Frédéric Lebaron, Lennart Rosenlund and Henry Rouanet. 'The Norwegian Field of Power Anno 2000'. *European Societies* 9, no. 2 (March 2007): 245–73.

Hourani, Albert. *Arabic Thought in the Liberal Age 1798–1939*. Cambridge: Cambridge University Press, 1983.

———. *A History of the Arab Peoples*. Second. Cambridge, MA: Belknap Press of Harvard University Press, 2003.

———. 'Ottoman Reform and The Politics of Notables'. In *The Modern Middle East: A Reader*, edited by Mary C. Wilson, Albert H. Hourani, and Philip S. Khoury, 83–109. Berkeley: University of California Press, 1993.

Hubbard, Ben, and Michael R. Gordon. 'Key Syrian Rebel Groups Abandon Exile Leaders'. *The New York Times*, September 2013. http://www.nytimes.com/2013/09/26/world/middleeast/syria-crisis.html.

Human Rights Watch. 'Tunisia: Events of 2005', January 5, 2006. https://www.hrw.org/world-report/2006/country-chapters/tunisia.

———. 'Tunisia: Suspension of Associations Arbitrary', August 13, 2014. https://www.hrw.org/news/2014/08/13/tunisia-suspension-associations-arbitrary.

Iannaccone, Laurence R. 'Religious Practice: A Human Capital Approach'. *Journal for the Scientific Study of Religion* 29, no. 3 (1990): 297–314.

ICG. 'Avoiding a Populist Surge in Tunisia'. *Crisis Group*, March 4, 2020. https://www.crisisgroup.org/middle-east-north-africa/north-africa/tunisia/b73-tunisie-eviter-les-surencheres-populistes.

———. 'Jihadist Violence in Tunisia: The Urgent Need for a National Strategy'. International Crisis Group, June 22, 2016.

Ignatius, David. 'A New Cooperation on Syria', May 12, 2015. https://www.washingtonpost.com/opinions/a-new-cooperation-on-syria/2015/05/12/bdb48a68-f8ed-11e4-9030-b4732caefe81_story.html.

Institut National de la Statistique. 'Gross Domestic Product (GDP), Second Quarter 2021', 2021. http://ins.tn/en/publication/gross-domestic-product-gdp-second-quarter-2021.

Integrated Judicial Council of Aleppo. 'Bayān Mushtarak Ṣādir 'an Majlis Al-Qaḍā' Al-Muwaḥḥad Bi-Ḥalab Wa-Muḥāmū Ḥalab Al-Aḥrār', February 19, 2013. https://www.facebook.com/qadaaalap/.

———. 'Bayān Tashkīl Majlis Al-Qaḍā' Al-Muwaḥḥad Bi-Ḥalab', December 2012. https://www.youtube.com/watch?v=fSbzb-2RAZ0.

International Crisis Group. 'Syria Under Bashar (I): Foreign Policy Challenges', February 2004. http://www.crisisgroup.org/en/regions/middle-east-north-africa/egypt-syria-lebanon/syria/023-syria-under-bashar-1-foreign-policy-challenges.aspx.

———. 'Syria Under Bashar (II): Domestic Policy Challenges'. International Crisis Group, February 2004. http://www.crisisgroup.org/en/regions/middle-east-north-africa/egypt-syria-lebanon/syria/024-syria-under-bashar-2-domestic-policy-challenges.aspx.

International Organization for Migration. 'Migration Data in Western Asia', 2022. https://www.migrationdataportal.org/regional-data-overview/migration-data-western-asia.

ISIS. 'Interview with Abū Muqātil At-Tūnusī', March 2015.

Islamic Front. 'Bayān', July 23, 2014.

Islamic State in Iraq and Syria. 'Structure of the Caliphate', July 6, 2016.

Jaffrelot, Christophe. *Hindu Nationalism: A Reader*. Princeton: Princeton University Press, 2009.

Jaouadi, Ridha. 'Al-Ḥamad Lillāh; "Jam'īyat Al-Lakhmī Al-Khayrīyah Lil-Tanmiyah" Mawlūd Jadīd Li-Taḥqīq Al-Karāmah Al-Insānīyah', June 19, 2012. https://www.facebook.com/RidhaJaouadi/posts/456740407690940:0.

———. *Getting Your Way: Strategic Dilemmas in the Real World*. Chicago: University of Chicago Press, 2006.

———. 'I'tilāf Al-Karāmah Laysa Ḥizbā Jadīdan', 2019. https://www.facebook.com/ridha.jaouadi.9.

Jasper, James M. 'A Strategic Approach to Collective Action: Looking for Agency in Social-Movement Choices'. *Mobilization: An International Quarterly* 9, no. 1 (2004): 1–16.

Jasper, James M., and Jan Willem Duyvendak. *Players and Arenas*. Amsterdam: Amsterdam University Press, 2014.

Jenkins, J. Craig. 'Resource Mobilization Theory and the Study of Social Movements'. *Annual Review of Sociology* 9, no. 1 (August 1983): 527–53.

Julani, Abu Muhammad al-. 'Bayān', July 11, 2014.

———. 'Jabhat Al-Nuṣrah Taḥmil 'alá 'Ātqhā an Takūn Silāḥ Hādhihi Al-Ummah', January 2012.

———. 'Jabhat Fatḥ Al-Shām I'lān Tashkīl', August 22, 2016. https://www.youtube.com/watch?v=s_9aqT0yg2o.

———. 'Tafrīgh Kalimah Al-Shaykh Abī Muḥammad Al-Jawlānī Al-Mas'ūl Al-'Āmm Li-Jabhat Al-Nuṣrah-Al-Manārah Al-Bayḍā' Li-Mujāhdī Al-Shām', April 10, 2013. http://almanaraalbaydaa.blogspot.com/2013/04/blog-post_1130.html.

Kandil, Hazem. *The Power Triangle: Military, Security, and Politics in Regime Change*. Oxford: Oxford University Press, 2016.

Karagiannis, Emmanuel. 'Hizballah as a Social Movement Organization: A Framing Approach'. *Mediterranean Politics* 14, no. 3 (November 1, 2009): 365–83.

———. 'Political Islam and Social Movement Theory: The Case of Hizb ut-Tahrir in Kyrgyzstan'. *Religion, State and Society* 33, no. 2 (2005): 137.

Keddie, Nikki. *An Islamic Response to Imperialism: Political and Religious Writings of Sayyid Jamāl Ad-Dīn 'Al-Afghānī'.* Berkeley: University of California Press, 1983.

Keddie, Nikki R., and Yann Richard. *Roots of Revolution: An Interpretive History of Modern Iran*. New Haven: Yale University Press, 1981.

Kelidar, Abbas Rashid. 'Religion and State in Syria'. *Asian Affairs* 5 no. 1 (October 1974): 16–22.

Kepel, Professor Gilles. *Jihad: The Trail of Political Islam*. Cambridge, MA: Belknap Press of Harvard University Press, 2003.

Khalaf, Rana, Oula Ramadan, and Friederike Stolleis. 'Activism in Difficult Times Civil Society Groups in Syria 2011–2014'. Beirut: Friedrich-Ebert-Stiftung, 2014. http://www.fes-syria.org/topics/civil-society/.

Khosrokhavar, Farhad. *Inside Jihadism: Understanding Jihadi Movements Worldwide*. Yale Cultural Sociology Series. Boulder: Paradigm Publishers, 2009.

Kitschelt, Herbert P. 'Political Opportunity Structures and Political Protests: Anti-Nuclear Movements in Four Democracies'. *British Journal of Political Science* 16(1) (1986): 57–85.

Koopmans, Ruud. 'A Failed Revolution-But a Worthy Cause'. *Mobilization: An International Quarterly* 8, no. 1 (2003): 116–18.

Koopmans, Ruud, and Paul Statham. 'Ethnic and Civic Conceptions of Nationhood and the Differential Success of the Extreme Right in Germany and Italy'. In *How Social Movements Matter*, edited by Marco Giugni, Doug McAdam and Charles Tilly, 225–52. Social Movements, Protest, and Contention; vol. 10. Minneapolis: University of Minnesota Press, 1999.

Krinsky, John. 'Fields and Dialectics in Social Movement Studies'. *Social Movement Studies* 20, no. 2 (March 4, 2021): 174–92.

Lacroix, Stéphane. *Awakening Islam: Religious Dissent in Contemporary Saudi Arabia*. Cambridge, MA: Harvard University Press, 2011.

———. 'Between Revolutionaries and Apoliticism: Nasir Al-Din Al-Albani and His Impact on the Shaping of Contemporary Salafism'. In *Global Salafism: Islam's New Religious Movement*, edited by Roel Meijer, 58–80. New York: Columbia University Press, 2009.

Landis, Joshua. 'What Happened at Jisr Al-Shagour?' *Syria Comment*, June 13, 2011. http://www.joshualandis.com/blog/?p=10202.

Lapidus, Ira M., and Edmund Burke, eds. *Islam, Politics, Social Movements*. Berkeley: University of California Press, 1988.

Leduc, Sarah. 'Far Left on the Front Lines: The Westerners Joining the Kurds' Fight in Syria'. *France 24*, February 23, 2018. https://www.france24.com/en/20180223-syria-afrin-foreigners-westerners-far-left-join-kurdish-revolution-fight-turkey.

Leenders, Reinoud. *Spoils of Truce: Corruption and State-Building in Postwar Lebanon*. Ithaca: Cornell University Press, 2012.

Lefèvre, Raphaël. *Ashes of Hama: The Muslim Brotherhood in Syria*. Oxford; New York: Oxford University Press, 2013.

Lewis, Bernard. *The Crisis of Islam: Holy War and Unholy Terror*. New York: Random House, 2004.

Lewis, Mary Dewhurst. 'Necropoles and Nationality: Land Rights, Burial Rites and the Development of Tunisian National Consciousness in the 1930s'. *Past & Present* 205, no. 1 (2009): 105–41.

Li, Darryl. 'A Jihadism Anti-Primer'. *Middle East Report*, no. 276 (2015): 12–17.

Lincoln, Jennifer. 'Manich Msamah and the Face of Continued Protest in Tunisia'. Jadaliyya (August 24, 2017). https://www.jadaliyya.com/Details/34515.

Lister, Charles. 'How Al-Qaida Lost Control of Its Syrian Affiliate: The Inside Story'. *CTC Sentinel*, February 15, 2018. https://ctc.westpoint.edu/al-qaida-lost-control-syrian-affiliate-inside-story/.

———. 'Profiling Jabhat Al-Nusra'. Brookings Institution, July 2016. https://play.google.com/store/books/details?id=CtyNAQAACAAJ.

———. *The Syrian Jihad: Al-Qaeda, the Islamic State and the Evolution of an Insurgency*. Oxford: Oxford University Press, 2016.

Ljunggren, Jørn. 'Elitist Egalitarianism: Negotiating Identity in the Norwegian Cultural Elite'. *Sociology* 51, no. 3 (June 1, 2017): 559–74.

Lobmayer, Hans Gunter. *Opposition Und Widerstand in Syrien*. Deutschen Orient-Instituts, 1995.

Local Council of Aleppo City. 'Bayān Min Al-Majlis Al-Maḥallī Li-Madīnat Ḥalab', May 9, 2016. https://www.facebook.com/TheLocalCouncilOfAleppoCity/photos/a.519158224797260.

Loehr, Daniel. 'Women, Media, Blasphemy, and the President: Four Constitutional Quarrels Explained', August 20, 2012. http://www.tunisia-live.net/2012/08/20/women-media-blasphemy-and-the-president-four-constitutional-quarrels-explained.

Lund, Aron. 'Going Home: An Interview with Tarif Al-Sayyed Issa'. *Carnegie Middle East Center* 22 (2015). https://carnegie-mec.org/diwan/61724.

———. 'Islamist Groups Declare Opposition to National Coalition and US Strategy', September 24, 2013. http://www.joshualandis.com/blog/major-rebel-factions-drop-exiles-go-full-islamist/.

———. 'The Jihadi Spiral', February 8, 2017. http://carnegie-mec.org/diwan/67911?lang=en.

———. 'Politics of the Islamic Front'. *Syria in Crisis*. Washington, DC: Carnegie Endowment for International Peace, 2014. http://carnegieendowment.org/syriaincrisis/?fa=54183.

———. 'Struggling to Adapt: The Muslim Brotherhood In a New Syria'. Washington, DC: Carnegie Endowment for International Peace, May 2013. http://carnegieendowment.org/2013/05/07/struggling-to-adapt-muslim-brotherhood-in-new-syria/g2qm.

———. 'Syrian Jihadism', Ulbrief 13, September 14, 2012.

———. 'Syrian Rebels Capture Idlib', March 29, 2015. http://www.joshualandis.com/blog/syrian-rebels-capture-idlib-by-aron-lund/.

———. 'Syria's Salafi Insurgents: The Rise of the Syrian Islamic Front'. Vol. 17. Swedish Institute of International Affairs, 2013. https://www.ui.se/globalassets/

ui.se-eng/publications/ui-publications/syrias-salafi-insurgents-the-rise-of-the-syrian-islamic-front-min.pdf.

Macfarquhar, Neil. 'A Battle for Syria, One Court at a Time'. *New York Times*, March 13, 2013.

———. 'A Bread Shortage Is the First Big Test of Transitional Council in Aleppo'. *New York Times, December*, December 15, 2012. http://www.nytimes.com/2012/12/16/world/middleeast/syrians-face-severe-bread-shortage-in-aleppo.html.

MacFarquhar, and Hwaida Saad. 'Rebel Groups in Syria Make Framework for Military'. *New York Times*, December 7, 2012. http://www.nytimes.com/2012/12/08/world/middleeast/rebel-groups-in-syria-make-framework-for-military.html.

Magnan, Pierre. 'L'Europe Veut-Elle Imposer Un Accord de Libre-échange 'Complet' à La Tunisie?', June 1, 2019. https://www.francetvinfo.fr/economie/emploi/metiers/agriculture/leurope-veut-elle-imposer-un-accord-de-libre-echange-complet-a-la-tunisie_3462665.html.

Mahmood, Saba. *Politics of Piety: The Islamic Revival and the Feminist Subject*. Princeton: Princeton University Press, 2005.

Malik, Shiv. 'The Isis Papers: Behind 'Death Cult' Image Lies a Methodical Bureaucracy'. *The Guardian*. The Guardian, December 7, 2015. https://www.theguardian.com/world/2015/dec/07/isis-papers-guardian-syria-iraq-bureaucracy.

Mansour, Ahmad. 'Abū Muḥammad Al-Jawlānī Amīr Jabhat Al-Nuṣrah'. Youtube, May 27, 2015. https://www.youtube.com/watch?v=-hwQT43vFZA.

Mardin, Şerif. 'Religion and Secularism in Turkey'. In *The Modern Middle East: A Reader*, edited by Şerif Mardin, Albert H. Hourani, Philip Khoury, and Mary Wilson, [347–74]. London: I. B. Tauris, 1993.

Marks, Monica. 'Tunisia's Ennahda: Rethinking Islamism in the Context of ISIS and the Egyptian Coup'. *Rethinking Political Islam Series*, 2015, 1–14.

———. 'Youth Politics and Tunisian Salafism: Understanding the Jihadi Current'. *Mediterranean Politics* 18, no. 1 (2013): 104–11.

Marzouki, Nadia. 'Tunisia's Rotten Compromise'. *Middle East Report*, July 10, 2015. https://hal.archives-ouvertes.fr/hal-03024063/.

———. 'Tunisia's Wall Has Fallen'. *Middle East Report Online*, January 2011. http://www.merip.org/mero/mero011911.html.

Mathieu, Lilian. 'L'espace des mouvements sociaux'. In *Lectures, Les livres*. Croquant (Éditions du), 2012.

———. 'The Space of Social Movements'. *Social Movement Studies* 20, no. 2 (March 4, 2021): 193–207.

Maton, Karl. 'Habitus'. In *Pierre Bourdieu: Key Concepts*, edited by Michael James Grenfell, 48–64, 2014.

McAdam, Doug. *Political Process and the Development of Black Insurgency, 1930–1970*. Chicago: University of Chicago Press, 1983.

McAdam, Doug, and Sidney G. Tarrow. 'Dynamics of Contention Ten Years On'. *Mobilization: An International Quarterly* 16, no. 1 (2011): 1–10.

McAdam, Doug, Charles Tilly, and Sidney G. Tarrow. *Dynamics of Contention*. Cambridge: Cambridge University Press, 2001.

McCarthy, John D., and Mayer N. Zald. 'Resource Mobilization and Social Movements: A Partial Theory'. *The American Journal of Sociology* 82, no. 6 (May 1977): 1212–41.

McCarthy, Rory. *Inside Tunisia's Al-Nahda: Between Politics and Preaching*. Cambridge: Cambridge University Press, 2018.

Meddeb, Hamza. *Ennahda's Uneasy Exit from Political Islam*. Washington, DC: Carnegie Endowment for International Peace, 2019.

Meijer, Roel. *Global Salafism: Islam's New Religious Movement*. New York: Columbia University Press, 2009.

———. 'Introduction'. In *Global Salafism: Islam's New Religious Movement*, edited by Roel Meijer. New York: Columbia University Press, 2009.

———. 'Taking the Islamist Movement Seriously: Social Movement Theory and the Islamist Movement'. *International Review of Social History / Internationaal Instituut Voor Sociale Geschiedenis, Amsterdam* 50, no. 2 (July 2005): 279–91.

Melucci, Alberto. *Challenging Codes: Collective Action in the Information Age*. Cambridge Cultural Social Studies. Cambridge: Cambridge University Press, 1996.

———. *The Playing Self: Person and Meaning in the Planetary Society*. Cambridge: Cambridge University Press, 1996.

Merone, Fabio. 'Analysing Revolutionary Islamism: Ansar Al-Sharia Tunisia according to Gramsci'. *Journal of North African Studies* 26, no. 6 (November 2, 2021): 1122–43.

Merone, Fabio, Théo Blanc, and Ester Sigillò. 'The Evolution of Tunisian Salafism after the Revolution: From La Maddhabiyya to Salafi-Malikism'. *International Journal of Middle East Studies* 53, no. 3 (August 2021): 455–70.

Merone, Fabio, and Francesco Cavatorta. 'Salafist Mouvance and Sheikh-Ism in the Tunisian Democratic Transition'. Dublin: Centre for International Studies, Dublin City University, 2012.

Mersch, Sarah. 'Tunisia's Ineffective Counterterrorism Law'. Washington, DC: Carnegie Endowment for International Peace, August 6, 2015. https://carnegieendowment.org/sada/60958.

Meyer, David S., and Suzanne Staggenborg. 'Thinking about Strategy'. In *Strategies for Social Change*, edited by Gregory M. Maney, Rachel V. Kutz-Flamenbaum, Deana A. Rohlinger, and Jeff Goodwin, 3–22. Minneapolis: University of Minnesota Press, 2012.

Misbar Syria. 'Al-Thawrah Al-Sūrīyah Jum'ah Al-'Azzah Jāmi' Al-Rifā'ī 25 Ādhār', March 25, 2011. https://www.youtube.com/watch?v=PcVmPGQsoIM.

Mische, Ann. 'Cross-Talk in Movements: Reconceiving the Culture-Network Link'. *Social Movements and Networks: Relational Approaches to Collective Action*, 2003, 258–80.

Mitchell, Richard P. *The Society of the Muslim Brothers*. Middle Eastern Monographs. Oxford; New York: Oxford University Press, 1969.

Mizouri, Amel. 'Khaṭīr Jiddā Al-Fīdiyū Rāshid Al-Ghannūshī Ra'īs Ḥarakat Al-Nahḍah', October 10, 2012. https://www.youtube.com/watch?v=5aFECUkDyug.

Moubayed, Sami. 'Syria's Abu Al-Qaqa: Authentic Jihadist Or Imposter?' *Terrorism Focus* 3, no. 25 (June 2006). https://jamestown.org/program/syrias-abu-al-qaqa-authentic-jihadist-or-imposter/.

Mousa, Amal. *Bourguiba Wa Al-Masāla Al-Diniya*. Tunis: Ceres Editions, 2006.

Muhajir, Muhammad Bin Salih. 'Al-Khulāṣah Fī Munāqashah I'lān Al-Khilāfah', August 2014. https://justpaste.it/gvna.

Multiple authors. 'al-Mawqi' al-Ta'rīfī bi-al-Shahīd Ṭarīf al-Sayyid 'Īsá', March 20, 2018. https://abualfida.com/.

Multiple rebel factions. 'Bayān Raqm 1: Ḥawla Al-I'tilāf Wa-Al-Ḥukūmah Al-Muftaraḍah', September 24, 2013.

Nabahani, Taqiuddin an-. *The System of Islam*. London, UK: Al-Khilafah Publications, 2002.

National Democratic Institute. 'Final Report, Legislative and Presidential Election'. National Democratic Institute, 2014. https://aceproject.org/ero-en/misc/tunisia-final-report-legislative-and-presidential-1/at_download/file.

Nessma TV. 'Mahdī Jum'ah: 149 Masjid Khārij 'an Al-Sayṭarah Wa-Barnāmjnā Wāḍiḥ Bi-Khuṣūṣ Taḥyīd Al-Masājid'. Youtube.com, March 4, 2014. https://www.youtube.com/watch?v=kdtm-4NH-3Y.

Netterstrøm, Kasper Ly. 'After the Arab Spring: The Islamists' Compromise in Tunisia'. *Journal of Democracy*, 26 no. 4 (October 2015). https://muse.jhu.edu/article/595928/.

The New Arab. 'Tunisia PM Fires Five Ministers amid Growing Constitutional Crisis', February 16, 2021. https://english.alaraby.co.uk/news/tunisia-pm-fires-five-ministers-amid-growing-constitutional-crisis.

Newlee, Danika. 'Hay'at Tahrir Al-Sham (HTS)', 2018. https://www.csis.org/programs/transnational-threats-project/past-projects/terrorism-backgrounders/hayat-tahrir-al-sham.

O'Bagy, Elizabeth. 'The Free Syrian Army', March 2013. https://understandingwar.org/sites/default/files/The-Free-Syrian-Army-24MAR.pdf.

Organisation Tunisienne du Travail. 'Al-Waqfah Al-Iḥtijājīyah Al-Silmīyah Bi-Sāḥat Al-Qaṣabah Bi-Al-'Āṣimah', August 18, 2014.

Orient.net. 'Ba'da Antkhābh Muftiyan 'Āman li-Sūriyā .. Min Huwa al-Shaykh Usāmah al-Rifā'ī?' *Orient Net*, November 21, 2021. https://orient-news.net/ar/news_show/194066.

Orient TV. 'Al-Duktūr Muḥammad Al-Shaykh Ra'īs Ḥukūmat Al-Inqādh Al-Sūria - Liqā' Khāṣṣ', January 19, 2018. https://www.youtube.com/watch?v=cQsajxyi5Z4.

Owen, Roger. *State, Power and Politics in the Making of the Modern Middle East*. 3rd ed. London: Routledge, 2004.

Pankhurst, Reza. *The Inevitable Caliphate?: A History Of the Struggle for Global Islamic Union, 1924 to the Present*. Oxford; New York: Oxford University Press, 2013.

Passy, Florence. 'Social Networks Matter. But How?' In *Social Movements and Networks: Relational Approaches To Collective Action*, edited by Mario Diani and Doug McAdam, 21–48. Oxford: Oxford University Press, 2003.

Passy, Florence, and Gian-Andrea Monsch. *Contentious Minds: How Talks and Ties Sustain Activism*. Oxford: Oxford University Press, 2020.

Perkins, Kenneth. *A History of Modern Tunisia*. Cambridge: Cambridge University Press, 2014.

Perthes, Volker. *Syria under Bashar al-Asad: Modernisation and the Limits of Change*. London: Routledge, 2004.

———. *The Political Economy of Syria under Asad*. London; New York: I. B. Tauris, 1997.

Pierret, Thomas. *Religion and State in Syria: The Sunni Ulama from Coup to Revolution*. Cambridge: Cambridge University Press, 2013.

———. 'Salafis at War in Syria: Logics of Fragmentation and Realignment'. In *Salafism After the Arab Awakening: Contending with People's Power*. London: Hurst, 2017.

———. 'The Struggle for Religious Authority in Syria', May 14, 2014. https://carnegie-mec.org/diwan/55593.

———. 'The Syrian Islamic Council'. *Thomas Pierret', The Struggle for Religious Authority in Syria', Carnegie*, May 13, 2014. https://carnegie-mec.org/diwan/55580.

Polletta, Francesca. 'It Was like a Fever . . .'. Narrative and Identity in Social Protest'. *Social Problems* 45, no. 2 (May 1998): 137–59.

———. *It Was like a Fever: Storytelling in Protest and Politics*. Chicago: University of Chicago Press, 2006.

Porta, Donatella della. 'Radicalization: A Relational Perspective'. *Annual Review of Political Science* 21, no. 1 (May 11, 2018): 461–74.

Porta, Donatella della, Teije Hidde Donker, Bogumila Hall, Emin Poljarevic, and Daniel P. Ritter. *Social Movements and Civil War: When Protests for Democratization Fail*. London: Routledge, 2017.

Posusney, M. P. 'Multi-Party Elections in the Arab World: Institutional Engineering and Oppositional Strategies'. *Studies in Comparative International Development* 36, no. 4 (2002): 34–62.

Qaraqūrī, Ilyās al-. 'Masājid Ṣafāqis Tajammu' Tabaru'āt Lil-Manāṭiq Al-Mankūbah Balaghat Akthar Min 50 Ṭunā Min Al-Mawādd Al-Ghidhā'īyah Wa 50 Ṭunā Min Al-Malābis', February 11, 2012. https://www.turess.com/sfaxien/7496.

Qasamṭīnī, Salīm al-. 'Jam'īyat 'Al-Lakhmī' Al-Khayrīyah Lil-Tanmiyah Mawlūd Jam'yātī Jadīd Bi-Ṣafāqis', August 4, 2012. https://www.turess.com/attounissia/65715.

Qasim Zaman, Muhammad. *The Ulama in Contemporary Islam: Custodians of Change*. Princeton Studies in Muslim Politics. Princeton: Princeton University Press, 2002.

Qilālah, Mahā. 'Tamma A'tiqālhu Wa-Al-Īfrāj 'anhu Fī Ẓurūf Ghāmiḍah: Min Huwa Al-Khaṭīb Al-Idrīsī Shaykh Al-Salafiyīn Fī Tūnis Wa-Ū'stādh Abū 'Iyāḍ', March 3, 2015. https://ar.africanmanager.com/تم-اعتقاله-والافراج-عنه-في-ظروف-غامضة-م/.

Qutb, Sayed. *Milestones*. Islamic Book Service, 2006.

Radio Mosaique fm. 'Riḍā al-Jawādī Yustaqīl min I'tlāf al-Karāmah', January 26, 2020. https://www.mosaiquefm.net/ar/أخبار-سياسة-تونس/677137/رضا-الجوادي-يستقيل-من-إئتلاف-الكرامة.

Redondo, Raúl. 'Tunisian Abir Moussi Promotes Classifying the Muslim Brotherhood as a Terrorist Organization', June 9, 2020. https://atalayar.com/en/content/tunisian-abir-moussi-promotes-classifying-muslim-brotherhood-terrorist-organization.

The Reform Front. 'Barnāmaj Jabhat Al-Iṣlāḥ', 2012.

Reuters. 'Al-Bājī Qāyid Al-Sebsy Y'alana Ta'sīs Ḥarakat "Nidā' Tūnis" Lil-Taṣady Li-Haymanah "Al-Nahḍah"', June 16, 2012. https://www.france24.com/ar/20120616-تونس-الباجي-قايد-السبسي-نداء-حزب-النهضة-الاسلامية.

Rey, Terry. *Bourdieu on Religion: Imposing Faith and Legitimacy*. Routledge, 2014.

Rizqī, Najlā' al-. 'Bi-Al-Asmā': Al-Masājid Al-Khārijah 'an Sayṭarat Wizārat Al-Shu'ūn Al-Dīniyyah', November 18, 2014. https://www.turess.com/aljarida/122105.

Rosen, Nir. 'Islamism and the Syrian Uprising'. *Foreign Policy*, March 8, 2012. mideast.foreignpolicy.com/posts/2012/03/08/islamism_and_the_syrian_uprising.

Roy, Olivier. *Globalized Islam: The Search for a New Ummah*. New York: Columbia University Press, 2006.

———. *Islam and Resistance in Afghanistan*. Cambridge: Cambridge University Press, 1990.

Rudloff, Bettina, and Isabelle Werenfels. 'EU-Tunisia DCFTA: Good Intentions Not Enough', November 22, 2018. https://www.swp-berlin.org/en/publication/eu-tunisia-dcfta-good-intentions-not-enough.

Rupesinghe, Natasja, Mikael Hiberg Naghizadeh, and Corentin Cohen. 'Reviewing Jihadist Governance in the Sahel'. *NUPI Working Paper*, 2021. https://nupi.brage.unit.no/nupi-xmlui/handle/11250/2758436.

Sadiki, Larbi. 'Intra-Party Democracy in Tunisia's Ennahda: Ghannouchi and the Pitfalls of 'Charismatic' Leadership'. Middle East Institute, November 25, 2020. https://www.mei.edu/publications/intra-party-democracy-tunisias-ennahda-ghannouchi-and-pitfalls-charismatic-leadership.

Salamé, Ghassane. 'Political Power and the Saudi State'. In *The Modern Middle East: A Reader*, edited by Albert H. Hourani, Phillip Khoury, and Mary Wilson, 579–600. Berkeley: University of California Press, 1993.

Salem, Norma. *Habib Bourguiba, Islam, and the Creation of Tunisia*. London; Dover: Croom Helm, 1984.

Salih, Yassin Al-Haj. 'The Syrian Shabiha and Their State - Statehood & Participation'. Heinrich Böll Stiftung, 2014. https://lb.boell.org/en/2014/03/03/syrian-shabiha-and-their-state-statehood-participation.

Sallaz, Jeffrey J., and Jane Zavisca. 'Bourdieu in American Sociology, 1980–2004'. *Annual Review of Sociology* 33, no. 1 (2007): 21–41.

SANA. 'Majmū'ah Musallaḥah Taḥtal Asṭaḥ Ba'ḍ Al-Abniyah Fī Madīnat Al-Lādhiqīyah', March 26, 2011. https://web.archive.org/web/20110811112527/http://sana.sy/ara/2/2011/03/26/338665.htm.

Sarkis, Mona. 'Hasserfüllte Milizennamen'. *Heise Medien*, August 10, 2012. https://www.heise.de/tp/features/Hasserfuellte-Milizennamen-3395244.html.

Savage, Mike et al. 'A New Model of Social Class? Findings from the BBC's Great British Class Survey Experiment'. *Sociology*, 47 no. 2 (2013), 219–50. http://journals.sagepub.com/doi/abs/10.1177/0038038513481128.

Savage, Mike. *Social Class in the 21st Century*. London: Penguin UK, 2015.

Sayed Khatab. '"Hakimiyyah" and "Jahiliyyah" in the Thought of Sayyid Qutb'. *Middle Eastern Studies* 38, no. 3 (2002): 145–70.

Sayf, Abī Barā'at al-. 'Al-Raṣāṣah L'bṭāl Maqāl Al-Khulāṣah', 2014.

Schwab, Regine. 'Insurgent Courts in Civil Wars: The Three Pathways of (trans)formation in Today's Syria (2012–2017)'. *Small Wars & Insurgencies* 29, no. 4 (July 4, 2018): 801–26.

Seale, Patrick. *Asad: The Struggle for the Middle East*. Berkeley: Berkeley: University of California Press, 1988.

Selvik, Kjetil. 'It's the Mentality, Stupid: Syria's Turn to the Private Sector'. In *Changing Regime Discourse and Reform in Syria*, 41–70. Boulder: Lynne Rienner Publishers, 2008.

Selvik, Kjetil, and Thomas Pierret. 'Limits to Upgrading Authoritarianism in Syria: Private Welfare, Islamic Charities, and the Rise of the Zayd Movement'. *International Journal for Middle East Studies* 41, no. 4 (2009): 595–614.

Sfaxien Association of Mosque Preachers. 'Al-Sha'b Yurīd Taḥkīm Shari' Allāh', March 15, 2012.

———. "Arīḍah Ilá Kull Min Yuhammahu Al-Amr', May 31, 2011. http://www.fichier-pdf.fr/2011/05/31/aridha-1/aridha.pdf.

SfaxTV. 'Al-Muẓāharah Al-Ghafīrah Jiddan Bi-Ṣafāqis 1 Juwiliyah', July 1, 2011. https://www.facebook.com/media/set/?set=a.238413969520326.73188.150210028340721.

S. H. 'La Coalition Al Karama obtient son visa et devient un parti'. *Business News*, May 12, 2021. https://www.businessnews.com.tn/La+Coalition+Al+Karama+obtient+son+visa+et+devient+un+parti+%0D%0A%0D%0A,544,108316,3.

Shābbī, Ṣabāḥ al-. 'Shahrān Sajanā Ma'a Ta'jīl Al-Tanfīdh Lil-Shaykh Ḥusayn Al-'Ubaydī', April 11, 2014. https://www.turess.com/assabahnews/84144.

Shadid, Anthony. 'Disparate Factions From Streets Fuel New Opposition in Syria'. *New York Times*, June 30, 2011. www.nytimes.com/2011/07/01/world/middleeast/01syria.html.

Sharbajī, Jawād. 'Ḥiwār Khāṣṣ Ma'a Al-Shaykh Usāmah Al-Rifā'ī .. Ra'īs Rābiṭat 'Ulamā' Al-Shām', December 22, 2013. http://www.enabbaladi.org/archives/14393.

Sheikh, Abu Jaber al-. 'I'lān Tashkīl Hay'at Taḥrīr Al-Shām', January 28, 2017.

Shu'ūr, Rāshid. 'Ṣafāqis-Fī Ittifāqīyat Sharākat Bayna Wizārat Al-Tashghīl Wa-Jam'īyat Al-Lakhmī: Iḥdāth 1000 Mawaṭin Shughl Fī Aqall Min 'ām Bi-Al-Wilāyah', September 25, 2012. http://www.turess.com/alchourouk/579432.

Siba'i. *al-Ishtirāqiya al-Islām*. Dar al-Maṭbuw'āt al-'Arabiya, 1959.

Sigillò, Ester. 'Islamism and the Rise of Islamic Charities in Post-Revolutionary Tunisia: Claiming Political Islam through Other Means?' *British Journal of Middle Eastern Studies* 49, no. 5 (October 20, 2022): 811–29.

Singerman, Diane. 'The Networked World of Islamist Social Movements'. In *Islamic Activism: A Social Movement Approach*, edited by Quintan Wiktorowicz, 143–63. Bloomington: Indiana University Press, 2004.

Skeggs, Beverley. 'Context and Background: Pierre Bourdieu's Analysis of Class, Gender and Sexuality'. *The Sociological Review* 52, no. 2 (October 1, 2004): 19–33.

Slackman, Michael, and Liam Stack. 'Syria Tense as Protesters Mourn Their Dead'. *New York Times*, March 26, 2011. www.nytimes.com/2011/03/27/world/middleeast/27syria.html.

SMART News Agency. 'Majlis Al-Qaḍā' Al-A'lá, Waḥdunā Mu'aẓẓam Maḥākim Ḥalab Wa-Rīfihā Bi-'Istithnā' Maḥākim Al-Nuṣrah Wa-Al-'Aḥrār', August 10, 2015. https://www.youtube.com/watch?v=2dSQvsWf9I4.

SNHR. 'On the 11th Anniversary of the Popular Uprising', March 15, 2022. https://snhr.org/blog/2022/03/15/on-the-11th-anniversary-of-the-popular-uprising-228647-syrian-civilians-documented-killed-including-14664-by-torture-with-151462-arbitrarily-detained-forcibly-disappeared-and-14-million-others/.

Snow, David A., and Robert D. Benford. 'Ideology, Frame Resonance and Participant Mobilization'. In *From Structure to Action: Comparing Social Movement Across Cultures*, edited by Bert Klandermans, Hanspeter Kriesi, and Sidney Tarrow, 197–218. London: Jai Press, 1988.

Snow, David A., E. Burke Rochford, Steven K. Worden, and Robert D. Benford. 'Frame Alignment Processes, Micromobilization, and Movement Participation'. *American Sociological Review* 51, no. 4 (1986): 464–81.

Snow, David A., Louis A. Zurcher, and Sheldon Ekland-Olson. 'Social Networks and Social Movements: A Microstructural Approach to Differential Recruitment'. *American Sociological Review* 45, no. 5 (1980): 787–801.

Soares, Benjamin, and Filippo Osella. 'Islam, Politics, Anthropology'. *The Journal of the Royal Anthropological Institute* 15 (May 2009): S1–23.

Souissi, Mounir. 'Al-Katātīb Al-Qur'ānīyah Fī Salb Istrātījīyah Tūnis Li-Mukāfaḥat Al-Taṭarruf', June 16, 2010. https://www.dw.com/ar/الكتاتيب-القرآنية-في-صلب-استراتيجية-تونس-لمكافحة-التطرف/a-5687991.

Stack, Liam. 'Syria, Claiming Heavy Toll in Town, Hints at Retaliation'. *New York Times*, June 6, 2011. http://www.nytimes.com/2011/06/07/world/middleeast/07syria.html.

Suhaylī, Afāq al-. 'Munīr Al-Talīlī (Wazīr Al-Shu'ūn Al-Dīnīyah) L « Al-Tūnisīyah » Qarīban Ilḥāq Iṭārāt Al-Masājid Bi-Al-Waẓīfah Al-'Umūmīyah', February 4, 2015. https://www.turess.com/attounissia/146773.

Sutton, Philip, and Stephen Vertigans. 'Islamic "New Social Movements"? Radical Islam, Al-Qa'ida and Social Movement Theory'. *Mobilization: An International Quarterly* 11, no. 1 (2006): 101–15.

Syrian Human Rights Committee. 'New Massacre in Sednaya Military Prison', July 2008. http://www.shrc.org/data/aspx/d0/3620.aspx.

Syrian Interim Government. 'al-Ahdāf wa-al-Haykalīyah', 2020. https://www.syriaig.net/ar/177/content/الأهداف%20والهيكلية.

Syrian Islamic Council. 'Bayān Ta'sīs Al-Majlis Al-Islāmī Al-Sūrī'. المجلس الإسلامي السوري, April 1, 2014. http://sy-sic.com/?p=179.

———. 'Dirāsah Da'āwá Al-Khilāfah Al-Islāmīyah', May 26, 2015. https://sy-sic.com/?p=1455.

Syrian Islamic Front. 'Mīthāq Al-Jabhah Al-Islāmīyah Al-Sūrīyah', December 12, 2012. https://docs.google.com/document/d/1fACS9tltlmZDmomlB1ZtiJLZaAckWOT0yhtRwoskgIE/edit?pli=1.

Syrian Islamic Liberation Front. 'Min Naḥnu?', December 16, 2013. https://web.archive.org/web/20131216225821/http://syrialiberationfront.net/%D9%85%D9%86-%D9%86%D8%AD%D9%86-%D8%9F-2/.

The Syrian Muslim Brotherhood. 'Mukhtaṣar: Al-Mashrū' Al-Siyāsī Li-Sūriah Al-Mustaqbal'. Damascus, 2004.

Syrian Salvation Government. 'Indhār', December 10, 2017.

———. 'Nashr I'lān Tijārīyah Ḥaṣrīyah - Bifa', October 13, 2018.

———. 'Nashr I'lān Tijārīyah Ḥaṣrīyah - Dogus', September 16, 2018.

Tamimi, Azzam. *Rachid Ghannouchi: A Democrat within Islamism*. Oxford; New York: Oxford University Press, 2001.

Tarrow, Sidney G. *Power in Movement: Social Movements and Contentious Politics*. 2nd ed. Cambridge: Cambridge University Press, 1998.

———. *Strangers at the Gates: Movements and States in Contentious Politics.* Cambridge: Cambridge University Press, 2012.

Tibi, Bassam. 'The Islamist Venture of the Politicization of Islam to an Ideology of Islamism: A Critique of the Dominating Narrative in Western Islamic Studies'. *Soundings: An Interdisciplinary Journal* 96, no. 4 (2013): 431–49.

———. 'The Totalitarianism of Jihadist Islamism and Its Challenge to Europe and to Islam'. *Totalitarian Movements and Political Religions* 8, no. 1 (March 1, 2007): 35–54.

Tobin, Sarah A. *Everyday Piety: Islam and Economy in Jordan*. Ithaca; London: Cornell University Press, 2016.

Touraine, Alain. *The Voice and the Eye: An Analysis of Social Movements*. Cambridge: Cambridge University Press, 1981.

Touraine, Alain, and David Mercy. *Critique of Modernity*. Oxford: Blackwell Publishing, 1995.

Ṭrābelsī, Ḥasan al-. 'Masjid Al-Lakhmī Yustaqbal Al-Shaykh Riḍā Al-Jawādī Imāmā Jadīdan La-Hu'. *Alhiwar*, March 16, 2011. http://www.turess.com/alhiwar/15903.

Tripp, Charles. *Islam and The Moral Economy: The Challenge of Capitalism*. Cambridge: Cambridge University Press, 2006. http://journals.cambridge.org/production/action/cjoGetFulltext?fulltextid=1220008.

Tuğal, Cihan. 'Transforming Everyday Life: Islamism and Social Movement Theory'. *Theory and Society* 38, no. 5 (2009): 423–58.

Tuniscope. 'Ta'yīn Imām Khaṭīb Li-Khuṭbat Al-Jum'ah Fī Jāmi' Al-Zaytūnah Badalan 'an Ḥusayn Al-'Ubaydī', January 23, 2015. https://www.turess.com/tuniscope/61367.

———. 'Wazīr Al-Shu'ūn Al-Dīnīyah: Lā Tūjad Jawāmi' Khārij Sayṭarat Al-Wizārah Ḥāliyan', November 4, 2017. https://www.turess.com/tuniscope/132498.

Tunisia Agence Presse. 'Bi-Sabab Al-Khaṭīb Al-Idrīsī: Wizārat Al-Shu'ūn Al-Dīnīyah Tlj' Ilá Al-Qaḍā' Lil-Naẓar Fī Masjid Khārij 'an Al-Sayṭarah', March 22, 2016. http://www.turess.com/africanmanager/311858.

Tunisian Front for Islamic Associations. 'Bayān', March 1, 2012. https://www.facebook.com/front.national.des.associations.islamiques/photos/384667544894920.

———. 'Bayān Al-Jabhah Al-Tūnisīyah Al-Jam'īyāt Al-Islāmīyah: Bi-Khuṣūṣ Tadnys Al-Muṣḥaf Al-Sharīf Wā-Al-ā'tidā' 'alá Muqadasātnā', March 22, 2012.

———. 'Bayān Al-Jabhah Al-Tūnisīyah Al-Jam'īyāt Al-Islāmīyah: Hawla Ba'ḍ Maẓāhir Al-Zulm Wa-Al-'Unf Fī Bilādunā', August 7, 2012.

———. 'Bayān Al-Jabhah Al-Tūnisīyah Al-Jam'īyāt Al-Islāmīyah: Ḥawla Khaṭar Al-Mudd Al-Shī'ī Bi-Tūnis Wa-Wājib Al-Taṣaddy La-Hu', September 1, 2012.

———. 'Bayān Ḥawla Aḥdāth Al-Qayrawān Wa Ḥayy Al-Taḍāmun', May 21, 2013.

———. 'Nuṣrat Li-Kitāb Allāh', March 22, 2012.

Tunisian Republic. 'Décret-Loi N° 2011-88', September 24, 2011. https://www.acm.gov.tn/upload/1410083987.pdf.

———. 'Tunisian Constitution', 2014. https://www.constituteproject.org/search?lang=ar&q=%D8%AA%D9%88%D9%86%D8%B3&status=in_force.

Tunisian Government. 'Al-Qānūn Al-Asāsī Raqm 26 Li-Sanat 2015 Tārīkh 7 Aghusṭus 2015 Bi-Sha'n Mukāfaḥat Al-Irhāb Wa-Man' Ghasl Al-Amwāl', August 7, 2015. https://cyrilla.org/ar/entity/qtybt6xdbebu5rv98w06yldi?page=1.

Tunisie Islamique. 'Al-Khiṭbah Al-Ūwlá Lil-Shaykh Riḍā Al-Jawādī Ba'da 20 Sanah (2011/01/28)'. *Facebook*, February 3, 2011. https://www.facebook.com/Tunisie.Islamique1/videos/187820314572412/.

'Uraysī, Āmāl al-. 'Tūnis: Muqatal Al-Qiss Al-Būlandī Yuthīr Makhāwif. . . Wa-Yu'ziz An'dām Al-Thiqah Bi-Al-Ḥukūmah', February 25, 2011. http://www.daralhayat.com/internationalarticle/237788.

van Dam. *The Struggle for Power in Syria: Politics and Society Under Asad and the Ba'th Party*. London; New York: I. B. Tauris, 1996.

Verter, Bradford. 'Spiritual Capital: Theorizing Religion with Bourdieu Against Bourdieu'. *Sociological Theory* 21, no. 2 (June 2003): 150–74.

Volkmann, Elizia. 'Tunisia: Kais Saied's Anti-Corruption War off to a Slow Start', July 29, 2021. https://www.aljazeera.com/news/2021/7/29/tunisian-presidents-anti-corruption-war-gets-off-to-a-slow-start.

Volpi, Frederic. *Political Islam Observed*. New York: Columbia University Press, 2010.

Volpi, Frederic, and Ewan Stein. 'Islamism and the State after the Arab Uprisings: Between People Power and State Power'. *Democratization* 22, no. 2 (2015): 276–93.

Wacquant, Loïc J. D. *Body & Soul: Notebooks of an Apprentice Boxer*. Oxford: Oxford University Press, 2006.

Wagemakers, Joas. *A Quietist Jihadi: The Ideology and Influence of Abu Muhammad Al-Maqdisi*. Cambridge: Cambridge University Press, 2012.

White, Benjamin Thomas. *The Emergence of Minorities in the Middle East: The Politics of Community in French Mandate Syria*. Edinburgh: Edinburgh University Press, 2011.

White, Jenny Barbara. *Islamist Mobilization in Turkey: A Study in Vernacular Politics*. Seattle: University of Washington Press, 2002.

Wiktorowicz, Quintan. 'Anatomy of the Salafi Movement'. *Studies in Conflict and Terrorism* 29, no. 3 (May 1, 2006): 207–39.

———. *Islamic Activism: A Social Movement Theory Approach*. Bloomington: Indiana University Press, 2004.

Wolf, Anne. *Political Islam in Tunisia: The History of Ennahda*. Oxford: Oxford University Press, 2017.

———. 'Snapshot – the Counterrevolution Gains Momentum in Tunisia: The Rise of Abir Moussi', November 18, 2020. https://pomed.org/snapshot-the-counter revolution-gains-momentum-in-tunisia-the-rise-of-abir-moussi/.

World Bank. 'Individuals Using the Internet', 2022. https://data.worldbank.org/indi cator/IT.NET.USER.ZS.

———. 'Overview', June 21, 2021. https://www.worldbank.org/en/country/tunisia/ overview.

World Islamic Front. 'World Islamic Front Statement Urging Jihad Against Jews and Crusaders', February 23, 1998. https://irp.fas.org/world/para/docs/980223-fatwa.htm.

Yassin-Kassab, Robin, and Leila Al-Shami. *Burning Country: Syrians in Revolution and War*. London: Pluto Press, 2018.

Yavuz, M. Hakan. 'Opportunity Spaces, Identity, and Islamic Meaning in Turkey'. In *Islamic Activism: A Social Movement Approach*, edited by Quintan Wiktorowicz and M. Hakan Yavuz, 270–88. Bloomington: Indiana university Press, 2004.

Zeghal, Malika. 'Constitutionalizing a Democratic Muslim State without Sharia: The Religious Establishment in the Tunisian 2014 Constitution'. In *Shari'a Law and Modern Muslim Ethics*, edited by Robert W. Hefner, 107–34. Bloomington: Indiana University Press, 2016.

———. 'Religion and Politics in Egypt: The Ulema of Al-Azhar, Radical Islam, and the State (1952–94)'. *International Journal of Middle East Studies* 31, no. 3 (August 1999): 371–99.

Zelin, Aaron Y. 'Up to 11,000 Foreign Fighters in Syria; Steep Rise among Western Europeans'. *The Washington Institute*, December 17, 2012. https://www.washingtoninstitute.org/policy-analysis/11000-foreign-fighters-syria-steep-rise-among-western-europeans.

———. *Your Sons Are at Your Service*. New York: Columbia University Press, 2020.

Ziadeh, Radwan. *Al-Islām Al-Siyāsī Fī Sūriyā*. Abu Dhabi: The Emirates Center for Strategic Studies and Research, 2008.

Zisser, Eyal. 'Appearance and Reality: Syria's Decisionmaking Structure'. *Middle East Review of International Affairs* 2, no. 2 (1998): 29–41.

INDEX